A MODERN HISTORY OF
JAPAN

A MODERN HISTORY OF
JAPAN

*From Tokugawa Times
to the Present*

ANDREW GORDON
Harvard University

New York   Oxford
OXFORD UNIVERSITY PRESS
2003

Oxford University Press

Oxford   New York
Auckland   Bangkok   Buenos Aires   Cape Town   Chennai
Dar es Salaam   Delhi   Hong Kong   Istanbul   Karachi   Kolkata
Kuala Lumpur   Madrid   Melbourne   Mexico City   Mumbai   Nairobi
São Paulo   Shanghai   Singapore   Taipei   Tokyo   Toronto

and an associated company in Berlin

Published by Oxford University Press, Inc.
198 Madison Avenue, New York, New York 10016
http://www.oup-usa.org

Oxford is a registered trademark of Oxford University Press

Library of Congress Cataloging-in-Publication Data

Gordon, Andrew, 1952–
    A modern history of Japan: from Tokugawa times to the present / Andrew Gordon.
      p. cm.
    Includes bibliographical references and index.
    ISBN 0-19-511060-9 (cloth)—ISBN 0-19-511061-7 (pbk.)
    1. Japan—History—1868– 2. Japan—History—Tokugawa period, 1600–1868. I. Title.

DS881.9 .G66 2003
952—dc21
                                                                              2002070916

Printing number: 9 8 7 6 5 4 3 2 1

Printed in the United States of America
on acid-free paper

Contents

Maps, Tables, and Figures

Maps

Tables

Figures

60984 81800

Preface

The experience of people in Japan over the past two centuries is a fascinating and fast-paced story of the changes of modern times. The main body of this text covers Japanese history from approximately 1800—the last decades of rule by the military lords (or shogun) of the Tokugawa family—to the end of the twentieth century.

These were centuries of extraordinary transformation worldwide. The point of departure, the years around 1800, marks an exceptional moment in world history as well as the early days of a profound, and related, transformation in Japan. The industrial revolution in Britain dramatically changed the balance of global economic and military power. Political revolutions in France and elsewhere gave birth to modern nation-states and modern nationalism, spreading not only new ideas about what was just and possible for human societies but also new forms of domination around the globe. This text begins by examining the intersection of these global shifts with a developing crisis in Japan's political and social order under the Tokugawa rulers.

In Part 2 we turn to Japan's modern revolution and the astonishing transformations of the late 1800s. This was the Meiji era, which took its name from the emperor installed in 1868. During the Meiji reign, Japan shifted swiftly and surprisingly from a semicolonized status to the position of an imperialist power. Part 3 examines Japan's imperial era, beginning with the nation's rise to global power and ending with the devastating experience of World War II and its aftermath. We conclude by investigating the postwar history of contemporary Japan and the issues facing people in Japan, and around the world, today.

THEMES OF CONNECTION AND MODERN EXPERIENCE

This book's title signals the importance of two themes: modernity and connectivity. A more typical title for a work such as this would be *Modern Japanese History*. Such a title would suggest that the Japanese-ness of the story is central. It would point readers to a peculiarly "Japanese" story that happened to unfold in an era we call "modern." This book is called *A Modern History of Japan* in order to shift the balance between Japanese-ness and modernity. It tells a peculiarly "modern" story as it unfolded in a place we call Japan.

In other words, the modern history of Japan has been inseparable from a larger modern history of the world. For this reason, a central theme of this book must be connectivity. Sometimes for better and sometimes for worse, ideas, events, material goods, and resources from abroad have influenced experiences in Japan profoundly, and vice versa. In this dynamic process, people in Japan have shared much with people elsewhere. This theme will be clear as we examine the topics of political, economic and social, and cultural history in the following chapters.

Although the crisis of the Tokugawa regime had internal causes, the collapse of Tokugawa rule was catalyzed by a changing international environment. A new group of leaders improvised a program of nation-building that reflected their understanding of the sources of Euro-American military and economic power. Their efforts proceeded in fits and starts, amid opposition and controversy. But their modernizing projects had much impact. From this time forward, the character of the nation-state became a central issue in modern history in Japan, as it did the world over, and struggles over how to organize political life are central topics of this book. These contests concerned ideas and institutions that were the focus of modern political life worldwide: constitutions and parliament, monarchy and democracy, rights for women as well as men, nationalism, imperialism, and the role of the military. We give attention to both the policies imposed by rulers and the political actions of ordinary people that influenced these policies.

The rise of capitalism is a related dimension of the modernizing project of the nineteenth and twentieth centuries in Japan, as around the world. The text examines the roles of both government and private citizens and the interactions of working people with managers. Relations between social classes, between men and women at work and in the family, and between farmers and city-dwellers were complex and consequential in Japan as elsewhere. Calls for harmony were frequent and sometimes effective, but conflict was frequent and often intense, and we pay close attention to such conflicts.

Conflict among nations and those aspiring to nationhood has been a third dimension of modern world history. Japan's regional and global role has been remarkable for its variety and above all for its devastating impact in the first half of the twentieth century. Japan was a dependent semicolony dominated by Western powers from the 1850s through the 1880s. The new nation became a colonial power almost equal to the Western powers by 1905. It turned to imperialist expansion and a war seeking hegemony over all of Asia in the 1930s and 1940s, with tragic consequences. It has since been a pacifist and passive nation in global politics. These contentious and changing relations among Japan, Asia, and the West are a major focus of the chapters to follow.

Diversity in the detailed texture of modern history is the other side of the coin of connectivity. The history of any place, Japan included, offers variations on the themes of wider world history. If connections and global interactions are central themes of modern history in Japan, it is also undeniable that some particular characteristics marked the thought and behavior of Japanese people. While this book highlights the shared experiences of modern times in Japan and elsewhere, it also identifies some experiences that made Japan distinctive. For example, particular characteristics of the samurai ruling class of the Tokugawa era shaped the changes that took place in the modernizing drive of the late nineteenth century. Another distinctive feature of Japan's modern history has been the powerful role of the Japanese state. The government has consistently sought to control the messy process of social and economic change, including relations among social classes and between men and women. Its actions sometimes provoked unintended consequences, but they were hardly ever unimportant.

It is important to recognize such particular features of modern history in Japan. It is even more crucial for scholars and students not to view Japan's history as uniquely unique or exotic. This pitfall exists partly because people in Japan have themselves been preoccupied, and sometimes obsessed, with defining and preserving something called "Japanese-ness." This has been the case at least from the nineteenth century through the present, so the widespread concern with defining "Japan" will be an important theme in discussions to follow of both elite and mass culture. Many aspects of so-called Japanese tradition, it turns out, were invented as myths of the modern era. On some occasions "Japanese traditions" were seen as obstacles to progress; at other times they were put forth as a model to the world. But just as Americans have sought to define and defend a peculiar "American way of life" (and continue to do so), and just as people in France or China or indeed anywhere on the globe have claimed and defended their "exceptional" characteristics, throughout modern history in Japan a deep interest in specifying and protecting "Japaneseness" has always been present.

ACKNOWLEDGMENTS

In preparing this book, I have been fortunate to have the help and advice of numerous people. Several graduate students at Harvard worked as research assistants, gathering information, preparing charts and tables, and checking numerous facts. For this help, I thank Jeff Bayliss, Ted Mack, Yoichi Nakano, and Emer O'Dwyer. Bayliss and Mack also helped draft passages concerning their particular areas of research, the histories of minorities in Japan and of literature and publishing, respectively. Cemil Aydin similarly advised me on the treatment of pan-Asianism. My colleague Helen Hardacre offered important advice on the treatment of religion in the 1990s. I am much indebted to colleagues who read and commented on the entire manuscript at the publisher's request, offering detailed and extremely helpful guidance. They include Gary Allinson, Timothy George, Barbara Molony, and two anonymous readers. My editors at Oxford University Press—Nancy Lane, Gioia Stevens, and Peter Coveney—were patient and supportive while offering important advice. The efforts of all of these people made this a far better book than it would have been otherwise. I am responsible for the shortcomings that remain.

WEBSITE

A companion website for this book can be found at www.oxfordjapan.org, containing key historical documents in translation, as well as paper topics, study questions, and links to numerous websites helpful for the study of the modern history of Japan.

A NOTE ON MACRONS AND PRONOUNCATION

Macrons are straight lines drawn over vowels—for example, ō or ū. They indicate that the vowel sound should be drawn out ("oh," rather than "o": in musical notation this would be the difference between a half note and a quarter note). For a handful of very well-known words, such as major cities and the main islands (Tōkyō, Ōsaka, Kyōto, Hokkaidō, Honshū, Kyūshū) or the Shintō religion, it is conventional to omit the macrons, even though the vowel sounds in these words are indeed drawn out as indicated here. We omit them in such cases in this book. Other place names, personal names, and Japanese terms are written with macrons.

A MODERN HISTORY OF
JAPAN

Introduction

ENDURING IMPRINTS OF THE LONGER PAST

The rulers who took power in 1868 initiated changes that amounted to a modern revolution in Japan. To understand this time of transformation one must first pay close attention to the political, social, and cultural order that came together in the 1600s and to the many changes of the 1700s and 1800s. That history, of what is called the Tokugawa era (after the name of the ruling family), is the focus of Part 1. Before examining this fascinating period, however, newcomers to the study of early modern and modern Japan must be introduced to key features of geography, politics and international relations, and culture stretching back much further in time, all of which remained important in the modern era.

GEOGRAPHY AND CLIMATE

The territory of present-day Japan consists of a long, thin chain of islands about one hundred miles from the Korean peninsula at the closest point and five hundred miles from the coast of China. The four main islands are Kyushu, Honshu, Shikoku, and Hokkaido (Japanese rulers did not control the land or people of Hokkaido until the nineteenth century). This archipelago extends diagonally from the northeast to southwest for about twelve hundred miles, roughly the length of the eastern coast of the United States. One is never far from the ocean; the most inland point in the country is no more than eighty miles from the coast. The total area of Japan is just under 150,000 square miles, roughly the size of Montana. The area covered by lowland plains does not exceed 13 percent of total land; that occupied by plateau adds another 12 percent. Over two-thirds of the total land surface is made up of steep mountain districts. Rain is plentiful. A rainy season in June and early July comes between spring and a hot humid summer. The rainy season produces less intense downpours than the monsoons of other parts of Asia, but it has sufficed to enable irrigation and rice cultivation to succeed.

Several aspects of this geographic situation are relevant to Japan's modern history. The distance from the southern island of Kyushu to the Asian mainland was close enough to allow sea journeys more than two thousand years ago, but it was far enough to have made this a perilous journey. Until modern times this distance made it possible but unusual to launch military invasions from the continent or expeditions of conquest from Japan. This moderate distance also allowed people living in present-day Japan, both before the modern era and more recently, to hold an ambivalent sense of their relation to the cultures of the Asian continent. The Japanese people have been alternatively proud of their Chinese inheritance and defiantly assertive of an independent identity.

The temperate, moist climate, especially in the regions from the midpoint of the main island of Honshu to the southwest, made agriculture possible and supported a growing population. Inhabitants numbered around five million in the early centuries of settled agriculture in the first millennium C.E. The population grew to about thirty million by the early 1800s. Two particularly large and fertile plains played key strategic roles at the center of economic, political, and cultural life. In west central Japan, the Kansai Plain was home to ancient and medieval cities in the vicinity of present-day Osaka and Kyoto. In east central Japan, the Kantō region is the largest plain in the country. The Tokugawa rulers developed the huge city of Edo out of a small fishing village along the coast in the Kantō Plain. After 1868, Edo was renamed Tokyo, Japan's famous modern capital.

While the geographic inheritance of climate and agricultural plains allowed the population to grow, the lay of the land separated people from each other. The Japanese islands are compact but mountains, forests, and lack of long flat rivers hindered transport and communication and made centralized political rule difficult. Looking at the political unity and strong national identity of people in Japan today, it is tempting to assume that such unity and shared identity are deeply rooted in a long continuous historical experience. This is not the case. For most of the premodern era, central authorities exercised limited control over regions beyond the immediate environs of their political capital. Power was especially fragmented over the three centuries before the Tokugawa family established its authority in 1600. And even during the era of Tokugawa rule, famous for its political order and peace, local rulers retained much autonomy. The extent to which the masses of common people shared an identity as possessors of a common Japanese culture was quite limited. In many ways, the idea that Japan is a unified place whose people comprise a coherent nation is a creation of modern times. The notion of "Japanese-ness" is an identity cobbled together in the face of a resistant geography.

POLITICAL INSTITUTIONS

The Japanese emperor has played a central role in modern history. The imperial institution is one of a handful of monarchies that have survived the revolutionary upheavals of the modern era. Indeed, one can argue that with the exception of the seventh and eighth centuries C.E., the monarchy in Japan has been more consequential in its modernized form of the nineteenth and twentieth centuries than at any previous time.

The current imperial family traces its hereditary line back to the early sixth century. It emerged as the Yamato family of chief priests and priestesses presiding over one of several clans contending for political supremacy (eight early monarchs were women). By the early 700s, this Yamato clan had achieved unchallenged political as well as sacred authority. It built a capital city and commissioned the writing of historical chronicles that invented a mythic genealogical line extending back from the sixth century C.E. through twenty-eight legendary rulers to 660 B.C.E. This ancient mythology was revived in the late nineteenth century as the orthodox "modern" view of imperial history.

The early phenomenon of strong, politically active emperors did not continue.

With a few exceptions, emperors from the ninth through the nineteenth centuries were of little political consequence. They continued to play a religious role as priests in the indigenous Shinto tradition, but other figures came to rule in the name of the emperor: first aristocratic families linked to the imperial court and then military families with diverse social and political bases. Thus, the high political profile of the modernized monarchy in the nineteenth century was a major break with the past.

Military figures with long histories played key roles in the revolutionary upheavals of the nineteenth century. The term *samurai* (as well as *bushi*) refers to Japan's warriors, a diverse group that figures prominently in the story to follow. Early samurai come into the historian's focus around the tenth century. They were provincial warriors who served aristocratic families in the capital or in the imperial court itself. The bow and arrow was their weapon of choice. In later centuries samurai achieved equality with, and then hegemony over, the aristocracy. The first military government, called a bakufu (or tent government), was founded in the coastal town of Kamakura in the Kantō region in the 1180s. Its chief won power by force of arms, but he then induced the emperor to legitimize this claim by conferring the title of shogun (generalissimo) upon him (the full title was Barbarian Quelling Generalissimo). More recent warrior rulers, including those of the Tokugawa family in power in the early modern period, likewise drew legitimacy from the imperial court by accepting the title of shogun.

The technology of war shifted over time, from bow and arrow to swords, and in the 1500s to firearms. In addition, the social and political organization of the samurai changed greatly. Earlier warriors engaged in individual combat. Regional warrior families were scattered through the countryside. Their control over the population was often weak. By the fifteenth and sixteenth centuries, more cohesive bands of warriors had come together under the leadership of military lords called daimyō (literally, "great name"). By the mid-1500s, political power was extraordinarily fragmented. The Japanese islands were divided into several hundred political units, or domains, under the control of ambitious and mutually suspicious daimyō lords, each of whom could mobilize a substantial force of samurai warriors. The political history of early modern Japan begins with a process of unification by which a few of these lords won hegemony over the rest.

PRIOR ENGAGEMENTS BEYOND THE ARCHIPELAGO

The first European missionaries and traders did not arrive in Japan until the 1540s, just before this unification began. They carried with them guns and God. Their firearms gave a boost to aspiring military rulers, accelerating the process by which the main islands came under unified political control. Their Christian religion had a smaller impact. By 1600, Spanish and Portuguese missionaries had converted as many as 300,000 people to the Catholic faith. But fearing that loyalty to a foreign god might lead to political disloyalty, Japan's rulers beginning in the 1590s sought to prohibit Christianity and to limit trade with Europeans. By the 1630s these restrictions were effectively imposed. In these ways, Europeans played an important but relatively minor role in Japan for a century before the modern era.

In contrast, other people in Asia, especially the Chinese and Koreans, played a major role in Japanese history for many centuries. Indeed, the premodern histories of the Chinese mainland, the Korean peninsula, and the Japanese islands are inseparable.

For centuries before modern times, relations among various rulers in Asia were loosely organized around a China-centered system of "tribute." Chinese emperors were the most powerful figures in the vast regions from Indochina to Northeast Asia. They viewed people outside their borders as possessors of less civilized cultures. They expected that emissaries of the rulers on the peripheries—called kings—would visit the Chinese capital, bow their heads low, present gifts, and praise the glory of the Chinese emperor, or "son of heaven." In exchange, the emperor promised protection and offered access to lucrative trade. Rulers on the Korean peninsula and in Vietnam were often unhappy at their subordinate role in tributary relations. They accepted the obligations (and economic benefits) of this system because they recognized the superior power—including occasional military invasions—that backed up Chinese requests for tribute. Although Japanese elites freely drew on the achievements of Chinese and Korean culture over many centuries, most of them—including the Tokugawa rulers—were also reluctant to accept the subordinate position implied by the system of tribute relations. Thanks to the barrier of the ocean, they were more successful in resisting claims for tribute. Even so, they had difficulty devising or imposing a different regional system until the nineteenth century. One major element of the modern revolution in Japan—which set it apart from its neighbors—would be the quick decision to embrace the Western system of diplomacy and international relations and to play the game of imperialist geopolitics on Western terms.

The premodern legacy of relations among people in Asia involved much more than such traditions of formal diplomacy. The Asian continent was the point of origin for almost all of the elements that came to define Japanese culture. Immigrants brought rice agriculture to Japan through China and Korea in the centuries from 300 B.C.E. to 300 C.E., and rice cultivation remained at the heart of economies throughout East Asia until the twentieth century. New military technologies also entered at that time. In the following centuries, both immigrants to and travelers venturing out of Japan imported a written language based on Chinese ideographic characters (kanji). They also imported political as well as religious ideas and institutions. These provided the foundation for the achievements of classical Japanese civilization during the Nara and Heian eras (700s through 1100s, C.E.). Important religious and economic relations with the Asian continent continued in the medieval era (1200s–1500s). For more than a millennium before the early modern period, people in Japan, and immigrants to Japan, imported and adapted the cultural forms of the Asian mainland.

Among these forms, Buddhism and Confucianism were traditions of particular importance in religion, philosophy, and political life. Buddhist religious practice was born in South Asia in the fifth century B.C.E. It flourished, reached China by the first or second century C.E., and spread further to the Korean peninsula. In the early 500s, the king of Paekche on the Korean peninsula introduced Buddhist writings and art to elite Japanese clans close to the emperor.

From the outset, Buddhism stressed that suffering was the essence of human life. A richly diverse body of thought and practice developed, first in India and later throughout Asia, with the goal of guiding people to a state of transcendence or enlightenment that could dissolve or overcome the suffering of human existence. Some

月 = moon (tsuki)

上、下 = above, below (ue, shita)

権利 = right (kenri)
[as in political rights]

Modern examples of Chinese written language imported into Japan. The character for moon
is a pictograph that visually conveys an image of a crescent moon. The characters for above
and below *more abstractly convey their meaning. More complex compounds, such as the term*
rights, *coined in Japan in the nineteenth century, combine such elements in a way that has
no direct connection to pictorial representation.*

Buddhists stressed meditation and ascetic practices. Others looked to prayer and appeals to greater powers for their salvation.

In Japan Buddhism reached an early peak of cultural and political prominence in the seventh and eighth centuries. These original sects later declined, but new sects, including the meditative Zen tradition and the more faith-based Pure Land and Nichiren Buddisms, continued to develop over the following centuries. Buddhism gradually extended its social reach into the countryside and among warriors and commoners as well as court aristocrats. A number of Buddhist temple complexes built up private armies or sought political influence. A few sects in the medieval era built extensive networks of independent political power. In the Tokugawa era, the Buddhist sects were brought under tight political control. Temples of one affiliation or another could be found in virtually every town and village, and rulers used them to keep track of the population. Through the centuries, Buddhism established itself in Japan as a vibrant cultural force. It was the source of new intellectual trends, such as the neo-Confucianism of medieval times, as well as the keeper of old traditions.

The moral and political dimensions of Confucian thought were important in Japan from ancient through modern times. Confucianism stressed the need for rulers to choose officials of the highest ethical and intellectual quality. Moral character was said to begin in the family with the piety and respect that children owed parents, fathers in particular. Superior men, with qualifications to lead others, were those who studied extensively and cultivated a benevolent spirit. Elites in ancient China created a system of examinations to test for such qualities, which they believed were reflected in mastery of the major Confucian texts. For nearly two thousand years, until the early twentieth century, Chinese emperors and political elites selected government officials on the basis of exam results. These Confucian ideas and writings first entered Japan in a similar fashion to Buddhism, via the Paekche kingdom. Confucianism, like Buddhism, reached a first peak of political importance in the seventh and eighth centuries. Chinese-style examinations were in use for a time. Japanese rulers consciously modeled their institutions on the Confucian practices of the powerful T'ang dynasty in China.

Over the following several centuries, Confucian thought and political practices declined in importance. But in medieval times, from the thirteenth to sixteenth centuries, Japanese Buddhist priests traveled to China and brought back a new development, neo-Confucianism, which was a revitalized interpretation of Confucianism that stressed the importance of direct reading of the classic Chinese texts of ancient times. The neo-Confucianism intellectual tradition was first developed by Zhu Xi, a brilliant Chinese thinker of the twelfth century (1130–1200). He revived and revised the Confucian tradition by stressing the need to ignore recent interpretations and turn directly to the original texts of Confucius and other early sages. For several centuries, the ideas of Zhu Xi were carefully studied in Japan by Buddhist monks. Neo-Confucianism struck a resonant chord in these monasteries of the medieval era among men labeled "Buddhist-Confucian" monks. As we will see, in Tokugawa times neo-Confucian ideas made their way into secular circles and became an important cultural and political force.

On occasion, severe tensions marred the relationship of Buddhist and Confucian adherents, as they jockeyed for aristocratic patronage or political power. But on the whole, the traditions and the advocates of Buddhist and Confucian thought coexisted in reasonable harmony in premodern times. Neither body of thought was primarily concerned with making an exclusive claim to truth and value. Both Buddhism and Confucianism became deeply rooted parts of Japanese culture.

Buddhism and Confucianism also came to coexist with the earlier religious practice of Shinto (the Way of the Gods). The term *Shinto* was in fact used for the first time in the eighth century to describe a diverse set of earlier ritual observances and sacred sites. The Shinto divinities were called *kami*. Many *kami* were linked to the cycle of agricultural and local community life. They were worshiped in small shrines throughout the land and were invoked in festivals and rituals over the course of the year. Shinto observances and beliefs focused on preserving purity and life in human society and nature. Other *kami* were protectors of powerful political families, chief among them the imperial family. This family claimed descent from a sun goddess, Amaterasu. Several grand shrines, above all the Ise Shrine in central Japan, developed in the early centuries C.E. as sacred ancestral sites of the imperial family.

Over the centuries Shinto priests, Buddhist monks, and Confucian scholars (and some who combined these roles in one person) integrated the Shinto pantheon and practice with Buddhist and Confucian traditions. From the eighth century, Buddhist temples and Shinto shrines were often located side by side. New doctrines in medieval times identified the various *kami* as manifestations of Buddhahood in a different form. In the early Tokugawa period, some Confucian scholars likewise stressed the similarity of Shinto and Confucian beliefs.

But a sense of difference among these three religious and ethical traditions did continue to exist, along with the possibility that their adherents would contend for ideological or political advantage. From early modern to modern times, the diverse elements of Japan's cultural past would be vigorously discussed and reinterpreted, sometimes being attacked as irrelevant or harmful impediments to modernity, at other times being exalted as the source of a special "Japanese" identity.

The Japanese islands in 1800 were home to a mainly agrarian population of about thirty million people. Commerce was dynamic and expanding. Urban life was energetic as well; roughly one-tenth of the population lived in cities or towns. Under the partially centralized rule of the Tokugawa family, the islands were part of a Northeast Asian regional system of trade and diplomatic relations.

But from a global perspective, these islands were a relative backwater. They were scarcely integrated into political or economic relations beyond East Asia. Sprouts of capitalism were visible, and signs of political crisis were widespread, but few would have predicted a revolutionary transformation of economy and society, or polity and culture, in the near future.

Yet by 1900, a multisided revolution had occurred. Japan was the only constitutional nation-state outside Europe and the Americas. It was the only non-Western imperialist power. It was the first, and at the time the only, non-Western site of an industrial revolution.

Equally extraordinary changes marked the twentieth century. The early decades saw energetic democratic movements. Sharp confrontations broke out between laborers and their bosses, between tenant farmers and their landlords. Modern times also brought innovation—and uncertainty—to gender roles. The first half of the century witnessed a political history of terror and assassination, an imperialist history of aggressive expansion, and a war that included some of the worst atrocities of a century that saw more than its share of murderous behavior. By the start of the twenty-first century, a pacifist Japan had become one of the most affluent societies in the world, but its people faced new, tough challenges as they looked to revitalize the economy, teach the young and support the old, and play a constructive global role.

The goals of this book are to sort out cause and effect in this history, recognize continuities as well as abrupt changes, and understand how people in Japan themselves understood their experience. These remain controversial and important subjects, part of the shared heritage of world citizens.

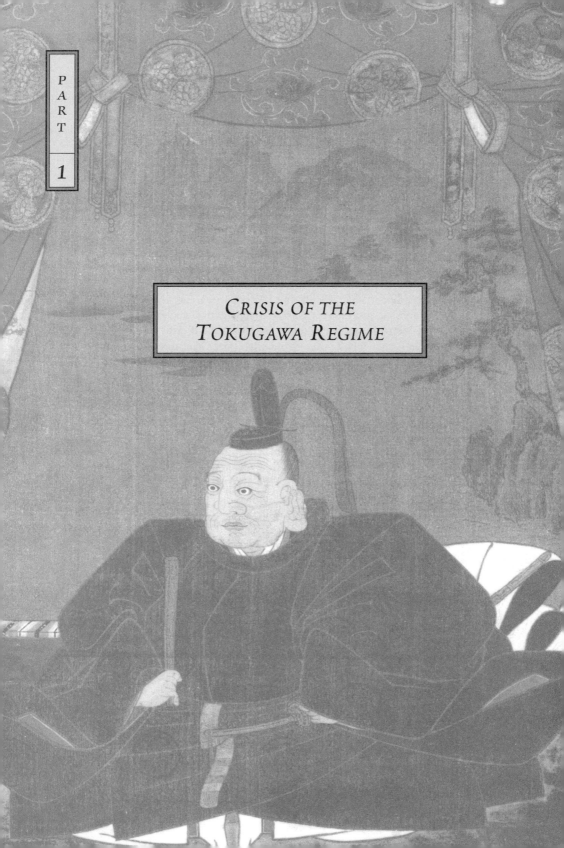

CRISIS OF THE TOKUGAWA REGIME

1

The Tokugawa Polity

The tumultuous changes of modern times in Japan unfolded against the backdrop of more than two centuries of unprecedented peace and social order. This era, called the Tokugawa period after the family name of Japan's military rulers between 1600 and 1868, has left a variety of images for later ages. The Tokugawa order was bolstered by harsh laws and restrictions on social and geographic mobility. Officials are said to have ruled by the motto, "Sesame seeds and peasants are very much alike. The more you squeeze them, the more you can extract from them."[1] At the same time, the Tokugawa centuries were an era of flourishing rural production and commerce and lively city life. One careful European observer wrote in the 1690s that "an incredible number of people daily use the highways of Japan's provinces, indeed at certain times of the year they are as crowded as the streets of a populous European city."[2]

Numerous formal restrictions coexisted with an energetic, at times rambunctious, population over the Tokugawa centuries. And important changes took place. These did not set the Tokugawa system on a smooth course toward modernity, but they were important nonetheless. By the nineteenth century, the regime faced grave problems. Underemployed warriors suffered a troubling identity crisis. Established institutions and ideas seemed inadequate to deal with new pressures at home and from outside. Rulers strongly committed to maintaining order faced social tensions and protests. A look at the origins of Tokugawa society and the emergence of these problems helps one make sense of the unexpected and hardly predictable modern transformations that began when the regime eventually collapsed.

UNIFICATION

The most important feature of Tokugawa history was the absence of warfare. The contrast to what came before was immense. From 1467 to 1477, the Ōnin War destroyed the ancient capital of Kyoto, the emperor's home since 794, a beautiful city of temples and aristocratic residences. For the next century, warfare was constant. Hundreds of thousands of samurai men in arms clustered around provincial military rulers called daimyō. These regional rulers jockeyed for control of land, people, and commerce.

Although war was a dominant theme of the age, this was by no means a century of unrelieved misery for all. Commerce flourished, and several cities emerged as relatively autonomous international trading ports. Some devotees of Buddhism organized powerful communities called *ikkō* (single-minded) sects. They too won autonomy from daimyō control.

Then, between the 1570s and 1600, three remarkable, often ruthless rulers pulled together an enduring political order. From the 1600s through the mid-1800s, people in Japan enjoyed over 250 years free of war. The warrior elite of daimyō and samurai retained their place as political rulers, but the character of the warriors changed dramatically. Immense change likewise came to economic and cultural life.

The first of the so-called unifiers was Oda Nobunaga.* He began as modest lord of the Owari domain in the vicinity of present-day Nagoya. In 1555 Nobunaga began his rise to power, soon embarking on a ruthless campaign of terror. He laid waste to the Buddhist strongholds, killing thousands of monks and burning great libraries and temples. In 1574, he overcame the independent villages whose residents supported the *ikkō* sect of Buddhism. By 1582, when he was assassinated by a treacherous underling, he had consolidated control over roughly two-thirds of Japan.

Viewed with fear and awe at the time, Nobunaga has not been remembered kindly by historians, who have called him "a magnificent savage," a "cruel and callous brute," even "a Japanese Attila."[3] But Nobunaga was more than a butcher. He also fashioned political institutions that his successors used to good effect in establishing and sustaining the Tokugawa peace. He encouraged or allowed relatively autonomous village organization as long as villagers paid taxes. He developed a bureaucratic program of tax collection, so that his vassals did not collect revenue directly from villages. Instead, specialized tax collectors did this, and they gave the loot in part to the vassals, in part to Nobunaga. He simultaneously separated the thousands of petty military lords from their fiefs. He took "proprietorship" from these men, and in exchange he guaranteed the petty lord an income reflecting the size and output of his land. In doing this, he established the right to reassign a subordinate lord.

For this system to work, a systematic survey of the land, its productive capacity, its size, and its ownership was crucial. Nobunaga pioneered in the use of surveys of the quality and quantity of agricultural land, and this constituted a foundation of the early modern political system. He also began the practice of disarming villagers and establishing a fairly sharp class boundary between warriors and farmers.

In the wake of Nobunaga's death, one lieutenant took up the banner as aspiring hegemon. This was Toyotomi Hideyoshi, a low-born foot soldier of unimposing appearance. His contemporaries dubbed him "the monkey." His wife is said to have called him a "bald rat." Epithets aside, he was a brilliant political strategist. In contrast to Nobunaga, who obliterated rivals and gave their lands to trusted underlings, Hide-

---

*A note on names: In the Japanese language people typically are identified with their family name first, followed by their given name (so-called first name), and we will follow this pattern in this book. Thus, Oda was this ruler's family name. His given name was Nobunaga. Historians refer to most important figures by their family name (for example, Prime Minister Ito), but a few especially famous or notorious figures in political or cultural life are called by their given ("first") names, much the way speakers of English refer to the British royal family members as "Charles" or "Elizabeth." Oda Nobunaga (as well as Toyotomi Hideyoshi and Tokugawa Ieyasu) are such figures in Japan. In these cases we follow the Japanese practice and use their given names.

yoshi pursued a politics of alliance-building. He attacked enemies who resisted, but he accepted oaths of loyalty from those who came over to his side. In such fashion, he extended domininion over all of Japan by 1591.

Hideyoshi continued and systematized the institutions of Nobunaga, and he added some twists of his own. He took hostages from the daimyō to ensure their loyalty. In 1588 he extended throughout his lands the practice of disarming peasants through so-called sword hunts. He also launched two massive and disastrous invasions of Korea in 1592 and 1597, seemingly with the intention of conquering China as well. Hideyoshi simultaneously turned against the Jesuit missionaries who had been winning converts in Japan since they first arrived in the 1550s. At the time of his death in 1598, Hideyoshi stood unchallenged at the apex of a federation of daimyō that covered the entire territory of Japan. He left behind a council of his most trusted lieutenants, called regents. They pledged to rule on behalf of his young son until the boy came of age. This was an unstable plan for succession, and a power struggle soon broke out among the regents.

THE TOKUGAWA POLITICAL SETTLEMENTS

These decades of swift political innovation culminated in rule by the Tokugawa family's bakufu, or military government. The first Tokugawa ruler was Ieyasu. One of his foreign biographers, a British scholar writing in 1937 with a sympathetic eye on the programs of Adolf Hitler in Germany, excused his ruthless side by noting that "the virtues desirable in the ordinary farmer or bourgeois are hardly of much use to a military dictator."[4]

Ieyasu was a harsh ruler. He was also a patient tactician who knew how to compromise. He was a peer of Hideyoshi, and his strongest potential opponent, but he held back from challenging the "bald rat." Ieyasu rather consolidated a base in the region of the eastern Kantō Plain, and he waited. Following on Nobunaga and Hideyoshi's models, he built up an effective domain government in the 1580s and 1590s. After Hideyoshi died, Ieyasu—who was one of the regents—lost little time in gathering his allies. In 1600 he destroyed the forces of the other regents, loyal to Hideyoshi's son, in the famous battle of Sekigahara. This gave him essentially unchallenged hegemony. In 1603 he had the emperor grant him the ancient title of shogun.

In 1605, just five years after Sekigahara, while he was still energetic and healthy, Ieyasu "retired." He put his own son, Hidetada, in the office of shogun to ensure a smooth succession. He continued to rule from behind the scenes until he died in 1616. The son had only seven unchaperoned years as shogun until his own death in 1623.

Ieyasu's grandson, Tokugawa Iemitsu, was the third shogun and a ruler almost as important as Ieyasu. His rule from 1623 to 1651 was the height of the Tokugawa dictatorship. It was Ieyasu and Iemitsu, in particular, who consolidated the institutions that remained in place when Western powers threatened to colonize Japan in the 1850s.

Ieyasu and Iemitsu built upon the achievements of Nobunaga and Hideyoshi to

Portrait of the Tokugawa regime founder Ieyasu. Although Ieyasu came to power by exercising military might, in this painting he is dressed in court robe and cap, which convey the message that his legitimacy also derived from the Emperor's grant of the title of shogun, or generalissimo.
Courtesy of Nikkō Tōshōgū Shrine.

put in place a series of what we can call "settlements." These various arrangements secured the Tokugawa position at the apex of political power. They neutralized all possible opposition, from daimyō and the emperor's court, to samurai, peasants, merchants, and priests. These settlements eliminated tensions of previous decades, even centuries. They brought to Japan the most stable political order in its history. Of course, historical processes of creating or sustaining institutions are never entirely stable. The settlements of the 1600s generated new contradictions that eventually eroded the Tokugawa order, but this was a gradual process that unfolded over the course of more than two centuries.

The Daimyō

Most of the specific Tokugawa policies had precedents in Hideyoshi's institutions of rule or those of Nobunaga, but Ieyasu and his successors implemented them more systematically. The settlement with the daimyō was one of the most important. Ieyasu enforced an order limiting castles to one per domain. He required daimyō to swear oaths of loyalty to him. He forbade them from concluding alliances among themselves and dispatched inspectors to make sure the daimyō were in compliance. Ieyasu further controlled the daimyō by mandating that all their marriages receive Tokugawa approval.

Ieyasu periodically required the daimyō to give him expensive contributions to building projects, including his great castle at Edo, which he established as his seat of power. But occasional coerced "gifts" of this sort were the closest Tokugawa Ieyasu or his descendants came to taxing the daimyō. The fiscal autonomy of domains was a significant limit to Tokugawa power. Following the precedent of Hideyoshi, Ieyasu opted to rule through a political system of alliances with weaker military rulers. He left roughly 180 daimyō in place as hereditary rulers of relatively autonomous domains as long as they showed respect and followed his orders.[5]

His grandson, Iemitsu, extended the Tokugawa reach considerably. Iemitsu established the right to confiscate daimyō lands and give them to other lords he considered more reliable. He also exercised power by ordering some daimyō to trade domains, which weakened them considerably. He confiscated portions of many domains and gave them to lieutenants under his direct command. These territories were called Tokugawa "house" lands. On other occasions he took the land of former opponents of the regime and granted them to his most loyal daimyō allies, called *fudai* daimyō. Through such steps, he was able to ensure the hegemony of the Tokugawa clan and its allies in other domains.

All told, Iemitsu redistributed control over about five million *koku*,[6] fully one-fifth of Japan's arable land. In these maneuvers, Iemitsu was especially tough on the daimyō who had opposed his grandfather in the battle of Sekigahara. These were called the *tozama*, or outer, daimyō. He protected his power base by building a concentric pattern of Tokugawa house lands close to Edo, surrounded by lands of allied *fudai* daimyō and Tokugawa relatives called *shinpan*. He placed the former opponents—the *tozama* daimyō—in lands at the farthest reaches of the three main islands.

Iemitsu also put in place one extremely important innovation, actually a dramatic extension of a pre-Tokugawa practice. This was the system of "alternate attendance" (*sankin kōtai*). It completes the picture of Tokugawa rule at the peak of hegemony over once-dangerous rivals. It had roots in the treatment of some daimyō by an earlier shogun, in the 1300s. The daimyō of this era were required to "attend" in the capital of the time, Kyoto, rather than live in domains, so the shogun could keep tabs on them. On several occasions in the late sixteenth century Hideyoshi likewise required leading daimyō to remain close by in "attendance." But this early form of attendance was not ongoing, scheduled, or universal. Between 1635 and 1642 Iemitsu regularized the attendance system.

Iemitsu required all daimyō to maintain residences in Edo as well as in their home domain. They would have to attend upon the shogun by residing in Edo in alternate years. Their wives and children had to remain behind in Edo when they went home for a year before the next period of attendance. This was a most effective system of political control. It created what were essentially hostage neighborhoods of daimyō families (although the conditions of these "hostages" were quite comfortable as long as they did not try to leave the city). The attendance system led to the watchword at the guard posts of Edo: Beware of women going out, guns coming in. These would have been signs of rebellion in the making. But for two hundred years, there were no serious challenges to the Tokugawa.

In addition to controlling them, attendance dramatically weakened the daimyō. It forced them to spend great sums to maintain several households, one back home and two or three in Edo. They also had to pay for their grand processions back and forth between the home castle and Edo. Daimyō lords typically used up two-thirds of their annual tax revenues on staffing their Edo residences. Forced attendance weakened the daimyō politically by removing them from a hands-on role in local rule, since they were absent half the time. In addition, a daimyō's sense of identification with his home domain was often weak because he would be raised by his mother and her staff in Edo, never setting foot in his own domain until adulthood.

The Imperial Institution

A second critical settlement gave the shogun effective control over the potentially most potent Japanese political symbol, the emperor. Ieyasu continued the Nobunaga and Hideyoshi policies of economic support for the court, raising it considerably from the genteel poverty of the previous century. The position of supreme military ruler, or shogun, was in theory a grant from the emperor. For this reason, the Tokugawa family could raise their own legitimacy by simultaneously enhancing imperial prestige and carefully controlling the emperor. To this end, the shogun promulgated a set of "laws for nobles." The shogun claimed the power to make court appointments and grant land incomes. He held an imperial prince hostage at the Tokugawa family's own shrine at Nikkō. To monitor the imperial court, he stationed his own deputy at a highly visible outpost in Kyoto, the Nijō palace not far from the emperor's palace, while he flattered the court with minor courtesies.

These policies presented the shogun as a virtual equal to the emperor. One result was to create significant confusion in the minds of Westerners in the mid-nineteenth century as to who was, in fact, the sovereign ruler. In 1857, the American trade negotiator Townsend Harris presented the shogun a letter from President Pierce addressed to "His Majesty the Emperor of Japan."[7] But at least among the samurai who joined political agitation against the Tokugawa in the 1850s and 1860s, the notion that legitimacy stemmed from the emperor remained powerful.

The Samurai

Several hundred thousand samurai warriors had been more or less permanently mobilized by hundreds of daimyō to fight the wars of the late 1500s. In a political system that closely resembled that of feudalism in Europe, these samurai had controlled small portions of land, called fiefs, as well as the peasants who farmed them. They had drawn tax income from this land to support their military endeavors. But controlling this land and its residents, and defending it from neighboring warriors, could be difficult. By pledging loyalty and offering military service to more powerful daimyō rulers, these samurai warriors gained protection from predatory neighbors as well as rebellious peasants. After the wars of unification ended, however, few of these samurai returned to supervise their lands directly. Instead, most became town- and city-dwellers. Many were instructed by their daimyō rulers to take up residence in the so-called castle towns that had sprung up around each domain's castle. Others were told to serve at the domain residence nearby the shogun's castle at Edo. Still others were posted as officers in rural towns, who oversaw a complex bureaucracy that surveyed land, assessed output, collected taxes, and kept local order. The samurai's fief lands came to be administered by these specialized officers of the daimyō or the shogun. The officials would collect tax revenues from the lands originally controlled by the samurai and forward the funds to the daimyō's castle or his Edo residence. The daimyō would then pay out to each samurai an amount equivalent to the expected income from that man's original fief.

The samurai in the city retained the right to wear two swords. Some served as policemen and keepers of order, but the majority no longer had official military duties. Assigned to a variety of administrative positions, or sometimes to none at all, the samurai received from the daimyō their annual salaries, called "stipends," reflecting the value of a fief of origin. But over time, the samurai's sense of connection to this fief became increasingly abstract and weakened. Samurai were subject to Tokugawa or domain law. Private vendettas of honor or loyalty were harshly punished in the interests of a broader concept of social order.

At first, with the unification wars still fresh in living memory, these citified samurai were a rough-and-tumble lot. Samurai gang wars—a *West Side Story* in the shadows of Edo castle—were frequent in the early 1600s. Over time, however, most samurai turned in swords for calligraphy brushes. They came to occupy a theoretically privileged but often quite confined position as a hereditary elite that managed the business of bakufu and domain. Assignments to high office, and prospects for promotion, came to depend on literacy, especially for samurai sons born into the middle and upper ranks. The samurai were transformed from warriors into bureaucrats. Those on the bottom of the salary scale lived in very modest, often impoverished, circumstances. During the Tokugawa era, roughly 6 to 7 percent of the population was from samurai families.

Villagers and City-Dwellers

The fourth settlement that bolstered the Tokugawa peace was that imposed upon the remainder of the population, the commoners, who were divided into several subgroups. In the 1630s, Tokugawa Iemitsu ordered all commoners to register with a Buddhist temple. The system was tightened in 1665 when the shogun ordered the temples to guarantee each person's religious loyalty. Villagers were not allowed to change places of residence or even travel without permission. The system of registration was thus a tool of political and social control. It was also a means to enforce the ban on Christianity that had been inconsistently imposed on the population since the 1590s.

The statuses of farmer and of merchant or artisan townspeople thus became fixed and hereditary. Roughly 80 percent of the population was farmers. The remainder were townspeople of various sorts. But despite many restrictions on what people in each status group were allowed to do, the Tokugawa did not micromanage the lives of ordinary people. Within the confines of a circumscribed world, commoners had considerable autonomy. It is true they needed permission to travel and were not supposed to move to cities. But enforcement of such rules was often quite lax. In practice, the bakufu and domain governments kept out of the internal affairs of villages, as long as the villagers paid their taxes. The bakufu collected taxes from a whole village, not from individuals. The village, in turn, retained the collective responsibility for managing internal affairs, maintaining order, and delivering criminals to the bakufu or domain authorities.

The settlement imposed upon city-dwellers, whether merchants or artisans, whether in bakufu centers of Edo or Osaka or in the hundreds of domain castle towns, was similar in broad outlines to that imposed upon villagers. As they had done with village headmen, samurai officials delegated responsibility for keeping order and regulating economic activity to councils of leading merchants. A group of city elders was given responsibility for enforcing laws, investigating crimes, and collecting taxes.[8]

The Margins of the Japanese and Japan

In the orthodox vision of the Tokugawa social order, which drew on Chinese Confucian ideas, society was divided into four classes arranged in a hierarchy of moral virtue as well as secular authority: warrior, farmer, artisan, and merchant. Many, however, did not quite fit into any of these groups. Some were people of respect or celebrity: Buddhist priests, actors, and artists. Others were subject to society's scorn, including prostitutes and various groups of outcastes. The main outcaste group was called *eta* (literally, "much filth," today a pejorative term). This was a hereditary group of unclear origins. Its members lived in scattered communities, where they performed tasks deemed unclean by mainstream society, such as burials, executions, and the handling of animal carcasses. The outcastes also included criminals assigned to a separate category of "nonpersons" (*hinin*), who were forced to subsist on jobs such as ragpicking.

In Edo in the 1600s, the entertainment quarters of brothels, theaters, and restaurants developed into a flourishing district called Yoshiwara, near the shogun's castle. Its presence offended moralistic officials and tempted samurai to neglect duty for the pursuit of male pleasure. But the rulers were practical men and were not inclined to ban prostitution. Instead, the bakufu authorities took the occasion of a fire that destroyed this district in 1657 to locate a new Yoshiwara on the far outskirts of the city. In addition to brothels, the district was home to teahouses, Kabuki theaters, and restaurants. Near the Yoshiwara district one found most of the city's Buddhist temples as well as its public execution grounds, which were supervised by the hereditary outcastes. All of these people—outcastes of various categories, as well as prostitutes and priests—were literally as well as conceptually relegated to the margins of society by the physical placing of their communities on the edge of cities.

The Tokugawa paid particular attention to religious institutions. Not only was the entire population required to register with temples, but the temples themselves were also closely regulated. Their numbers and locations were specified, and they were required to report annually to the bakufu (or the daimyō). Such rules were intended to prevent Buddhist temples from growing in strength, as they had in the past, to a point where they might challenge secular authority.[9]

Another important marginal status group were the Ainu people, who trace complex roots back to aboriginal inhabitants of the Japanese islands. For centuries preceding the Tokugawa era they maintained a relatively separate culture in the northern reaches of Honshu and the northern island called Ezo (present-day Hokkaido). In Tokugawa times the Ainu numbered roughly twenty-five thousand. For the most part, they subsisted by hunting and gathering. The northernmost daimyō, of the Matsumae domain, was given the responsibility for trading with the Ainu, and also for keeping them at bay. The Ainu occupied an ambiguous status on the margins of society. In the Tokugawa order they were not viewed as fully part of the civilized world of Japanese people. But neither were they considered fully part of the barbaric world of foreigners.

Foreigners were the final key group kept carefully on the margins. The foreign relations of Tokugawa Japan are often summed up in a single word, "seclusion," or by two words, "closed country." Indeed, in the 1600s the Tokugawa did cut off trade with countries that insisted on selling religion together with material goods. This ruled out the Spanish and the Portuguese, who had been active in both pursuits since the 1540s. Their emissaries would not abandon missionary work for the sake of worldly profit.

From 1633 to 1639, the same years during which he initiated the policy of alternate attendance, Iemitsu issued a series of edicts that restricted the interaction of people in Japan with those outside. He prohibited the Japanese from voyaging overseas to the west of Korea or to the south of the Ryūkyū Islands (Okinawa). He restricted the export of weapons and banned the practice and teaching of Christianity and the travel of Catholics to Japan. In 1637–38, peasants in the Christian stronghold of Shimabara (near Nagasaki) rebelled, moved by a combination of economic grievances and a millenarian hope for spiritual deliverance. Bakufu forces viewed this as a challenge by traitorous Christians. They suppressed the rising brutally, killing perhaps thirty-seven thousand people, young and old, men and women. Iemitsu also expelled the Portuguese traders. Their last ships left Nagasaki in the summer of 1639. Finally, he forbade all remaining foreigners from traveling inland or from selling or giving books to anyone in Japan.

The English had already abandoned the Japanese trade in 1623. The Spanish followed in 1624. When the Portuguese were forced to leave, only the Dutch remained. They were content to keep their religious ideas to themselves and focus only on trade. They took up residence on a tiny outpost in Nagasaki harbor, a landfill island called Dejima.

These steps had a major impact. They sharply reduced Japanese ties to the West for over two hundred years, from the 1630s to the 1850s. This was a critical time in European history. It was the era of the industrial and bourgeois revolutions and the colonizing of the New World. It encompassed the entire colonial period in North America and the first seven decades of the history of the United States.

But to simply understand the Tokugawa foreign policy as one of seclusion is ultimately quite misleading. Not until much later in the Tokugawa era, in the 1790s, did people within Japanese society identify "seclusion" as the defining essence of the system. From the rulers' perspective at the time, by issuing these edicts the Tokugawa had simply ousted those Westerners who insisted on promoting a religion that appeared to be a political threat. They still tolerated some Western trade and continued to cultivate foreign relations in Asia, except to forbid private travel abroad. They promoted officially sponsored trade and diplomatic travel, both for its own sake and to maintain domestic hegemony.

Satsuma domain was allowed to trade with the Ryūkyū Islands (Okinawa). This was a source of Chinese goods throughout the Tokugawa era. Even in 1646, despite the uncertainty of wars in China as the Qing established their dynasty, bakufu officials in Edo decided that Satsuma should maintain this trade. The bakufu also continued trade with China through Nagasaki throughout the Tokugawa era. This provided access to intelligence as well as goods.

The Tokugawa also maintained important economic and political relations with Korea. These links were reopened just about a decade after Hideyoshi's invasion. The Japanese set up an outpost in Pusan much like the Dutch trading house in Nagasaki. This trade reached a tremendous volume. The domain of Tsushima, a small island with almost no agriculture located about halfway between Kyushu and southern Korea, handled this trade. By 1700 it earned profits comparable to the rice tax revenue of the largest domains in Japan.

In addition, the Tokugawa made active use of foreign policy to shore up their political legitimacy, especially through the exchange of embassies with Korea. Diplomatic relations with Korea were carried out beginning in the early 1600s. The Koreans sent twelve major embassies to Japan between 1610 and 1764, roughly one visit each ten to fifteen years. Each embassy brought from three hundred to five hundred members. They would come on occasions of congratulation, such as the birth of a shogunal heir or the accession of a new shogun. There were no missions in the reverse direction. While the Japanese actively sought to have Koreans come, the Koreans never invited the Japanese, and they rebuffed occasional Japanese inquiries.

A similar diplomatic relationship developed between the Ryūkyū Islands and the bakufu. The Ryūkyūans sent twenty-one embassies of congratulation between 1610 and 1850. With China, however, the Tokugawa established no official relations. The Japanese refused to conduct relations in a way that acknowledged Chinese superiority, as the Chinese wanted.

Through these several diplomatic initiatives the Tokugawa rulers rejected the premises of a China-centered order emblematized by the tribute system to which other Asian rulers submitted. They were attempting to develop a vision and a reality of a different regional order. This was not a blatantly hegemonic vision. The Koreans were treated with a certain respect. They were not expected to prostrate themselves or to convey symbolic servitude, as they were in visits to the Chinese court. They interacted more or less as equals (although the Japanese clearly placed themselves as superiors to the Ryūkyūans).

Through such diplomacy, the Tokugawa sought to legitimize its domestic position as the hegemon of Japan. It hoped in particular to impress the many daimyō with the respect shown by foreigners to the Tokugawa. This goal is most evident in the way the Korean embassies were used, especially in 1617 and in 1634 around the time of the so-called expulsion edicts. The *tozama* and collateral lords were all commanded to attend a reception for 428 Korean visitors, a grand procession, and a visit to Ieyasu's grave. They were to be impressed by the many gifts to the Tokugawa and the congratulations given by the Koreans on unification of the country. Over the ensuing decades, Korean missions served to show the elite daimyō and top samurai that Japan's domestic political order was respected by a wider world.

By the late 1700s, this system of foreign relations had implanted a firmly held belief among bakufu officials and daimyō, and many informed samurai and educated, wealthy villagers, that legitimate rule must exclude relations with the West. In the feisty words of Aizawa Yasushi, a very important critic of Tokugawa policies in the 1820s:

> Recently the loathsome Western barbarians, unmindful of their base position as the lower extremities of the world, have been scurrying impudently across the Four Seas, trampling other nations underfoot. Now they are audacious enough to challenge our exalted position in the world. What manner of insolence is this?[10]

Three decades later, such views clashed head on with the Western belief in the universal validity of its civilization—backed by the force of gunboats. As this happened, the Tokugawa order fell apart.

The settlements described in this chapter were worked out in the main under Tokugawa Ieyasu. They were consolidated by his grandson Iemitsu. The settlements were described at the time as eternal reflections in social order of a natural hierarchy of cosmic or sacred origin. They constituted a system that one pioneering American historian of Japan, John W. Hall, called "rule by status."[11] By this phrase he meant that the separate statuses of daimyō, samurai, court noble, villager, merchant or artisan, priest or prostitute, and outcaste or Ainu all had their own laws. Each status had its own relationship to the Tokugawa rulers. People were in theory restricted to their status niche, but they were given responsibility for self-regulation as well.

Tokugawa rulers could be harsh and arbitrary in their efforts to uphold order and their own position. But the political regime of these centuries was durable, and it was able to accommodate considerable change over time. It brought unprecedented peace to the Japanese islands. The economy grew substantially. The cultural life of both city and countryside was often vigorous and creative. Judged against the standards of the previous centuries in Japan, these achievements were considerable.

But the flexibility and the reach of the Tokugawa order had limits. Compared to the Western nation-states that projected their military and economic power into Japan in the 1850s, the Tokugawa polity was a clumsy and divided structure. It was incapable of taxing the economic resources of the entire country, or of mobilizing human resources throughout the land, and it could not sustain a monopoly on the conduct of international relations. By the early nineteenth century, powerful underlying tensions, both socioeconomic and ideological, had significantly weakened the political and social control of the Tokugawa rulers.

2

Social and Economic Transformations

The formal status order of the Tokugawa system hardly changed for over two centuries. But this structure of political institutions rested on shifting socioeconomic ground. Two centuries of economic growth and social change eroded the boundaries between status groups and generated new tensions among the primary status groups of farmer and samurai. These tensions produced intense pressures for reform.

How intense? Was Tokugawa Japan a society on the verge of revolution by the early 1800s? Almost certainly not. In the absence of the turmoil generated by a renewed Western presence, the Tokugawa regime might well have endured for decades beyond the 1860s. But it is equally true that the reach and rapidity of the modernizing projects of the new Meiji regime owed much to gradual earlier changes in the cultural and socioeconomic spheres, as well as to growing calls for reform in late Tokugawa times. The chemistry of Japan's nineteenth-century revolution involved a powerful reaction between external catalysts and internal elements.

THE SEVENTEENTH-CENTURY BOOM

Cities throughout the Japanese islands were growing in size and number in the sixteenth century on the eve of the Tokugawa unification. Contending military rulers (the daimyō) fueled this urban growth by pulling their samurai warrior followers into semipermanent garrisons in castle towns. In addition to samurai, these towns were populated by service personnel: quartermasters, artisans, and traders clustered around the fortresses.[1]

But the fortunes of the daimyō waxed and waned in the power struggles and warfare of the late 1500s. The foundation of these towns and their merchants was similarly shaky. Not until the Tokugawa regime consolidated its hold and gave new stability to the federated domains of the land did urban centers became more stable. When this happened in the seventeenth century, an unprecedented flourishing of cities and of commerce resulted. In most domains, the samurai become permanent city-dwellers. Even a small domain's castle town would have about five thousand samurai residents, living on salaries and spending it all in the city.

A single innovation was most responsible for promoting both urbanization and the economic integration of separate domain economies with Osaka and Edo. This

TABLE 2.1 Major Cities circa 1720

City	Population
Tokyo	1,000,000
Osaka	382,000
Kyoto	341,000
Kanazawa	65,000
Nagoya	42,000
Nagasaki	42,000

Source: Sekiyama Naotarō, *Kinsei Nihon no jinkō kōzō:
Tokugawa jidai no jinkō chōsa to jinkō jōtai ni kansuru
kenkyū* (Tokyo: Yoshikawa Kōbunkan, 1969).

was the system of alternate attendance (*sankin kōtai*). Without it, the domains were likely to have developed as independent small states. The rural periphery of each castle town would have supplied the center in a self-contained local economy. Economic interaction between domains would have been relatively limited.

The population centers in domain castle towns did in fact develop economic links to their rural hinterlands. But in addition, the travel and residence requirements of the alternate attendance system promoted a massive traffic across domain borders in people, in cash, and in goods and services. The attendance system drained the coffers of the daimyō, who paid for the travel. But it led to expanded interregional trade and specialized local production for distant city markets, above all those of Edo and Osaka.

The Tokugawa capital of Edo was the largest urban center and the regime's administrative center. It was dominated by the grand castle of the shogun and by a huge population of both Tokugawa and domain samurai, forced to live in attendance on the shogun. Nearly as large, and more caught up in contests of getting and spending, was the Tokugawa commercial hub of Osaka. Driving the city's economy were a dozen or more leading rice traders. They handled the businesses of converting rice paid as taxes from throughout Japan into cash, which the daimyō could then disburse to their samurai retainers stationed in Edo; the traders also then sold the rice to city-dwelling consumers.

Both these cities, and the roads between them, teemed with life. One witness to this was Englebert Kaempfer, a German doctor who served as physician at the Dutch trading outpost in Nagasaki. He journeyed to Edo as part of the annual Dutch tribute missions in 1691 and 1692.

The country is populous beyond expression, and one would scarce think it possible, that being no greater than it is, it should nevertheless maintain and support such a vast number of inhabitants. The highways are in almost continuous rows of villages and boroughs: you scarce come out of one, but you enter another; and you may travel many miles, as it were, without knowing it to be composed of many villages.[2]

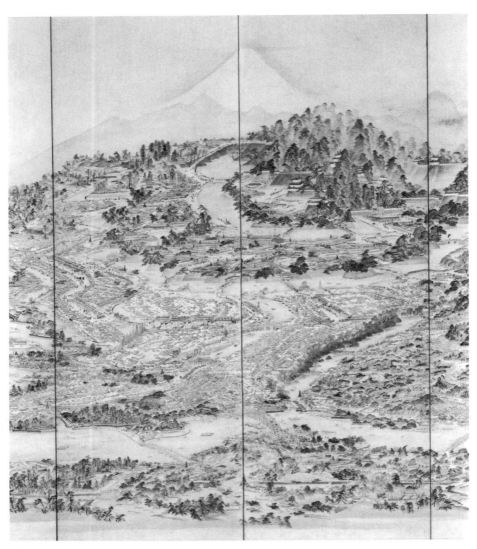

A bird's-eye view of Edo, the Tokugawa bakufu's capital city, in 1809. Mount Fuji stands snowcapped in the background. The shogun's castle is in the upper right, with daimyō and other samurai residences forming a ring around the castle moat. Commoner quarters, mainly for merchants, shopkeepers, and artisans, are in the foreground. The Sumida River runs across the bottom, marking the edge of the city at that time.
Courtesy of Tsuyama City Museum.

Nihonbashi (literally, Bridge of Japan), the central point in the city of Edo, in 1640. This painting nicely conveys the bustle of commerce and crowds in the capital. Boats passing beneath the bridge carry wood, rice, fish, and other commodities. Walking above is a great mix of samurai, commoners, monks, and street performers.
Courtesy of the Idemitsu Art Museum.

They were also crowded and dirty places. The commoner districts of Edo in the 1700s were even more densely populated than residential portions of Tokyo in the late twentieth century, one of the world's most crowded cities.

Overall, by 1700, roughly 5 or 6 percent of Japanese people lived in cities with populations greater than 100,000. Europe at this time was less than half as urban by this measure; only 2 percent of Europeans lived in cities of this size. If we define cities to include smaller places, the extent of urbanization is equally impressive. By 1700 about 10 percent of the people of Japan, or about three million people, lived in towns or cities of over 10,000 inhabitants. Edo, with its million souls, was the largest city in the world. Kyoto and Osaka, each with about 350,000 residents, were comparable to London or Paris. By any measure, Japan was one of the most urban societies in the world in 1700.

The growth of cities had several profound economic effects. For one, an infrastructure of transportation and communications was created and maintained both to supply the city-dwellers with material goods and to allow the huge parades of daimyō, each accompanied by hundreds of followers, to move back and forth.

Overland transport and travel were facilitated by an extensive road system. Two main roads linked Edo to Kyoto and then Osaka, the Tōkaidō route along the sea and the Nakasendō trail though central Japan's mountains. Other spokes radiated in all directions from Edo to points north, south, and west. To lodge these travelers, networks of inns sprung up. Equivalent in status and luxury to five-star hotels were the fifty-three officially designated inns along the Tōkaidō route for daimyō and top samurai travelers, while commoners put up with humbler accommodations. When daimyō attendance processions crossed paths with the many commoners on various commercial errands or on pilgrimages to shrines, the bustle was considerable.

This detail from a landscape print of the 1840s by the renowned artist Hokusai conveys a sense of the traffic on the main overland routes in the eighteenth and early nineteenth centuries, prompted by growth in local manufacturing and interregional trade as well as travel.
Courtesy of Keio University.

Travel became so common by the late eighteenth century that a lively publishing industry developed to produce maps, travel diaries, and the Tokugawa equivalent of the modern travel guidebook. Some of the advice offered by one travel writer in 1810 seems quite familiar to the contemporary tourist: "[L]odge only at well-established inns. . . . [E]ven when you are hungry, do not overeat. . . . [D]rink only clean water. Do not drink carelessly from an old pond or a mountain spring." Other advice concerned particular status groups only. Ordinary samurai were reminded that "when retiring for the night, put your sword or swords under the bedding. Halberds or lances should be placed by your side." Highly ranked travelers could find sensible tips on "preventing sickness when riding in a palanquin," such as drinking "boiling water to which has been added some juice squeezed from the ginger root." But of greatest interest to historians are bits of advice that reveal how Tokugawa society was marked by a particular status order and a particular concern to respect the rules of that order:

> Guests at an inn should enter the bath in the order arranged by the staff. Yet sometimes a difficult situation arises when the inn is busy and the order for bathing becomes confused. On such occasions, examine the appearance of the other guests, and if there is a person of high status among them, allow him to go first. The question of who will bathe before whom can easily lead to quarrels.[3]

The roads moved things as well as people. To this end, a busy packhorse transport industry sprung up, leading thousands of teamsters to jostle for road space with travelers. Historians have analyzed the records of these shippers, which reveal the density of economic activity by the 1700s. Consider, for example, the case of one main transport center along the Nakasendō trail, the inland route from Edo to Kyoto. Numerous secondary routes dotted with small towns and villages fed into the major "highway." At its midpoint stood the town of Iida. Roughly twenty-one thousand fully loaded packhorses departed in a typical year, taking local products to distant markets. This comes to sixty loads per day, every day of the year. If one assumes the teamsters operated only in daylight, then we have about five packhorses per hour departing Iida. And these precise records only cover business originating in this town. The volume of through traffic is estimated at five to ten times more. A popular saying in the 1700s, probably just slightly exaggerated, claimed that one thousand horses a day passed through. In this rather remote inland town, then, one must imagine traffic jams in the town center—and an active trade in scoops and shovels. Coastal shipping was actually more economical than overland hauling, and the cargo boat trade flourished as well. The cash needs of Edo-ites were huge. Daimyō from all over Japan had to get their tax rice to market, convert it to cash, and get the cash to Edo to support their households and attending samurai. Those in central and southwestern Japan used Osaka as the port to which rice was shipped and sold to merchants. The river at the heart of Osaka by the early eighteenth century was jammed with boat traffic, and the shores were lined with imposing merchant warehouses. The rice traders were the commercial kingpins of their day. They loaned money to daimyō lords and accumulated great fortunes.

In addition to people and things, an increasingly complex economy moved money, and not just cash. The daimyō who sold their rice in Osaka needed the proceeds in Edo. This led merchant houses to maintain branches in the capital. They would hand over funds to a daimyō in Edo upon receipt of his tax rice in Osaka. The merchants also began to issue these funds as credit in advance of the harvest. In essence, these traders created a rice-futures market. In exchange for cash in advance, a daimyō would issue a promissory note pledging expected tax rice to a merchant banker. These notes could be bought and sold at prices that would fluctuate in anticipation of the value of the harvested rice.

In this increasingly complex and productive economy, the cities were the magnets for commerce, and the towns, roads, and seaways were the nodes and arteries of economic life. The villages, in turn, provided most of the raw materials that were consumed and processed.

In important ways, the Tokugawa government stopped at the village gate. Only rarely did samurai overseers or police reside in the village. Neither domain nor Tokugawa governments imposed taxes directly on individual households. The entire village was assessed for taxes. The village headman and elders were responsible for dividing up the burden among the villagers. This left villagers relatively free to manage their affairs and to produce for the market once they met their basic obligations of rice tax.

In this situation, farmers improved their practices, and agricultural production and output grew substantially in the Edo era. Reliable general data do not exist, but production records that survive for individual fields show that output in the 1700s and early 1800s sometimes doubled over a fifty-year span.[4] Behind these gains lay not so much new technologies as slight improvements and better diffusion and use of existing ones. Some changes were as simple as the increased use of hoes and better tools for threshing. In addition, farmers adopted more productive strains of seed rice. They made more use of fertilizers such as ground dried herring. And they improved their irrigation systems through greater use of water-ladders.

One underlying change that made this diffusion of better practices possible was literacy. Educated samurai, as well as some priests and farmers (including quite a few women), began to offer classes to country people at unofficial schools. These typically met at Buddhist temples in villages. More and more children of farmers learned to read, both boys and girls. Improvement-minded farmers began to write "how-to" manuals describing effective agricultural techniques. These circulated widely from the seventeenth century onward. Estimates vary, but it seems that between one-third and one-half of Japanese men and perhaps one-fifth of women were literate by the early 1800s.[5]

With peace, and with rising output on the land, the population of Japan grew sharply in the 1600s. No reliable national censuses were taken, but the combination of scattered temple records and records of tax yields suggests that from 1600 to 1720 the agricultural population grew from about 18.5 million to 26 million farmers. If one adds in about 7 million city-dwellers and nonfarmers—merchants, artisans, and samurai families—the total reaches the vicinity of 33 million. The population appears to have nearly doubled in about 120 years, an impressive sustained growth rate of 0.8 percent each year.

RIDDLES OF STAGNATION AND VITALITY

The economic and social evidence for the 150 years that followed this seventeenth-century boom presents an apparent riddle of simultaneous stagnation and vitality. On the negative side of the ledger, one is first struck by the shrinking of the largest cities in the heart of the main island, castle towns in particular. Data available from thirty-seven major castle towns show an average loss of population of 18 percent from 1700 to 1850. Cities in the economically advanced southwestern provinces suffered the most severe population loss. The only growing towns were in remote locations.[6]

In addition, overall population growth came to a virtual halt between the 1720s and 1860s. Several devastating famines killed thousands in the late 1700s. In the Tenmei famine of 1786, the worst weather in decades led to crop failures, starvation,

Water-ladders such as this, which allowed farmers to irrigate fields more effectively, were among the technologies that spread in the Tokugawa era, allowing agricultural productivity to rise.

Courtesy of the library of the Historiographic Institute, University of Tokyo.

and deserted villages. Reports reached the cities of unburied corpses piling up, and even of cannibalism. Again, in the 1830s, widespread famines were chronicled, which generated death tolls from hunger and related disease in the tens or even hundreds of thousands in some prefectures. The detail of the reports is convincing: People were

This painting conveys something of the devastation of the Tenmei famine of the 1780s. An emaciated mother chews leather as her child desperately seeks to nurse. Other family members chew leather or animal carcasses. The famine was caused by flood, cold weather, and volcanic eruptions, especially devastating in the northeast of the main island of Honshu. Tens of thousands died of starvation.
Courtesy of the National Archives of Japan.

eating leaves and weeds or even straw raincoats; officials were issuing directives giving peasants permission to bury the dead without waiting for official permission.

Beyond famine, one puzzling and disturbing phenomenon was the practice of infanticide. For reasons that remain controversial to this day, it was apparently not unusual for farming families to abandon or kill unwanted infant children, both boys and girls. Both moralists at the time, and most historians until the 1970s, viewed infanticide as the last resort of desperate peasants. But careful analysis of demographic records such as temple registers suggests another interpretation. At least in some villages, evidence of infanticide is stronger for the wealthier farmers. It may have been a form of family planning taken not only by the poorest to avoid starvation but also by successful farmers to prevent numerous offspring from carving a stable homestead into tiny units that could not support a family.[7]

In the face of these trends, complaints from the cities mounted in number and intensity. Samurai officials viewed famines and infanticide as evidence of the moral failings of the rulers as well as the ruled. The elite was failing in its obligation to leaven hierarchy with enough benevolence to allow peasants at least to survive (and pay taxes). Closer to home, living costs for city-dwelling daimyō and samurai mounted. Few domains successfully increased revenues to cover these costs, even though they could have more aggressively taxed the rising output of the peasants. Daimyō and samurai instead took loans from merchant houses, and often had trouble repaying them. By the early nineteenth century, the world seemed out of joint to the bureaucratized samurai elite. Laments like the following were common:

> Today's samurai have lived in luxury for nearly two hundred years . . . and have seen no fighting for five or six generations. Their military skills have disappeared, and . . . seven or eight out of ten of them are as weak as women.[8]

The city merchants were little happier. The shogun and leading daimyō had the political clout to simply repudiate their debts. They did this with fair regularity. Merchants had little recourse but to swallow the loss and issue new loans. Of equal concern, upstart rural producers were competing effectively with the officially certified urban purveyors of goods and services. One 1789 complaint comes from the city of Okayama, a castle town with about twenty thousand commoners and a sharply declining population:

> Commerce in this city has steadily declined and many small merchants find themselves in great difficulty. On the other hand, ships from other provinces stopping at places such as Shimoshii Village and Saidaiji Village have steadily increased, bringing trade in the country to a flourishing condition. People used to come into the castle-town from the surrounding area to shop, but now people from the castle-town go to the country to shop. Country shopkeepers used to come to the towns to receive goods on consignment, but now town shopkeepers send agents to the country to arrange to receive goods on consignment. . . . Farmers and tradesmen have exchanged positions. Naturally this has impoverished many people in the town.[9]

Such reports, whether from samurai administrators, scholars, or city merchants, reflect the anxiety of people offended at the violation of the natural hierarchy of the world as it ought to be. They also reveal that in the world as it was, the misfortunes of daimyō or officially favored merchants were someone else's gains. The Okayama author's lament that "farmers and tradesmen have exchanged positions" is a reaction to the evidence on the other side of the economic ledger: A tremendous surge in rural production and commerce took place in the eighteenth and early nineteenth century.

One document from a small town that tripled in size from 1757 to 1855 as it came to specialize in weaving recounts that "weavers who came to make a living hired women operatives to spin and weave, and people came crowding into the town from other provinces, renting houses there and even in surrounding hamlets."[10] Other sources describe weaving operations of thirty to fifty to even one hundred employees.

A host of other industries developed throughout the countryside, including the production of sake (rice wine) and food staples like miso, soy sauce, vinegar, refined oil, or dried fruits. In the spinning and weaving of silk, cotton, and rougher fabrics, complicated networks of home-based production grew up. Brokers orchestrated as many as a dozen steps in the production process, each with its network of specialized producers. Similar production networks emerged for lacquerware, ceramics, or wooden bowls for everyday use; for paper and paper products; for candles, rope, clogs, and fabric dyes; and for ornaments such as combs and hairpieces. By the 1800s these and many other products had long ceased to be monopolized by city artisans or urban markets. This change can be called the "proto-industrialization" of the countryside. It was defined by an increased scale of operations and specialized production networks serving long-range markets. These networks were deeply embedded into the rural society and economy. A significant and growing minority of the rural population, both men and women, began to work for wages outside of the family in a variety of manufacturing endeavors. Some concluded annual or seasonal contracts. Others became part of a casual daily-wage labor force.

This economic development sometimes set upstart rural producers against established city traders and artisans. At the same time, within the countryside it set a prospering, entrepreneurial upper crust against embattled smallholders or tenant farmers. The latter struggled to survive in a world of increased danger as well as opportunity.

In Tokugawa Japan poorer peasants had few effective means of legally protesting. If taxes or debts were too high, they could simply run off to another domain, and some did. But this was a risky choice both legally and economically. Petitioning the authorities for relief through proper channels was not illegal, but if the claim was rejected the petitioner faced the risk of punishment. Any other form of petitioning outside channels was illegal, as were all collective, mass actions. But such violations of order took place, and they did so with increased frequency over time.

The trend was clearly toward more protests. These included mass petitions and demonstrations as well as attacks on officials or the wealthy. Over time, an important shift took place toward more aggressive actions. The relatively passive act of literally running away or the humble act of submitting a petition had together accounted for nearly half of all peasant "protests" from 1600 to 1650. By the first half of the 1800s these actions accounted for just 13 percent of all protests, while acts classified as "direct attacks" and "smashings" now accounted for 43 percent.[11]

TABLE 2.2 Peasant Protests, 1600–1867

Years	Total Number of Protests	Protests per Year
1600–1700	420	4.2
1700–1800	1,092	10.9
1800–1850	814	16.2
1851–1867	373	21.9

Source: Stephen Vlastos, *Peasant Protests and Uprising in Tokugawa Japan* (Berkeley: University of California Press, 1986), p. 46.

Some of these protests set rural producers angry at restrictions on commerce against officially privileged urban rivals. But many actions, in particular those called "smashings" in the slang of the day, took place within the countryside and within the peasant class, as poor peasants attacked rich neighbors. The protesters often destroyed the homes and looted the warehouses of successful farmer-producers. They sometimes distributed the contents at a roughly calculated "fair price." They rarely inflicted physical harm on people. Those on the receiving end of attacks were typically landlords, moneylenders, traders, and manufacturers (often the same person filling several of these roles). They were the people, for example, who lent money at usurious rates to smallholders seeking to cultivate mulberry trees and raise silkworms on the side. Protests could arise if prices fell and loans could not be repaid. The smallholding peasants were taking advantage of opportunities brought by the spread of trade and rural industry. Simultaneously, they feared the increased vulnerablity that came as commerce and the market penetrated the village. They deeply resented the success of wealthier farmers who took advantage of their position to charge high interest on loans and profit at the borrower's expense.

In this social and economic world, one also found important tensions between prescribed roles and evolving practice for men and women. The orthodox ideals of Tokugawa society held that women should be kept ignorant and in the kitchen. The classical statement of this attitude was a Chinese-inspired text called *The Greater Learning for Females*. This manual has been attributed to a Confucian scholar, Kaibara Ekiken, writing in the 1670s. It may well have been written by someone else, perhaps even Ekiken's wife, who was herself a scholar. Whoever wrote it, the work circulated widely. It contained nineteen chapters offering general principles for educating women and specific injunctions to submissive behavior. As one scholar notes, "[the author] proclaimed that female genitalia, while necessary for the reproduction of male heirs, were linked to dull-wittedness, laziness, lasciviousness, a hot temper, and a tremendous capacity to bear grudges."[12]

Social practice often defied such harsh prescriptions. Women played crucial productive roles both within the household economy, as they had in the past, and outside it. They occasionally acted as managers or co-managers of wealthy farming households and of merchant or artisan establishments in the towns. Women in more modest peasant families would take in piecework tasks such as spinning or weaving from rural textile brokers, and city-dwelling women took in piecework as well. In addition, young women often left home as wage laborers on seasonal or longer term contracts. As in earlier times, girls from wealthy farm families worked as domestic servants in the noble households of Kyoto, and those from impoverished homes worked as prostitutes in city or town brothels. In such cases, the parents would receive substantial advances against expected wages. Their daughters were obliged to work off the debt of these contracts over periods of from three to six years.

Other jobs for women outside the home were new variations on this theme. Much of the labor force in the flourishing spinning and weaving centers of the countryside was female. These workers, like those in the sex trade, often traveled considerable distance and lived at their work sites. They resided in small weaving establishments that contracted in advance with the parents for stints of a season or more. All these forms of wage labor—in homes, brothels, and factories—were to endure and to play a central role in the later economic and social history of modern Japan.

Men outside the upper ranks of the samurai were also a good bit more flexible in their daily practice than the ideology of gender separation and hierarchy might suggest. Both Tokugawa and early Meiji evidence shows that they played an active role in child care and housework. The written injunctions of a wealthy merchant to his son in 1610 included orders to handle tasks such as preparing food for servants, buying and storing firewood, and sorting garbage: "If a man does not take these troubles upon himself, he can never run a household successfully."[13] The household was both a workplace and a residence, and domestic labor was not tightly cordoned off as a female sphere of activity. An American traveler in 1878, Isabella Bird, wrote of an early morning rural scene of "twelve or fourteen men sitting on a low wall, each with a child under two years in his arms, fondling and playing with it, and showing off its physique and intelligence."[14]

How does one reconcile the undeniable evidence of famine and infanticide, of population decline in cities and large towns, and of increased social protests with equally strong evidence of social vitality and expanding rural trade and manufacturing? We can reconcile these conflicting bodies of evidence first by recognizing the uneven distribution of resources between and within classes and between regions. A second factor explaining the divergent fate of social classes and regions was the relatively limited integration of the Tokugawa economy into Asia-wide or global trading networks.

Cities declined while smaller towns prospered. These country places had several advantages. They were located near raw materials and water power, close to growing rural markets, and close enough to city markets. They were sustained by tight networks of personal relations among traders and producers. These links were important to stable economic relations in the absence of systematic commercial law. They benefited from the ability of rural workers to shift between farming and other occupations. They were free from the taxes and guild restrictions that hampered city merchants more closely under the watch of Tokugawa or domain authorities. Within the countryside as well, some regions did better than others. In particular, rural production and trade proliferated most extensively in regions from central Honshu southwest to northern Kyushu, while northern Honshu lagged behind.

The flourishing of some portions of the countryside at the expense of cities offers an interesting contrast to the experience of Europe in the 1600s and 1700s. There, the rural economy tended to grow, but urban centers did not simultaneously decline. The difference lies in the surging foreign trade that Europeans pursued so aggressively. It added to urban employment, allowed food imports, and seems to have encouraged overall population growth as well as migration to cities.

In Tokugawa Japan, international trade was only of modest importance. Japanese in the seventeenth and eighteenth centuries did export considerable volumes of silk and copper to China through the port of Nagasaki, as well as large amounts of silver to Korea. This trade supported employment in the vicinity of Nagasaki, in mining regions, and in silk-producing areas from Kyushu in the south to Kyoto and Osaka in central Japan. Even so, Japan's foreign trade did not play a role as an engine of economic and urban growth to the extent that it did in Europe over the same centuries. Instead, an inward-focused and rurally focused growth took place.

Economic fortunes varied by class as well as by region. As the economy became more complex and productive, it offered both opportunities and risks. This was a process of change in which the harsh consequences of failure were not buffered by systematic social welfare policies. Instead, the disparities of wealth and power in villages grew wider. The rural upper crust became more literate and mobile. Rich farmers had land and cash to invest. They had the education and information to make better decisions.

Tokugawa society was never egalitarian. Toward the end of this era, reformers sometimes put forward the notion that the early age of Ieyasu was a golden era when villages were populated by family farmers of equal means. This was a myth. Its proponents were often rebels seeking to "rectify" a world that in fact had always included impoverished villagers dependent on the benevolence of domain lords or village leaders for tax relief or loans to survive lean years. But dependent villagers of the early Tokugawa era tended to be servants or branch family members. Their poverty was buffered by the patrons' sense of an obligation to care for their charges.

Paternalistic benevolence did not vanish by the 1800s, but it seems to have become less reliable. Dependent commoners were increasingly connected to their betters by wage labor contracts rather than kinship ties. They were more often in need of such relief, but less able to count on it. The gradual but significant rise in social protest over the Tokugawa era was a response not to inequality in general, which was not new, but to a new *type* of inequality, that of the market. Rulers and the wealthy were attacked not so much for their status itself, but for a failure to exercise the duty of benevolence understood to come with status.

3

The Intellectual World of Late Tokugawa

Faced with widespread symptoms of distress and decline, from chronic daimyō and samurai debt to devastating famine and increased instances of violent protests, both rulers and ruled produced vigorous critiques of their changing world. The gist of such statements often looked backward as well as forward: Reform was needed to return the world of the present to the better times of the past. Ironically, as is often the case, conservative reforms actually set in motion a chain of events that made a return to that past impossible. To understand the cultural and intellectual ferment of late Tokugawa times, one must begin by examining the ideal world that reformers wished to restore.

IDEOLOGICAL FOUNDATIONS OF THE TOKUGAWA REGIME

For any political order to endure as long as the Tokugawa system did, it cannot rely solely on the coercive power of hegemon and henchmen. Authority has to be grounded in an accepted concept of legitimate rule. Like all aspiring rulers, Oda Nobunaga and Toyotomi Hideyoshi faced this ideological dilemma. They faced it, however, with a particular intensity. Because they had used coercion so nakedly, they had greater than usual need to convince people of the legitimacy of their rule. Both of these men, as well as Tokugawa Ieyasu, sought to ground their authority upon religious as well as secular symbols and ideals.

Nobunaga promoted himself as a divine ruler even as he went to war against popular religious sects and killed tens of thousands. He demanded that samurai "venerate" him. In exchange he offered not only military but also divine protection. He asserted that the service rendered in this life would benefit a loyal vassal in the next life. He issued proclamations demanding worship of him for those wishing to gain wealth and happiness. He also came to present himself as the embodiment of "the realm" (*tenka* in Japanese, literally "under heaven"). Unlike earlier military hegemons, he rejected a shogunal position because this would have placed him symbolically subordinate to the emperor as recipient of imperial confirmation. He had vassals use the phrase "for the *tenka*, for Nobunaga" in their pledges of loyalty. He thus identified himself with the realm, which was itself defined in terms of being all under heaven. He claimed sovereignty in a way that was similar to, but predated, Louis XIV of France, with his famous declaration that "I am the state" ("l'état, c'est moi").

Hideyoshi shared this tendency for self-deification. He hosted the emperor as an equal at his palace in Kyoto. His consort was made equal in status to the emperor's mother. The status of his son was made that of the emperor's son. He also presented the Korean invasions as sacred national campaigns, replete with ceremonies at a Shinto shine. Although the Shinto religious tradition sees blood as a source of grave pollution, Hideyoshi sponsored a "blood festival" in his own honor. In death he arranged for construction of a shrine to himself, as Great August Deity, with nationwide branches.

The Tokugawa clan continued these programs of personal deification that rivaled the sacred claims of the imperial court. Ieyasu controlled and dictated even the petty behavior of the court families, and he received foreign embassies in their presence. Iemitsu, for his part, in 1634 made a grand procession to the emperor's home city of Kyoto with 309,000 men.

Tokugawa Ieyasu also built the grand shrine at Nikkō. In the twentieth century this has become one of Japan's premier tourist sights, but Ieyasu was not seeking tourist yen or dollars. He sought self-deification in the overstated, baroque tradition of his immediate predecessors. He knew of Nobunaga's glorious Azuchi Castle, destroyed shortly after Nobunaga's death, and he consciously sought to wipe out and replace Hideyoshi's shrine network. He specified that he was to be buried at Nikkō. In a symbolic move of posthumous politics this shrine was located at the same distance from his Edo castle as the Grand Imperial Shrine at Ise was from the imperial palace in Kyoto. He claimed for himself the posthumous name of "Great Incarnation, Shining Over the East." The phrase invoked both the Buddhist concept of reincarnation and the Shinto image of brilliant light. He also made himself into an Asia-wide, even universal, god: In Iemitsu's time Korean embassies paid their respects at Nikkō, as did official delegates from the Ryūkyū Islands, and even the Dutch. In location, in ritual use, and in nomenclature, Iemitsu was seeking to displace Ise as the premier sacred political symbol in the land. In 1645 he elevated the Nikkō Shrine to the level of a *gū*, the same term used for Ise. Imperial messengers were forced to pay respects at Nikkō, not vice versa.

While the Tokugawa bolstered their claim to rule by seeking to symbolically deify the persons of the rulers, they also anchored their legitimacy in philosophical claims of religious and secular traditions. From diverse sources in the first century of Tokugawa rule, there emerged broad agreement on several core ideas concerning the proper political and social order. First, hierarchy is natural and just. Second, selfless service and accepting one's place within a hierarchical society are great virtues. Third, Tokugawa Ieyasu was the great sage founder, source of all wisdom. The order he created was said to be rooted in the order of the cosmos.

A complicated mixture of Buddhist, Shinto, and neo-Confucian elements underlay this ideological synthesis. A samurai-turned-Zen priest named Suzuki Shōsan (1579–1655) was one source of this ideology. He argued that the present life was an occasion to repay obligations to benefactors (lord, parents). One existed not for oneself, but for lord and society. One served them by observing one's proper place. Suzuki enjoined commoners to follow their "calling" through motivated performance of their daily work. The result, he taught, would be salvation in the next life. A Shinto cleric named Yamazaki Ansai (1618–82) searched the Shinto tradition for a "Japanese way" of thought to explain the world he knew. He used numerology to argue for a parallel or correspondence between teachings of the ancient Japanese gods and the Chinese sages, and from this he built an argument in favor of the Way of the Tokugawa.[1]

Finally, numerous thinkers, in an increasingly diverse and contentious intellectual world by the end of the 1600s, drew on neo-Confucian ideas to educate rulers and ruled on the character of the just political order. Since medieval times, the neo-Confucian ideas of Zhu Xi, stressing the importance of direct reading of ancient Confucian texts, had been studied in Japan primarily by Buddhist monks. An important new academy in Edo began to change this. It was founded by Fujiwara Seika and his follower Hayashi Razan. These men convinced the bakufu to support their endeavors in the form of an officially favored think tank. In 1630 the bakufu provided funds for their buildings, centered on a "Sages Hall" to honor Confucius that opened in 1633. In 1670, the Hayashi academy was officially recognized as a shogunate university. As secular scholars, the Hayashi came into conflict with Ieyasu and Iemitsu's Buddhist advisors. They disapproved of promoting Confucian learning beyond their monasteries. The Hayashi scholars succeeded in challenging the intellectual primacy of monasteries, but from the outset they faced challenges themselves from rival secular scholars and academies. In this process, much scholarship in Japan was brought into a secular realm in which the students were not only samurai but also well-to-do commoners. The Hayashi scholars and their rivals stressed the practical value of knowledge as they mobilized Confucian ideas to support the state.

At the heart of the neo-Confucian synthesis developed by these thinkers was the principle of reason, or *ri*. This immutable natural law was said to be the basis of all learning and conduct. It permeated the physical universe and the social world of humans as well; thus laws of nature and laws of society had the same metaphysical basis. Chinese and Japanese neo-Confucianists both counseled the active "investigation of things" of the physical *and* social world to discover the role of principle in it. Observation was said to confirm that *ri* governed the relations of the heavenly bodies. It placed earth at the base, the sun above, and the stars in motion around both. Similarly, the ruler stood above, the people at the base. All humans, as well, had proper relations to each other: father-child, husband-wife, ruler-subject, friend-friend, sibling-sibling. In Japan specifically, the shogunal ruler was said to stand above the rest of the people. The emperor, descended from the supreme heavenly body, the sun, delegated power to him. The people—in the four primary statuses of samurai, farmer, artisan, and merchant—stood below him, with samurai as aides to ruling power. Early in the Tokugawa era, this order of things was literally and figuratively enshrined as the sacred creation of the sage Ieyasu. The first goal of all Tokugawa reformers—even those from opposed philosophical traditions—was to sustain it.

CULTURAL DIVERSITY AND CONTRADICTIONS

The neo-Confucian synthesis represented the world of nature and of humans as seamless and orderly. In fact, numerous Japanese people of the Tokugawa era, including Confucian scholars themselves, understood their world as a complex place. The pieces did not always fit together; human desires and political loyalties might oppose orthodox notions of the proper society. As they explored these contradictions, an expanding body of participants invigorated and diversified the intellectual and cultural life, both in cities and in the countryside, among commoners and the samurai elite. Debate began in the 1660s, just as neo-Confucian teachings were being validated with bakufu patronage. The debate continued for nearly two hundred years. A wide variety of individuals and schools argued over the proper interpretation of Confucianism. Those working within the Confucian tradition also faced challenges from scholars drawing on entirely different schools of thought.

The school of Ancient Learning (*Kogaku*) was perhaps the most significant challenge to neo-Confucian thought from within the tradition of scholarship that sought to interpret Confucius for the present era. A series of great scholars elaborated the Ancient Learning ideas. The most famous was Ogyū Sorai (1666–1728). The school derived its name from the insistence that proper knowledge rested on unmediated understanding of the ancient texts of Confucius himself. They argued that neo-Confucian interpretations of Zhu Xi, or his followers in Korea, China, or Japan, had failed to understand the true meaning of old words. This position is rather ironic. Zhu Xi's own point of departure in the 1100s was also a call to ignore intervening interpretations and return directly to the ancient Confucian texts.

Sorai revered Confucius and the ancient Chinese kings who built political institutions upon Confucian ideas. He stressed that the samurai needed to model their behavior on the ancient Confucian rulers by cultivating virtue and devotion to duty. He asked them to model present-day institutions on the ancient systems as well. At the same time, Sorai recognized that the "way," or the political-ethical order, of the early kings was something they themselves had created by virtue of their high intelligence and insight. It was not directly imposed by divine sources. This implicitly opened the way for rulers in later ages, such as Tokugawa Japan, to make appropriate adjustments, provided they based these on proper understanding of ancient texts, rituals, and institutions.

At issue for Sorai, his contemporaries, and their successors was the problem of how to justify creative political action and institutional innovation. Society was manifestly changing before their eyes, but it was supposed to be rooted in ancient ideas and practices. Sorai was committed to the support of a timeless and changeless "way" that originated in ancient China. As a shogunal advisor in the early 1700s, some of his policy proposals called on the bakufu to adopt ancient Chinese tax systems or bureaucracies. But he was also enough of a realist to argue that rulers of his own time should take some innovative steps such as allowing peasants to buy and sell land.[2]

By the early 1700s, merchants joined samurai scholars such as Sorai in the active study and critique of both ancient texts and the contemporary world. In Osaka and its environs, in particular, a number of academies emerged under commoner patronage.

The most important, given official status by the Tokugawa rulers, was called the Kai-tokudō Merchant Academy. Recent study of the Kaitokudō scholars has changed the longstanding view among historians that the Tokugawa merchant class accepted a subordinate place in a Confucian status order and made no claim to a political role. The Kaitokudō scholars in fact argued that politics and economics were inseparable. They placed samurai and merchants in functionally equivalent roles; the former were to run the bureaucratic administration, while the latter managed economic affairs that were of importance to the entire society.

To be sure, the Kaitokudō intellectuals did not challenge the samurai's right to rule. One cannot make a simple analogy between Tokugawa merchant thinking and that of the European urban bourgeoisie that began to oppose aristocratic power in the eighteenth century. But these Tokugawa era teachings did emphasize the interdependence and relative equality of *virtue* and public function between merchants and bureaucrats. Such notions formed an important part of a cultural world that lived on into later times, when country and city merchants alike became captains of industry dedicated to enriching the nation as well as themselves.[3]

Part of the cultural ferment of Tokugawa times played out not only among strait-laced samurai-scholars, or in equally sober academies supported by merchants, but also in the entertainment quarters of the great cities, especially Osaka and Edo. Here, theaters and book shops stood beside teahouses and brothels. Here, samurai mixed with commoners in the audience of puppet and Kabuki plays. The scripts of these plays drew on scandalous gossip and flamboyant crimes to address profound themes of the conflicts between duty and desire, between public law and private loyalty.

The Tokugawa era cities were home to flourishing prose fiction, poetry, and pictorial arts that celebrated the lives of commoners and rogues and gently challenged the high-minded moralists of established order. Ihara Saikaku, for example, wrote popular fiction that poked fun at religion, at merchants and their greed, and at human desires. His works focused on people at the bottom of society and made heroes and heroines of them. In "The Woman Who Loved Love" he offers a wicked parody of the search for religious truth by telling the story of a courtesan's search for the ideal lover. The final episode has the courtesan standing at a temple, gazing at one hundred figures of the Buddha, each one reminding her of a former lover. Another Edo writer with a different sort of critical sensibility was the poet Matsuo Bashō (1644–1694). His elegant haiku celebrated the natural world and a vanishing past. Resident in the great city, his work nostalgically appreciated the quiet countryside to which he periodically escaped.

an old pond . . .	furuike ya
a frog leaps in,	kawazu tobikomu
the sound of water	mizu no oto[4]

An unprecedent market for literature and art also sustained the Tokugawa cultural product perhaps best known outside Japan today, the woodblock print, or *ukiyo-e*. The term literally translates as "pictures of the floating world." The term "floating world" referred to the ephemeral entertainments of the world of brothels and theaters. As woodblock art began to flourish in the middle of the Tokugawa era, prints of famous courtesans and star Kabuki actors were produced in huge numbers. The painters them-

Woodblock landscape prints became very popular and sophisticated in the late Edo era. This view of "Evening Snow at Uchikawa" is by the renowned print artist Hiroshige, from 1835 or 1836.
Courtesy of Keio University.

selves became luminaries of the cultural scene. Later print artists also turned to the genre of the landscape. They produced many celebrated works that paralleled in pictorial form Bashō's exploration of the countryside. Prints were also frequently integrated with text; one inspiration for the twentieth century comic book (*manga*) was probably the printmaking of the Tokugawa era.

Two theatrical traditions emerged at the heart of urban cultural life: the Kabuki and the *bunraku* puppet theater. The former began as a means by which prostitutes, male and female, drew crowds who might be enticed to purchase sexual services as well. Performances were often held in outdoor theaters in dry riverbeds, alongside carnival entertainments such as bear and tiger acts or sumo wrestling. In 1629, the bakufu banned female actors from the Kabuki in an effort to suppress prostitution. Ironically, the Kabuki survived. Some say it improved as a result. It certainly became more distinctive. The brilliant performances of female impersonators (the *onna-gata*) came to be the defining highlight of the Kabuki theater. Here in the theater of the seventeenth and eighteenth centuries, one finds an early example of the postmodern idea that gender identity is not fixed in a person's physical body, but is the changeable result of performance.

The *bunraku* puppet theater was a second great innovation of Edo era culture. Its "performers" were puppets of roughly two-thirds life size. Up to three men manipulated each puppet. A highly skilled singer-actor chanted the several parts and the narration, backed by musical accompanists. The puppet theater was attractive to writers since they had no uppity actors to deal with, and the literary qualities of the plays were developed beautifully. The greatest *bunraku* playwright was Chikamatsu Monzaemon (1653–1725). His works were noteworthy for treating the tragic lives of common people, including scandalous contemporary events such as domestic murders.

Chikamatsu brilliantly captured the tensions within Tokugawa thought and society. His works often explore conflict between duty or obligation, on one hand, and human feeling on the other (*giri* versus *ninjō*). *Love Suicide at Sonezaki*, based loosely on a real story, tells of a paper seller who falls hopelessly in love with a prostitute. His relatives criticize him and his business fails. He pawns his wife's kimono to buy out his lover's contract. With his wife and family ready to disown him, he and his lover, torn by guilt as well as desire, run away to commit suicide. In the end, duty destroys desire, but the audience is left to wish it had not.

Chikamatsu explored a similarly conflicted outcome with more immediate political implications in *The Tale of the 47 Rōnin* (*rōnin* were samurai without a daimyō or master to serve). Chikamatsu wrote a puppet theater version of the story in 1706. In the 1740s, a Kabuki version was written, called *Chūshingura*, and this became the most frequently staged play of the Tokugawa era (it continues to be a hugely popular subject of cinema and stage in modern Japan). The puppet and Kabuki scripts thinly disguised their origin in an actual incident of 1703 by relocating the events several centuries earlier. The story celebrates the loyalty of samurai warriors whose master was disgraced and executed at the hands of a political enemy. To avenge this act, they break the law by attacking and killing the nemesis of their former master. As with the domestic tale of the Sonezaki suicide, the violation of law and order is ultimately punished. The forty-seven retainers are required by the authorities to take their own lives as the price of their successful pursuit of personal revenge. But these loyalists are heroes in death, both in the actual event and in the play, which exposed a crucial tension in the Tokugawa political world: To whom was ultimate loyalty owed?

Playwrights and actors explored these tensions to the delight of large audiences. Tokugawa political advisors and scholars sought to contain these cultural forms and to resolve the problems they explored. The entertainment quarters themselves were bounded by walls and physically isolated on the edges of town. Samurai were told not to enter their gates. The bakufu and domains enacted what are called "sumptuary laws" to keep social behavior in line with hereditary status. These orders restricted the dress permitted to samurai of various ranks and to merchants and other commoners. They prescribed who could be carried around town in palanquin chairs. They limited building size in accord with status and rank. Laws even regulated eating and drinking habits, forbidding to farmers the unspeakable luxury of tea. Peasants were to content themselves with hot water.

The fact that many of these injunctions were continually reissued is strong evidence that many people ignored them. To this extent, the bakufu dictatorship had a limited reach. Nonetheless, the laws set a sober tone, and the tensions of this era have echoes in recent times. As in many societies, a moralistic tendency to condemn luxurious living and glorify austerity persists to the present day in Japanese cultural life and public policy. Yet, another side to popular culture celebrates the accumulation of wealth and the stylish consumption of abundant goods.

The authorities also placed limits on subject matter appropriate for Kabuki, and they regulated the times and numbers of performances. This was part of a broader effort to contain the tensions of the Tokugawa order. Ogyū Sorai's opinion to the shogun on how to deal with the vendetta of the forty-seven *rōnin* addressed the tension between the virtue of loyalty to a particular lord and the value of order to society as a whole. He acknowledged that their deed was righteous. It was sparked by a proper sense of shame—a determination "to keep oneself free from any taint." Even so, he concluded that laws for the entire country must be upheld, and the men must be punished. An "act of violence without official permission" was intolerable. If "general principles are impaired by special exceptions, there will no longer be any respect for the law in this country."[5]

Other tensions were ultimately impossible to contain. One was the conflict between merit and heredity. A Confucian ruler was qualified for his status by merit. In China, merit was cultivated by study and confirmed by an examination. Examinations had been used in Japan in earlier centuries, but in the Tokugawa era the samurai faced no such tests. They had a hereditary claim to rank and to income. Official appointments were roughly pegged to these birthrights. For much of the Tokugawa era, people made little effort to reconcile the contradiction between meritocratic principle and hereditary practice. Scholars and rulers alike preached the importance in principle of recruiting the wise and the strong to domain and bakufu offices. Yet hereditary rank and family income continued to be the most important influence on a samurai's career path in practice.

As the perception deepened in the 1700s that society faced a crisis, complaints increased about the failure of rulers to appoint "men of talent" to high office. The term "a daimyō's skill" became an insult. Numerous thinkers in the 1700s and 1800s— what one historian calls "merit reformers"—called on rulers to regenerate the system by appointing men of talent. Their stated goal was to preserve and strengthen the existing regime. But their critiques clearly implied that to deny men of talent indefinitely would threaten the legitimacy and survival of the ruler.[6]

A second ultimately subversive tension centered on the relationship of the emperor to the shogun. On one hand, the Tokugawa rulers closely watched and supervised court life. They used shrines such as that at Nikkō as well as foreign diplomacy to symbolically assert a more or less independent source of legitimacy. But the emperor in theory had appointed Ieyasu and his successors as shogun. Across the Tokugawa centuries, aspiring political actors outside the Tokugawa ruling circle, and some on the edges of it, sustained the idea that Tokugawa authority was delegated and conditional. The Mito domain, for example, was a branch of the Tokugawa house. It was potentially eligible to supply an heir to the shogun should the direct line fail. Its daimyō of the late 1600s, Mitsukuni, would don court robes every New Year's morning and bow toward Kyoto. He would tell his vassals, "My Lord is the emperor. The present shogun is the head of my family."[7] Given such opinions, it was virtually inevitable that in a moment of great crisis those who lost faith in the Tokugawa rulers would look to the emperor to support their insurgent acts.

REFORM, CRITIQUES, AND INSURGENT IDEAS

Beginning in the early 1700s, chronic debt and a belief that the regime faced a moral as well as a fiscal crisis sparked the first of several official drives to reform. Each was shorter than the previous round. None had enduring impact. The eighth shogun, Yoshimune, in office from 1716 to 1745, presided over the first of these campaigns, called the Kyōhō reforms (after the reign name of the emperor at the time). From 1767 to 1786, the shogunal advisor Tanuma Okitsugu initiated a number of unorthodox economic reforms intended to expand government income. His profligate habits gave conservative opponents an opening to attack him. He was forced from office in disgrace. His nemesis and successor as chief shogunal advisor was Matsudaira Sadanobu. He launched the Kansei reforms (1787–93). These aimed to stabilize consumer rice prices, cut government costs, and increase revenues. The final reform, of the Tempō era (1841–43), had similar objectives. Although the bakufu's measures were ineffective, reformers enjoyed some success in a few domains.

Two different approaches characterized these reforming endeavors. One might be called "hardline Confucianism." This was the spirit of Yoshimune's reforms of the early 1700s and Matsudaira's brief efforts toward the end of the century. In addition to praising austerity, railing against luxury, and cutting government costs, they sought to shore up the status system by a policy of moral persuasion. Samurai were told both to study harder and to commit themselves anew to the martial arts. Matsudaira promised that those who proved their talent and diligence would be promoted to responsible posts even if they were lower-ranked samurai. He also tried to eliminate unorthodox ideas with an order in the 1790s that reaffirmed Zhu Xi Confucianism as the official philosophy of the bakufu. This edict also put in place stricter censorship, including a ban on pornography. It implemented a system of annual examinations at the shogunal academy responsible for training top officials. In theory, this opened the door to men of talent within the bakufu. In practice, the exams remained heavily biased against samurai of humble origin.[8]

In contrast, the program of Tanuma Okitsugu, who preceded Matsudaira in the bakufu from 1777 to 1786, and some of the subsequent Tempo era reforms of the 1830s, sought to encourage or exploit change. The spirit here is comparable to what historians of Europe refer to as mercantilism, or policies by which the state promotes economic development to bolster its power. Like Matsudaira, Tanuma promoted efforts of farmers to reclaim land, which would expand the tax base. He went further than his predecessor, however. He promoted bakufu cooperation with merchants with the goal of licensing or taxing their operations. He supported trade with China, hoping to export finished goods in exchange for silver. He also encouraged science and translations of Western books.

The hardline effort to return to a golden past was ideologically attractive but not feasible. The converse attempt to accept and profit from change was practical, but it was ideologically suspect and hard to justify. The Tokugawa rulers lacked the unity or will to pursue such a course. Some of the outer domains proved more flexible. This left them in a good position to contend for power in the mid-nineteenth century crisis.

Calls for drastic reform were not limited to rulers and their advisors. Even in the early 1700s, the spread of commerce and education fostered increasing ties between literate merchants and samurai in cities and an upper crust of literate and prosperous farmers in the country. This rural upper class had begun to develop an interest in political and economic matters reaching beyond the village boundaries.

These families were the patrons of temple-based schools in the countryside. In some cases they sent children to official domain academies that were mainly intended for samurai. Once educated, these farmers—including a minority of women as well as men—would correspond with teachers and writers in the cities concerning cultural matters. They exchanged and evaluated Chinese poetry. They discussed ancient Japanese literature or Confucian philosophy. They sent their children to be servants at court families in Kyoto or at merchant houses in Osaka or Edo.

In a number of regions, such educated farmers became followers of a group of intellectuals who formed the School of National Learning. One pioneer of this scholarly tradition was Motoori Norinaga (1730–1801). He was reacting in part to the extreme worship of Chinese thought in the work of men like Ogyū Sorai. He and his followers shared Sorai's reliance on ancient texts. Like Sorai, they used these texts on behalf of contemporary critiques and calls for reform. But Norinaga asserted that Japanese people should seek knowledge in their native genius, and not in alien Chinese sources.

Norinaga's search for a pure Japanese culture led him back to the earliest Japanese literature, including historical chronicles (the *Kojiki*, 712 C.E.) and prose fiction (the *Tale of Genji*, eleventh century). He found in these works what he glorified as core values of the Japanese people: a sympathetic, emotional understanding of others and the intuitive ability to distinguish good and evil without complex rationalization. He exalted Shinto as a tradition of thought that posited a gradual continuum from humans to gods. The latter inhabited a mysterious realm only just beyond human reach, not radically transcendent. The emperor, in such a vision, was a crucial being who mediated between the realms of spirit and humans.

The network of National Learning scholars and rural adherents expanded significantly in the early nineteenth century. Norinaga's own work did not address politics explicitly, but his followers, in particular Hirata Atsutane (1776–1842), politicized his ideas in the early 1800s. They articulated ideals of loyalty to "Japan" that went beyond the narrower loyalty to a daimyō and his domain, which made up the primary political identity for most people in the Tokugawa era. Most inhabitants of Japan, that is, considered their domain to be their "country." The word *kuni*, in fact, which in modern times came to refer to a national unit (Japan), was applied to the domains of the Tokugawa era. Hirata's ideas looked beyond domain loyalty to a sort of nationalism that characterized the responses of people to the Western powers in decades to come. The network of registered Hirata disciples numbered 3,745 after his death in the 1850s.[9] Many of these, in turn, stood as teachers and promoters of National Learning doctrine to others.

Hirata exalted Japan as the land of the Shinto gods. He elevated Japan to a superior place in the international order. He and his followers viewed external and internal signs of distress as evidence that the current rulers were failing their obligations to gods, emperor, and people. The supporters of National Learning did not lead the attack that overthrew the Tokugawa. But they formed part of a climate of opinion that made great upheaval and change—on behalf of a national entity that transcended the Tokugawa system—more likely and easier to achieve.

One of the most profound and directly consequential critiques of the status quo came from scholars of the Mito domain, home to a potential rival branch of the ruling Tokugawa line. The most important of these was Aizawa Yasushi (1782–1863), an advisor to the Mito daimyō and the author of an incendiary text called the *New Theses* (*Shinron*). This work mixed an explicitly anti-Western message with an implicitly anti-bakufu critique. Written in 1825, Aizawa's text was secretly copied and circulated among dissident samurai in the 1840s and 1850s.

The *New Theses* condemned the weakness of the ruling elite. Daimyō and their top aides were said to be living in dissolute luxury. They had failed to prepare for the unprecedented foreign threat of Western ships, whose visits were increasing year by year. The bakufu was condemned for keeping other domains weak to ensure its own hegemony, thereby weakening the whole of Japan against outsiders. The populace was said to be gullible and disloyal. As Aizawa was fond of writing, the commoners were "stupid." He was terrified that Christian missionaries would easily be able to convert the masses and destroy Japan's essence as the land of the gods.

Aizawa wanted the rulers to recruit men of talent. He wanted them to reemphasize morality for the people and serve as moral exemplars. These were relatively ordinary proposals for a Tokugawa reformer. Aizawa also called for greater centralized power to meet the common threat. The *New Theses* put forward this advice to enable the Tokugawa to strengthen themselves and the entire realm. Despite this intent, the call for greater reverence for the emperor and dramatic domestic reform to deal with the foreign threat was potentially subversive to the Tokugawa.

Knowledge produced in the West was called "Dutch learning" because the Dutch traders in Nagasaki were its primary source. It was another source of potentially transforming ideas. The bakufu forbade the import of "Christian books" beginning in the 1640s, but books on practical topics such as surgery or navigation were allowed, and a small flow of Western books, as well as Chinese translations, arrived in Japan over the following decades.[10] This prohibition was relaxed in 1720. A modest tradition of Dutch-language scholarship of the West took root, primarily in Nagasaki. Its practitioners looked into Western natural science, medicine, and botany in particular and compiled a dictionary and maps. This remained a disinterested academic study until the 1840s, when the so-called Dutch scholars turned to study of military technology.

National Learning, the reformism of the Mito school, and Dutch-mediated Western learning appealed primarily to subelites of the rural upper crust and to educated samurai of middle to lower ranks. Its appeals were most powerful on the margins of the Tokugawa order, in the countryside, in outer and collateral domains with traditionally tense relations with the shogunate, or in far southern Nagasaki.

One other potentially subversive strand of thought was nurtured among poorer peasants. It was expressed in the increased instances of rebellion mentioned in the previous chapter and in powerful new religious movements. Several newly founded popular religions of late Tokugawa times each won thousands of believers. These include the Kurozumi (1814), Tenri (1838), and Konkō (1857) religions, among others. Each was founded by a man or a woman who experienced a divine revelation or a miraculous cure. They drew diversely on Shinto or Buddhist elements. These religions gained support from masses of peasants who had come to expect that a great change was imminent. Such a change would "rectify the world" (*yonaoshi*) to a proper state of equality and prosperity for all. Some religions counseled patient waiting for the moment of renewal, but adherents might also be stirred to act to hasten the day of salvation in this world. The authorities viewed these groups with much anxiety.

In addition, the rural villagers of Tokugawa Japan cut loose in several astonishing moments of mass pilgrimage. These were called *okage-mairi* or *Ise-mairi*, after the Ise Shrine that was the destination of many of the pilgrims. Such events erupted at roughly sixty-year intervals through the Tokugawa period. They intensified sharply in the last two iterations. Observers reported in 1771 that about two million peasants packed their bags and took to the road to Ise. At the same time, reports circulated of objects such as Shinto shrine amulets—small good luck charms—floating down from the sky. This was repeated in 1830 on an even more extraordinary scale. Roughly five million people (in a country of perhaps thirty million) took to the road and visited Ise over a span of about four months. They jostled, sang, shouted, begged, and sometimes stole from and fought with each other all the way to the shrine. Mass pilgrimage was not in itself a revolutionary act, but it did heighten widespread expectations of change.

In sum, one thread running through the work of many Tokugawa thinkers and critics by the early 1800s was a widespread sense that the times were disjointed. Things were not as they should be. Action was needed to set them right. Setting things right generally meant returning to an idealized golden age of early Tokugawa times. Even Aizawa Yasushi intended his work to help the bakufu regenerate itself. But only slightly below the surface, many were drawn to the idea that an entity and interest larger than the bakufu, centered on the emperor, should be the focus of reform. In a dramatically new context created by Japan's humiliating, coerced entry into a Western-dominated world order in the 1850s, these calls for action mixed with the discontent and frustrated ambitions of many people. This proved to be a potent, increasingly nationalistic brew, in which reforming ideas had revolutionary consequences.

4

The Overthrow of the Tokugawa

In the decades around 1800, whalers, merchant ships, and gunboats from Europe and the United States appeared in Japanese waters with alarming frequency, pressing their claims with increasing persistence. They were powerful symbols and emissaries of the capitalist and nationalist revolutions that were just then transforming Euro-American societies and reaching beyond to transform the world. In Japan they turned a chronic low-grade crisis into an acute, revolutionary situation. For decades, the superintendents of the Tokugawa order had been somehow muddling through. Shogun and daimyō managed to handle the combined pressures of social discontent among peasants and samurai and fiscal crisis in their own treasuries. Into this mix came heretofore unknown foreign power—military, economic, and cultural—raising unprecedented demands for a new sort of international relationship. Suddenly the Tokugawa bakufu's very legitimacy was called into question.

Even so, for some time it appeared that the Tokugawa system might bend without breaking. By the mid-1860s the bakufu had moved to remodel the military, adjust the balance between domain and shogunal power, and import new technology. Foreign diplomats divided their bets. The British were officially neutral, but their chief representative maintained unofficial ties with the insurgent outer domains, and some of their merchants offered direct support. The French backed the Tokugawa reformers seeking to superintend the process of integrating Japan into the Western diplomatic and economic order.

By hedging their bets the British turned out to be smarter gamblers. In the end, the Tokugawa rulers had too much of an investment in the old order. Rulers of outer domains were often cautious, as well, and they sometimes suppressed the rebels in their domains. But at critical moments they supported the initiatives of new actors, lower on the social scale. These were the "men of action," self-styled heroes hoisting a banner to "honor the emperor and expel the barbarians." They forced the Tokugawa from power and then launched one of the great revolutions of modern history.

THE WESTERN POWERS AND THE UNEQUAL TREATIES

The first harbingers of renewed Western interest in Japan came by land. Russian explorers had reached the far eastern shores of the vast Siberian forests in the 1780s.

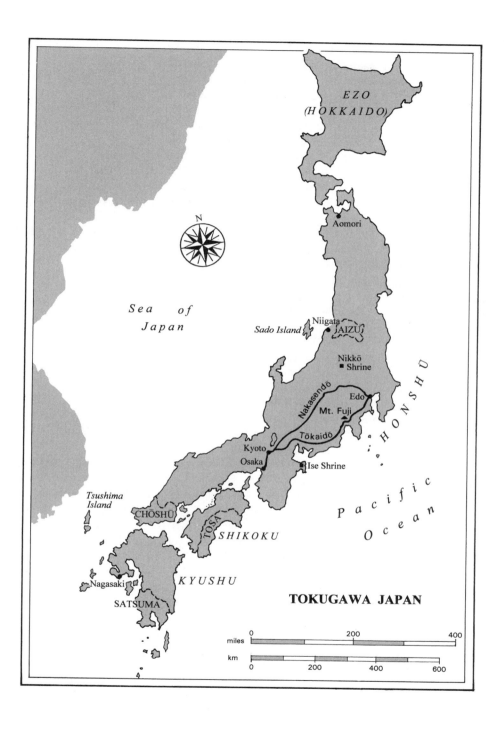

Sea of Japan

EZO (HOKKAIDO)

Aomori

Niigata
Sado Island
AIZU

Nikkō Shrine

Nakasendō
Mt. Fuji
Edo
Tōkaidō

HONSHU

Kyoto
Osaka
Ise Shrine

Tsushima Island

CHŌSHŪ

TOSA

SHIKOKU

Pacific Ocean

Nagasaki

KYUSHU

SATSUMA

TOKUGAWA JAPAN

miles
0   200   400

km
0   200   400   600

From there, they charted the coastal waters while trappers and traders worked the northern islands of Sakhalin and the Kuril chain, and then Hokkaido. In 1792 in Hokkaido, and again in 1804 in Nagasaki, Russian traders asked the bakufu to grant trade privileges, but they accepted a polite Tokugawa refusal. These overtures marked the start of several decades of sporadic but increasing and occasionally violent incursions. In 1806–07, Russian naval officers led destructive attacks on Japanese settlements in Hokkaido, Sakhalin, and Etorofu islands.

One year later the British joined the chase. The warship *Phaeton* entered Nagasaki harbor in 1808 and threatened to attack the Dutch (the two nations were enemies in the Napoleonic wars). In 1818 a British ship sailed into Uraga bay, near Edo. The bakufu quickly rejected their request to begin trade relations. In response to such visits, the bakufu in 1825 issued an order that imposed the most extreme interpretation yet of "seclusion" policy: expel by force any foreign ship in Japanese waters. As a result, when the American merchant ship, the *Morrison*, made a similar plea for trade in 1837, it met an even harsher reply: a volley of harmless cannon fire. A few years later, in 1844, the Dutch made an overture from their long-established base in Nagasaki. They submitted a polite entreaty to the bakufu from King William II. They explained that the world had changed: The Japanese could no longer remain safely disengaged from the commercial networks and diplomatic order that the Western powers were spreading thoughout the globe.

The Dutch argument was backed by the shocking evidence of the recent Opium Wars in China. The Chinese in 1839 had tried to ban the socially disastrous opium trade. The British defended "free trade" with force. By 1842 their gunboats had imposed their will on the Chinese. In a treaty that anticipated Japan's future, the British forced open new ports to trade and forced the Chinese to accept tariff levels set by the British. They won the extraterritorial right to impose British law on Chinese soil, administered by British officials in cases involving British subjects.

Those Japanese who knew of this result were deeply troubled. The chief bakufu official, Mizuno Tadakuni, noted that "this is happening in a foreign country, but I believe it also contains a warning for us."[1] Tokugawa officials politely rejected the Dutch advice to avoid a future war by quickly signing trade treaties—first with the Dutch, of course. But they did make some changes. In 1842, the bakufu relaxed the 1825 policy of shoot first, ask questions later. Westerners adrift in Japanese waters were to be given fuel and provisions and sent peacefully on their way. In addition, the bakufu heeded some of the advice of protonationalist reformers such as the Mito scholars. Chief councillor Abe Masahiro implemented a gradual buildup of coastal defenses in the Tokugawa heartland after he took office in 1845. He also allowed other domains to do the same.

Foreign pressures and bakufu responses combined in ways that ultimately weakened the bakufu. At the same time, they strengthened an emerging national consciousness among a growing body of political actors. The Opium War confirmed the worst fears of all who viewed the Western barbarians as insatiable predators intent on conquest as well as profit. This gave the basic stance of seclusion a more powerful rationale than ever. Yet any effective practical response had to avoid war while domains and bakufu bolstered their defenses. At the very least, this required short-term retreat from hardline seclusion and the import of some of the Western technologies that enabled this threat in the first place. The bakufu was trapped between a rock and a hard place. It could hardly avoid the appearance of weakness as it tried to build strength.

It is tempting to dismiss the xenophobic arguments of so many Japanese at this time as both futile and irrational. In Asia, at least, the Western powers did not see territorial conquest as their only viable option. They wanted trade more than territory. But paranoid views sometimes rest on firm ground. Western ideologies of free trade were buoyed by a moral certitude and expansive reach that did not take no for an answer. They certainly did not rule out colonization. People in late Tokugawa Japan, who believed they had nothing to gain from any increased contact with the barbarians from the West, were correct to feel threatened. Their way of life, from the material to the political, was about to change irrevocably.

In 1853, Commodore Matthew Perry of the United States arrived in Japan as the most determined carrier yet of this simple message: Agree to trade in peace, or suffer the consequences in war. His mission marked a new step in the American advance to the West. With Atlantic waters nearly exhausted, American whalers had been venturing far across the Pacific. Having taken California from Mexico in 1848, the Americans had a new sense of commercial and military ambition in the Pacific. They also wanted to compete with the British. Most immediately, Perry wanted the Japanese to sell coal to naval ships and allow provisioning stops to whalers.

His appearance in Edo bay in July 1853, and his return the following year, occasioned much baffled and excited interaction. During the return visit in 1854, the Japanese sought to intimidate the intruders with an exhibition of sumo wrestling. The Americans were not impressed. One described in his diary an event of "shoving, yelling, tugging, hawling, bawling, twisting, and curvetting about, with seemingly no aim whatever." He concluded, "It was a very unsatisfactory trial of strength, there were one or two falls, but after all, any wrestler that I have heretofore seen of half the muscle would have laughed at them."[2] On the other hand, the Americans brought some of their latest technology, including a one-quarter scale locomotive engine and a 370-foot circle of track. "Steam was up, an Engineer got on the tender and one of the [bakufu] Commissioners sat on the car, it was set going and ran round at a speed of 18 miles an hour."[3] The Japanese official, his robe flapping in the wind, was reported to be delighted at the ride.

Such episodes notwithstanding, Perry was a hard-nosed and humorless man. He left a harsh message in July 1853 with a promise to come back for an answer: "The undersigned, as an evidence of his friendly intentions, has brought but four of the smaller [ships of war], designing, should it become necessary, to return to Yedo in the ensuing spring with a much larger force."[4] This episode sparked panic among the population in and around Edo. It also sparked an extremely unusual step, indeed unprecedented, by the bakufu. Hoping to rally a consensus for its choice to make some concessions and avoid a war, the bakufu actually requested that daimyō submit their advice in writing on how best to deal with the Americans.

True to his word, Perry sailed back to Japan in early 1854 with a substantial fleet of nine ships, including three steam frigates. The bakufu agreed to allow American ships to stop over in the relatively remote ports of Shimoda and Hakodate. The Americans also won the right to station a consul in Shimoda. The terms of this Treaty of

Kanagawa were extended to the European powers—France, Britain, the Netherlands, Russia—as well. This bakufu concession stopped short of an immediate opening to trade, but the Western powers quickly pressed their advantage. The first American consul, Townsend Harris, took up residence in Shimoda on the southern tip of the Izu peninsula in 1856. Harris backed his demand for a trade treaty with the plausible threat that the British would drive an even tougher bargain. This first comprehensive treaty of trade, he noted, would surely serve as the model for the other powers.

By February 1858, the bakufu negotiators signed a treaty that very nearly replicated the Opium War settlement with China, without a shot having been fired. They were well aware that their domestic opponents would take advantage of this step to attack the bakufu. But they believed they had no better choice. A war would be futile. Other negotiators would be no less demanding.

The treaty opened eight ports to trade. Most notably, the Japanese surrendered tariff autonomy and legal jurisdiction over the treaty ports. Tariffs on goods entering or leaving Japan were set in the treaty. Japan's government had no power to change them. Foreign nationals accused of crimes in Japan would be tried in consular courts presided over by foreign judges under foreign laws, a practice known as extraterritoriality. In short order, the bakufu made similar agreements with the other Western powers.

These "unequal treaties" were humiliating in theory and in practice. It is true, and worth mentioning, that the Americans accepted Japanese insistence that opium trade be outlawed, and the British did not object. Had opium entered Japan freely, it might have changed the subsequent course of Japanese history in significant ways. Nonetheless, the treaties imposed a semicolonial status upon Japan. Politically and economically, Japan became legally subordinate to foreign governments. Over the next few decades, petty insults were heaped one upon the other. Numerous nasty crimes went lightly punished, if at all. In the 1870s and 1880s, these injustices—a rape unpunished or an assault excused—came to be front page material in the new national press. They were experienced each time as a renewed blow to pride, yet another violation of Japanese sovereignty.

Yet it would be misleading to conclude simply that these treaties trampled a *preexisting* national pride and sovereignty. Rather, from the early 1800s through the 1860s, the very process of dealing with the pushy barbarians *created* modern Japanese nationalism. Among shogunal officials, in daimyō castles, and in the private academies where politically concerned samurai debated history and policy, a new conception took hold of "Japan" as a single nation, to be defended and governed as such. As this happened, the Tokugawa claim to be Japan's legitimate defender began to wither.

THE CRUMBLING OF TOKUGAWA RULE

The immediate economic impact of the new treaty-port trade was substantial. Foreign merchants discovered that gold in Japan could be purchased with silver coins for about one-third the going global rate. They were delighted. In the first year of trade they bought massive amounts of gold. They sold it in China for triple the purchase price. In 1860, the bakufu staunched this financial hemorrhage by debasing its gold coins to bring them in line with world standards. This expanded the money supply and caused sharp inflation. In addition, foreign demand caused silk prices to triple by the early 1860s for both domestic and foreign purchasers. At the same time, imports increased of lightly taxed, inexpensive foreign goods, especially finished cotton. This helped consumers but drove many Japanese producers out of business.

Consumers and producers alike responded with violent protest. City-dwellers were furious over rising grain prices. At the peak of inflation in 1866 they destroyed hundreds of rice merchant shops in large food riots in Edo and Osaka. Similar protests hit smaller towns and villages in the regions surrounding each city. The year 1866 also saw a surge of unrest among silk producers. In the Bushu region to the west of Edo, about six thousand farmers and silk producers embarked on a weeklong campaign of violent protest. They marched from village to village, expanding their forces en route. They smashed the homes of their creditors, the rural upper class of village headmen, landlords, and moneylenders.[5] Bakufu troops eventually subdued them.

The rioters usually targeted fellow Japanese as their exploiters. They blamed urban rice merchants and rural moneylenders in particular. But many people in the 1860s, including silk producers who might have profited from increased demand and prices for their product, blamed the difficult plight of the common people on foreign traders and by implication the Japanese government that agreed to trade in the first place. The poetry written by rural disciples of Hirata Atsutane's School of National Learning conveys this sentiment passionately. Consider these words of Matsuo Taseko, a woman who produced silkworms in the Ina Valley in mountainous central Japan:

> It is disgusting
> > the agitation over thread
> > in today's world
> Ever since the ships
> > from foreign countries
> > came for the jeweled
> > silkworm cocoons
> > to the land of the gods and the emperor
> people's hearts
> > awesome though they are,
> > are being pulled apart
> > and consumed by rage.[6]

The popular anger reflected in riots and in such poems did not lead directly to the overthrow of the Tokugawa. But it certainly encouraged anti-Tokugawa activists who blamed the bakufu for impoverishing the people and dishonoring the emperor.

The forced opening of the treaty ports had a more immediate political impact as well. As it sought to keep the foreigners at bay, the manner in which the bakufu dealt with the daimyō and an expanding body of political activists around the country reduced the bakufu's legitimacy and hastened its demise.

In 1853, the bakufu's chief councillor, Abe Masahiro, had asked the daimyō to present their opinions on responding to Perry's first visit. Through consultation, he hoped to build consensus for a difficult decision. This was a domestic political "opening" that paralleled the more famous "opening" to the West. It had the unintended consequence of revealing bakufu weakness. It inspired dreams of power among leaders in key domains that had long traditions of frustrated political ambition. These included the outer domains of Satsuma, Chōshū, and Tosa, which had opposed the Tokugawa in their rise to power in 1600. Their daimyō and samurai still tended the flame of anti-Tokugawa sentiment over two centuries later. Closer to home, the powerful Mito domain—a branch of the Tokugawa family—emerged as a strong voice for change in both policy and the balance of power between bakufu, daimyō, and imperial court, as did other collateral domains such as Echizen and Aizu. Mito was headed by the staunch anti-foreign daimyō, Tokugawa Nariaki. It was home to the equally anti-foreign, pro-emperor (although nominally pro-Tokugawa) scholarship of men like Aizawa Yasushi.

The next dramatic sign of Tokugawa weakness came in 1857–58, in a tangled fiasco involving dispute over the shogunal succession and the signing of the treaty with the United States. The shogun himself, Iesada, was a weak and ailing young man with no heirs. His head councillor was the most important figure within the bakufu. In the face of daimyō criticism of his handling of Perry's demands, Abe Masahiro had resigned from this position in 1855. His successor, Hotta Masayoshi, faced two immediate challenges. With Iesada dying of illness, he had to oversee the choice of a new shogun. With Townsend Harris restless in Shimoda, he had to conclude treaties with the Americans and other powers without alienating the restive daimyō. His choice for shogun, and that of the inner circle of the *fudai* daimyō who monopolized the shogun's council, was a weak, controllable figure, a twelve-year old daimyō from the collateral domain of Kii. Arrayed against this, and also against the treaties, were the powerful reformist and anti-foreign daimyō of Mito, Satsuma, and several other domains. They promoted the son of Tokugawa Nariaki (the Mito daimyō), a reputedly talented young prodigy named Yoshinobu.

At this juncture, Hotta decided to strengthen his hand in both foreign policy and the succession dispute by seeking the emperor's ratification of the treaty with Harris. Laden with gifts, he broke longstanding precedent with an elaborate visit to Kyoto to receive the imperial blessing. In response, the Emperor Kōmei took an equally unprecedented step into foreign and domestic policy decisions: He refused to support the bakufu. His own anti-foreign leanings were bolstered by court officials and reformist daimyō, Tokugawa Nariaki in particular. The emperor told Hotta that he disapproved of the treaty. He signaled his support for Nariaki's son as the next shogun.

Greatly humiliated on both counts, Hotta had no choice but to resign. The Tokugawa could no longer count on the support of the imperial court. Bakufu prestige had suffered a huge blow. With this episode, a complex three-sided political dance began. It would continue for ten years. Bakufu diehards, especially councillors from smaller *fudai* domains, wanted to bolster traditional Tokugawa authority by carrying out foreign policy and military and financial reforms on their own terms. They were opposed on the elite level by powerful daimyō of the outer and collateral domains and officials in the imperial court. These prominent contenders for power used anti-foreign, pro-emperor rhetoric as they sought to shift the center of political authority in their direction. The third party to this dance was of lower status. These were the so-called loyalist samurai, or "men of high purpose" (*shishi*). They propelled events forward with acts of political terror aimed at domestic opponents or foreign enemies.

These loyalists were most often angry young men from the middling to lower ranks of the samurai class. They were joined by a number of politically engaged members of the rural and urban elite, including a handful of activist women. These were crucial figures in the revolutionary history of ideas and political action in Japan. The samurai loyalists were fiercely proud people who understood themselves by virtue of birth and training to be servants of their lords and, beyond that, of a larger and vaguely defined realm of Japan epitomized by the emperor. In the tradition of Tokugawa officialdom, they combined civil and military cultivation. They schooled themselves in Confucian classics while they trained in fencing and swordsmanship. Reflecting this dual training, they felt a twofold responsibility to think and to act: to propose solutions to the problems of the moment and to selflessly realize them in practice.

One harbinger of such sentiment and behavior was Ōshio Heihachirō. In the 1830s he was a samurai of low rank in the Osaka city government. Ōshio was schooled in a stream of Confucian thought that stressed the importance of righteous individual action. Outraged that top officials ignored his calls to help impoverished commoners at the time of the Tempō famine in 1838, Ōshio led a fierce uprising of Osaka residents. His forces burned down fully one-fourth of the city before being suppressed by bakufu troops.

In the 1850s, groups of similarly angry and action-oriented dissidents coalesced in domains throughout Japan. They were especially influential in several domains in which they enjoyed a sympathetic hearing from the daimyō and top officials, especially Satsuma, Chōshū, Tosa, and Hizen. The most famous cluster of loyalists were the students of Yoshida Shōin, a charismatic scholar-samurai in Chōshū. Yoshida himself was executed in 1859 during a bakufu crackdown on dissent. His followers went on to play leading roles in overthrowing the Tokugawa and consolidating the new Meiji regime. The inns and temples in castle towns and in Kyoto that served as clandestine meeting places for these activists trace a path toward revolution similar to the "freedom trails" in American cities like Boston or Philadelphia that offer a sense of history to later ages.

The loyalists drew intellectual inspiration from an eclectic mix of idealism and practical reformism. They supported direct, violent action. They believed the existing system denied due respect and authority to "men of talent" such as themselves. They exalted the emperor, and they hated the foreigners who had forced their way into Japan. They put hate into action by assassinating not only domestic enemies, but foreigners as well. Among their victims were Townsend Harris's Dutch interpreter and a well-known British merchant. But—and this is a crucial point—although they set off on their political path with crude and hopeless notions of standing up to foreign gunboats with razor-sharp swords and expelling the barbarians immediately, many loyalists quickly tempered their extremism with practical experience.

In particular, those who lived long enough to tell the tale came to see the need to learn from the West and perhaps even coexist with it. An archetypical case is that of Tosa loyalist Sakamoto Ryōma. In a scene that is a favorite of historical dramas to this day, Sakamoto charged into the residence of a bakufu official one day in 1862. With sword drawn, he stood intent on killing this man, who was modernizing the Tokugawa navy along Western lines. His target, Katsu Kaishū, convinced the would-be assassin to first hear him out. In the course of an afternoon Katsu saved his own

Young samurai from Satsuma and Chōshū, who have just led a successful revolt against the Tokugawa shogun in the name of loyalty to the Meiji emperor, are here photographed in To-kyo in 1869. On the left end, Itō Hirobumi of Chōshū; on the right end, Ōkubo Toshimichi of Satsuma. The two younger men in the middle were sons of the daimyō of Satsuma domain.
Courtesy of Ishiguro Takaaki.

life and persuaded Sakamoto that modernizing reforms were inevitable. Over time, people like Sakamoto developed a profound understanding of Western ideas, institutions, and technologies that would become deeply rooted in Japan.

POLITICS OF TERROR AND ACCOMMODATION

The Tokugawa bakufu thus faced a triple threat, from foreign powers, restive daimyō, and hot-headed samurai. It responded to this new situation with inconsistent policies. Its leaders lurched from accommodation to a hardline policy and back. They hoped all the while to strengthen the bakufu and share as little power as possible. Hotta's successor as ranking bakufu official, Ii Naosuke, repudiated the politics of consensus-seeking. He tried to revive the traditional Tokugawa dictatorship. He went ahead without imperial approval to sign the Harris treaties in July 1858. He appointed the weak child-candidate as shogun. He told the court and outer daimyō to keep out of bakufu affairs, foreign policy and shogunal succession included. Ii carried out the dramatic Ansei Purge (after the era name) in 1858. He forced several reformist daimyō to resign, placed Tokugawa Nariaki under house arrest, and executed or imprisoned sixty-nine anti-bakufu samurai activists.

This crackdown proved too little, too late to put the anti-bakufu genie back in the bottle. In March 1860 a group of Mito loyalists assassinated Ii just outside a gate to

Edo castle. They saw him as a hateful tyrant who had killed their comrades and betrayed the emperor. Ii's worried successors in the bakufu council returned to an accomodationist line. Their goal was to win back the support of the court and powerful daimyō with strategic concessions, while cracking down on the extremist samurai. The emperor's capital of Kyoto was the literal and symbolic battleground for all contestants.

The consensus-building policy of the new Tokugawa leadership sought "unity between court and bakufu (*kōbu gattai*)." This slogan meant different things to different people. For the bakufu, the idea was to make conciliatory gestures, such as arranging a marriage between the emperor's sister and the newly installed young shogun. The powerful outer daimyō of Satsuma, Chōshū, and Tosa and the collateral houses of Mito and Aizu had other ideas. To them, unity of court and bakufu meant a major shift of decision-making authority to a council of lords centered in Kyoto. Such a system would have reduced the shogun to a position of first-among-equals, as a loyal imperial servant.

The bakufu concluded it had no choice but to accept some of these strong calls for reform. In 1862 it agreed to end the venerable system of alternate attendance as an economic step to allow domains to save money. This also, of course, loosened the bakufu's increasingly precarious grip on daimyō political activity. The bakufu agreed that the daimyō could spend these funds on strengthening "national" defense by building up their domain armies and navies, another step that could bolster the daimyō opposition. The bakufu also agreed to appoint three powerful daimyō as special advisors to the shogun.

The bakufu hoped that such steps would drive a wedge between samurai radicals and their domain leaders, allowing it to crack down on the former. This did not happen immediately. Instead, loyalist samurai from all over Japan converged on Kyoto in 1862 and 1863. The city became a hotbed of agitation among court officials and anti-foreign loyalists from many domains, people willing to sacrifice their own lives in the name of expelling the foreign barbarians and honoring the Japanese emperor. The supposedly pure motives of these devoted youths, and the sheer drama of their conspiracies and actions, left a potent legacy of political inspiration to later generations. They also forced the bakufu to take further controversial steps to regain control.

In 1863, the loyalists convinced the Emperor Kōmei to formally request that the shogun immediately expel the Western barbarians. The bakufu responded by sending the shogun to Kyoto (the first such procession since Iemitsu's grand visit in 1634) to discuss the matter. This trip represented a dramatic shift of geopolitical power. The bakufu expected that its new daimyō "allies" in the politics of court-bakufu unity would help persuade the emperor to revoke the expulsion request. Powerful daimyō, most notably the lord of Satsuma, understood that immediate explusion was impossible. But they kept silent. Indeed, the Satsuma lord quietly left Kyoto at a crucial moment in the negotiations. With expulsion advocates in control of the court, the shogun had no choice but to return to Edo after accepting a certain date, June 25, 1863, as the exact moment to expel the barbarians.

The bakufu officials were well aware that their forces could not carry out this order. The deadline passed quietly in Edo. But in Chōshū at the far southern tip of the main island, loyalist soldiers in the domain army launched a cannon attack on an

American ship. American and French warships immediately retaliated. They landed at Shimonoseki and destroyed several shore batteries, although the Chōshū attacks continued for some weeks. As the treaty powers considered further retribution, the bakufu and Satsuma forces finally joined hands to drive the Chōshū loyalists and the anti-bakufu court advisors out of Kyoto.

The bakufu moved to shore up control. It organized a militia under the control of the Aizu daimyō to keep a tight rein on activities in Kyoto. It promised to fulfill the "immediate" expulsion order in due course by closing the port of Yokohama in the near future. The court, shorn of its most radical elements, accepted this pledge. But the immediate crisis persisted for another year. In 1864 loyalist samurai from all over Japan retreated to Chōshū, where domain leaders allowed them to stay and conspire. From there, they mounted a new attack. They marched on Kyoto, with plans for a coup to capture the emperor and liberate him from Tokugawa control. They were met and routed by a combination of Satsuma and Aizu forces loyal to the bakufu.

The bakufu followed this advantage with a punitive expedition to Chōshū. As the price for allowing the Chōshū domain to survive, the bakufu demanded that the daimyō execute the leaders of the attack on Kyoto, and he agreed. Satisfied that Chōshū was now controlled by a more moderate faction of samurai, the bakufu armies returned home. Advocates of a moderate politics of court-bakufu unity seemed to have regained the initiative.

BAKUFU REVIVAL, THE SATSUMA-CHŌSHŪ INSURGENCY, AND DOMESTIC UNREST

With hindsight, it is easy enough to see that the appearance of bakufu victory was deceiving. This was not obvious at the time, however. Chōshū was disgraced. Newly energetic leaders headed the bakufu. What *was* obvious was that the turmoil of the previous several years had set in motion a train of events that would transform Japan to some extent no matter who was in charge. Far-reaching social and political reforms were imposed both within the bakufu and in some key domains, especially in Chōshū. These centered on opening military and civil administration more broadly to talented men of various backgrounds and streamlining the larger political structure.

Within the bakufu, the finance commissioner, Oguri Tadamasa, led a drive to reorganize the military along Western lines beginning in 1865. Oguri even contemplated abolishing the domains entirely and creating a centralized national government. He received important advice and financial support for these efforts from the French minister to Edo, Leon Roche. But he also ran into opposition from conservative bakufu officials and from Tokugawa vassals anxious to protect their hereditary privileges. His programs of administrative and military reform did not go as far as those undertaken in some domains. In the summer of 1866 he received some powerful support when a new shogun, Tokugawa Yoshinobu, took office. This was the same man whom reformist daimyō had promoted for the position of shogun in the political struggles of 1857–58. Now that he had the chance to rule, Yoshinobu resolved to work with Oguri and Roche to remake the bakufu into a Western-style national government. Conservative interests within the bakufu continued to resist change. But the reforms these men tried to introduce were quite similar to those implemented by the new Meiji regime several years later. Even had the bakufu "survived," it would have done so by transforming itself into a political system not unlike that which replaced it.

This did not happen for two related reasons. Given a taste of power, the leaders of the outer domains, above all Satsuma and Chōshū, were unwilling to return to a subordinate position under Tokugawa rule. And most important, samurai within their borders—at times in defiance of domain rulers—undertook dramatic reforms. They consolidated military strength sufficient to challenge and defeat the Tokugawa armies.

The Chōshū loyalists had been defeated and lost power in 1864, but the bakufu had not rooted them out completely. Surviving remnants continued to organize militia using Western arms and military techniques. In a breakthrough social innovation, the organizers of these militia, in particular Takasugi Shinsaku, allowed (and sometimes forced) peasants to join. After 250 years during which peasants were strictly forbidden from bearing arms and training as soldiers, they were given a chance to join battle. Whether they saw this as a chance for individual glory or a role in a grander cause, these farmer-soldiers and their samurai partners built units with high morale as well as skill. In 1865 Takasugi's forces fought a victorious civil war in Chōshū. They retook control of the domain government. As in Satsuma, the Chōshū treasury was well stocked owing to effective fiscal reforms initiated decades earlier. This allowed the domain to purchase arms and ships from British merchants and build a formidable force.

Without such a drama of civil war, Satsuma had also been modernizing its military forces. Domain finances were healthy thanks to a mercantilist policy of promoting and taxing trade and the production of commercial crops, sugar in particular. In addition, Satsuma shared with Chōshū an extremely high ratio of samurai to commoners, a tradition of enmity to the Tokugawa, and the ability to escape close bakufu scrutiny because of its distant location. This made the two domains appear to be natural allies. In fact, it took much cajoling by outsiders to bring them together.

The key figure here was Sakamoto Ryōma, the Tosa samurai who had turned from anti-foreign assassin to open-the-country reformer after his encounter with the bakufu official Katsu Kaishū. Sakamoto brokered a secret alliance between Satsuma and Chōshū in 1866. The two domains promised to support each other in the case of a bakufu attack on either one. This was not long in coming, for the Tokugawa could not tolerate the return of the loyalists to power in Chōshū. In the summer of 1866, the bakufu army embarked on a second expedition to the southwest to punish Chōshū. It demanded support from other domains, but Satsuma—bound by its secret alliance— and several others refused to send troops. The expedition ended in a stunning defeat for the poorly motivated bakufu forces.

The defeat and retreat of this large army across the length of the main island were public humiliations that made the fall of the Tokugawa regime inevitable and sparked widespread popular expectation of change, even of apocalyptic deliverance. Some peasants reacted to the impending collapse with uprisings to resist taxes or attack the authority of village elites. Such incidents were widespread in the final two years of bakufu rule. Especially in 1866, at least 35 urban riots and 106 peasant uprisings took place. They were concentrated in the months following the failed bakufu attack on Chōshū.

More unusual and intriguing was the carnival of dancing and celebrating that swept the central regions from Osaka to Edo in late 1867. In Osaka, Kyoto, Nagoya, and numerous other towns, small good luck charms somehow began raining down from the sky. Authorities in a few cases caught people tossing these from rooftops, in effect seeding the clouds. Whether or not the charms were of truly magical origin, they had powerful effect. In places where they fell, people took to the streets for days of drunken dance and carousing. They defied orders to cease. Their songs—written down by observers at the time—reveal a sharp awareness of the political contest underway and its likely outcome in defeat for the Tokugawa. One British writer descibed the scene in Osaka in 1867:

> Crowds of people in holiday garb, dancing and singing "ee ja nai ka, ee ja nai ka (isn't it good)," houses decorated with rice-cakes in all colours, oranges, little bags, straws and flowers. The dresses worn were chiefly red crepe, a few blue and purple. Many of the dancers carried red lanterns on their heads. The pretext for these rejoicings was a shower of pieces of paper, bearing the names of the two gods of Ise, alleged to have taken place recently.[7]

With such extraordinary outbursts in the background, key actors in the bakufu and major domains struggled over the precise manner in which the era of Tokugawa rule would end. At stake was the question of who would have a voice. Would the bakufu be replaced by an inclusive, in some rough sense "representative" form of government, perhaps a council of daimyō? Or, would a narrow group of insurgents be able to monopolize power in a new regime? The issue was not quickly resolved. It would remain at the heart of Japanese political life for decades.

Once again, it was the Tosa daimyō, advised by Sakamoto Ryōma and Gotō Shōjirō, who played a crucial role as intermediary. The Tosa objective was to replace bakufu rule with a roughly British model: bicameral rule by a council of lords and a second council representing lesser samurai, and perhaps commoners. By November 1867, the shogun, Tokugawa Yoshinobu, had been persuaded to accept this plan. He was to step down from his post and "return" ultimate power and sovereignty to the emperor. But the Tokugawa would retain control of their own considerable lands. Yoshinobu expected the Tokugawa house would continue to play an important role in the ruling council of lords.

This compromise, even with its huge reduction of Tokugawa power, did not satisfy the insurgent forces in Satsuma and Chōshū or their allies in the imperial court. In December 1867 the Satsuma and Chōshū armies marched on Kyoto. They took control of the imperial palace. In early January 1868 the insurgents prompted the Emperor Meiji, who had just recently taken the throne upon his father's death in 1867, to announce an imperial "restoration." The bakufu was to be abolished. It would be replaced by a new government of nobles and daimyō under the emperor. The Tokugawa would have no place at all. Yoshinobu resisted, but his troops were easily defeated in a battle just outside Kyoto. He retreated to Edo, but in April 1868 his military commander, Katsu Kaishū, turned over Edo to the insurgent forces without a fight. Katsu was convinced that peacefully setting up a new political order was preferable to fighting to the death for a lost cause.

Not all the Tokugawa supporters shared this commitment to a larger, national political order centered on the emperor. Samurai in several domains in northern Japan, in particular, did not trust the insurgents. They feared the new rulers from Satsuma and Chōshū would shut them out of the new regime. They resisted with arms and put up a stiff fight. The last pockets of bakufu and allied domain resistance were not crushed until eighteen months after the official "restoration" of the emperor in January 1868. As many as three thousand men died in the fiercest attacks, which targeted the holdout domain of Aizu.

The old regime thus collapsed, not without some turmoil and bloodshed, and with great political drama. Over the years of anti-foreign and anti-bakufu activism, participants on all sides had greatly shifted their visions of the desired political or social order. In the early 1860s, some had traveled to Europe or the United States on missions sent by their domains or by the bakufu. For the most part they abandoned crude plans for immediate "expulsion." They developed a rather sophisticated appreciation of the potential of Western technologies and even political institutions.

Some had moved further by 1868. They had abandoned even the position of strategic concession, that one should learn from the barbarians to overcome and expel them in a decade or two. They had decided instead that Japan might permanently become part of a global order of nation-states. These activists were beginning to create a sense of a nation, at least in their own ranks. Beyond them, the masses of people, by no means as stupid or ignorant as many samurai believed them to be, held fervent expectation for change, perhaps deliverance. Few lamented the passing of the bakufu. But few identified themselves with the new order, either. Who would lead the new regime, and how would it be structured? Together with charms floating down from the skies, these and many fundamental questions seemed almost literally up in the air when the reign of the Emperor Meiji was announced in 1868.

MODERN REVOLUTION

1868–1905

5

The Samurai Revolution

The "restoration" of the young Emperor Meiji in 1867–68 was little more than a coup d'état. A relatively small band of insurgents had toppled the Tokugawa bakufu. They stated their intent to restore direct imperial rule, but this was not likely to occur. Strong emperors who exercised power directly had been exceptional in Japanese history. Political contenders at the time feared that the rebels from Satsuma and Chōshū would simply form a new bakufu and use the name of the emperor to rule from a narrow base of power. After all, beyond the political upheaval in Kyoto and Edo, little had changed. The islands of Japan were still divided into nearly two hundred relatively autonomous domains. Each maintained its own treasury and army. The samurai were still receiving stipends, which they viewed as a hereditary birthright. The daily life of the countryside and cities had gone through some tumult. But the scattered peasant rebellions were short-lived.

However, if we compare this situation of 1868 in any aspect—political, economic, social, cultural—to that of just a decade later, the changes are breathtaking and fully merit the term *revolution*. Of course, no society ever totally severs itself from its past, and Japan was no exception. But the range and depth of change were astonishing to observers at the time. It remains so when looking back after 150 years. One of the most insightful contemporaneous observers was a British scholar named Basil Hall Chamberlain. He lived in Japan for over thirty years beginning in 1873. In 1891, he wrote:

> To have lived through the transition stage of modern Japan makes a man feel preternaturally old; for here he is in modern times, with the air full of talk about bicycles and bacilli and "spheres of influence," and yet he can himself distinctly remember the Middle Ages. The dear old Samurai who first initiated the present writer into the mysteries of the Japanese language, wore a queue and two swords. This relic of feudalism now sleeps in Nirvana.
>
> His modern successor, fairly fluent in English, and dressed in a serviceable suit of dittos, might almost be European, save for a certain obliqueness of the eyes and scantiness of beard. Old things pass away between a night and a morning.[1]

Although Chamberlain here stresses how unusually swiftly the events of this "transition stage" unfolded, his writing also suggests that Japan's transition was part of a broader global shift. And indeed, the revolution that began in the 1860s was a Japanese variation on a global theme of modern revolution. Changes that took place in societies around the world in the nineteenth and twentieth centuries also unfolded in Japan.

Although sharing much with a global history of modernizing societies, the Japanese revolution did take place through a process that differed from the revolutions in Europe of the late eighteenth and the nineteenth centuries. In Europe, members of newly powerful classes, especially the urban bourgeoisie, challenged and sometimes overturned the privileges of long-entrenched aristocrats. By contrast, in Japan of the Meiji era it was members of the elite of the old regime, the samurai, who spearheaded the attack on the old order. Their role has led many historians to describe Japan in the nineteenth century as undergoing a "revolution from above" or an "aristocratic revolution."[2]

In the twentieth century, other modernizing revolutions also unfolded through a process in which members of elite groups undermined their own well-established positions while they restructured the political order. The Japanese mode of modern revolution was not unique. Rather, it contrasted with earlier Western revolutions and resembled some later ones. This sort of elite-led revolution took place in Japan because of particular features of the samurai class, both weaknesses and strengths. On the negative side, change was possible because the samurai were not a securely landed elite. They were essentially salaried employees of their lords. Although this status was hereditary, it was less rooted in property than a European-style feudal estate, a Chinese gentry holding, or a Korean aristocratic status (*yangban*). The samurai had less to lose than elites in such societies. They were hard-pressed to protect their privilege as hereditary government employees once the new rulers decided to revoke it. Some did protest the actions of their former comrades bitterly, but others were either unable or unwilling to resist. On the positive side, many of the activists in the restoration movement had already developed a commitment to serving and building a realm that went beyond the narrow confines of a single domain. This emerging national consciousness offered a compelling reason for many to accept programs of far-reaching change.

PROGRAMS OF NATIONALIST REVOLUTION

The leaders of the new Meiji government in 1868 were thrilled at the ease and speed with which they overcame the Tokugawa. They remained insulted by the unequal and coerced foreign presence and worried about the prospect of continued foreign encroachment. They were simultaneously fearful of resistance from domestic opponents. Domain armies remained in place, after all. Some had considerable stocks of Western arms.

The Meiji revolutionaries were motivated by fear of these challenges. They were also moved by their own sense of the ongoing problems of the Tokugawa order: military and economic weakness, political fragmentation, and a social hierarchy that failed to recognize men of talent. Propelled by both fear and discontent with the old regime, they generated an ambitious agenda, through a process of trial and error, aiming to build a new sort of national power.

Political Unification and Central Bureaucracy

Their first dramatic step was to abolish all the daimyō domains, thus dismantling a political order in place for 260 years. By 1868, almost immediately after the restorationist coup, top leaders of the new provisional government such as Kido Kōin of Chōshū and Saigō Takamori of Satsuma decided that the politically fragmented system of domains had to be overhauled. They acted with careful tactics and reached their goal in just three years. One British observer marvelled at this and other changes in 1872: "[F]our years ago we were still in the middle ages—we have leapt at a bound into the nineteenth century—out of poetry into plain useful prose."[3]

The move toward an integrated national polity began in March 1869. The new government convinced key daimyō of prestige and power, especially those of Satsuma, Chōshū, Tosa, and Hizen, to voluntarily surrender their lands back to the emperor. As the patrons of many of the coup planners, these men were guaranteed respect and a voice in the new order if they wished. In fact, they were all quickly reappointed as domain governors with handsome salaries. Nonetheless, the "return of lands" established the principle that all lands and people were subject to the emperor's rule. By early 1870, all daimyō had formally returned their lands and taken appointments as governors of their domains, but they retained significant autonomy, as in the past.

Preparing the ground for the complete abolition of the daimyō domains, the Meiji reformers worked to place domain governments in sympathetic hands. They pressed the daimyō to appoint men of talent and often modest rank to key adminstrative posts. Such people would be likely to welcome further reform. Kido Kōin and other top officials in the Meiji government also won support of powerholders in many domains, both daimyō and their followers, by promising them posts in the new central government. They backed such persuasion by threat of force, creating an imperial army primarily from Satsuma and Chōshū samurai. It was untested, but it was stronger than any single domain's forces or any likely combination of forces.

Having bought off potential opposition leaders and built support in key domains with these measures, the government in August 1871 had the emperor announce that all domains were immediately abolished. They were replaced with "prefectures" whose governors were appointed from the center. This was much more than a renaming of domains into prefectures. It was a stunning change, with immediate visible consequences. The central government would now collect taxes from domain lands. The daimyō were ordered to move to Tokyo. Many castles were dismantled. Within just three months, the number of political units was consolidated dramatically, from 280 domains to 72 prefectures. Most of the new governors were not former daimyō. They were middling samurai from the insurgent domains now controlling the government.

This decree was accompanied by a large payoff to the daimyō themselves. They were granted permanent yearly salaries equivalent to roughly 10 percent of their former domain's annual tax revenue. Daimyō were simultaneously relieved of all the costs of governing. Most were quite content to take early retirement on such generous terms. Thus, within the short span of three years, a political order in existence for over two and a half centuries simply disappeared. The Tokugawa bakufu, on the one hand, and the hundreds of semi-autonomous domains on the other, no longer existed.

Simultaneously, of course, the Meiji leaders had to erect a new national political structure to govern these domains turned prefectures. For several years they groped in this direction, experimenting with a confusing variety of political forms. They bolstered their claim as restorationists by labeling these first government offices with ancient Chinese terms used by the Japanese court in the Heian period (794–1192). In early 1868, the Sat-Chō rebels and court officials placed themselves atop a provisional government to rule in the name of emperor. Later that year they established the Council of State as the highest political authority and monopolized its highest posts. The organization of this council was revised in 1869 and again in 1871. Later in 1871 it was replaced by a tripartite set of ministries of the Center, Left, and Right, further subdivided into various functional ministries (Finance, Foreign Affairs, Public Works, Home Affairs).

This format proved relatively effective. It persisted until 1885, when the Meiji leaders inaugurated a cabinet system modeled explicitly along European lines. At the head of this government was a prime minister. He presided over a cabinet that ran the bureaucratic agencies—the several ministries—of the Japanese state. This structure was codified in the Meiji constitution of 1889, discussed in detail later in this chapter. Although this constitution provided for a deliberative assembly (the Diet), state ministers were responsible not to the Diet but to the emperor.

In the early Meiji years, the ministerial staff was recruited mainly by personal connections from the ranks of Satsuma and Chōshū samurai and their allies. But the government rather quickly moved toward a more impersonal, merit-based mode of recruitment. In 1887 it began a system of civil service examinations. From this point on, performance on this exam became the primary qualification for service in the prestigious ranks of the ministries of the Japanese imperial state.

The creation of this bureaucratic state was a step of great importance in the history of modern Japan. The Meiji rulers inherited a Tokugawa legacy of bureaucratic rule by civilianized samurai. They extended its reach by eliminating domains. They deepened its reach by replacing the clumsy Tokugawa administrative machinery of overlapping jurisdictions with functional ministries with clearly defined responsibilities. They bolstered its legitimacy by putting the meritocratic ideals of the Tokugawa system into practice. And finally, they elevated its prestige by defining the bureaucratic mission as one of service to the emperor. They gave the state a greater legitimacy and power than it had ever held in the past.

Eliminating the Status System

The second great change of early Meiji was even more remarkable. It was achieved at greater cost. By 1876, less than a decade after the restoration coup, the economic privileges of the samurai were wiped out entirely. The coup leaders expropriated an entire social class, the semi-aristocratic elite from which they came. They met some stiff, violent resistance, but they managed to overcome it. This remarkable change amounted to a social revolution.

The government moved to expropriate the samurai primarily for financial reasons. The government reduced samurai stipends when it abolished the domains, but in the mid-1870s these payouts still consumed a huge chunk—roughly half—of state revenues. The new rulers had other uses in mind for this money. They believed that the samurai gave back relatively little value for their high costs. Their ranks included many talented people sitting idle. Their time-honored military skills, focused on swords and archery, were useless. Thus the samurai's stipends were basically welfare for the well-born.

This case for expropriating the samurai was clear enough to government leaders soon after the restoration. But taking this step was a major undertaking. It took nearly a decade and enraged many former samurai. In particular, many of those who had supported the restoration drive, but remained in their domains after 1868, felt betrayed by their former comrades now running the Meiji government. The latter moved in small steps first, as they had with domain abolition. In 1869 they reduced the large number of samurai ranks to two, upper samurai (*shizoku*) and lower samurai (*sotsu*). In 1872 a large portion of the lower samurai were reclassified as commoners (*heimin*), although they retained their stipends for the moment.

In 1873, the government announced that stipends would be taxed. The next year it announced a voluntary program to convert stipends to bonds. The right to a stipend could be traded for an interest-bearing bond with a face value of five to fourteen years of income (in general, the lower the stipend, the higher the multiple). The bond would pay interest ranging from 5 to 7 percent, with smaller bonds paying higher rates. The income stream from all but the most generous bonds was a good bit lower than the annual stipend. Few samurai volunteered for this program.

The government made this program compulsory in 1876: All stipends were converted to bonds. In contrast to the well-compensated daimyō, many samurai suffered significant losses. Their annual incomes fell by anywhere from 10 to 75 percent. They further lost pride and prestige: The right to wear swords was denied to all but solidiers and policemen.

The elimination of samurai privilege allowed the new regime to redirect financial and human resources alike and was part of a larger transformation of society from a system of fixed statuses to a more fluid, merit-based social order. The other side to the abolition of samurai privilege was the end to formal restrictions on the rest of the population. At least in theory, this constituted social liberation. In 1870, all non-samurai were classified in legal terms as commoners (*heimin*). With some important gender-based exceptions noted later, the restrictions of the Tokugawa era on modes of travel, dress, and hairstyle were eliminated. Restrictions on occupation were abolished. The government ended legal discrimination against the hereditary outcaste groups of Tokugawa times such as *eta* and *hinin*. These terms came to be considered slurs and were replaced in official language by the label *burakumin* (literally, "village people," in reference to their segregated villages). The descendants of these outcastes, however, continued to face prejudice and discrimination.

Some commoners fared well. Not surprisingly, many of those with education and money, in particular the landowners, moneylenders, and petty manufacturers at the upper levels of rural society, thrived in the more open social order of the Meiji era. Others, especially those with weak claims to farmland, lived in desperate poverty. They depended on the unreliable benevolence of landlords to survive illness, crop failures, or price declines. Although the samurai lost their income and social privilege, they were educated and ambitious. Many landed on their feet. Others invested their bonds in new businesses and failed miserably. Still others took up arms against the new government or joined political movements on behalf of a parliament and constitution.

The literature of the Meiji period offers one window into the excitement, the opportunities, and the risks of this era of change. One example is this comment by the narrator of *Footprints in the Snow*, a vibrant and widely read novel set in the 1880s and written in 1901 by Tokutomi Roka:

> The race will go to the swift, not the empty-headed! The real testing-time in politics will come after the Diet gets going in 1890—and in everything, not only politics: the further Japan advances on the world stage, the more opportunities for the really able![4]

The Conscript Army

Even before the samurai were fully dispossessed, the Meiji leaders decided they had to renovate the military from the bottom up. Key figures from Chōshū were deeply impressed at the superior performance of their mixed farmer-samurai militias in the restoration wars. These men—Kido Kōin, Ōmura Masujirō, and Yamagata Aritomo—argued forcefully for a conscript army drawn from the entire population. Their views were controversial, to say the least. In October 1869 a group of samurai in Kyoto, outraged at the conscript proposal, assassinated Ōmura. And among top government figures, the Satsuma men saw things differently from the Chōshū clique. They came from a domain where nearly one-fourth of the population had been samurai. They feared arming ignorant and potentially rebellious commoners. They wanted to ensure a major role for samurai in the new Meiji order. The champion of this position was Ōkubo Toshimichi, who ranked with Kido as one of the two most powerful leaders in the first decade of the Meiji era. At first he prevailed, with the support of Iwakura Tomomi, the most important court noble in the Meiji government. In April 1871 the government created an imperial army of just under ten thousand samurai recruited from the restoration forces.

The conservative military leadership seemed to be in control, but their ascendance was short-lived. Yamagata Aritomo returned from a trip to Europe fully convinced that mass conscription was the key not only to building military strength but also to disciplining a loyal populace. By 1873 his arguments had prevailed. The government decreed a system of universal conscription. Beginning at the age of twenty, all males were obligated to give three years of active service and four years on reserve status.

The draft was not popular. The 1873 decree noted several exemptions, for household heads, criminals, the physically unfit, students and teachers in many prescribed schools, and government officials. It also allowed people to buy their way out for a huge fee of 270 yen. This sum represented more than the annual wage of a common laborer. Large numbers of people sought to qualify for exemption or somehow scrape together the buyout fee. The army had trouble meeting the quotas for what the government itself labeled a "blood tax" (following European terminology). In 1873–74 angry crowds attacked and destroyed numerous registration centers in sixteen riots; nearly 100,000 people were arrested and punished.

As this resistance makes clear, the strong discipline and fierce loyalty shown by Japanese soldiers in later decades were by no means timeless traditional elements of

Japan's "national character." Such resistance also took place in Europe and in the United States, where large anti-draft riots erupted during the Civil War. In Japan as elsewhere, a patriotic spirit that could induce willing military service—a key element of modern nationalism—had to be drummed into the masses of people over several decades. Japan's army passed its first major test when it put down a large samurai rebellion in 1877. An imperial rescript of 1882 addressed to soldiers and sailors enjoined youths to serve the emperor with loyalty and valor. Teachers and texts in the new public school system echoed the message. The navy was built up in the 1880s and 1890s. By the mid-1890s, Japan's military was strong enough to move from the task of keeping order at home to that of imposing its will overseas. Military service came to be accepted as the patriotic obligation of Japanese men by most recruits and their families.

Compulsory Education

Parallel to its program of military reform, the Meiji government instituted a new system of education with remarkable speed. With grand language, in 1872 it declared four years of elementary education to be compulsory for all children, boys and girls: "In a village there shall be no house without learning, and in a house, no individual without learning." This important step reflected the new leaders' understanding of the sources of Western power. Observation of European and American societies convinced leaders such as Kido Kōin that mass schooling, like mass conscription, was a fundamental source of the economic and military power of the West. Their initial models were primarily American and French, and the 1872 decree established a system of elementary and middle schools and national universities. At the outset, the government announced that schools were to encourage practical learning as well as independent thinking. By this means commoners would find their own way to serve the state.

Mass compulsory education was a bold initiative, and a risky one for the government. Tokugawa thinkers such as Aizawa Yasushi had complained endlessly of the "stupid commoners" who would easily be tricked by demagogic Christian missionaries into betraying the authorities, even the emperor. Such attitudes could have led the Meiji leaders to hold back from imparting literacy and potentially subversive "enlightenment" to imperial subjects who were expected to follow orders. The Meiji leadership consciously took this risk. They concluded that an ignorant populace would be a greater danger to their projects to build political and economic power. They also developed rather different views of the value of learning for girls and boys. The former were expected to learn the skills needed for future domestic roles as wives and mothers as well as loyal subjects of the emperor. The latter were expected to take their knowledge into a wider public realm of endeavor in the cause of building the nation.

Reactions to compulsory education were mixed. The era's literature conveys the excitement of many young men at the opportunity to better themselves and serve their country, if possible in the new capital of Tokyo. In *Footprints in the Snow*, Tokutomi also evoked the enthusiasm for learning of the early 1880s:

> About the end of August a letter came from Matsumura with a tremendous piece of news. "Tremendous news." For us boys, in those days, these words could have only

one meaning: Matsumura was leaving next month, to study in the capital—in Tokyo! You could feel his excitement in the hardly legible scrawl; his handwriting was none too firm at the best of times, but this! The characters fairly danced their way down the page in a kind of dishevelled ecstasy.[5]

Not everyone was so happy at the obligation to attend school and the opportunity to graduate. The elementary schools were to be financed by a 10 percent local surcharge to the national property tax. In the 1870s angry taxpayers reacted to compulsory schooling as they had to the draft: They rioted. Crowds of people destroyed at least two thousand schools, usually by setting them afire. This represented close to one-tenth of the total number of schools. The passive resistance of simply not going to school was even more widespread. Rates of attendance for school-age boys and girls stood at 25 to 50 percent of the eligible population for the first decade of the new system.

But eventually, as with serving in the military, attending school became a well-accepted obligation of the emperor's subjects. By the end of the nineteenth century, rates of elementary school attendance reached levels of 90 percent or more. By 1905, 98 percent of school-age boys and 93 percent of girls were attending elementary schools as the law required. As compulsory education took root, the idea that one's life course—at least that of young men—should be open at the outset and should reflect one's talent and efforts became one of Japan's most fundamental and widely held social values. In Tokugawa Japan, a major tension set the merit ideal—that men of talent should hold office—against the hereditary status system. The Meiji social revolution resolved this ideological tension clearly in favor of merit.

The Monarch at the Center

Finally, one of the most portentous new departures of the revolutionary years of early Meiji was the decision to put the emperor at the very center of the political order. The restoration activists carried out their coup in the name of the Meiji emperor. But once in power, they held no consensus on what to do with him. The populace was not particularly committed to the emperor as a political symbol. Nor was the emperor an impressive young man, whether in court garb or in Western military uniform.

After the emperor's triumphal progress from Kyoto to Edo in 1868, the early Meiji government struggled to decide where to locate a permanent capital. Some officials supported moving the capital permanently to Edo (renamed Tokyo, or Eastern capital), some wished to send the emperor and capital back to Kyoto, and still others spoke of establishing two capitals. Not until 1889 was the decision for Tokyo made permanent. The government called the emperor's Tokyo residence a "temporary court" until that year, when it officially renamed it the "Imperial Palace."[6]

Over these same two decades, as the capital moved, the image of the monarchy was transformed as well. The government heaped more and more symbolic weight upon the emperor and empress. The empress and her retinue adopted Western clothes in the 1880s as part of the effort to project an image of the monarchy as a modern institution. The emperor also underwent a striking metamorphosis to become the symbol of a modern monarch. The contrast between his earlier portraits and the famous portrait prepared by an Italian artist in 1888 best illustrates this dramatic change. The

Photograph from 1872 of the Meiji emperor in court dress on a Japanese-style chair. The young emperor appears rather ill at ease.
Sudō Mitsuaki, *Meiji Tennō gyoden* (Tokyo: Kaneo Bun'endō, 1912). Courtesy of T. Fujitani.

This 1873 photograph of the Meiji emperor in Western military dress, with a Western hairstyle, moustache, and beard, on a European-style chair, reflects the government's desire to project a modern, Westernized image of the new emperor and nation. The emperor's posture suggests a young man not yet fully at home in this new role and image.
Sudō Mitsuaki, *Meiji Tennō gyoden* (Tokyo: Kaneo Bun'endō, 1912). Courtesy of T. Fujitani.

This photograph of an 1888 portrait of the adult Meiji emperor was enshrined in all public schools. The portrait was the work of a well-known Italian painter, Eduardo Chiossone. It provided the official image of Japan's new modern monarch, contrasting sharply with the less imposing youthful images of just fifteen years earlier. This contrast indicates not only the maturation of the emperor but also the new certainty and authority of the government's use of his image.
Watanabe Gintarō, *Gotaisō goshashinchō*, vol. 1 (Tokyo: Shinbashidō shoten, 1912). Courtesy of T. Fujitani.

painting was subsequently photographed and enshrined in schools throughout the nation. It has defined the Meiji emperor's image ever since.

At the same time, the constitution greatly elevated the emperor's legal and cultural authority. From the 1880s through the 1930s, the imperial institution became an all-too-powerful unifying force. It served as a touchstone for personal, social, and national identity. It came to link individuals to immediate communities of family, workplace, and neighborhood—and beyond that to the imagined community of nation and empire.

BUILDING A RICH COUNTRY

The Meiji leaders, especially those who traveled abroad, were profoundly impressed with the energies unleashed by industrial capitalism. Manufacturing and trade seemed as important a source of European national power as did battleships and cannons. Economic strength, in fact, appeared to be the base that supported the military super-structure of European states. Kido Kōin was typical of his colleagues in the new government. While traveling in the United States and Europe in 1872 he filled his diary with references to the "astonishing," the "indescribable," or the "magnificent" achievements of Western architecture, education, and industry.[7]

Motivated by such awestruck views of Western learning and industry, government leaders undertook numerous steps to realize the foremost Meiji slogan of building a "rich country, strong army" (*fukoku kyōhei*). Some initiatives were indirect measures to build the infrastructure of an industrial economy. Others were direct measures to construct and operate mines and factories as government projects.

The most important economic reform of the 1870s was the new tax system. The new Meiji government began its life in poverty. It drew revenue from a narrow base of former Tokugawa lands and borrowed funds from some of the major Osaka merchant houses. When it replaced autonomous domains with centrally managed prefectures in 1871, it inherited the huge obligation of samurai stipends and daimyō pensions, but it also gained the opportunity to draw taxes from all the former domains. In 1873, the government announced a new national land tax designed by Ōkubo Toshimichi. It was intended to stabilize state revenues at a level roughly comparable to the sum total of bakufu and domain taxes.

The significance of the new tax system went beyond securing revenue. It changed the economic relationship of individual landowners to the state and to each other. In the Tokugawa system, land ownership had been decided by custom in villages. Revenues were collected in lump sums from villages, not from individuals. There was no state-supervised system of title deeds or land registration and no officially sanctioned market in the purchase and sale of land. In addition, taxes were based on assessed yield, not assessed value. They were usually collected in kind (in rice). This meant that the government and not the taxpayer stood to lose (or gain) from fluctuating commodity prices: If the price of rice fell, so did government revenue.

The tax system of 1873 changed all this. It provided for a national land survey, conducted in the mid-1870s, that matched an owner to every piece of land and issued deeds. It also assessed the market value of all plots of land. Finally, it set the land tax at 3 percent of assessed value. This new system gave the government a predictable annual revenue. The new tax system also brought the national government into a direct economic relationship with individual (male) household heads. It shifted the risk and the opportunity of commodity price changes onto the taxpaying farmer. A farmer would have to sell a larger portion of his crop to pay the tax if grain prices fell. He would conversely profit from inflation. This made people aware of their economic and political ties to the state as they had never been before. Not surprisingly, taxes and state budgets became two of the most contentious political issues of the Meiji era.

Over a period of decades, the new government used a portion of these tax revenues for public works and institution-building projects to create the infrastructure of a capitalist industrial economy. It dredged harbors and built lighthouses to improve coastal shipping. It built telegraph lines beginning in 1869, and in 1871 it opened a postal system modeled on British practices. It encouraged the founding of joint stock companies among private investors. By the mid-1880s it had established a uniform national currency, the yen, backed by a central bank modeled along European lines.

Most important of all, the government took the lead in building a railroad network. The first line connected Tokyo to Yokohama and was completed in 1872. It was extended as far as Kobe by 1889. The government also encouraged private investment in railroads. Many former daimyō and high-ranking samurai pooled their pensions to join wealthy commoners in a railroad investment boom in the 1880s that helped bring a modern stock market into existence. By 1890, Japan boasted fourteen hundred miles of railroad, about 40 percent owned and operated by the government, the rest in private hands.

As it did all over the world, the "iron horse" had a huge cultural as well as economic impact. It changed people's sense of time, of distance, and of social behavior. As in the West several decades earlier, Japanese observers in the 1870s and 1880s invoked now-hackneyed metaphors. The train was a projectile "faster than an arrow"; it was a conveyance that "shrunk the world." They also noted that trains, with their precise timetables, promoted punctuality. These changes came slowly. Complaints about "lax and perfunctory" railway performance were common into the early 1900s. Nevertheless, the fact that customers were complaining itself indicates that attitudes had changed. The advent of trains meant that for the first time in Japanese history, it became important to calculate time to the minute—rather than the half-hour. This promoted the use of watches and clocks. Gradually, increased attention to precise timekeeping spread among the entire population.[8]

Beyond projects of infrastructure building, the Meiji government played an unusually direct role in building and operating industrial enterprises. Government leaders were convinced that private investors lacked the initiative and the knowledge to run modern factories. They were also convinced that foreign investment was dangerous. They had learned this lesson from their earlier study of "barbarian affairs," which taught them that the British and French had gotten their start in colonizing the Middle East through loaning money to local rulers. Foreign capital was not banned outright. But it was certainly not welcomed.

As a result, the first modern industrial enterprises in Japan were financed largely from domestic sources, especially from the national treasury. In the 1870s, the state financed and ran a number of so-called model enterprises: shipyards, coal and copper mines, engineering works, arsenals, and cotton-spinning, silk-reeling, glass, sugar, and

even beer factories—about two dozen large enterprises in total. Although it was reluctant to use foreign money for these projects, it was for a time quite anxious to
import foreign people as consultants and managers. At great expense in the 1870s,
the new government engaged several thousand "hired foreigners" (*oyatoi gaijin*) from
over twenty nations. This term had a pejorative connotation suggesting that the foreigners brought no value beyond detailed technical expertise. These technicians and
experts offered important advice in a wide range of economic and social endeavors.
They were handsomely paid. Most received salaries at the level of top officials in the
Japanese government.

Economic historians disagree over the importance of the government's role in
orchestrating economic development in Japan. Some stress that the total investment in
state enterprises was far less than in the military; that the government only built twenty
or so factories, a few mines, a telegraph system, and some rail lines; and that none
of these turned a profit. Indeed, most of the "model factories" lost money. In the early
1880s the government sold the money losers among its enterprises at bargain prices
to private investors. The few more successful ventures, primarily coal and metal mines,
were sold later in the decade at more competitive prices. But to dismiss the significance of this experience is too narrow. A first generation of managers and engineers
had been trained. A small industrial wage labor force had been created. These state
enterprises constituted an important launching pad for further growth.

In fact, the government initially had hoped to encourage private investors in new
industrial fields, but it could not entice or force the Edo era merchants, or landlords,
or others, to take the risk. As Ōkubo Toshimichi wrote in 1874, "the volume of goods
produced arises partly from the industriousness of the people, but more fundamentally
it must depend upon prior guidance and encouragement by the government and its
officials." Ten years later, after the model factories had been sold off, officials were
hardly more optimistic. One leading bureaucrat wrote in 1884 that "the Japanese people [are] generally unaccustomed to handling foreign machinery. They are so ignorant
of the science of mechanics that they cannot easily open an ordinary Western lock.
Even if they order machinery from abroad, they cannot operate it."⁹ It is probably
fairer to say that the people lacked experience and were appropriately cautious given
the risks faced by these early endeavors, than to call them ignorant or clumsy. But in
any case, it seems certain that few of the "model factories" would have been started
so soon by private individuals or groups.

These state activities were important for another reason as well. They generated
faith, both within the government and outside it, in the potential and the importance
of the state's role in supporting economic development. The idea that the state should
take a hands-on stance as promoter of the economy, as opposed to a more detached
role as referee and regulator, took root in this era. It remained powerful throughout
the twentieth century. The experience of running domain monopolies in Satsuma and
Chōshū during the Tokugawa era may have given impetus to the government's economic programs. But the hands-on state role was less a heritage of traditional Japanese
economic thinking than it was a well-considered new choice made by the Meiji leaders. They were developing a view that the world was divided into competing national
economic units. They saw Japan as a latecomer. They were desperate to catch up and
to escape semicolonial dependence. To this end, they turned to a German philosophy

of state-led development, in particular to the economic thinking of Friedrich List, rather than to the British laissez-faire logic of Adam Smith. Other Asian political elites have followed their lead, with consequences that remain controversial to this day.

STANCES TOWARD THE WORLD

The revolutionary Meiji agenda of the 1870s drew inspiration from a fervent curiosity about Euro-American technology and ideas. This openness to the West is remarkable when compared to the expulsionist rhetoric and action of the 1850s and 1860s, which had been indulged in by some of the very people who led the new government. They typically began to change their attitudes by accepting the foreign presence and foreign technologies as an expedient measure: One had to learn barbarian tricks to defeat them. But many of the Meiji leaders went on to develop a more profound appreciation for the enduring power of Western things and ideas.

Travel abroad was the most important educational experience for the young rulers of the Meiji state. In the 1860s both Satsuma and Chōshū, as well as the bakufu, sent students to study in Europe. These experiences gave future government leaders such as Itō Hirobumi and Inoue Kaoru of Chōshū and Ōkubo Toshimichi of Satsuma and business leaders such as Shibusawa Eiichi valuable firsthand exposure to the West. But the most important venture abroad was the Iwakura Mission of 1871–73. Several dozen people, including some of the most powerful figures in the new government (Iwakura Tomomi, Ōkubo, Kido, and Itō) spent eighteen months traveling through the United States and Europe. They observed all manner of institutions and practices, from schools and factories to parliaments. The economic power of modern industry and the social power of the educated citizens and subjects of the Western nation-states impressed the mission members profoundly. This experience powerfully motivated the ensuing shopping spree in the mall of Western institutions, from central banks and universities to post offices and police forces.

This newfound respect for the value and power of Western ideas coexisted with ongoing anger at the unequal political relationship between Japan and the Western powers. The primary reason for sending the Iwakura Mission in the first place was to revise the terms of the unequal treaties of 1858. This prospect was slapped down sharply by the Americans and Europeans whenever it was raised. The Japanese were told they had to bring their legal and political system up to European standards before treaty revision could even be considered.

In such a context, the West continued to be seen as a source of danger as well as opportunity. Dangers included not just foreign armies and navies. The Meiji leaders viewed democratic political ideas with great concern. They decided that parliaments could be divisive institutions rather than sources of unity and strength. From an early point they worried about how to encourage popular support without inviting dangerous political challenge or mass rebellion.

In addition to political turbulence, the West was seen as a potential source of social anarchy. This was often described with reference to topsy-turvy relations between men and women. The diaries of *bakumatsu* and early Meiji travelers to the

West are full of horror at the casual intimacy of men and women, and the unpleasant boldness of the latter. Such observers came to believe—wrongly perhaps—that the status of women in the West was higher than in Japan. Some Meiji men worried that they might face demands by women for equality in marriage or society at large.

The Meiji leaders and prominent intellectuals held similarly ambivalent attitudes toward Asia. On one hand, they sometimes called for an Asia-wide (or "pan-Asian") solidarity against the predatory imperialism of Western powers. At the same time, the 1870s saw the first clear signs of a high-handed Asian diplomacy backed by a scornful attitude that placed Japan above its Asian neighbors. In this view, Japan was Asia's natural hegemon. It would lead its benighted neighbors to modernization and equality with the West, whether they liked it or not.

This attitude surfaced with a vengeance in 1873 while the Iwakura Mission was abroad. Saigō Takamori, a zealous patriot from Satsuma, prodded the caretaker government to plan an invasion of Korea. Japanese traders in the early 1870s were pushing the Korean government to open trade relations. When the Koreans firmly refused, Saigō proposed an invasion to force the issue. In addition to considerations of national pride, Saigō and his supporters in the government such as Tosa samurai Itagaki Taisuke, hoped to ensure for the samurai invasion force a proud role in the new Meiji order.

Neither advocates nor opponents of invasion seemed particularly troubled by the irony that their behavior replicated that of the offensive Westerners in the 1850s. But the members of the Iwakura Mission strongly opposed the plan on strategic grounds. Their travels were daily making them more certain that before Japan could project its power outward, it needed to enact major reforms at home. Alarmed at news of the impending invasion, Kido and Ōkubo cut short their itinerary and returned to Tokyo, where they managed to squash Saigō's plan. They did not, however, repudiate the notion that Japan might impose its will on its neighbors by force.

Instead, they agreed the next year (1874) to a smaller action against the island of Taiwan. Taiwanese aborigines had killed several dozen shipwrecked Okinawan sailors—inhabitants of the Ryūkyū Islands—in 1871. The new Japanese government sought to include these islands in its territories, so it had demanded reparations, but the Chinese government also claimed control of the Ryūkyū Islands and had refused to pay. In 1874, with Ōkubo Toshimichi now in charge of the government, Japan sent a punitive military expedition of three thousand soldiers to Taiwan. They lost over five hundred men to tropical disease and made no significant military gains. But the Japanese government did extract a modest reparation payment from China.

The fact that military action came three years after the original incident reveals it to have been in part a strategic concession to the continued strong emotions of the faction in the government that had pushed to invade Korea in 1873. In addition, however, Japan's young government initially sought to use the expedition to establish military colonies on the island with the long-term goal of "civilizing" the native inhabitants. Japanese leaders were influenced in their thinking by Western diplomatic practice of the time, which justified colonization when carried out in the name of a mission to civilize native populations. The plan to set up colonies was not made public, and it was shelved as the expedition began in fear that it might incite a war with China.[10] But through the planning and execution of the Taiwan expedition new ground was broken. Japan's rulers not only established a precedent for gunboat diplomacy but also articulated among themselves the concept of a Japanese mission to bring "civilization" to the rest of Asia.

The rulers also established an expanded set of borders to the Japanese nation in this first decade of nation-building. The northern island known to the Tokugawa rulers as Ezo, home to the Ainu, was formally incorporated into the Meiji state as the prefecture of Hokkaido in 1869. Over the following years, Meiji rulers sent former samurai and others, including prison labor, north to open farmland in this newly claimed territory. A decade later, in 1879, Japan forced the Ryūkyū king to abdicate and incorporated the Ryūkyū Islands as the prefecture of Okinawa. But the matter of integrating the inhabitants of these territories as members of the Japanese nation was not resolved simply by drawing new borders. The Ainu living in the northern island of Hokkaido were included in the new system of family registration of 1872, by which the government defined people as "Japanese." But they were marked off from the rest of the nation in these registers with the label "former native," and they were not drafted for military service until the 1890s.[11] Okinawans were drawn into the nation even more slowly, for fear that a full-scale "Japanization" program would provoke conflict with China. Not until the late 1890s and early twentieth century were policies such as the draft or the new land tax system extended to Okinawa. While people in the newly claimed borderlands thus were recognized as Japanese subjects from early in the Meiji era, the policies to include them in the nation were ambivalent and slow to develop.

For more than a century, historians have been arguing over how to describe the profound changes of the first decades of the Meiji era. Early historians typically used the French and other European revolutions since the late eighteenth century as their model, describing the changes set in motion by the Meiji restoration as an incomplete or distorted revolution. If one accepts the premise that France in the 1790s furnishes the paradigm for a true revolution, then the changes in Japan indeed were not "complete." If one argues that the untrammeled ascendance of a capitalist bourgeoisie that attacks and defeats an aristocratic old regime is the essence of modern revolution, Japan's changes do appear "distorted." After all, it was a faction of the samurai "aristocracy" more than an emerging class of bourgeois capitalists that imposed the Meiji changes.

Even in recent years, many historians, both in Japan and outside it, have explicitly or implicitly understood the history of the Meiji era and the early twentieth century from this sort of comparative perspective. But such an analysis is not helpful. It arbitrarily imposes a Eurocentric model onto world history and does not make sufficient effort to understand the history of other places on their own terms.

The great changes of the Meiji era constituted a sort of modern "revolution from above" because they were imposed by members of the hereditary samurai elite of the old regime. But until 1868, many of these leaders had been frustrated, insecure, and ambitious men in the middle to lower ranks of the samurai class. They held greater privilege than the mass of the population, but to call them aristocratic revolutionaries from above and leave it at that is misleading. It leaves us with an image of men who were cosseted in privilege and then gave it up. It was precisely their intermediate status and their insecure salaried position, coupled with their sense of frustrated ambition and entitlement to rule, that account for the revolutionary energy of the Meiji insurgents and their far-reaching program of reform. This was a revolution of a frustrated subelite.[12]

In addition to avoiding Eurocentric comparisons, it is crucial to recognize that the Meiji revolution, like modern revolutions the world over, was an ongoing, turbulent process. Public schools, the new tax system, and the draft were imposed upon an often defiant population. The unequal treaties remained extremely controversial. Beginning with the birth of the new Meiji regime, the question of who would participate, and on what terms, was of the greatest importance to a quickly expanding public. The Meiji revolution had changed much but settled little.

6

Participation and Protest

In Japan of the Tokugawa era, the idea that common people could play a legitimate political role hardly existed. Commoners were to be the object of political action, not actors in their own right. A good ruler kept the common people alive, but barely so. In one stern Edo era injunction, attributed to Tokugawa Ieyasu, "peasants should be neither dead nor alive." Alternatively, peasants were likened to oil-producing sesame seeds: "The harder you squeeze them, the more you extract."[1] Political debate among educated samurai often centered on what one might call the "stupid commoner" problem. Thus, Aizawa Seishisai in 1825 had written:

> [T]he great majority of people in the realm are stupid commoners; superior men are very few in number. Once the hearts and minds of the stupid commoners have been captivated, we will lose control of the realm. . . . The barbarians' religion [Christianity] infiltrated Kyushu once before, and spread like the plague among stupid commoners. Within less than a hundred years, 280,000 converts were discovered and brought to justice. This indicates how fast the contagion can spread.[2]

What to do to keep the plague of barbarians from capturing the hearts and minds of the stupid commoners? Aizawa's solution in the early 1800s was certainly not to seek commoner loyalty by drawing them into politics as active participants. He wanted to indoctrinate them more thoroughly than before with a sense of the glorious essence of the emperor and their need to be loyal to him.

The Meiji political elite extended Aizawa's reasoning in some very important ways. They came to anchor the new political order in the absolute sovereignty and transcendance of the imperial institution. But in order to do this, they sought to keep the emperor outside of politics and above it. The effort contained contradictions and a certain danger. The logic of the emperor-centered polity offered the potential for various actors to claim to represent the imperial will.

Despite (and in some ways because of) government efforts to contain and indoctrinate the populace, the Japanese political world was quickly opened up to far more of the "stupid commoners" than the early Meiji leaders—not to mention Aizawa—could have possibly envisioned. Already in the early 1880s popular movements had some impact on the critical decision to promulgate a constitution. In the late 1880s political agitation in the streets of Tokyo derailed diplomatic negotiations to revise the unequal treaties between Japan and the Western powers. In 1890 a parliament, called the Diet, was opened. Elected representatives immediately began to play a significant political role. The political debates and practices of the first decades of the Meiji era opened the way to this unexpected outcome.

POLITICAL DISCOURSE AND CONTENTION

Already in the closing decades of the Tokugawa era, the door to legitimate political participation was being pushed open a few significant cracks in practice and in theory. Daimyō large and small had been invited to offer opinions to the bakufu on how to handle the black ships of Perry and their long-nosed passengers. A belief that an expanded public was entitled to play a role in politics also spread beyond the daimyō elite. In the 1850s and 1860s, samurai of various ranks and some of the more affluent commoners in the cities and countryside were meeting at a variety of sites to discuss contemporary issues. Their activities were diverse. Schools, study groups, and cultural groups such as poetry circles were among the most important incubators of a sense of political awareness in the late Tokugawa countryside. Many people, not only the privileged or powerful, were gripped with a sense that great change was approaching. They came to feel concerned and sometimes even moved to act.

Especially as the fall of the bakufu loomed imminent in 1866 and 1867, people from all walks of life came to believe that vast, unpredictable changes were on the way. In the final months of Tokugawa rule, showers of good luck charms and impromptu carnivals in city streets were signs of this vague expectation of change. More focused and immediately relevant were proposals worked up in several domains to create deliberative assemblies. These bodies were supposed to play a major role in any new governing structure. Among the most important was Sakamoto Ryōma's plan, supported by the Tosa and Echizen daimyō, for a bicameral national assembly. The upper house would be composed of court nobles and daimyō. Samurai and perhaps even commoners would be represented in the lower house.

As the new government anxiously looked to consolidate its power in early 1868, its leaders knew very well that such proposals, and the desire to participate, were widespread among allies as well as potential opponents. They were anxious both to tap into and to control these energies. One very important brief statement of such a strategy was the Charter Oath of 1868 (also called the Five-Article Oath), issued in March in the name of the emperor after considerable internal debate by the new government. It read as follows:

> By this oath we set up as our aim the establishment of the national weal on a broad basis and the framing of a constitution and laws.
>
> 1. Deliberative assemblies shall be widely established and all matters decided by public discussion.
>
> 2. All classes, high and low, shall unite in vigorously carrying out the administration of affairs of state.
>
> 3. The common people, no less than the civil and military officials, shall each be allowed to pursue their own calling so that there may be no discontent.
>
> 4. Evil customs of the past shall be broken off and everything based upon the just laws of Nature.

5. Knowledge shall be sought throughout the world so as to strengthen the foundations of imperial rule.

This remarkable document, especially articles 3–5, expressed a spirit of reform that informed the revolutionary changes imposed by the new government over the next decade. Equally important were the first two articles. They promised to involve some portion of the population in a process of "public discussion" (in Japanese, *kōgi*). This was to be carried out in "deliberative assemblies" with unspecified powers. These ambiguous promises were touchstones for much of the political contention of the following decades. Political activists within and outside the government struggled to give the articles specific meanings that suited their interests and visions.

The government, for its part, later in 1868 built on the vocabulary of the Charter Oath when it founded a bicameral "national deliberative assembly" (the Kōgisho). This body was comprised of two houses, along the lines of the Tosa proposal of two years earlier. The assembly was appointed, not elected, but it had legislative powers. The new rulers modified the governing structure several times over the next two decades. This first assembly was discontinued early on, by July 1869. A second consultative assembly replaced this body. It lasted for about a year before it, too, was adjourned permanently. But the early Meiji government had at least nodded in the direction of "widely established" deliberation by creating such assemblies.

Simultaneously, those outside the government looked to realize the promise of the Charter Oath with great enthusiasm. The question of whether to create a constitutional order was a central concern of the expanding world of public debate in the early Meiji years. Of greatest interest was the possible place of assemblies and popular representatives within a constitutional system. Debate on these matters played out in the thriving new forums of opinion journals and newspapers of what has come to be called the "Japanese enlightenment" of the 1870s.

In this decade a vigorous and partisan press emerged. The first daily newspaper in Japan, the *Yokohama Mainichi Shinbun,* was established in 1871. A daily newspaper began publication in Tokyo the following year. Called the *Nichinichi (Daily) News,* it is predecessor to today's *Mainichi Shinbun.* Such publications quickly became the center of public debate over the direction of the Meiji government. They called for establishment of a parliament. Less political and more commercially oriented papers began publishing at the end of the 1870s, with the founding of the *Asahi Shinbun* in Osaka in 1879 (this paper also survives to the present). These newspapers quickly developed mass circulations. The ensuing competition led to mergers of many smaller papers. By the end of the 1870s, a core of powerful newspapers was located in Tokyo and Osaka, and local papers were found in most prefectures.

Translations of Western books formed an important part of this expanding cultural output. A vast range of political thought was translated. By the late 1870s curious readers could dip into the works of John Stuart Mill and Jean-Jacques Rousseau. Works of conservative German statism and the social Darwinism of Herbert Spencer were translated and found enthusiastic readers among an increasingly educated public.

The most important single publication of the 1870s enlightenment was probably the *Meiji Six Journal (Meiroku Zasshi).* The most important intellectual voice of this journal, and indeed of the entire Meiji era, was certainly Fukuzawa Yukichi. The journal took its name from the year of its founding (1873). It was published by the Meiji Six Society, of which Fukuzawa was a founding member. He and his colleagues played an immensely important role in both introducing and promoting Western ideas in Japan. Fukuzawa's many writings are estimated to have sold a total of several million copies from the 1860s to 1890s. His *Conditions in the West*, published in three volumes from 1866 to 1870, was a best-selling introduction to Western institutions, customs, and material culture. His major works of the 1870s, *Encouragement of Learning* and *Outline of Civilization*, promoted a vision of a new Japan marked by a spirit of practical learning, free and skeptical inquiry, and a spirit of independence and equality of opportunity among the population.

At the heart of the writings of Fukuzawa and colleagues such as Nishi Amane and Nakamura Masanao (who introduced the utilitarian ideas of John Stuart Mill to Japan) was a belief in the inevitability and value of "progress" toward a state of "civilization." These men saw the nation-states of the contemporary West as the fore-front of world civilization. They valued the strivings of individuals in Japan not so much for the sake of individual happiness as for their contribution toward national progress and strength.

MOVEMENT FOR FREEDOM AND PEOPLE'S RIGHTS

From the 1870s into the 1880s, such ideas mixed with earlier hopes for expanded participation and social renovation to spark much political debate. The most significant political drive was the "movement for freedom and people's rights." This was a beast of many faces, a varied series of popular initiatives that posed a major challenge to the new Meiji government. Two fundamental questions concerned the politically aware men, and some women, who sustained the popular rights movements. First, what sort of new political structure should be adopted? Second, who would participate? Dis-cussion very quickly focused on the need to write a fundamental document that would answer these questions, that is, a constitution.

By the early 1870s, a simple logic framed virtually all political discourse, both among those serving in the government and those on the outside. The strongest states in the world were in the West. They had constitutions. Japanese people wanted to form a strong state, so they needed a constitution, too. The premise of this syllogism was that national power was of primary importance. Constitutions were seen by the rulers, and by most of those who objected to the narrow base of the new government, not mainly as guarantees of individual freedom and happiness or welfare. They were at their root documents whose basic laws would contain and mobilize the energies of the populace on behalf of a great national mission to build wealth and power.

From 1872 to 1873 a consensus in support of adopting a constitution of some sort emerged within the government. At almost the same time, and with a particular plea for a representative assembly, the call for a constitution became the rallying cry for a variety of non-government, or anti-government, organizations. These were formed in localities scattered around the country. They gradually came to coordinate their efforts and form the national networks that comprised the core of the Movement for Freedom and Popular Rights. As the new Meiji leaders gradually concentrated political power in the hands of a narrow group of former samurai from Satsuma and Chōshū, the popular rights activists were able to make increasingly credible charges that a new "Sat-Chō" dictatorship had replaced the old Tokugawa tyranny.

The first local popular rights group was founded in the former Tosa domain in early 1874 by Itagaki Taisuke. The group was called the Patriotic Public Party (Aikoku Kōtō). The priority given to the concept of patriotic action on behalf of the nation is significant. Itagaki had left the government several months earlier in a rage when the plan to invade Korea was overturned. Unlike Saigō Takamori, who took his anger in the direction of armed rebellion, Itagaki and his allies submitted a memorial to the government calling for a national assembly. They argued that free discussion and representative government were necessary to build a strong nation, as in this statement in their famous "Memorial on the Establishment of a Representative Assembly" of January 1874:

> The object which our government ought therefore to promote is by the establishment of a council-chamber chosen by the people to arouse in them a spirit of enterprise, and to enable them to comprehend the duty of participating in the burdens of the empire and sharing in the direction of its affairs, and then the people of the whole country will be of one mind.[3]

This manifesto won wide attention. Itagaki himself gained a reputation as the premier advocate of parliamentary constitutional government. The reputation was only partly deserved. Itagaki was an opportunist who more than once left his fellow activists in the lurch to return to the government with high rank. His organizing began with a relatively narrow base of support, primarily among former samurai. In addition to calls for political reform, he focused on winning relief for the once-proud, now impoverished samurai. Further, despite the calls for free deliberation, some former samurai supporters of the movement inherited the violent spirit of the *bakumatsu* "men of action," for whom pure motives were sufficient to justify dramatic acts of political terror.

Itagaki's initial organizations soon collapsed. But by the late 1870s, a fast-spreading interest at the grass roots of society in a constitution and parliament sustained a renewed movement for popular political participation. In the years from 1879 to 1881, in particular, local activists formed nearly two hundred political societies in the cities and countryside. Members included both farmers and former samurai. They undertook an unprecedented popular mobilization that gradually came together into two national political parties, with all the features of such bodies except the chance to contest national elections. They had dues-paying members in local units. They wrote bylaws to allow local groups to send representatives to national conventions to hammer out a platform and action program. These groups held rallies and founded journals. Leading members barnstormed on speaking tours of the Japanese countryside, holding grand fund-raising banquets with local supporters. They also collected tens of thousands of signatures on hundreds of petitions demanding a constitution and a parliament, which they submitted to the government.

In addition, the popular rights movement gained power by appropriating traditional symbols for its cause. Supporters performed plays with Tokugawa-vintage *bunraku* puppets, whose kimono were adorned with the written characters for "freedom"

Popular rights movement puppet, with characters for "freedom" (jiyū ＝ 自由) embroidered on the front of the kimono. These puppets were used in the bunraku *theater so popular in cities during the Tokugawa era. This newly designed puppet costume shows how the call for popular rights and freedoms was integrated into popular culture and broadcast beyond an intellectual elite.*

Courtesy of Tōru Senuma.

(*jiyū*). New children's rhyming songs echoed the call for popular rights. And the ideas of many activists mixed Confucian concepts of the ruler's obligation to practice benevolent government with Western ideas of natural human rights in political affairs.

What was particularly noteworthy about political life in Japan at this time is the self-generated activity of so many people at the grass roots of society. They came together in ad hoc study groups to read and debate, to write petitions or manifestos, or even to draft model constitutions. Some met in relatively elegant townhouses in Tokyo. Others met in crude rural huts. Some of their efforts lay buried in storehouses for the better part of a century, finally to be discovered in recent years by scholars practicing a so-called people's history, which searched for the political creativity of common people in such documentary remains.

Popular rights activity took place in a variety of forums. Groups called "industrial societies" were formed in the countryside to discuss issues such as new farming techniques, cooperative experimental stations, or high rates of taxation. Landowners and leading local families were usually the organizers. Typical members included village heads, teachers, local merchants, shrine officials, and doctors. The government decision to establish a Ministry of Agriculture and Commerce in 1881 was a step to co-opt and control such local energies.

Popular political education and activism also took place in city-based study groups. These were comprised primarily of journalists and educators, often former samurai, who made up the urban intelligentsia of the Meiji era. The most famous study societies evolved into Japan's leading private universities: Fukuzawa Yukichi's group developed into Keio University, and Ōkuma Shigenobu's organization formed the core of Waseda University.

Parallel to these urban academic groups were many rural cultural societies and political associations. These were the most numerous organizing units of the political ferment for popular rights. In contrast to those in rural "industrial societies," the members of these study groups tended to be former samurai. They read and discussed political philosophy as well as economic and agricultural texts. Often their deliberations led to a decision to take action, most typically in the form of submitting a petition to the Meiji government calling for a constitution and popular assembly.

The total membership of such organizations was a small minority of the entire population of Japan. But measured against the standard of the Tokugawa past, it seems appropriate to regard the glass of political activism in the 1870s and 1880s as half full rather than half empty. A larger portion of the populace than ever was engaged in the great political issues of Japan's modern emergence.

First and foremost among the issues so intensely debated was the place of the emperor. What would his powers and role be, in relation to bureaucrats, parliament, and the populace as a whole? With the rare exceptions of intellectuals strongly influenced by the model of France and its Declaration of the Rights of Man and Revolution, in Meiji Japan one finds no "republicans" in the classic sense of that term. That is, all parties to the political debate wanted the emperor to be a sovereign figure at the center of the political order. But there were vigorous discussions of how such an order was to be arranged, and one finds rather little evidence of the taboos and sense of awe that later came to be so oppressive in any discussion of the emperor. Some local groups talked freely of sharply restricting the emperor's powers. One of the most famous "draft constitutions" was discovered in a farm storehouse outside the town of Itsukaichi in 1967. It included an article giving the national assembly power to "pass judgement on and revise proposals emanating from the bureaucracy and from the Emperor."[4]

The proper extent of rights and powers of the people was the second, closely related issue at the center of public debate. The privately drafted constitutions typically provided for elected assemblies with powers over the purse and some authority to make treaties with foreign nations, draft legislation, and control the executive branch. For example, the Itsukaichi document, considered to stand on the moderate side of the various drafts discovered in recent decades, stipulated that

> if the government transgresses the constitutional principles of religion, morality, free-dom of belief, and individual freedom, or if it does not respect the principle of the equality of all people and the right to property as written in the constitution . . . then the national assembly shall have the power to argue resolutely against . . . and prohibit such acts.[5]

This was not a very practical legal provision. It did not specify who would decide when the government "transgresses constitutional principles." But it is a clear example of a grassroots interest in limiting the power of the state.

The peak of popular rights activism came from 1880 to 1881. Groups all around the country collected at least 250,000 signatures on more than one hundred petitions submitted to the government in Tokyo. Hundreds of local organizations joined into a national federation that organized three "preparatory conventions" in Tokyo. The del-egates to the third such gathering met in October 1881. They declared themselves a "political party," the Liberal Party (Jiyūtō), and immediately held their first national convention. The party platform called for popular sovereignty and the convening of a constitutional convention.

A few months later, in early 1882, a second group coalesced around Ōkuma Shigenobu. This former samurai activist from the domain of Hizen had just been ousted from his position as government minister, in part because he advocated a con-stitution that provided for a powerful parliament on a British model. His Progressive Party (Kaishintō) was more moderate than the Liberal Party in its demands. It had strong support among the emerging business elite.

It is no coincidence that in October 1881, precisely as this political mobilizing was reaching a peak of intensity and size, the Meiji government had the emperor announce that a constitution would be written and promulgated by 1890. The leaders who took this step were spurred by a sharp sense of crisis. In 1879 Yamagata Aritomo had written to Itō Hirobumi that "every day we wait, the evil poison [of popular rights agitation] will spread more and more over the provinces, penetrate into the minds of the young, and inevitably produce unfathomable evils."[6] Two years later, in 1881, Itō's trusted aide, Inoue Kowashi, wrote in a similar spirit. He wanted the government to quickly write a conservative, state-centered constitution:

> If we lose this opportunity and vacillate, within two or three years the people will become confident that they can succeed and no matter how much oratory we use . . .

public opinion will cast aside the draft of a constitution presented by the government, and the private drafts of the constitution will win out in the end.[7]

The popular rights movement was an important factor influencing the timing and direction of the government's decision to adopt a constitution. But the Meiji leaders were not simply caving in to the opposition. They had already decided that constitutional government was needed to secure international respect for Japan and to mobilize the energies of the people behind projects to build a "rich nation and strong army." In 1878 they took a first step in this direction by establishing elected prefectural assemblies nationwide, with advisory powers only. The government hoped thereby to win the support of the rural elite of property owners (voting rights were limited to those who paid the highest land taxes). In fact the assemblies often became hotbeds of popular rights agitation.

The unprecedented popular rights campaigns of petitioning and speechmaking influenced the decision to adopt a constitution in two ironic ways. First, they led the government to adopt repressive censorship laws. The first set was promulgated in 1875. These were tightened the following year and reinforced once more in 1887. Second, the campaigns also intensified the determination of government figures to write a conservative constitution modeled on the Prussian constitution of 1854. This document gave the king and his ministers much power and limited the rights of the people. For the Meiji rulers to write a constitution that upheld their vision of limited civil rights and marginal popular participation was not particularly difficult. Actually using the constitution to enforce such a vision would prove much harder.

SAMURAI REBELLIONS, PEASANT UPRISINGS, AND NEW RELIGIONS

Several other sharp challenges to the authority of the new government took place in these decades. Volatile reactionary demands to stem the pace of change or turn back the clock exploded in the 1870s. Commoners opposed to the military draft destroyed registration centers. Those upset at compulsory education and local school taxes demolished thousands of newly built schools. In addition, several rebellions of the expropriated former samurai took place in the mid-1870s.

These samurai uprisings had some motives and goals in common with the less violent popular rights agitation. They shared anger at being left out of the decision-making process. Frustrated former samurai in the 1870s saw two ways to influence the new government. Some tried to write new rules of participation. Others forced the issue with swords and guns. In addition, both the popular rights activists and the samurai rebels shared a very bellicose stand on foreign policy. They were in fact more aggressive than those in the government. Thus, when the debate over a Korean invasion split the government in 1873 both Itagaki Taisuke and Saigō Takamori quit their posts. Itagaki launched the popular rights movement. Saigō eventually led an armed rebellion.

Saigō's insurrection, the Satsuma rebellion, was the largest of several. In 1874 another member of the war faction who left the government, Etō Shinpei, led a force of twenty-five hundred warriors in an attack on the prefectural government of Saga

Police interrupting a speaker at a popular rights rally in the 1880s draw the wrath of the crowd for this suppression. In response to the agitation for popular rights, the government tightened censorship laws and stationed police observers on the stage at all political rallies. Speakers who crossed the line of acceptable rhetoric with strong anti-government statements were first cautioned, and then halted. For audience members, part of the excitement of attending these rallies was the possibility of watching or joining such a raucous moment.
Courtesy of Meiji Shinbun Zasshi Bunkō, Faculty of Law, University of Tokyo.

(in Kyushu). They wanted to reinstate their daimyō and reclaim their samurai stipends. Similar but smaller insurgencies, each involving several hundred former samurai, took place in Kumamoto and Fukuoka prefectures in 1876, also both in Kyushu. All these actions were quickly suppressed by troops of the new government, and the leaders were executed.

During these years, Saigō himself returned to his home of Kagoshima (the former Satsuma domain), also in Kyushu. There he founded a private military academy. His local support was so strong that Kagoshima prefecture had effectively seceded from the national government by 1876. The prefecture forwarded no taxes to Tokyo. It ignored other social reform orders of the Meiji government. Then, in the winter of 1877, Saigō set off with a force of fifteen thousand soldiers from Kagoshima on a march ultimately headed for Tokyo. His goal was to overthrow the government and restore samurai privilege. As the rebels proceeded through strongly anti-government territory into the neighboring prefecture of Kumamoto, Saigō's army quickly mushroomed to forty thousand men. It attacked the government troops who occupied Kumamoto castle. This siege failed when a large government army (over sixty thousand men) arrived to reinforce the local garrison. Three weeks of bloody fighting ended in a massive defeat for the rebels. They suffered about twenty thousand casualties. More than six thousand goverment soldiers were killed, and ninety-five hundred were wounded. Saigō committed suicide rather then be captured and executed. To this day, he remains a popular hero, revered as an exemplar of pure motives and loyalty to a cause, however hopeless. But his defeat made it clear that there would be no turning back to the old social order. Farmer conscripts had proven their worth against the samurai troops. Armed resistance to the new government was widely recognized to be impossible.

Even so, the poverty suffered by some farmers in the following years led them to raise arms against vastly superior forces on several occasions. These peasant uprisings were sparked especially by high levels of debt suffered by tenant farmers and small-scale producers of silk cocoons. Government economic policies of the early 1880s brought on sharp deflation. Rice and raw silk prices fell to roughly half their 1880 levels by 1884. Since overall prices fell by just one quarter, farmers who depended heavily on revenue from the sale of rice and silk products fared worse than others. Ambitious small landholders, sparked by dreams of just a bit more income in a new era of opportunity, had already taken loans to convert hillside fields to mulberry production for raising silkworms. They suddenly had to borrow even more simply to pay their taxes, which did not decrease with deflation. Many defaulted and lost their fields to moneylending landlords.

In numerous prefectures, especially in the silk-intensive regions in the Kantō region, these farmers organized groups with names such as Debtors Party or Poor People's Party. They demanded that creditors, usually local landlords, reduce or cancel their debts or suspend demand for payments. The largest uprising took place in the Chichibu region about fifty miles west of Tokyo. In early November 1884, six thousand men raised a ragtag army. They attacked and destroyed government offices and debt certificates. Marching from village to village, they drew in new supporters and trashed the homes of moneylenders. Local police were overwhelmed. The government eventually called in the army, and after about ten days the Meiji state's troops put down this rebellion rather easily. Five leaders were later tried and executed. A number of local Liberal Party members took part in these rebellions, and some of the rebels called themselves "soldiers of the Liberal Party." The party's national leadership was not involved, but they nonetheless disbanded the party rather than risk accusation of supporting insurrection.

In addition to armies of samurai rebels and parties of poor farmers, a number of powerful new religions constituted a third challenge to the new government. Some of these, such as the Tenri and Konkō religions, had been founded in the late Tokugawa decades. Others, such as the Maruyama and Ōmoto religions, emerged early in the Meiji era. By the late 1870s the Maruyama and Tenri organizations each claimed several hundred thousand adherents. These religions typically began when a founding figure, often a woman, became possessed of divine inspiration and wrote down or dictated the sacred scripture of the sect. Their teachings often called for restraint in this life in the expectation of salvation in the next. But as in Tokugawa times, they also preached messages of present-day deliverance through a sudden equalization of wealth, so-called *yonaoshi*, or "world rectification." They shared fury at the inequitable social and economic system with supporters of the Debtors and Poor Farmer's parties. On occasion this led to similar sorts of violent action and rumors of organizational links. In one incident in 1884, for example, just a week after the Chichibu uprising, supporters of the Maruyama sect in Shizuoka prefecture demanded immediate equalization of wealth and launched attacks that destroyed government offices.

These challenges to the new regime had complex social and regional sources. Former samurai, wealthy farmers, and poor farmers were three groups behind popular rights activism, while the former samurai and indebted farmers were main supporters of armed rebellion or new religions. Ironically, samurai resistance, whether through the popular rights movement or via rebellion, was strongest in the areas of greatest support for the 1868 restoration. These samurai, in Kyushu and Tosa above all, had expected to play a role in the new government that they brought to power. When they became disillusioned at its course, or felt excluded, they were more likely than others to act. Peasant protests were greatest in areas of commercialized farming, especially silk-producing regions where farmers were most vulnerable to the fluctuations of national and international markets.

PARTICIPATION FOR WOMEN

The turbulent social responses to the Meiji revolution also involved extensive questioning of gender roles and ideologies. Horror at the anarchic mixing of men and women in the West had been apparent in the writings of some of the earliest Japanese official travelers. In 1860, for instance, Muragaki Norimasa wrote this account of a bakufu mission to the United States, which was entertained at a ball at the State Department:

> Men and women moved round the room couple by couple, walking on tiptoe to the tune of the music. It was just like a number of mice running around and around. It is indeed odd that the Prime Minister should invite an ambassador of another country to an event of this sort! My sense of displeasure is boundless; there is no respect for order and ceremony or obligation.[8]

He was equally aghast when a young American woman had the impudence to quiz him rather naively about Japanese political and social customs at a state dinner.

Despite such views, the new government cautiously encouraged select women to play an active role in support of its programs. It included five young women (ages nine through sixteen) in the group of students who accompanied the Iwakura Mission. These youths stayed on in the United States to receive an American education and become model women for constructing a new Japan. Compared to the young men who accompanied the mission, they received less attention and support. One returned almost immediately; one died in America. Two returned and married comfortably into the ruling elite, leaving little independent legacy. But the youngest of these students, Tsuda Ume (nine years old when she left Japan), became a powerful figure promoting expanded social roles for women. Upon her return, she founded a college for women today known as Tsuda University, and she became a leader in women's education.

In these same years, a vigorous debate on appropriate roles and rights for women and men unfolded among those outside the government. At least in the documentary sources left to historians, this debate began with men discussing how women ought to be treated. The best known forum was the *Meiji Six Journal*. Some of the most important intellectuals of the time, including Fukuzawa Yukichi and Mori Arinori (later to be minister of education), wrote on the meaning of equality between men and women, the value of education for women, and the demerits of legally recognizing concubines and giving their children rights of inheritance.[9] Opinions on all these issues ranged widely. But as in the West in the late nineteenth century, the mainstream of reformist sentiment was decidedly cautious. Contributors to the *Meiji Six Journal* took care to distinguish between equal respect for men and women in their separate spheres, which they usually encouraged, and equality of political or legal rights in society at large, which they rarely favored. Commentators feared that the latter would only bring divisive conflict between the sexes and destroy social harmony. Consider, for example, this 1875 essay by Sakatani Shiroshi:

> The words equal rights, therefore, should not establish equality in life generally, although they may provide equality in the bedchamber. If today we establish this equality between the sexes in all aspects of life, we shall reach the point where the men will strive to oppress the women while the women attempt to oppress the men. . . . In sum, the word "rights" includes evil.[10]

Some women took their own steps to give meaning to the concepts of civilization and enlightenment that had been put forward in the first instance for men only. In one example, the early Meiji government promoted dramatic change in personal grooming for samurai men in 1871. It issued an order "encouraging them" to abandon the old top-knot for a Western haircut. Once the emperor did this, most samurai men followed his model. Some women in Tokyo then decided to make a similar change on their own. They organized an association calling for shorter and more practical hairstyles. They set an example with their own short cuts. The government responded in 1872 by outlawing short hair for women. According to this order of the state, even older women who had health reasons to wear short hair had to get a license to do so, at least if they were to go to a barbershop or hairdresser for the procedure.

Other women took demands for change into the political forum of the Movement for Freedom and Popular Rights. For a brief span from the late 1870s into the early 1880s, women played a significant role both as speakers and in large numbers as members of the audience at popular rights rallies. A few stalwarts, most famously Kishida Toshiko and Fukuda Hideko, began to make well-attended speeches advocating equal political and legal rights for women and men. Kishida condemned what she called outmoded notions of "contempt for women and respect for men." She defined "progress" and "civilization" as a situation in which women would have political and economic rights on a par with men. She called for education for women and equality within the family. She attacked the legality of concubines, which gave a man's wife and her children no greater claim on the husband's resources than a mistress had.

Fukuda later recalled in her autobiography:

> Listening to her [Kishida Toshiko] speech, delivered in that marvelous oratorical style, I was unable to suppress my resentment and indignation . . . and began immediately to organize women and their daughters . . . to take the initiative in explaining and advocating natural rights, liberty, and equality . . . so that somehow we might muster the passion to smash the corrupt customs of former days relating to women.[11]

For the men in the popular rights movement, a speaker like Kishida was both a threat and an opportunity. She increased the likelihood that the government might crack down on the movement. But she was a marvelous draw who brought enthusiastic and curious crowds into lecture halls or open-air rallies.

For their part, the Meiji rulers by the 1880s had concluded that their own wives might play a semipublic role as models and representatives of the nation to the world. Muragaki's shock at American dancing in the 1860s became an old-fashioned attitude. Elite men and women took up ballroom dancing and entertained foreigners at grand parties in the heart of Tokyo. And in public discussions among men, even in the government, the idea that women might support the nation with a political role had some support. Top officials as well as journalists discussed whether it might not be appropriate for female as well as male children in the imperial line to ascend to the throne. In the mid-1880s some prominent government figures supported this idea.

The two major popular rights parties both collapsed in 1884 because of factional infighting, the taint of association with peasant rebellions, and state repression. Their leaders soon regrouped. But the close alliance between male party politicians and activist women was not revived, even after the constitution was promulgated. Women interested in political or social action turned to activity as teachers or writers or organized nominally apolitical groups such as the Tokyo Women's Reform Society.

The government was in large part responsible for this retreat in women's political activity. It decided to limit imperial succession to males. On the eve of promulgating the constitution in 1889, it issued a series of laws that barred women from joining political organizations, speaking at or attending political gatherings, or even sitting as observers in the Diet gallery. These measures provoked a flurry of outraged commentary by leading women educators and social reformers, such as Shimizu Toyoko and Yajima Kajiko. They particularly ridiculed the ban on observing Diet proceedings. They asked: Did this mean that Japan's male elites expected their own behavior to offer a harmful example to observers? A number of male politicians and journalists echoed this question. The government backed down on this one point and allowed women into the Diet gallery. But most men in the popular rights movement were closer to their government colleagues than to their erstwhile female allies in their discomfort with the notion of political rights for women; the other more substantial prohibitions remained in force.

As Japan's rulers were promoting change, they were anxiously seeking to manage and control it. A fear of allowing women to transgress narrow boundaries of proper place and behavior remained powerful. The rulers' ambivalent reformism was particularly strong when it came to defining appropriate roles for women in realms as personal as hairstyles and as political as speaking at public rallies.

TREATY REVISION AND DOMESTIC POLITICS

Although the two parties that emerged at the forefront of the popular rights movement both collapsed in 1884, energetic popular activism continued through the decade. If anything, despite the folding of the Liberal and Progressive parties, the government's ability to impose its will against popular wishes decreased in the late 1880s. Nowhere was this as clear as in the tortured effort to negotiate more equal treaties with the Western powers. The government's plan to partially revise these treaties in the mid- to late 1880s sparked opposition and emotional discussion of Japan's proper place in the world. In addition, like the controversial question of the constitution in the 1870s, the treaty issue in the 1880s stimulated powerful demands for a political order that respected the popular will.

The Iwakura Mission had failed in its effort of 1873 to open negotiations to revise the "unequal treaties." For the rest of the decade, the government focused on more limited goals. It offered to open more ports to foreign trade if the Western powers would return partial Japanese control over tariffs. The British refused any concessions, and these efforts came to naught. In the early 1880s a new foreign minister, Inoue Kaoru, pleaded with more success for a multi-national conference in Tokyo to discuss treaty revisions. Ministers from all the treaty powers finally gathered in Tokyo in May 1886. By the following April they had drafted an agreement that Japan could regain tariff autonomy and nearly complete jurisdiction over the treaty ports. In exchange, Japan would open all its territory to foreign residence and commerce.

There were two crucial limitations in the agreement. First, it called for the Japanese government to submit the text of the new Japanese legal codes, just being drafted at that time, to all the powers for their inspection before new treaties could take effect. In addition, the agreement committed the Japanese government to hire foreign judges to sit in Japanese courts and hear cases concerning foreigners. A vociferous chorus of protest arose in response. People complained that these conditions allowed intolerable ongoing violation of Japanese sovereignty. One key government official, Minister of Agriculture and Commerce Tani Kanjō, quit his post in anger at the proposed changes. He blasted them as worse than the status quo. He became a somewhat reluctant popular hero. Former Liberal and Progressive party activists renewed their organizing nation-wide. They flooded the government with petitions against treaty revision on these terms. The major newspapers ran fierce anti-revision editorials. Roughly two thousand youths streamed into Tokyo to protest the proposed changes. They held demonstrations and mass visits to government offices. In the words of one official, "The hearts of the people are stirred to an extreme degree, and this invites the collapse of the cabinet."[12] In the face of this protest, the government was indeed forced to abandon the proposed revisions, and Inoue resigned as foreign minister.

His successor, Ōkuma Shigenobu, fared little better. He managed to negotiate a slightly more favorable set of revisions with the treaty powers in 1889, but these also ran into a mixed reaction within the government and strong opposition outside it.

Once again, petitions demanding completely equal treaties poured into the capital. In October 1889, a member of an ultra-nationalist political organization, the Genyōsha, hurled a bomb at Ōkuma and then committed suicide by cutting open his stomach. Ōkuma lost a leg but survived. The government abandoned the revision plan, and the cabinet resigned.

The participants in the turbulent politics of treaty revision mixed the fierce, violent politics of the *bakumatsu* "men of action" with a Western-style politics of editorial writing, petitioning, and lobbying. They ranged from knowledgeable democratic nationalists to small-time thugs looking for action. They carried forward an enduring anti-foreign sentiment and loyalty to the emperor from the final years of the Tokugawa era. They combined these older views with a new belief that only a political system that gave freedom and political rights to the people could bring national strength and international respect.

THE MEIJI CONSTITUTION

As the government polished the final drafts of the constitution, these agitations—which forced two cabinet ministers to resign—vividly reminded the Meiji rulers of the messiness and danger of popular participation in politics. It is no surprise that the document formally promulgated in a grand ceremony in 1889 was written and presented in a way that sought to maximize the power of the state and minimize that of the people.

The constitution was drafted secretly in 1886 and 1887 by a talented group under the direction of Itō Hirobumi and Inoue Kowashi. Itō had studied European constitutions in Europe. He brought first-rate foreign legal advisors back to Japan, most prominently a German professor of law, Hermann Roessler. The document was discussed by top government officials in 1888 in a body newly created for this purpose, the Privy Council. This council continued to function as an extra-constitutional advisory group once the constitution was promulgated. It served as one site where the Meiji leaders could manage the political system. This small group of leaders came be know as the Meiji "oligarchs" (*genrō* in Japanese), a term coined by the press in 1892. The original oligarchs were the key men, such as Itō Hirobumi and Yamagata Aritomo, who had come to dominate the cabinet and the bureaucracy in the 1880s. The *genrō* were an informal body, in the sense that there was no constitutional provision for them. But informal did not mean ambiguous or unclear. The identity of the oligarchs was well known.[13] For the rest of their lives, they continued to pull the strings of politics, but as they grew older they stepped back from the front lines of political battle to positions such as leadership of the Privy Council.

The constitution was handed down, quite literally, as a gift from the emperor to his prime minister and the people on February 11, 1889. It began, in the preamble, with an unequivocal declaration of imperial sovereignty: "The right of sovereignty of the State, We have inherited from Our Ancestors, and We shall bequeath it to Our descendants." Cabinet ministers were to be responsible to the emperor and not to the Diet. However, the prospect of direct imperial despotism was checked in a general way in the preamble, which went on to state that "Neither We nor [our descendants] shall in the future fail to wield the [rights of sovereignty], in accordance with the provisions of the present Constitution and of the law." In the constitution itself, the power of the bureaucracy in relation to the throne was bolstered by the requirement that cabinet ministers cosign all imperial orders. The constitution gave a special independence to the military general staff, via the "right to supreme command." This was article 11, which specified that the military was directly responsible to the emperor. The constitution granted a variety of civil rights to the people. All of these, however, were made conditional on "limits established by law."

The Diet itself was composed of an elected House of Representatives and a House of Peers. In preparation for the latter, the government had instituted a European-style system of peers in 1885. It variously titled about five hundred prominent court, government, and military officials as prince, marquis, count, viscount, and baron. Members of the House of Peers consisted of some of these figures, in addition to distinguished individuals appointed by the emperor and a handful of the highest taxpayers in the nation. This house was intended to be one more restraint on popular participation.

Even so, the constitution left important room for the electorate to assert its wishes. The definition of eligible voters was to be set by law, and the Diet had power to write and pass laws. It also had the crucial power to approve or veto the annual state budget. The government created a loophole with a clause that provided for the previous year's budget to automatically take effect if the Diet failed to pass the new budget. But as costs of government steadily increased, this escape hatch was of little help. Once the constitution took effect, the Meiji oligarchs were forced to take heed of the wishes of Diet representatives far more than they had expected or hoped.

The promulgation of a constitution and the convening of an elected Diet meant that Japan was a nation of subjects with both obligations to the state and political rights. Obligations included military service for men, school attendance for all, and the individual payment of taxes. Rights included suffrage for a few and a voice in deciding the fate of the national budget. The fact that these rights were limited to men of substantial property is important. Under the first election law, only about 1 percent of the total population paid sufficient taxes to qualify for the vote. Clearly the constitution was expected by its authors to contain the opposition. But to stress only the limitations placed on popular rights by the Meiji constitution is to miss its historical significance as a source of future change. The undeniable fact was that a constitutionally mandated, elected national assembly—with more than advisory powers—now existed. This clearly implied that a politically active and potentially expandable body of subjects or citizens also existed. Indeed, as the oligarchs decided to adopt a constitution, they were acutely aware that such a body politic was in the process of forming itself and developing its own ideas about the political order.

7

Social, Economic, and Cultural Transformations

In just three decades, from the 1860s to the 1890s, the Japanese economy emerged as an Asian powerhouse. It came to be called "the Workshop of Asia," a cliché that persisted far into the twentieth century. By the 1890s, textile manufacturers dominated home markets. They began competing successfully with British firms in China and India, as well. Japanese shippers were competing with European traders to carry these goods even to Europe.

Taking a long view, the economic takeoff of Meiji Japan was a formidable achievement. This is the case whether one compares Japan to other countries or compares the standards of living within Japan in the 1860s to those of decades later. But the immediate impact of the industrial revolution was disastrous for many people in Japan. Especially hard hit were members of two large, overlapping groups: small-scale family farmers and young women workers. Huge numbers of farmers lost their lands to moneylenders, and hundreds of thousands of teenage girls experienced the hardship of labor in the thread mills, the weaving sheds, the match factories, and the expanding brothels of the new Japan.

A divided judgment applies also to the cultural transformations of these decades. Japanese writers and artists embraced new forms from novels to oil painting, while older traditions from poetry writing to *bunraku* chanting showed ongoing vitality. But a profound anxiety that something was being lost in the headlong rush to a Western-focused modernity surfaced with increasing intensity in the 1880s and 1890s. This worry pushed intellectuals to improvise new concepts of Japanese "tradition." It also linked up with the fear of social disorder and political challenge among state officials. They responded by putting in place oppressive limits on individual thought and behavior.

LANDLORDS AND TENANTS

Agrarian society played a critical role in the economic transformation of Meiji Japan. It was a vital source of the labor power, food, tax revenues, and export earnings that made the industrial revolution possible.

From 1880 through 1900 Japan's population rose from about thirty-five to forty-five million people. At the same time, the rural, agricultural population declined slightly. Millions of people migrated from villages to towns or from towns to major cities. They moved as well from agriculture to commerce and manufacturing industries. Given these shifts, a demographic crisis could be avoided only by food imports or increased domestic output. Until about 1920, Japanese farmers supported the growing population with increased output. Agricultural productivity steadily increased for two reasons. The best practice of existing farms, previously limited to the most advanced areas, diffused more broadly. In addition, new crops, new seeds, and more fertilizer came into use. The precise extent of the increased productivity of land is a subject of controversy. Estimates of annual increase in output vary from 1 to 3 percent.[1] Even if the lower estimate is more accurate, the productivity gain was substantial and crucial. It fed a growing population. It also preserved scarce foreign exchange for imports of industrial and military technologies rather than food.

In fact, the agrarian sector was a crucial source of state tax revenues used for a wide range of modernizing projects. The land tax accounted for about 80 percent of government income in the 1870s and early 1880s. This fell to around 60 percent by the early 1890s when new taxes were imposed on consumer goods, including necessities such as soy sauce and salt and virtual necessities such as sugar and sake. But taxes on agricultural land still provided the majority of the government's revenues.

Simultaneously, farmers brought in crucial foreign exchange by exporting tea and silk products. A silk blight in Europe in 1868 opened the way for a booming export trade in silk cocoons raised in small sheds on family farms. When the European blight ended, the emphasis shifted to exports of silk threads. Between 1868 and 1893 Japanese raw silk production rose almost fivefold, from 2.3 million pounds to 10.2 million pounds. Most of this was sold overseas. Silk accounted for 42 percent of all Japanese export revenues during this quarter-century.

Agriculture had a further indirect economic impact through the export of people. After tea and silk, the third highest source of foreign exchange earnings in Japan around the turn of the century came from emigrant laborers who sent a portion of their earnings in Hawaii, California, or Latin America to relatives in their home villages.

Silk thread was often spun and woven in small factories in rural locations. The owners and operators were members of an entrepreneurial rural elite. The members of the upper crust of agrarian society played a crucial role in building a capitalist economy in Japan. They invested in and ran factories, paid large amounts of taxes, and sent their children on to higher education. Their educated sons, in particular, went on to leading positions in business, politics, or bureaucracy. They also foreclosed on high-interest loans to impoverished neighbors, and they hired the daughters of such farmers to work fourteen-hour days in spinning and weaving sheds. These landlords were playing a part in a much larger story of economic policy and its social consequences.

The huge costs of putting down the Satsuma rebellion, on top of the numerous costly projects to build the economy and military, left the Meiji government faced with a drastic revenue shortfall in 1878. It responded first by printing money. The result was a surge of price inflation. This only worsened the deficit, since tax revenues were based on land assessments that did not automatically rise with inflation. The real value of taxes fell. Japanese farmers briefly prospered.

In 1881 Finance Minister Matsukata Masayoshi, one of the surviving Satsuma activists of the 1860s and among the most important Meiji leaders, launched draconian fiscal and monetary policies. Seeking to halt the inflation, he cut state expenses sharply. By 1880 the government had already fired most of the foreign advisors hired in the 1870s. It now sold off the unprofitable government industries that these advisors helped build. Matsukata also shrunk the money supply by shutting down the printing presses that had produced cheap paper money in the late 1870s and returning to a silver-backed currency.

The result has come to be called the Matsukata deflation of the early 1880s. Agricultural commodity prices crashed by as much as 50 percent by 1884. To survive, small-scale landholders took new loans from moneylenders who were often nearby wealthy landlords. Thousands defaulted and lost their fields to these neighbors. One response was the wave of rebellion led by the Debtors or Poor Farmers parties in places such as Chichibu.

A related result of the great deflation was a dramatic shift in landownership. Like the rise in agricultural production, the precise increase in the number of tenant farmers is still subject to debate. A conservative estimate holds that the proportion of agricultural land worked by tenants rose from 30 percent in the late 1870s to 40 percent in the late 1880s. Even by this account, at least one-tenth of the arable land of Japan changed hands in one decade. The financial program of shock therapy indeed stabilized Japan's economy by the end of the 1880s. It was also a devastating experience for millions of people.

INDUSTRIAL REVOLUTION

The Meiji state had begun to put in place the infrastructure of a capitalist industrial economy by the early 1880s. It continued to build the economic foundation over the next two decades: railway lines, a new code of commercial law, specialized banks to provide long-term credit to industry. But relatively small numbers of private investors struggled with limited success to produce manufactured goods profitably through the rest of the 1880s. Then, in the two decades spanning the turn of the century, Japan's industrial economy took off. Manufacturing output rose 5 percent annually over these years. This was a much stronger performance than the worldwide annual growth rate of 3.5 percent. Japan's production even outpaced that of the United States, where industry was also booming. American manufacturing doubled from 1895 to 1915. In Japan manufacturing rose 2.5 times over the same period.

Industrialization was led by the textile industry. From the 1890s through 1913, output of silk quadrupled. By the eve of World War I, three-fourths of these threads were produced by machine, whereas earlier most silk had been reeled by hand. In addition, about three-fourths of silk output was being exported each year. Production of cotton thread increased at similar rates. Mechanized production also replaced hand spinning. And about half of the cotton output came to be exported, mainly to China and Korea.

Coal and metal mining was a second leading sector in Japan's early industrial era. Mineral production in Japan increased 700 percent from 1876 to 1896. After textiles mills, mines were the nation's major employers of wage labor. About half of the output from coal fields in Kyushu and Hokkaido provided fuel to Japanese factories. Most of the rest supplied steamships calling in Japanese ports. In addition, by the early twentieth century, the Ashio copper mine and refinery was one of the largest producers of this metal in the world.

A revolution in transport supported these new industries. By the late 1880s, Japan's railway lines extended over one thousand miles. By 1900 the total stood in excess of thirty-four hundred miles. The building of this rail system was a formidable technical feat in a mountainous country. And the rail system promoted other industrial ventures, most importantly textiles and coal mining, by lowering the transport cost of raw materials to factories and cutting the cost of sending finished goods to domestic markets and to harbors for export.

Rapid industrialization brought with it important innovations in social and economic organization. A boom in private railroad investment in the late 1880s sparked a more generalized "private company boom." Between 1886 and 1892, private investors established fourteen new railway companies. The total length of private lines was more than double that of government lines. This investment boom spread to spinning and mining and beyond. The experience taught some investors hard lessons in how to organize joint stock companies or trade in the stock market when the "enterprise mania" culminated in Japan's first modern financial crisis in 1890. The stock market crashed. Many poorly conceived speculative enterprises failed. But the boom also had some enduring impact. Most of the new railroad companies were solid ventures. They and a number of other new businesses survived the panic of 1890 to become leaders in the private sector of the economy.

The most distinctive feature of Japan's emerging system of capitalism was the central role played by monopolies that later came to be called zaibatsu (the term literally translates as "financial clique"). Several of the zaibatsu—most notably Mitsui and Sumitomo—had roots in merchant houses dating back to the Tokugawa era. Others, including the famous Mitsubishi zaibatsu, were founded from scratch by entrepreneurs in the Meiji era. In all cases, it was the 1870s and 1880s when these combines began to coalesce in their modern form. Their founders exploited long-standing close ties to the government and synergistic links between key industries to found their business empires. The Mitsui family, for example, had been dry-goods retailers in Kyoto and Edo since the 1670s. They had been moneylenders to the shogunate through the end of its days. In the 1860s, Mitsui's general manager cultivated ties to anti-shogunal forces as well. The family built on these ties after 1868. It handled a portion of the new government's tax collection operations, and from this founded the Mitsui Bank in 1876. The same year, it founded a general trading company. Soon thereafter Itō Hirobumi, the minister of public works at the time, offered Mitsui Trading Company an exclusive contract for sale of coal from the government's Miike mine. As Itō neatly put it, "We will not be tight. You can acquire the coal at cost price and get started on it directly."[2] Mitsui made immense profits from this arrangement. In 1888 it bought the mine outright, although it paid a handsome price to the government. It also sold much of this coal to British steamers, and these contacts helped Mitsui Trading open branch offices in Shanghai, Hong Kong, and then London. This dynamic triad of banking, mining, and trading came together in the 1880s. In the following decade, Mitsui built on this base and used its profits to acquire or found engineering (Shibaura), cotton-spinning (Kanegafuchi), and paper pulp (Ōji) companies and numerous other firms.

With slight differences in emphasis—shipping, then shipbuilding and railroads, were more important to the Mitsubishi combine—other zaibatsu emerged in similar fashion in the 1880s and 1890s. Although the founding families retained financial control of the each zaibatsu complex, from the start they avoided the drag of nepotism. Owners recruited able young men from outside the family and delegated important management responsibilities to them. This practice clearly separated ownership from management of Japanese business at a comparatively early stage in modern industrial development.

Why did these highly concentrated zaibatsu emerge to such prominence? Part of the answer must be that all capitalist economies generate momentum toward concentration. A glance at the railroad, steel, oil, tobacco, and financial empires of Americans such as Vanderbilt, Carnegie, Rockefeller, Duke, and Morgan makes clear that powerful monopolies were not unique to Japan. But the zaibatsu were unusual in their broad reach. They were not limited to particular industries or even to particular fields such as finance or manufacturing. Each zaibatsu spanned the entire range of business endeavor from trade and shipping to finance, mining, and all sorts of factory production. One cannot explain their emergence simply by referring to factors found in all capitalist economies.

One persuasive interpretation links the dominant position of entities such as the zaibatsu (or the bank-centered monopolies of late nineteenth-century Germany or state-run businesses in Russia) to the relative "lateness" of Japanese, German, and Russian economic development. A late-developer, the argument goes, can only catch up and compete internationally by swiftly mobilizing scarce resources of capital, skilled labor, and technology in new industrial endeavors. Only large organizations are able to do this. In some late-developing cases, the state will play this mobilizing role. In others—such as Japan—the lead will be taken by a mix of government projects and huge private combines.[3]

This logic of late development helps explain why the zaibatsu emerged. But it cannot fully account for the impressive performance of Japanese capitalism of the Meiji era, which was certainly unprecedented outside the West. The Tokugawa economic and demographic heritage was one factor. From well before the time of the Meiji reforms, one found widespread entrepreneurial and manufacturing skills with potential application in modern industry and a sophisticated network of commercial finance and coastal transport. In addition, population growth was slow, which allowed agricultural revenues to be shifted to new fields.

Building from this base, the ability of Japanese producers to draw from a pool of relatively inexpensive labor was a crucial part of the story. In the late nineteenth and early twentieth centuries, Japanese industry became steadily more mechanized. Nonetheless, labor productivity (the monetary value of goods or services produced by an average worker) lagged far behind the value of output per worker in advanced economies of the West. With relatively less productive workers, the only way Japan's economy could have been competitive was if the workers were relatively low paid.

Indeed, they were. Comparatively puny wages for relatively unproductive workers was crucial to the strong performance of Japanese manufacturers in these decades.

The proactive role of the state was another important factor. The state built an economic infrastructure and provided a base for the early zaibatsu in the 1870s and 1880s. In the following years the state took the lead in promoting—indeed enabling— the development of capital-intensive, higher technology industries. This was an area in which Japan lacked a comparative advantage in labor costs. For example, through the 1890s Japanese railroad companies imported locomotives and rails from the West because Japanese ironmakers or engineering firms either did not exist or were unable to offer competitive products. In the early twentieth century, the government took key steps that changed the situation on both the supply and demand side of this economic equation. On the supply side, it used government funds to found the Yahata iron and steel mill in 1896. State funds were also used to subsidize the shipping industry as well as private manufacturers in machine-making, engineering, and shipbuilding. On the demand side, the government nationalized almost all intercity railroads in 1906. It used this control of the railroads to direct orders for locomotives and rails to Japanese producers. It simultaneously placed tariffs on competing imports.[4] All these steps combined to nurture private sector heavy industries that otherwise would not have come into existence at this time or on such a scale.

Finally, the visible hand of the state was complemented by significant competition and entrepreneurship in the private sector. Young men inspired by dreams of great personal wealth found patrons who sent them abroad, where they apprenticed to European or American spinning mills, paper mills, engineering works, and the like. They returned home to manage factories and occupy top positions in the expanding zaibatsu. Multiple engineering and shipbuilding firms competed for government railway or naval procurements. Private steelmakers spun off from Yahata to compete with it. Tariffs offered these emerging Japanese firms some protection from foreign imports in the early twentieth century, but they were forced by domestic competitors to increase productivity and quality.

Japan's economic growth thus depended on a dynamic mix of state and private initiative. In parallel fashion, the ethos of the business elite mixed ideals of service to the nation with a drive for personal wealth. Japanese capitalists, like state bureaucrats, did not exalt the creativity of the market pure and simple. Neither did they laud the untrammeled pursuit of profit as the ultimate social benefit. Rather, they drew on Confucian language to put forward a philosophy of what might be called "selfless" profit-seeking.

Shibusawa Eiichi made this point with particular force. He was the most important financier and industrialist of the Meiji era. As an energetic entrepreneur he introduced the concept of joint-stock companies to Japan. He founded some of Japan's first successful large-scale textile mills, pulp mills, and private banks. Shibusawa preached the virtues of self-reliance, but he also argued strongly against the view that "through individualism or egoism the State and society can progress most rapidly." He countered that "I cannot support such a theory. . . . Although people desire to rise to positions of wealth and honor, the social order and the tranquillity of the State will be disrupted if this is done egoistically." In the words of a like-minded Meiji era trader, "the secret to success in business is the determination to work for the sake of society and of mankind as well as for the future of the nation, even if it means sacrificing oneself."[5]

THE WORK FORCE AND LABOR CONDITIONS

Such idealistic public statements probably reflected the sincere beliefs of many business leaders. Yet the goal of developing industry for the nation rarely led to generous treatment of working people. Female laborers—often the teenage daughters of the farm families who suffered in the Matsukata deflation—bore a particularly heavy burden.

By 1911, government statistics reported that just under 800,000 people labored in factories or mines with ten or more employees. About 475,000 of these worked in textile mills, either cotton or silk spinning or weaving. More than four out of five textile workers were women. They typically were required to live in company-owned dormitories that were locked at night. When fires occasionally broke out, these literally became death traps. A belief that women were fragile creatures was widespread among the upper classes of the time, but it had little impact on the treatment of the female textile laborers. They worked twelve to fourteen hours a day or more, compared to about twelve hours per day on average for males in industries such as machine manufacturing. Their wages were 50 to 70 percent of those paid to men in the same industry, and 30 to 50 percent of average male wages in heavy industries. Wages were based on the results of competition over output and quality. Discipline was harsh and sometimes arbitrary. Sexual harassment by male supervisors cannot be documented with numerical certainty, but it was a constant theme in the songs of these women.

Finally, the poorly ventilated mills were incubators of disease, especially tuber-

TABLE 7.1 Labor Force Numbers, Early Twentieth Century

	1902			1911		
	Men	**Women**	**Total**	**Men**	**Women**	**Total**
Textiles	32,699	236,457	269,156	67,128	408,257	475,385
Machine/tool manufacturing	33,379	983	34,362	67,271	3,817	71,088
Chemical engineering	38,615	43,683	82,298	47,159	22,414	69,573
Food and drink	16,837	13,316	30,153	34,202	12,922	47,124
Miscellaneous	20,729	11,579	32,308	37,831	20,123	57,954
Electric or gas utilities	475	21	496	4,476	40	4,516
Mining and refining	42,888	7,230	50,118	59,321	8,924	68,245
Total: All Industries	**185,622**	**313,269**	**498,891**	**317,388**	**476,497**	**793,885**

Source: Nihon rōdō undo shiryō. Dai 10 kan. Tōkei-hen, edited by Rōdō undō shiryō iin-kai. (Tokyo: Chūō kōron jigyō shuppan, 1959), pp. 104, 106.

culosis, which was the AIDS of its day: debilitating, incurable, and fatal. This disease had been a chronic but limited problem in Tokugawa times. It became an acute epidemic from the late nineteenth into the early twentieth century. The means of transmission were poorly understood. Women who contracted the disease in the mills were sent home to rest, and die. They spread the plague to their home villages.

The alternative to textile labor was not a life of leisure. Those who stayed with their families in rural villages had to help out with equally or more demanding farm labor. The memoirs of many textile workers offer divided judgments. They present a grim picture of unhappiness at harsh discipline and punitive incentive wages. They also recall pleasant friendships with other workers, full stomachs, and better food than on the farm. Wages were low compared to those of men, but they were high compared to most alternative work for women, such as unpaid labor on a family farm or home-based piecework for a manufacturing broker.

One job that paid higher wages to young women was prostitution. After textiles, the sex industry was the largest employer of women in the late nineteenth century.

Textile workers such as these young women in a silk-reeling factory in Nagano prefecture in the late Meiji era would have been among those singing the official or the "underground" songs about factory life. They are pulling threads off cocoons in very hot water in the basins in front of them. This photograph, in which the women are wearing makeup and elegant hairstyles, would appear to be a staged public relations shot authorized by the manufacturers to project a positive image of the workplace.
Courtesy of Okaya Silk Museum.

Prostitution was legal. Brothels were licensed and regulated by the state, although there were many unlicensed practitioners as well. At the turn of the century, about fifty thousand licensed prostitutes worked in Japan, not far below the sixty thousand women in cotton spinning mills (although less than the number in silk spinning and far less than in weaving). If the pay was relatively high, so too were the costs in health, in dignity, and in loss of freedom. Families often took substantial advances in "selling" a teenage girl to a brothel. She could not quit until the advance was repaid, which usually took three to five years.

It is not easy to discover how women workers in the early industrial era viewed their situation. Most had only an elementary education. They did not leave behind extensive memoirs. Until recent decades they have not been seen as important subjects of history writing. But some clues survive in accounts of social reformers, journalists, and government surveyors. Not surprisingly, statistical surveys of factory labor show that many women responded to poor conditions by quitting. Annual rates of turnover in excess of 100 percent of the work force were common. A famous government study, entitled *Workers' Conditions*, published in 1902 using data from the Kanega-fuchi Cotton Spinning Mill, the largest in Japan, offers some dramatic numerical evidence of this. At the start of the year 1900, the company employed 4,500 women. Even though it cut back the work force to about 3,500 women by the end of the year, the company was forced to hire 4,762 new workers over these twelve months because of massive attrition. Fully 4,846 female employees "escaped or fled" their jobs, 692 were fired, 255 left due to illness, and 31 (nearly 1 percent) died.[6]

On occasion these workers came together in acts of collective protest. From 1897 to 1907, textile workers went on strike thirty-two times at spinning mills and weaving sheds large and small to demand higher wages or improved working conditions. Most of these actions lasted only one or two days, or a few hours. Few succeeded. The fact that the women lived in tightly supervised company dormitories made it difficult for them to organize protests or link up with social activists outside the factory walls. If they did protest, they were typically fired and had no choice but to return home.

The improvised songs of the textile workers were written down by observers. They reflect the attitudes that led to high quit rates and strikes. They reveal the anger and despair of the workers, but also dreams of better lives for themselves and pride in their contribution to Japan's national income and power. This pride was the message promoted every day by the mill supervisors and recruiters. They taught an offical message to silk spinners as they hiked together across mountain passes on the way to the factories:

Raw silk,
Reel, reel the thread.
Thread is the treasure of the empire!
More than a hundred million yen worth of exports,
What can be better than silk thread?
Factory girls,
We are soldiers of peace.
The service of women is a credit
To the empire and to yourselves.

There are trials and hardships, yes,
But what do they matter?

The songs that the women improvised on their own were different:

If a woman working in an office is a willow,
A poetess is a violet,
And a female teacher is an orchid,
Then a factory woman is a vegetable gourd.

Or,

How I wish the dormitory would be washed away,
The factory burn down,
And the gatekeeper die of cholera,
At six in the morning I wear a devil's face,
At six in the evening a smiling face.
I want wings to escape from here,
To fly as far as those distant shores.[7]

Communities of skilled male factory workers also came into being in Japan's early industrial era, although their numbers were smaller than the number of women factory laborers. By 1902, approximately 33,000 men worked in shipbuilding, machine and machine tool industries, and railroad companies. Another 40,000 worked in mines and metal refineries—alongside a significant minority of female coal miners. An additional 100,000 men labored in a wide variety of different industrial sites.

These men mixed a sense of humiliation at the condition of their lives, and even self-loathing, with pride, assertiveness, and a commitment to self-help. They were footloose. Unlike the well-known "lifetime employees" of the decades after World War II, male workers in early industrial Japan believed that the only way to become a skilled worker deserving of the name was to gain experience at a number of factories, learn diverse skills, and thus advance. These men were as quick to leave their jobs as were the textile women. But where the young women were often escaping to leave factory work altogether, the men—called "traveling workers"—were job-hopping as part of a career strategy. They typically aspired to save money and start up their own small factory. A few succeeded.

They also organized a number of strikes, and in the 1890s undertook a few short-lived drives to organize unions. A union of metalworkers founded in 1897 enrolled nearly three thousand at its peak. But turnover among members was high, and by 1899 the union was losing support. In 1900 the government passed a Public Order Police Law that made organizing difficult, and the union collapsed. Strikes and labor organizing reflected anger at dignity denied as much as a desire for higher pay. The best organized strike of the era took place among locomotive engineers at the Japan Railway Company in 1899. They argued that "our occupation is not base but noble; it should be accorded respect, not contempt." One core demand of the workers was for a change in the wording of their job title, which conveyed an image of low-grade status in comparison to clerks and station-masters whose jobs required less skill and who bore less weighty responsibility.[8]

Male workers in a lathe shop of the Shibaura Engineering Works in 1896. A supervisor, in Western cap and formal dress in the center, stood at the top of the workplace hierarchy, and tensions between such supervisors and the ordinary workers were common. Workmen in jobs that drew on traditional artisan skills tended to wear the Edo era craftsman's coat (lower left).
Courtesy of Toshiba Corporation.

Their bosses saw such skilled workers as notoriously unreliable. One manager at a major engineering firm vented his anger in a magazine for young boys after a visit to the United States in 1908. Well-educated young workers were uppity and did not know their place, he fumed. Older laborers were stubborn men who relied only on past experience, so that "teaching them anything is like trying to teach a cat to chant Buddhist prayers." Unlike America, he claimed, where workers were docile and "carried out a job after just one order . . . in Japan things don't get done without constant instructions and the lot of a supervisor is difficult."[9]

This negative view of workers must be viewed critically. It contrasts sharply with testimony from many workers themselves. They told of their determination to study, improve their skills, and one day open their own small workshop. The managerial view that employees were stubborn and poorly disciplined did not reflect a genuine deficit of talent or energy among laborers. It reflected the unwillingness of these workers to devote themselves to bosses who offered unreliable treatment.

SPREAD OF MASS AND HIGHER EDUCATION

In the 1880s and 1890s, as protest against compulsory schooling decreased and attendance rose, the government also changed the curriculum. It became clear that commoners were using their education to read newspapers and sign petitions that criticized the government. The Ministry of Education responded with a more state-centered, moralistic curriculum. The leader in this shift away from the more liberal and pragmatic spirit of public education in the 1870s was Mori Arinori, a former Satsuma samurai who served as minister of education from 1886 to 1889. Under his leadership the ministry put in place tighter central controls over textbooks. Mori also introduced a regimented system of teacher training in government schools, complete with military drills. The government promoted Confucian ideals of loyalty, obedience, and friendship in the schools. It also turned to German advisors as it adopted a moralistic curriculum that stressed lessons of filial piety and loyalty to the state.

The culminating statement of this conservative reform came in the Imperial Rescript on Education, promulgated in the name of the emperor on October 30, 1890. The document reflected the beliefs of high government officials and their advisors that the goal of education was learning to serve society and the state. These officials argued that the early Meiji education system betrayed this objective by stressing individual initiative. But officials disagreed on the wisdom of grounding a statement of the state-centered purpose of education primarily in Confucian rhetoric. Confucian scholars such as Motoda Eifu, a tutor to the Meiji emperor, wanted to establish loyalty and filial piety as unshakeable social values. Pragmatists such as Itō Hirobumi resisted a narrow imperial statement of orthodox morality. They feared it might draw the throne into political debates.

The result of this debate was a somewhat schizophrenic document. Parts of the rescript invoked core Confucian values concerning human relations:

> Ye, Our subjects, be filial to your parents, affectionate to your brothers and sisters; as husbands and wives be harmonious, as friends true; bear yourselves in modesty and moderation; extend your benevolence to all. . . .

Other phrases invoked a spirit of allegiance to the state that was common to the nationalism of nineteenth century Euro-American political systems:

> . . . advance public good and promote common interests; always respect the Constitution and observe the law; should emergency arise, offer yourselves courageously to the State. . . .

Binding together these moralistic injunctions to filial piety and patriotism were statements linking such values directly to the emperor and his ancestors. The rescript began with the claim:

> Our Imperial Ancestors have founded Our Empire on a basis broad and everlasting, and have deeply and firmly implanted virtue. . . .

It ended with a stirring charge:

> The way set forth here is indeed the teaching bequeathed by Our Imperial Ancestors, to be observed alike by Their Descendants and the subjects, infallible for all ages and true in all places.

In the years after its promulgation, this document took on a sacred aura of remarkable power. Together with a portrait of the emperor, a copy was enshrined in every school in the nation. It was read to the assembled students on ceremonial occasions. Stories circulated of heroic school principals who risked—or lost—their lives when they dashed into burning buildings to retrieve the imperial rescript or photograph. Students had trouble making full sense of the rescript's archaic language. But they could understand the basic messages: The imperial institution made Japan a special place and subjects should obey authorities ranging from parents all the way to the emperor.

The spirit and structure of higher education were rather different from that of the rescript and the elementary schools. By 1905, about 104,000 students, roughly 10 percent of the eligible population, went on to attend a variety of middle schools. The "normal schools" trained students, young boys as well as some girls, for careers as teachers. In addition, a huge variety of vocational middle schools prepared youths for careers as technicians, clerks, or engineers. A small minority of middle-schoolers continued to climb the education ladder by attending private and public higher schools. Some of these schools undertook to educate young women. In 1899 the government required each prefecture to found at least one higher school for girls. A number of Western missionary groups also opened higher schools for young women. The most prestigious higher schools were seven national institutions for young men. Beginning with the First Higher School, in Tokyo, these were founded between 1886 and 1901. Together they admitted 5,300 male students per year.

Beyond this, at the pinnacle of the system, stood seven imperial universities, also for men only. Among the universities, it was Tokyo Imperial University, its law faculty above all, that provided the best ticket to the upper reaches of the bureaucracy or the business world.

Schooling beyond the lower elementary level was voluntary. It was limited to those who could pass the entrance examinations and whose parents could afford the tuition and the loss of a working child's income. Ironically, as students climbed to the higher reaches of this very hierarchical order, they were encouraged to think more freely. The higher schools and universities in particular gave the students a large degree of autonomy. Students organized the school's extracurricular life on their own. In the classroom they were encouraged to read widely in Western philosophy and political thought. This openness at the top reflected the thinking of Mori Arinori, the minister of education who oversaw the founding of the higher schools. His goal was to nurture an elite of patriotic future leaders of the nation. He believed such people needed to learn initiative and responsibility. For this purpose, they had to be given autonomy in their formative years.

Literature offers one view of the social and psychological world of the students of this era. One of the great writers of the era, Natsume Sōseki, framed his memorable novel of 1914, *Kokoro*, around the experience of two generations of university-educated characters. In a tale of death and suicide, he offered a grim but powerful

An artist's rendition of the ceremony of reading the Imperial Rescript on Education to elementary school students in the early twentieth century. The principal holds and reads the rescript. The photograph of the emperor's portrait is on view in the ark in the center behind opened curtains. This ritual mimics precisely the ceremony of 1889 at which the emperor handed over the constitution itself, as his "gift" to the prime minister and the nation. Yushima Elementary School, Tokyo.

statement of the alienated existence of the modern man. Sōseki's novel was preceded by the real case of one unfortunate Tokyo Imperial University boy named Fujimura, who threw himself off the famous Kegon waterfall in 1903. He left a note that could have been written by a character in *Kokoro*:

> Ensconced in the vastness of space and time, I with my meager body, have tried to fathom the enormity of this universe. But what authority can be attributed to Horatio's

philosophy? There is, after all, only one word for truth: "incomprehensible." My agony over this question had brought me, at last, to a decision to die, and yet now, standing at the precipice, there is no anxiety in my heart. For the first time, I realized that great sorrow is at one with great happiness.

This suicide became a media event: Postcards, picturebooks, and souvenirs were spawned by it, as well as imitators. One historian claims there were almost two hundred death leaps from the same falls over the next eight years.[10]

Such episodes capture only one aspect of the culture of late Meiji Japan. Other memoirs and novels (such as Soseki's slightly more cheerful *Sanshirō*) show the city and the university as sites of dreams, adventure, and longing. Young boys, and young girls at a few private higher schools, came to the city with ambition and energy. They fell in love with its anonymity and excitement. They cherished its sense of motion and change. Reading Western literature and philosphy was a standard element of higher education at the time. It sometimes sparked a flamboyant sense of rebellion and assertion. Meiji youths read Kant, Rousseau, and Mill, among others. The decades around the turn of the century were exciting times for many youths privileged to go beyond elementary education and think about their role in the "new Japan."

CULTURE AND RELIGION

The Meiji era drive to construct a modern nation of "civilization and enlightenment" remade the Japanese cultural landscape as well as the economy and political system. Beginning in the 1870s, government officals, educators, and artists began to explore what it might mean to "Westernize" the entire spectrum of cultural life. This sometimes took place in a force-fed spirit of "whole-package" modernization. Organizers of the Japanese military, for example, decided in 1871 that if Western armies all had military bands, and if Japan was to remake its military on Western lines, then Japanese forces had best follow suit. They quickly established a new, enduring tradition of Western-style military music. In a similar fashion, in 1880 the Meiji government engaged a Boston public school teacher to bring "proper" modern music education into the new Japanese schools. He helped prepare the first school children's songbook in 1881. Half the tunes were Western melodies with new lyrics by Japanese poets. "Auld Lang Syne" became a syrupy ballad about "the light of fireflies." Other songs were older Japanese melodies rearranged into Western-style harmonies.[11]

In a similar practical spirit that mixed a commitment to building a strong nation with the vocation of an artist, important painters in the 1870s and 1880s gained government support to promote Western styles of oil painting. They drew on the experience of some Edo era painters with Western art media and styles, such as the use of vanishing-point perspective in eighteenth-century woodblock prints. The Meiji government set up art contests and schools to teach Western techniques. Also, beginning in the late 1880s Japanese writers such as Futabatei Shimei, Mori Ōgai, and then Natsume Sōseki began to produce widely read works of prose fiction in forms comparable to Western novels.

New forms of theater were slower to develop, even as older forms came under fire. In Tokugawa times leading practioners of Noh theater had been patronized with stipends by the shogunate and daimyō. The Meiji reforms cut off this source of support, and the Noh theater briefly floundered. Kabuki had a firmer popular audience, but it too faced problems in early Meiji years. Western-oriented reformers criticized it as "decadent" (because plots were set in brothels) or feudalistic. The emphasis in the 1880s and 1890s was on "reform" of the Kabuki theater. Playwrights brought in Western dress and plots centered on modern life, but these new plays proved most unpopular.

Despite such broadly based efforts to modernize or Westernize Japanese culture, older forms persisted and even flourished, often without state support. Statistics are not available, but musical traditions from *shamisen* and *koto* playing to the chanting of puppet-theater narratives (*jorūri*) may actually have increased in popularity even as schoolchildren learned new Western tunes. The Kabuki survived its critics. Leading actors called for the preservation of the classical plays, and the Edo era repertory remained most popular.

Beginning in the mid-1880s, a drive to preserve or revive a so-called traditional Japanese culture emerged in a mood of confrontation with Western-oriented reformers. Leaders included both Westerners and Japanese. Two of the most famous such cultural missionaries to the world were Ernest Fenellosa and Okakura Kakuzō. Fenellosa came to Japan to teach philosophy in 1878 after graduating from Harvard University with a strong background in the history of art. He developed an abiding love for Japanese art and culture. Okakura began as his student and became a close colleague.

The two worked together for many years. As Motoori Norinaga and his followers had done in the 1700s in reaction to the popularity of Chinese thought, they articulated and vigorously promoted a notion that Japan in particular, and the Orient in general, was home to a glorious spiritual and aesthetic sensibility. This contrasted sharply in their view to the materialism of the West. More reactionary cultural conservatives picked up such themes to simply attack Western influence in Japan. Okakura and Fenellosa spoke in less combative Hegelian terms of a superior "synthesis" of a global culture that would result from the interaction of East and West.[12]

There is an important twist in this cultural history of mid- to late Meiji Japan. Western imports coexisted, mixed, and sometimes conflicted with a resilient set of indigenous cultural forms. As this happened, many older cultural forms were dramatically reshaped. Later generations came to view these as "traditional" and typically Japanese. In the process they articulated new concepts of "Japanese-ness." The Noh theater, for example, survived in part because government officials promoted it as a Japanese parallel to Western opera. They treated visitors such as former American President Ulysses Grant (in 1879) to command performances. Noh performance took on ritualistic aspects that had not been present before. Modern martial arts such as judo, sports such as sumo wrestling, and arts such as the cultivation of bonsai plants were both transformed in practice and took on symbolic meaning as emblems of Japanese-ness for the first time.[13]

This modern process of inventing traditions was striking. But neither it nor the concern to preserve spiritual values at a time of materialistic modernization was peculiar to the history of Japan or of the non-Western world. In modernizing Europe no less than in Japan, artists and poets were among many who turned to their own past to find or invent spiritual traditions in the face of a modernity seen as inhumane or excessively materialistic.

Religion faced similar turmoil and transformation in the Meiji era. Evangelical religious organizations with indigenous roots, founded in the Tokugawa era, expanded dramatically in the Meiji era. Another newly energized religious movement of the Meiji era was Christianity. Approximately sixty thousand "hidden Christians" (*kakure kirishitan*) had survived the often fierce persecutions of the Tokugawa era. They were still practicing their faith when the bakufu collapsed. In 1873, the Meiji government repealed the bakufu's anti-Christian laws, but offered no specific protection to religious activity. The 1889 constitution guaranteed a limited religious freedom "within limits not prejudicial to peace and not antagonistic to duties as citizens."

In this ambiguous context, Catholic, Russian Orthodox, and Protestant missionaries returned to Japan in the 1870s. They enjoyed just moderate numerical success. Christians remained well under 1 percent of the population. But these men and women played a disproportionately large role in Japanese cultural and political life. In the late nineteenth and early twentieth centuries Christian activists became leaders of social reform movements including socialism and the labor movement. Such people were committed to following the dictates of individual conscience that in theory transcended or opposed the dictates of the state. In the face of a government that made an all-encompassing claim on the loyalty of imperial subjects, this was a brave position. It often proved impossible to sustain. Many Christians responded by defining their religion as an entirely apolitical commitment.[14]

The Meiji state consistently took an active role in managing all religious practice as part of its effort to establish legitimacy. It created a national organization of Shinto shrines for the first time in Japanese history. The important Ise Shrine had long been associated with the emperor, but before 1868 Shinto consisted primarily of decentralized local shrines for the worship of community deities without close ties to the state. The government set up a Department of Shinto in 1868. In 1870 it issued a proclamation stating that the nation was to be guided by the "way of the *kami* (Shinto deities)." In 1871 Shinto shrines were officially designated as government institutions for the observance of "national rites." Many government officials as well as religious figures questioned the wisdom of this close relationship over the next several decades. But the state continued to patronize Shinto and to stress its close links to the newly important imperial institution. The process culminated in 1900 when the Home Ministry created a Shrine Office and a nationally certified priesthood. In these ways the notion that Shinto was the ancient religion of all Japanese was invented by the modern state-builders of Meiji times, as were the institutions to promote this idea.

As Shinto was elevated and transformed, the Buddhist priesthood and worshipers faced criticism and persecution. The government ended the semiofficial status of Edo era Buddhist temples with the Separation Edict of 1868. This banned Buddhist priests from holding simultaneous positions in Shinto shrines. It replaced the Edo era requirement that every person register at a local Buddhist temple with a system of compulsory registration at local Shinto shrines. These steps crystallized a more explicit awareness among ordinary people that Shinto and Buddhist practices and dieties indeed were different. They also sparked a wave of popular attacks on Buddhist temples. These peaked in 1871 when numerous temples, statues, and relics were destroyed.

Some Buddhists fought fire with fire. They staged demonstrations and riots of their own. They demanded the freedom to preach Buddhist doctrine. They called for the ouster of Christianity. From the 1870s through the 1890s, Buddhist priests and thinkers followed contradictory impulses as they sought to protect themselves and regain popular and official support. Some issued strong calls for the state to respect freedom of religion. Others sought legitimacy by jumping on the bandwagon of a reactionary nationalism that criticized Christianity and the materialist West for destroying Asian spirituality. Still other critics took an opposite tack and condemned Christianity for betraying the rational spirit of modernity. Among the most prominent of such voices was that of Inoue Enryō, a philosopher and teacher. He founded an important institute of philosphical studies in 1885 and argued that Christian beliefs in a divine being were actually less rational or modern than relatively nontheistic Buddhist ideas.

AFFIRMING JAPANESE IDENTITY AND DESTINY

The dizzying pace of change in Japan of the Meiji era provoked varied reactions. For some, change offered liberation and personal opportunity. For some, it offered a chance to achieve collective, national glory. For others (or for these same people at other times), change meant danger, decadence, and loss of moral virtue. Such fears broke to the surface in at least three arenas of discussion and policy: fear of political disorder, fear of gender disorder, and cultural concern to answer the question, Who are "we Japanese"?

Fear among government leaders that a restless populace might challenge their political control led to the decision for a conservative constitution modeled on Prussian lines. It sparked the push for military drills in the schools. It inspired the call for a spirit of sacrifice for the state in the Imperial Rescript on Education. Fear of gender anarchy amidst a headlong rush to modernity had surfaced early in the decision to ban women from adopting short hairstyles in 1872. It emerged again when the government sharply restricted women's political activity in 1890.

The third great fear in the face of the changes of the Meiji era was present before Perry's ships appeared. It was crystallized in the phrase, "Expel the barbarians." This was the notion that outsiders from across the seas would poison the souls of Japanese people, convert them perhaps to Christianity, and demolish their true identity. In the early Meiji years, these fears were submerged for the most part. Government leaders and many others joined a rush to modernize. The dominant view through the 1870s and early 1880s was that the essence of being a Japanese patriot was to embrace change. Loyal Japanese were told to help build the army and the state along Western lines.

But lurking behind such reforming projects—and breaking to the surface in occasional rebellions—was a logic that differentiated people in Japan from those elsewhere. It lead to the question: To what ultimate end are we making these changes? As we build railroads and adopt a European-style constitution, do we have a unique identity as Japanese people? If so, what is it?

Many people raised such questions, especially from the mid-1880s onward. Some of the most pointed and thoughtful early questioners included a group of young men who in 1888 formed the Society for Political Education (Seikyōsha) and began to publish a magazine called *The Japanese*. These writers feared that as the nation followed a path toward so-called civilization, it might "forfeit our national character and destroy all elements of Japanese society." As one wrote: "What is today's Japan? The old Japan has already collapsed, but the new Japan has not yet risen. What religion do we believe in? What moral and political principles do we favor? It is as if we are wandering in confusion through a deep fog, unable to find our way."[15]

Fears of political disorder, gender anarchy, and the loss of a cultural soul resolved themselves to some degree, although never definitively, around the turn of the century. By this time a sort of political, social, and cultural orthodoxy was articulated widely by political leaders such as Itō Hirobumi and by major journalists and scholars as well.

First and foremost, these anxieties were met by a turn toward the emperor as a political and cultural anchor. The Meiji oligarchs unambiguously anchored the political order in the emperor, who invoked "the supreme power We inherit from Our Imperial Ancestors" to promulgate an "immutable fundamental law" in the form of the constitution.

The symbolic management of the imperial institution was a risky project. On one hand, the oligarchs desperately wanted to keep the emperor above politics so that their opponents could not do as they had done in the 1860s, and turn the emperor against the government. Simultaneously, they were committed to using his image and words to ensure political order, as in the Imperial Rescript on Education. And just as some in the government had feared, a small incident within months of the rescript's promulgation sparked a huge controversy. In January 1891, an "installment ceremony" for an imperially autographed copy of the rescript took place at the First Higher School in Tokyo. The principal asked all present to bow to the imperial signature. But Uchimura Kanzō, a Christian and an English teacher at the school, aware that the constitution guaranteed "freedom of conscience" to all subjects, refused to do so. He believed that such a bow amounted to "idol worship" and violated his faith.

Within a few days, a huge storm of protest at this act of disloyalty erupted in the press. Uchimura soon repudiated his action and repeatedly made public bows to the rescript on other occasions. But the outcry eventually forced Uchimura to resign his position. The incident prompted some of the nation's most prominent philosphers and educators to defend the forced bow to the rescript as a constitutional act. They argued that the moral essence of both documents was a public one. Obedience to the state and emperor, that is, was presented as the highest secular obligation, one that transcended private ethics or religious belief.

Parallel to its efforts to elevate and reinforce ultimate imperial authority, the state dealt with fears of gender anarchy and its desire for loyal subjects of both sexes by articulating an important new concept aimed at women. This was the ideal of the "good wife and wise mother." A member of the Meiji Six Society, Nakamura Masanao, first put forward this slogan. It had restrictive implications of course. A woman's vocation was to be that of nurturer. Her role was to be centered on the home. Women were barred from politics, from inheritance, and from any independent legal standing in civil law.

But the idea that the primary duty of women was to serve in the twin roles of good wife and wise mother was not purely reactionary or restrictive. In some ways it was an innovative effort to change the role of women in a new era. In Tokugawa Japan, women, especially samurai women, had been seen as relatively unteachable and not much in need of formal education. They were not given any public role of importance. In the Meiji formulation, wise women needed schooling. To raise children well in a new era, the mother had to be literate. She had to know something of the world beyond the home. If her sons were to serve the state in the military, the home had to play a quasipublic role as incubator of these soldiers. The notion of "good wife, wise mother" that Meiji government officials began to promote aggressively around the turn of the century was new in that women were to be educated. It was also new in that women's work at home, and also in the factory, was valued as a form of service to the state.

The imperial institution took part in this project to prescribe new roles for women and for men. The emperor gave the signal that men could wear Western haircuts by adopting that style himself. The empress mixed old and new styles of personal grooming. On one hand, her traditional hairstyle signaled to women that they should keep their hair long and braided up. On the other hand, her Westernized facial appearance encouraged women to stop shaving their eyebrows or blackening their teeth. Both raised hair and blackened teeth had been marks of beauty in the elite culture of the Tokugawa era and before, but the latter practice was changed with support from the throne in the face of Western examples and criticisms.

Beyond politics and gender, people such as Okakura, Fenellosa, and the writers in the magazine *The Japanese* at the turn of the century began to define "Japanese culture" as the essence of their identity. Like the ideology of "good wife, wise mother," this was not a purely reactionary turn. The men in the Society for Political Education agreed that Japan's government should build national economic and military strength by using Western technology. But they also developed an idea of particular "Japanese" values that should be cultivated in the process. Perhaps the most powerful value was said to be a unique conception of beauty, an aesthetic sense rooted in art and the natural environment. A special aesthetic and moral sense could serve as a cultural anchor in a time of great change. Such concern to defend "Japanese-ness" reinforced stereotypes of feminine virtue as well, for Japan's traditional culture was defined by such writers in feminine terms centered on beauty and grace. From the late nineteenth century to the present day, this desire to define a Japanese essence has been a near constant concern, at times an obsession, of Japanese intellectual and cultural life.

Official orthodoxy was neither perfectly secure nor unchallenged. Despite the promulgation of the Imperial Rescript on Education with its stress on loyalty, and its oppressive interpretations and uses, dissenters did emerge in the following decades. They ranged from feminists to socialists and communists. They would challenge the orthodoxy of imperial supremacy and win thousands of adherents. But it is certain that the political and cultural reactions of late Meiji restrained these trends. They defined and limited the cultural as well as social and political terms of debate, as people sought to make sense of the continuous changes that were now part of Japan's modern condition.

The Meiji changes remain among the most controversial topics in Japanese history. In 1968, the Meiji centennial set off a ferocious debate on whether one should celebrate anything at all. The shadow of World War II defined this debate, and to some extent it still does. Critics argued that an authoritarian, emperor-centered Meiji system of politics and culture combined with an economic order that impoverished the peasantry and limited the domestic market to pave the road to a disastrous war fifty years later. Since the 1960s, a more positive view of the Meiji era has become widespread in Japan and abroad. This narrative of progress stresses that in 1889 Japan became the first non-Western nation to adopt a constitutional political system, while at roughly the same time it became the first non-Western industrial, capitalist economy. These were indeed impressive political and economic achievements. After all, much of the non-Western world at this time was subjected to increasing economic and political subordination under the expanding hegemony of Euro-American nation-states. Some of the "advanced" Western nations were no less authoritarian than the new Meiji system. But like all modern revolutions, the changes of the Meiji era left a complex legacy of progress and pain.

8

Empire and Domestic Order

The Meiji revolution transformed the domestic space of Japan. Railroads linked the countryside in newly intimate fashion to ports and urban centers such as Tokyo, Yokohama, Osaka, and Kobe. The Meiji revolution also transformed the relationship between Japan and the world. By the end of the nineteenth century, Japan had shifted from a relatively marginal position to a dominant place in Asia. It was seeking control over Korea and had won colonial control over Taiwan. It gained formal equality with the Western powers by revising the unequal treaties, and it established a strategic position as junior partner to the British. It both absorbed and exported products and people, importing grain from Korea, selling textiles to China, and both sending and receiving men and women to and from Asia and the Americas as laborers and students. People in Japan were making themselves an integral part of a broader East Asian and global system.

Just as Japan's domestic transformation had global causes and consequences, its drive for empire had domestic roots and ramifications. The nation-building projects described in the previous chapters inspired a new patriotism among masses of Japanese people. This bolstered the assertive external agenda of the government. Nation-building projects also sparked calls for participation and reform, which struck the same rulers as threatening or even subversive. They responded with programs to shore up the domestic social and political order. They also made empire a potent symbol of the identity and unity of the Japanese people.[1] In these ways, imperialism reflected and also contributed to a changed relationship of Japanese subjects to their state.

THE TRAJECTORY TO EMPIRE

The most important focus of Japanese overseas activity in the 1870s and 1880s was the Korean peninsula. In 1876, Japan employed gunboat diplomacy to force the Treaty of Kanghwa on Korea. This opened three ports to trade with Japan and gave the Japanese extraterritorial jurisdiction. Both the process and the result were little different from those pursued by Commodore Perry in Japan two decades before. Japanese traders used this opening to economic advantage. They sharply expanded exports to Korea, primarily by reselling European manufactured goods first imported to Japan.

115

They also began to import significant amounts of rice and soybeans from Korea. Japan was the destination for about 90 percent of exports from Korea through the 1870s.

The Japanese government sought to forge a close political relationship to Korea in the 1880s, which would supersede Korea's intimate and dependent ties to China rooted in the centuries-old tribute system. Its goal was to promote a regime in Korea that was independent of both China and Russia and deferential to Japan. In the strategic thinking of Yamagata Aritomo, the most important geopolitical strategist among the Meiji leaders, Korea was to be part of a buffer "zone of advantage" protecting Japan's home-island "zone of sovereignty."

As one step to secure this zone, in 1881 Japan sent military advisors to help modernize the army of the Korean court, at the time led by the reform-minded King Kojong. He and his top aides were impressed at the modernizing projects underway in Japan, but they faced powerful conservative and anti-foreign opposition. Over the following years, political turmoil left Korea vulnerable to outside pressures. The Japanese government, members of Japan's mainstream political opposition, and Japanese political adventure-seekers and gangsters with shadowy ties to the government all sought to exploit this opening. In 1882 anti-foreign opponents of the king killed several of the Japanese military advisors and took power in a coup. The Japanese responded by forcing the new government to offer an indemnity and accept Japanese troops stationed in Seoul to protect Japan's diplomats there.

Both the Japanese government and private citizens continued to support the reformist "independence" faction in Korea. Its members understood independence somewhat differently from the Japanese. They wanted greater independence from the Qing rulers in China as well as independence from other foreign powers, Japan included. But they were interested in Japanese assistance, and some of their leaders had received education and funding in Japan. Support for the reformers set the Japanese against the conservative Korean government, which still accepted a close relationship with China. It also pitted Japan against the Chinese rulers, who were intervening far more in Korean politics than they had in their long-standing role as patron of a tributary state.

In 1884 one reformer, Kim Ok-kyun, led a coup d'état with secret promises of support from the Japanese legation in Seoul. Kim had been influenced by Fukuzawa Yukichi in Tokyo a few years before. Fukuzawa had advised him to promote nationalism and modernize Korea along Japanese lines. Kim's rebel forces assassinated conservative ministers and seized the Korean king, but two thousand Chinese troops intervened to put down his coup. Crowds of Koreans angry at the Japanese role behind the uprising joined the counterattack. They killed ten Japanese military advisors and about thirty other Japanese residents.

The Japanese press and political organizations responded with furious calls for revenge. Japan and China were close to war. Some former Liberal Party activists even organized private militias. They hoped to send these across the sea to promote Korean "independence." But in the government, the bloody and economically disastrous Satsuma rebellion was still a fresh memory, and a major military buildup was just underway. The Meiji rulers were reluctant to send their forces overseas just yet. Neither did they want private adventurers to get out of hand. In the Osaka Incident of 1885, Japanese police thwarted a secret plan to lead a militia expedition to Korea. They arrested the key conspirators, including Ōi Kentarō, a popular rights activist, and

Fukuda Hideko, a leading advocate of women's rights. The government also upset domestic opponents by reaching a compromise agreement with China in 1885, the Li-Itō pact. This was concluded between Itō Hirobumi and the Chinese minister in charge of Korean affairs, Li Hongzhang. The two sides pledged to take their military forces out of Korea and offer advance warning of any plan to return.

These incidents of 1881 through 1885 established a pattern that would repeat itself several times over the next twenty-five years as Japan carved out a colonial empire in Asia. The Japanese press and political opponents of the government would put forth a rhetoric of Asia-wide (pan-Asian) solidarity as they beat the drums on behalf of causes such as Korean independence from China or Asian equality with the West. Their vision of Asian unity placed Japan in charge, as tutor and military hegemon. The Japanese government would rein in but not repudiate such voices, as it moved more cautiously in a similar direction. Korea would remain the principal but not the sole overseas site of expanding overseas control. It was the place where the Japanese military, diplomatic officers, and civilian "patriots" opposed the Chinese, the Russians, the British (who also sought a foothold on the peninsula), and of course the Koreans. Many of the latter developed a forceful new nationalism that rejected Chinese as well as Japanese, Russian, or any foreign domination.

One key to explain the timing of the Japanese push was the ongoing project to build a powerful military, both as a force to keep order at home and as an instrument of empire. In the 1880s and early 1890s, the government funded a substantial buildup of the navy as well as the army. In addition, Yamagata consolidated institutions of military command that were as insulated as possible from popular and Diet control. Looking to German models, he founded elite officer training academies and a military general staff with direct responsibility to the emperor. This structure gave the military field command considerable independence from the prime minister and even from the ministers of the army and navy.

In the short run, Yamagata's policies put in place a relatively cautious military command. These men resisted the more reckless popular jingoists. They used force outside Japan only in favorable situations. In the long run, the lack of external constraint would enable the military itself to engage in reckless bids for conquest.

After the Li-Itō agreement in 1885, the Japanese government kept a low profile in Korea for nearly a decade. The Chinese gained control by stationing "advisors" at the Korean court to reform the Korean military and communications network. In addition, Russian diplomats won increased influence at the court, where some Koreans viewed them as a counterforce to excessive Chinese authority. This in turn led the British to occupy a small island off the Korean coast. The British demanded that Russia pledge to respect Korean territorial "integrity" before they withdrew in 1887. The United States also joined the contest for influence in Korea. Several Americans served as foreign affairs advisors to the throne from 1886 into the 1890s.

With foreign powers pressing from all directions, Korea's own leaders desperately maneuvered to gain some breathing space and independence. This proved impossible. In the early 1890s long-simmering peasant anger at economic distress and the foreign presence erupted in a major uprising, the Tonghak rebellion. In 1894 this led directly to a war between China and Japan, fought in Korea.

The Tonghak was a religious movement whose adherents blamed their impoverished plight on both the Korean elite and foreigners—the Japanese in particular but the Chinese as well. By the spring of 1894, Tonghak rebels had taken control of much territory and a major provincial capital, and the Korean government asked China to send troops to put down the uprising.

The commitment of Chinese troops gave the Japanese government an opening it was hoping for, leading to the outbreak of the Sino-Japanese War of 1894–95. Japan's military buildup had by now given it a rough naval parity with China. Yamagata Aritomo and other top leaders decided the time had come to secure the upper hand in Korea. In the name of "protecting Japanese residents," in June 1894 they sent eight thousand troops to Korea and demanded an equal voice with China in administering Korea's internal affairs. The Chinese refused. Japan responded by seizing control of the Korean royal palace in July and forcing the Korean court to declare war on China.

This war was in fact a battle between China and Japan. It consisted primarily of naval engagements, and it ended in complete Japanese victory by April 1895. In the peace treaty concluded at the Japanese port of Shimonoseki, Japan made clear its aspirations for an area of advantage well beyond Korea. It won control of Taiwan and some nearby islands, as well as the Liaodong peninsula and railroad building rights in southern Manchuria. Taiwan indeed became a Japanese colony, although not at the simple stroke of a pen. Japan had to send an army of sixty thousand troops to put down fierce Taiwanese resistance to Japan's initial colonial occupation, and forty-six hundred Japanese troops died from combat or disease. The Southern Manchurian Railway did become the foundation of an expanding Japanese presence in Manchuria, but in a tripartite intervention in 1895, the Russians worked with French and German diplomats to force Japan to return the Liaodong peninsula (see map on p. 191).

The outcome of the Sino-Japanese War had a huge impact around the world and in Japan. The Western powers and their publics had expected the Chinese to prevail, and in Western eyes Japan came out of the war with vastly increased prestige as the model modernizer of the non-Western world. In one typical example of the astonished reaction to Japan's swift rise to the status of a global power, the *Times* of London quoted Lord Charles Beresford in April 1895:

> Japan has within 40 years gone through the various administrative phases that occupied England about 800 years and Rome about 600, and I am loath to say that anything is impossible with her.[2]

At home, the war inspired a huge outpouring of nationalist pride. It won the government strong support in the Diet for its previously controversial budget proposals. The press led a chorus of contempt for the Chinese "who ran from battle disguised in women's clothes." It praised the righteousness of Japan's war on behalf of "civilization."[3] The unifying effect of expansionism was a lesson not lost upon the government, which indeed went into the war in part to shore up support at home.

The war proved economically as well as politically valuable. As part of the peace settlement, Japan gained an extraordinary indemnity of 360 million yen from China. This amounted to about four and a half times Japan's annual national budget of the year before the war. Most of the bounty (300 million yen) went to military spending. A small portion was invested in a modern, state-run iron and steel mill at Yahata on the island of Kyushu. Indirect benefits were substantial. Military procurements helped industries such as arms production. By taking pressure off the rest of the budget, this indemnity allowed the government to grant huge subsidies to the shipping and ship-building industry.

Parallel to this successful drive for empire of the 1890s, the Japanese government also achieved its long-sought goal of treaty revision. After the failed attempts to ne-gotiate new treaties with the Western powers in the 1880s (discussed in Chapter 6), a new round of negotiations took place from 1890 to 1894. In July 1894, barely two weeks before the start of the Sino-Japanese War, Japan and Britain signed a new treaty. It stipulated a full end to extraterritoriality in 1899. It returned tariff autonomy to Japan less immediately; the new treaty limited Japanese duties on most imports to 15 percent or less until 1911. In contrast to the treaty proposals of the 1880s, the new treaty was to take effect without the much-criticized transitional period when foreign judges would sit on Japanese courts. The other powers soon followed suit and signed similar treaties.

Now that the constitution was in effect, public support for the treaties was more important to the government than ever. Although the constitution gave the emperor power to make treaties, it also permitted the Diet to "make representations to the Government as to laws or upon any other subject." An unpopular treaty could provoke serious disruption of Diet proceedings and impede passage of other laws or the budget.

As matters turned out, with the Sino-Japanese War in the background, opinion in the press and the political parties wholeheartedly welcomed the new treaties, with one noteworthy reservation. The old treaties gave Westerners special privileges, but they also restricted foreigners to a few residential enclaves, the so-called treaty ports. For-eigners were not allowed to live or own property in the Japanese interior. In exchange for the end to extraterritoriality, Japan agreed to end these prohibitions in 1899 and accept so-called mixed residence. This sparked a surge of fears of everything from the unbridled spread of foreign materialism and gender equality to "foreign insects poisoning the nation."[4]

The hysteria soon subsided; the new treaties and mixed residence took effect without incident. The insect invasion did not come to pass, although both capitalism and feminism had enduring impact (the former more than the latter). In Japanese popular and official thinking at the turn of the century, as at the start of the Meiji era, Western institutions and technologies were sources of strength, but the West and West-erners remained a menacing presence. The intervention by the Russians, French, and Germans that had forced return of the Liaodong peninula to China in 1895 only increased this view. One famous journalist, Tokutomi Sohō, recalled that "the retro-cession of Liaodong dominated the rest of my life. After hearing about it I became almost a different person psychologically. Say what you will, it happened because we were not strong enough. What it came down to was that sincerity and justice did not amount to a thing if you were not strong enough. . . . Japan's progress . . . would ul-timately depend upon military strength."[5]

Despite such views, other international trends around the turn of the century offered some prospect that strength might grow from more peaceful ground. Japan's overseas trade expanded sharply before and after the Sino-Japanese War. From 1880 through 1913 both imports and exports increased eightfold in volume, roughly dou-bling every decade. This was more than twice the growth rate of world trade overall.

As a result, the yearly value of imports and exports as a proportion of the total national product rose from about 5 percent in 1885 to 15 percent by the eve of World War I.[6] Japan was able to grow economically by importing both raw materials and sophisticated machinery and exporting manufactured goods, textiles in particular.

Emigration was another important international element in Japan's economic growth. Japanese business leaders and writers beginning in the 1880s envisioned emigration as a way to allow impoverished Japanese to better their own lives and to enrich Japan by sending their earnings home. Emigrants were few at first. By 1890 no more than five thousand Japanese were living in Hawaii, one thousand in California, and a comparable number in Korea and China. But emigration surged in the next two decades, strongly encouraged by the Japanese government. By 1907 there were sixty-five thousand Japanese in Hawaii and sixty thousand in the continental United States. The wages sent home by these emigrants, for the most part agricultural laborers, accounted for about 3 percent of all Japanese foreign exchange earnings in these years.[7] Some prominent Japanese at the time considered this peaceful emigration and trade to be an alternative to colonization by force. But most Japanese journalists, intellectuals, and government officials came to see economic expansion and emigration as partners to, and not substitutes for, an expanding colonial empire backed by a powerful military.[8]

From 1895 through the early 1900s, Korea remained their primary strategic concern. The Shimonoseki treaty of 1895 forced China to recognize Korea as an "independent" state. With this provision, the Japanese expected to keep the Chinese at bay. They tried to dominate the Korean government by stationing advisors in Seoul to administer Meiji-style reforms. But Korean leaders were unhappy with Japanese control and the direction of reforms. They continued to play foreign powers against each other by turning to Russia for help. Over the next decade, the Russians came to rival the Japanese position in Korea. They challenged it in Manchuria as well by seizing the Liaodong peninsula in 1898.

Japanese leaders responded with several initiatives to regain control in Korea and establish themselves as an imperial power in Asia. In 1900–01 Japan sent ten thousand troops to China—the largest single national contingent—to join the multinational force that put down the Boxer Rebellion. This rebellion involved several months of violent attack on foreigners in Peking and the port city of Tientsin. The rebels were members of a secret society that practiced traditional calisthenics (hence, the Westerners called them Boxers) and other rituals said to make them immune to bullets. But the Boxer forces could not, after all, resist foreign troops. Japan joined the subsequent peace conference as an equal to the other powers and won the right to station a "peace-keeping force" in the vicinity of Peking.

In the wake of the Boxer uprising, the Japanese drew closer to the British, while the Russians kept their troops in Manchuria and sought to extract further exclusive concessions from China before leaving. The Japanese and British formalized their cooperative ties with an alliance in 1902. By this agreement the British recognized Japan's special interests in Korea. Each nation pledged to aid the other if Russia and a fourth party attacked either one. Such a combined attack never took place. Nonetheless, with a colony in Taiwan, troops in Peking, and an alliance with the British, Japan had secured a place as one of Asia's imperial powers.

Over the next several years, Japanese leaders sought above all to solidify hegemony in Korea. One option viewed with favor by Itō Hirobumi in particular was a diplomatic deal with the Russians. Japan would grant them primacy in Manchuria if they would retreat in Korea. Through 1903, the government negotiated in a half-hearted way with Russia. In fact, Japan was unwilling to concede full control of Manchuria to the Russians, and the latter were equally insistent on maintaining a Korean presence. In addition, political parties, journalists, and leading intellectuals, including a group of prominent Tokyo Imperial University professors, held rallies and issued increasingly forceful calls for war. This strengthened the hand of hawkish voices among the Japanese negotiators. The atmosphere—and the role of a jingoistic press—was quite similar to that in the United States on the eve of the Spanish-American War of 1898. By February 1904, the Japanese government had decided to secure its position in Korea as well as Manchuria by force. It declared war on Russia. This began the Russo-Japanese War, Japan's second major military struggle over Korea in a decade.

From the outset, leaders of the Japanese army and navy viewed this war as a risky endeavor. Confirming their fears, the military results were mixed. Japan won a string of land battles as it advanced north on the Korean peninsula toward Manchuria. The army also prevailed in January 1905 in a half-year siege of Port Arthur at the tip of the Liaodong peninsula. In May 1905 the navy destroyed the Russian fleet off the coast of Korea. Yet the Japanese could not rout the Russian forces completely, and their own human and material losses were high. Japanese armaments were running short. Funds were scarce. The Russians also had motive to stop fighting. They feared that a continued war would incite revolutionary movements back home.

In May 1905 the Japanese oligarchs secretly asked the American president, Theodore Roosevelt, to mediate. A treaty of peace was negotiated at Portsmouth, New Hampshire, and signed on September 5, 1905. The settlement reflected the uncertain military situation. The Japanese gained control of Russian railway lines in southern Manchuria and took over Russian leases in two Manchurian ports as well. They also won recognition of their exclusive rights in Korea. But aside from territorial rights on the southern half of the virtually uninhabited Sakhalin island, Japan emerged with no outright gains of land and no financial compensation. This contrasted sharply with the Sino-Japanese War. Public opinion at home was severely disappointed.

Nonetheless, Japan was now clearly in control of Korea. Its advisors in fact ran the government. The Japanese army, through the office of resident general, administered Korean foreign relations. The resident general increased his power in 1907 when Japan forced the Korean monarch to resign and disbanded the Korean army. Japan then annexed Korea outright as a colony in 1910. Until 1945, the offices of the governor general of Korea, appointed by the emperor, held complete military, judicial, legislative, and civil authority.

From the end of the Russo-Japanese War through the annexation, Japanese international relations remained troubled. The Koreans and Chinese deeply resented and often resisted Japanese domination. The United States had become a naval power in the Pacific in the 1890s. American hostility to Japanese immigration grew sharply in the early 1900s. In 1907–08 the United States forced Japan to accept the so-called Gentleman's Agreement. This limited Japanese immigration to close relatives of people already there. In addition, the United States had adopted its "Open Door policy" in 1899, which insisted that all nations have equal access to any of the ports open to trade in China. This position set the Americans against Japanese claims to hold special rights in Manchuria.

But at the very least, Japan's position in Taiwan and Korea was secure from international challenge; Korea had been shifted from a "zone of advantage" to a "zone of sovereignty," now ringed by an expanded area of advantage. A broad range of foreign opinion admired these achievements, using invidious racial comparisons. Beatrice Webb, the famous British socialist, wrote during a 1911 trip to Asia that the Chinese were "a horrid race." She voiced similar scorn for Koreans. But the Japanese, she said, "shame our administrative capacity, shame our inventiveness, shame our leadership."[9]

The Japanese state in this way acquired economic privilege beyond its borders. It eroded, then denied, the political autonomy of other people. Several actors and forces drove Japan to become an imperialist power. First, indigenous intellectual traditions developed by scholars of National Learning or those of the Mito domain rejected both Sino-centric and Western models of international relations. They claimed a special place for Japan as a divine realm that "constitutes the head and shoulders of the world and controls all nations."[10] The new rulers of Meiji Japan drew on such attitudes as they looked to secure Japan's position in Asia and enshrine the emperor as the pillar of the domestic order as well. The jingoistic press, the public, and adventurers seeking pan-Asian unity with Japan at the head were inspired by such ideas as well.

Second, the Meiji rulers accepted a geopolitical logic that led inexorably toward either empire or subordination, with no middle ground possible. They saw the non-Western world being carved up into colonial possessions by the strong states of the West. They decided that Japan had no choice but to secure its independence by emulating the imperialists. Thus, Yamagata Aritomo developed the strategic vision of zones of sovereignty ringed by zones of advantage. As this doctrine took root in a world of competing powers, it contained a built-in logic of escalation. Conceivably Japanese leaders could have defended national independence and prosperity in Asia by promoting trade and emigration with both neighbors and distant nations, without seeking an imperialist advantage. But no leaders believed this was possible. The behavior of other powers hardly encouraged them to change their minds.

Third, influential Japanese also developed substantial overseas business interests, especially in Korea. Trade to and from the peninsula grew sharply from the 1880s. Leaders of the financial world staked important claims as well. In 1878, led by the great entrepreneur Shibusawa Eiichi, Japan's First National Bank began opening Korean branches. It became the major financial institution in Korea by far, a combination of a commercial and a central bank handling customs, currency issue, loans, and insurance to traders. Shipping lines and railway promoters were also prominent players in the Korean economy. The sum total of these activities was modest in comparison to the entire Japanese economy, but the leading Japanese businessmen active in Korea were politically influential figures in Japan. They had particularly close ties to Itō Hirobumi, who served as the first resident general in Korea after the Russo-Japanese

War. Itō paved the way toward formal annexation by forcing the Korean king to abdicate in 1907. He was assassinated in 1909 by a Korean nationalist.

Military and economic domination were two sides of a single coin. All of Japan's elites as well as the vigorously opinionated public saw Korea, and Asia more generally, as a frontier for Japan's expanding power and prestige. The move to empire was thus "overdetermined." That is, it was propelled by connected logics of military power, competitive geopolitics, expanding trade and investment, as well as nativist ideals of Japanese supremacy. These ideas were reinforced in turn by the racialist thinking so dominant in the West at this time.

CONTEXTS OF EMPIRE, CAPITALISM, AND NATION-BUILDING

From the Meiji restoration through 1890, civilian bureaucrats and the military had ruled in the name of the sovereign emperor. Itō Hirobumi and his colleagues who wrote the Meiji constitution of 1889 gave the Japanese people a limited political voice through the elected lower house of the Diet. But they expected bureaucrats and generals to continue to rule without significant accountability to the broader populace.

Things did not turn out as planned. A vigorous drive for participatory, parliamentary politics emerged from the 1890s into the early twentieth century. Its supporters accepted, and even embraced, both imperial sovereignty and the emergence of Japan as an imperialist power in Asia. But they sharply challenged the leaders in the bureaucracy and military. The anchors put in place by Japan's rulers around the turn of century failed to bind people completely to their rulers' wishes.

Three related projects of Japan's modernizing elite provided the context for the unexpectedly turbulent politics of the late nineteenth and early twentieth centuries: the drive for empire, the industrial revolution, and policies of nation-building.

Imperialism shaped domestic politics in large part because it was expensive. Beginning in 1896 the government consistently sought new taxes to enforce Japan's foothold on the Asian mainland. People protested these impositions, even though they approved of the result. The imperialist project had a more indirect political impact as well. The numerous parades and demonstrations of the Sino-Japanese and Russo-Japanese wars gave new legitimacy to public gatherings, especially in cities. As the government mobilized people behind wars it unwittingly fostered the belief that the wishes of the people, whose commitment and sacrifice made empire possible, should be respected in the political process.

The rise of industrial capitalism in late nineteenth-century Japan brought on a related set of politically important changes. Expansion of heavy industry beginning in the interwar decade around the turn of the century was financed in part by fruits of empire such as the demand for arms production and the Sino-Japanese War indemnity, which subsidized steelmaking and shipbuilding in particular. Industrialization then produced a growing class of wage laborers, skilled male workers as well as female textile workers. These people tended to cluster in the cities, especially Tokyo and Osaka. They played key roles in political agitations of the early twentieth century.

Further, as industry and commerce expanded, the number of retail shops, wholesale enterprises, and small factories increased in both new and old industries. Small

Mother and children receive word of husband/father's death in the Sino-Japanese War. Painted in 1898 by Matsui Noboru. Such paintings conveyed the grief of the survivors, but they sought to do so in a way that suggested the nobility of sacrificing one's life for the country and exalted the stoic response of the family members. Ironically, when this painting—a proud possession of the Imperial Household Agency—was used in a high school textbook in the 1960s to illustrate the character of prewar society and politics, the Ministry of Education refused to authorize the textbook. A major controversy ensued for decades when the author (Ienaga Saburō) sued the government for its action.

Museum of the Imperial Collections, Sannomaru Shōzōkan, Imperial Household Agency.

Politician making a speech from a theater balcony in central Tokyo on September 5, 1905,
the day of the Hibiya riot in protest of the terms of the treaty that ended the Russo-Japanese
War. Political rallies of this sort were not usually accompanied by violence. Many hundreds
of such events, some indoors and some in the open air, were convened each year in major
cities in the 1890s and early 1900s, especially, of course, as elections approached.
Tokyo Sōjō Gahō.

business proprietors—whose Euro-American counterparts are called *petty bourgeoi-*
sie—had to pay various local and national taxes. But in the first thirty years of Diet
politics, their tax payments rarely qualified them to vote. The burden of taxation
without representation, familiar to students of history elsewhere, greatly angered these
people. They launched several energetic anti-tax movements from the 1890s to the
1920s.

The impact of nation-building programs on politics was also profound. The simple fact that the constitution created an elected Diet sent to any attentive person a message that Japan was a nation of subjects with some degree of political rights in addition to duties. Obligations to the state included serving in the military, attending school, and paying taxes. Rights for men included suffrage and a voice in deciding the fate of the national budget. Electoral politics encouraged a vigorous partisan press, political parties, and other practices of democratic political systems: speech meetings and rallies, speaking tours and demonstrations. By the 1890s, hundreds of legal, open political rallies were convened each year in major cities. This was something new in Japanese history.

The right of even a few men to vote for members of a national assembly implied that a potentially expandable body of politically active subjects existed. Virtually all political leaders and most followers in these early days of the twentieth century were men of means and education: landlords, capitalists, and an emerging class of urban professionals such as journalists and lawyers. But the formerly parochial, apolitical, and often impoverished commoners of Japan, some women as well as men, were swelling the ranks of political rallies and movements. They, too, were developing a sense of themselves as members of the nation, ready to voice opinions on foreign and domestic policy.

THE TURBULENT WORLD OF DIET POLITICS

Called into being by the Meiji constitution, the bicameral Diet had the power to pass laws and approve the government's annual budget. From the time of the first election in 1890, it immediately became a focal point of Japanese political life.

The election law promulgated together with the constitution in 1889 limited both suffrage and office to men of substantial property. It allocated three hundred seats across 257 districts to the House of Representatives (some large districts were given two members). The first men elected to the Diet were primarily landlords. In addition, a sprinkling of businessmen and former bureaucrats won seats, as did some urban professionals such as journalists, publishers, and lawyers. Roughly one-third of these representatives were former members of the samurai class.

The House of Peers, in contrast, was not elected. Members were appointed by the emperor from several categories, including the hereditary peerage created in 1885, males in the imperial family, and the highest taxpayers in the nation. A few imperial appointees won posts for distinguished government service or scholarship. The Peers collectively formed a privileged and extremely conservative group of top former bureaucrats, former daimyō, a few members of the Tokugawa family, as well as the wealthiest men in the nation. They were intended to restrain any liberalizing pressures from the House of Representatives.

Diet members voted on legislation introduced either by government ministers or by the representatives themselves. They voted on the budget, and they debated numerous other matters. One controversial issue was the expansion of the electorate. Beginning in late 1897 some Diet representatives joined with activists in the press to promote the suffrage movement. In 1900 the government lowered the tax qualification for voting from 15 to 10 yen per household. This step doubled the electorate from about 1 percent to 2 percent of the population.

From the first sessions in the 1890s, members of the Diet discussed social problems as well. They looked into the health and conditions of factory workers, and they debated the merits of protective "factory laws" on European models. Government officials argued in favor of steps such as limited hours of night work for women and children. Representatives allied to textile magnates and other industrialists fiercely opposed such a law. They reached a compromise in 1911 with passage of the relatively weak Factory Act. Diet members also addressed issues of foreign policy. They uniformly rallied behind the flag during Japan's wars of imperialist expansion, but they just as consistently balked at the high cost of the military during peacetime and resisted proposals to expand the size of the military.

But in the early years of Diet politics, local issues loomed largest. Taxes and their uses were certainly the most controversial matters. Landlords in the Diet pushed the government not to rely solely on the land tax, and the Diet passed a new "business tax" in 1896. It levied a charge on businesses that rose in proportion to numbers of employees and buildings as well as revenues. Over time, the proportion of national revenues derived from the land tax declined substantially. Not surprisingly, Diet representatives with close ties to leading capitalists launched a vigorous campaign to repeal the business tax.

As they struggled with these issues, ministers of state and elected representatives simultaneously wrangled over what to do with tax revenues. Should they go primarily to the army and navy? Should they be used for local projects such as harbor improvements and roads? If so, in which districts? As elsewhere, this was the everyday stuff of parliamentary politics in modern Japan.

The first six Diet sessions took place from 1890 to 1894. They were contentious in the extreme. On one side stood the government: cabinet ministers appointed by the emperor, who supervised a bureaucracy of state employees selected by the new civil service examination system. Against the government stood the members of opposition political parties. Their members consisted mainly of former popular rights activists. They grouped into a Liberal and a Progressive party for the first election, in July 1890, and together won a majority with 171 seats. The oligarchs were able to pull together a pro-government party of just 79 members. The opposition immediately pushed to cut the budget. The no-nonsense prime minister, Yamagata Aritomo, was inclined to override this opposition and even dissolve the Diet. But in order to make the first session a smooth one, he compromised and a budget was passed.

The next several sessions, through 1894, saw repeated confrontation between the Diet members in the Liberal and Progressive parties and hardliners among the oligarchs, in particular Yamagata and Matsukata Masayoshi (prime minister initially from 1891 to 1892). The Diet members were intent on cutting the budget. The oligarchs had little use for parliament. They tried to invoke the emperor's name, with some success, to force politicians to support the government position. The Home Ministry had the job of supervising elections. It often pressured voters to support government candidates with police violence and bribery. (See Appendix A for full list of Prime Ministers.)

The second Diet election in 1892 was particularly violent. No less than twenty-five voters died, and several hundred were injured in fighting at the polls. Even so, the opposition parties together retained a majority of seats. In this and the following three sessions, the government resorted to threats, bribes, admonitions issued by the emperor, and dissolution of the Diet to pass its agenda. Japan's experience with parliamentary politics got off to a very rocky start.

The start of a move toward a more cooperative politics of compromise began with the Sino-Japanese War. Members of the Diet enthusiastically supported the war. They put political struggles with the government on hold under Prime Minister Itō's wartime unity cabinets. For his part, Itō also came to support a cooperative political strategy. He was willing to offer Diet representatives bureaucratic posts and a voice in the allocation of funds in exchange for their support of the government budget.

After the war, the cooperative mood receded for several years. Although Matsukata Masayoshi (prime minister once more from 1896 to January 1898) did appoint the party politician, Ōkuma Shigenobu, as foreign minister, he was not willing to concede as many favors as Ōkuma's party sought. He dissolved the Diet after suffering a no-confidence vote. Similar reluctance to share the spoils of office with party men doomed the cabinet of the hardline oligarchic leader Yamagata Aritomo, prime minister from November 1898 to 1900.

The year 1900 marked the start of Itō Hirobumi's final stint as prime minister. The turn to the twentieth century inaugurated an era of gradually more stable compromise between state ministers and elected Diet politicians. Itō committed himself to a strategy of compromise and alliance with Diet representatives. In 1900 he organized a new political party, called the Friends of Constitutional Government (Rikken Seiyūkai, abbreviated as Seiyūkai). The core of the Seiyūkai was comprised of former members of Itagaki's Liberal Party. After Itō resigned as prime minister in 1901, the prime minister's office alternated for twelve years between Yamagata Aritomo's right-hand man, a general from Chōshū named Katsura Tarō, and Itō's close protégé, Saionji Kimmochi, a liberal-minded court noble who helped lead the Seiyūkai. Katsura held office three times (1901–06, 1908–11, 1912–13), and Saionji served twice (1906–08 and 1911–12). Each man ruled by making alliances with the Seiyūkai, which was becoming an increasingly cohesive force in the House of Representatives. Saionji cooperated out of conviction. He believed a more inclusive body of men of substance would bring political and social stability to Japan. Katsura was more suspicious of the parties. He made reluctant deals of convenience or necessity.

The other truly important political figure in these years was a well-to-do son of a former samurai family, Hara Kei. He was the effective leader of the Seiyūkai from about 1904.[11] His varied career reflects his character as a master networker. He began with a brief stint in the government, then turned to journalism, where he was a successful editor. In the 1880s he was recruited into the Foreign Ministry, then returned to journalism in the early 1890s, before entering the Seiyūkai party as secretary general in 1900. He was elected to the Diet in 1902 and held a seat until his death.

Hara was the master of what one historian has called "the politics of compromise," practiced behind the scenes to increase the power of elected politicians and political parties.[12] Hara traded his party's support of the government budget for one of two sorts of political goods. The first was government office, especially cabinet positions, for party members. This helped ensure the second, which was public spending in member districts for roads, harbor improvements, schools, and railroad lines. He perfected Japan's version of "pork barrel" politics, a practice that has continued ever since.

One key deal came in late 1904. Hara offered to support Katsura's wartime budget in exchange for a promise that the Seiyūkai president, Prince Saionji, would be the next prime minister. Katsura honored the bargain, and the Seiyūkai was able to place its members in every cabinet through 1912. Through such maneuvering, the Seiyūkai became more cohesive and bureaucratic, while the bureaucracy became more partisan. When a party leader such as Hara served as home minister, he would advance the careers of ministry bureaucrats who pledged allegiance to his party by promoting them to higher posts in prefectural government or the police. In return, such men provided sympathic policing of local and national elections, which gave the Seiyūkai a powerful boost at the polls.

From its founding in 1900 through 1912 the Seiyūkai was the only effective political party in the national Diet. At this point, the greatest political confrontation since the inauguration of Diet politics in 1890 took place. It unfolded just months after the death of the Meiji emperor in July 1912, which began the reign of his son, the Taishō emperor. The political battle that began that autumn was aptly labeled the "Taishō political crisis."

Novelist Natsume Sōseki has left the most memorable evocation of the emperor's death as a symbol of the passing of an era in his famous novel of 1914, *Kokoro*. The main character concludes, "I felt as though the spirit of the Meiji era had begun with the emperor and had ended with him."[13] Millions of people shared the belief that the modernizing nation stood at a moment of transition. This impression intensified powerfully when General Nogi Maresuke and his wife committed suicide on the day of the emperor's funeral. Nogi had become a military hero for his role in the Sino-Japanese War, but his leadership in key battles of the Russo-Japanese War had been disastrous, leading to huge casualties in futile attacks. His suicide appeared to be an act of atonement for this failure. The press blared out headlines of this shocking final act of loyalty of a military couple to their ultimate commander, the emperor.

The major political battle that unfolded as the Taishō emperor began his reign confirmed the popular sense that a new era had begun. The crisis erupted in November 1912. Prime Minister Saionji had for some time faced strong pressure from the army to provide funds for at least two new divisions. This was part of a plan to expand the military that had been approved by the government in general outline in 1906. But Saionji wanted to reduce government expenses, so he refused funding for the divisions. At this point, the army minister resigned. The military further refused to supply a replacement (by law, the ministers of the army or navy had to be active duty officers). Unable to form a cabinet, Saionji resigned.

At this point the Seiyūkai held a majority in the Diet as well as strong popular support. The press and leading intellectuals viewed the military's tactics as an affront to "constitutional government." By this term they meant a system that respected the power of the elected members of the Diet. Business leaders were less ideologically committed, but they supported the Seiyūkai drive to cut government expenditures. When Katsura Tarō replaced Saionji as prime minister and refused any concessions to the Seiyūkai, all of Katsura's opponents joined forces in the unusually vigorous

Movement to Protect Constitutional Government. They issued manifestos and held dozens of well-attended indoor and outdoor rallies. These reached a peak in February 1913.

Katsura, for his part, understood that he needed a base of some sort in the Diet. He believed he could win the support of nationalistic representatives who would defect from the Seiyūkai. But when he launched a new party, the Rikken Dōshikai, in December 1912, he drew a mere eighty-three members. Not one man came over from the Seiyūkai. Katsura faced an aroused populace outside the Diet and a no-confidence vote within it. He was increasingly desperate, so he turned to the emperor as other oligarchs had done before. He had the emperor issue a rescript calling on Saionji to cooperate.

At this point something quite unusual happened. Seiyūkai members called Katsura's bluff, while the demonstrations continued outside. In one of the most memorable speeches in the brief history of the Diet, Ozaki Yukio, a famous advocate of parliamentary government, declared on February 5 that Katsura and his supporters

> always preach loyalty, as if they alone know the meaning of loyalty to the Emperor and love for the country, while in reality, they conceal themselves behind the throne and snipe at their political enemies. Do they not indeed seek to destroy their enemies by using the throne as a parapet and the imperial rescripts as bullets?[14]

Katsura had tried and failed to use the emperor to influence a partisan political battle. By one account he "turned deathly pale . . . His facial expression was like one being sentenced to death."[15]

Several days later, major riots broke out in Tokyo and other cities. On February 10, anxious crowds gathered outside the Diet, hoping to learn firsthand of Katsura's expected resignation. When word spread that the Diet would not convene that day, the crowd turned violent. Groups of rioters destroyed thirty-eight police sub-stations in Tokyo, and they attacked pro-government newspapers. Several people were killed, and hundreds were injured and arrested. Hara wrote fearfully in his diary that "if [Katsura] still refuses to resign, I think a practically revolutionary riot will occur."[16]

Katsura did in fact resign. The surviving oligarchs (Yamagata and Matsukata, plus Saionji) asked a navy man, Yamamoto Gonnohyōe, to form a new cabinet, with the understanding that the Seiyūkai would have a place in it. Hara bitterly disappointed the leaders of the Movement to protect Constitutional Government. They wanted him to hold out for complete party control of the new cabinet. Instead, he accepted three posts, including one for himself as home minister, and some key policy concessions. Yamamoto agreed to revise regulations that had given the military a de facto veto over cabinet formation. In the new rules, not only active duty officers but also *retired* military men could serve as army and navy ministers in the cabinet. Yamamoto also widened the doorway to party influence in the bureaucracy by making the vice minister's position a political appointment in addition to the minister's. He also reduced the budget and cut the size of the bureaucracy.

In this fashion, it became clear at the end of the Meiji emperor's reign that political rulers could not ignore the power of elected representatives in the Diet, and that one party above all, the Seiyūkai, had fashioned a cohesive system to control a majority of Diet representatives. But it is also important to note that while Katsura thus lost the political battle of 1913 in humiliating fashion, his hastily formed Dōshikai party would persist and improve its fortunes. The tumultuous events of these months had put in place a structure of two-party rivalry that persisted through the 1930s.

THE ERA OF POPULAR PROTEST

The riots that marked this Taishō political crisis go a long way toward explaining why Hara accepted a compromise that betrayed the hopes of hardline advocates of "constitutional government." On one hand Hara insisted that landlords and business leaders deserved a political voice through their representatives such as his Seiyūkai party. But no less than his rivals in the bureaucracy or military such as Katsura or Yamagata, he was terrified by the specter of aroused and politically focused masses. He did not want to encourage them or their leaders.

Such fear was not paranoia. The first twenty years of the twentieth century not only saw the Diet and its representatives win seats at the table of elite politics but were also a time of chronic public disturbance. One historian has dubbed this "the era of popular riot."[17] The prospect of popular unrest mixing with new ideologies of political radicalism eventually led the oligarchs and party politicians to join hands to secure social order and their own positions of privilege.

In addition to the riots during the Taishō political crisis of 1913, crowds of Tokyoites took violent steps to air their grievances on eight occasions between 1905 and 1918, and similar riots took place in other cities.

The first riot came in 1905. The treaty announced after the Russo-Japanese War had greatly disappointed most Japanese people. The war had been eight times as expensive as the Sino-Japanese conflict a decade before. War dead numbered sixty thousand fallen in battle, plus twenty thousand taken by disease, four times the toll of the Sino-Japanese War. The government and the press had led people to expect an indemnity and territorial gains. But the peace settlement offered neither.

Members of the Diet, intellectuals, journalists, and the mass of the populace were all furious. Dietmen formed groups to oppose the treaty. They called for a rally to convene at the Hibiya Park in the heart of Tokyo on September 5, 1905. The police forbade it. A crowd gathered anyway, heard speeches, and spilled out in all directions to launch a massive three-day riot. Violence broke out in numerous cities nationwide. Tokyo was reported to be in a state of anarchy. Seventeen rioters were killed. No less than 70 percent of the city's police substations were destroyed.

For Japan's bureaucratic and military rulers, the Hibiya riot was a frightening event. By their actions as well as in speeches, people were saying that if they were to pay for empire, and die for it, their voice should be respected in politics. Although the people were vociferous supporters of empire and the emperor, they were condemning his ministers for ignoring what they called "the will of the people." The men who organized the rallies and led the riots called in their speeches for a political system that would respect the shared wishes of the people and the emperor. Several such "wishes" emerged with particular clarity. People wanted lower taxes, hegemony in Asia, the respect of the West, and the freedom to assemble and make these demands.

For a time, men of substance in the Diet were willing to encourage these voices.

TABLE 8.1 Riots in Tokyo, 1905–18

Date	Main Issues	Secondary Issues	Site of Origin	Description
Sept. 5–7, 1905	Against peace ending the Russo-Japanese War	Against clique government; for "constitutional government"	Hibiya Park	17 killed; 70 percent of police boxes, 15 trams destroyed; pro-government newspapers attacked; 311 arrested; violence in Kobe, Yokohama, rallies nationwide
March 15–18, 1906	Against streetcar fare increase	Against "unconstitutional" behavior of bureaucracy, Seiyūkai	Hibiya Park	Several dozen streetcars smashed; attacks on streetcar company offices; many arrested; increase revoked
Sept. 5–8, 1906	Against streetcar fare increase	Against "unconstitutional" actions	Hibiya Park	113 arrested; scores injured; scores of streetcars damaged; police boxes destroyed
Feb. 11, 1908	Against tax increase		Hibiya Park	21 arrested; 11 streetcars stoned
Feb. 10, 1913	For constitutional government	Against clique government	Outside Diet	38 police boxes smashed; government newspapers attacked; several killed, 168 injured (110 police); 253 arrested; violence in Kobe, Osaka, Hiroshima, Kyoto
Sept. 7, 1913	For strong China policy		Hibiya Park	Police stoned; Foreign Ministry stormed; representatives enter Foreign Ministry to negotiate
Feb. 10–12, 1914	Against naval corruption; for constitutional government	Against business tax; for strong China policy	Outside Diet	Dietmen attacked; Diet, newspapers stormed; streetcars, police boxes smashed; 435 arrested; violence in Osaka
Feb. 11, 1918	For universal suffrage		Ueno Park	Police clash with demonstrators; 19 arrested
Aug. 13–16, 1918	Against high rice prices	Against Terauchi cabinet	Hibiya Park	Rice seized; stores smashed; 578 arrested; incidents nationwide

Crowd storming and setting fire to the home minister's residence during the Hibiya anti-treaty riot of 1905, dramatically rendered in a special issue of the Japan Graphic *(the* Life *magazine of its day). The issue was titled "The Riot Graphic." Although the surface cause of the riot was a perceived weakness in foreign policy, the home minister was a particular target of popular wrath because he was responsible for policing and suppressing political organizing. The police themselves were often attacked as well.*
Tokyo Sōjō Gahō.

They called for rallies during political upheavals in 1912–13, and again in 1913–14, knowing full well that riots might follow, because they stood to benefit if popular energies discredited the oligarchs. But this was an alliance of temporary convenience. By the end of World War I, elite politicians came to see that they shared with bureaucrats and military men an interest in social order and control that was threatened from several directions.

They identified one such threat in Japan's first generation of socialists. Interest in Western socialism, now translated into Japanese, began to increase in the late 1890s. A group centered on Abe Isoo, Katayama Sen, and Kōtoku Shusui announced the founding of a Social Democratic Party in 1901, but the Katsura cabinet banned the party that same day. Socialist supporters nonetheless continued their activities, launching a weekly paper, the *Commoner News* (*Heimin Shinbun*) in 1903. In addition to reporting on labor unrest, the paper offered a singular voice of opposition to the Russo-Japanese War.

This small group of socialists staked out increasingly militant positions after the war. In 1906 they led protests against increased streetcar fares that ended with minor riots. In 1908 sixteen of them were arrested at a rally featuring flags emblazoned with the words "Anarchism" and "Communism." Three years later, a handful of activists in the socialist camp plotted to assassinate the Meiji emperor. The police uncovered the plan and used it as pretext to arrest a far larger number of socialists. Twelve of these people were executed in what came to be called the Great Treason Incident of 1911. This harsh and widely publicized action silenced left-wing activists for several years.

One of the conspirators executed in 1911 was a woman named Kannō Suga. In addition to supporting socialism, Kannō and several other unconventional women pioneered the feminist cause in the early twentieth century. Like socialism, their ideas inspired fear and loathing among male rulers. Their major publication, founded in 1907, was called *Women of the World* (*Sekai Fujin*). It covered the conditions of Japanese women workers in mines, textile mills, and brothels. It also offered news of suffrage and peace movements of women in other countries.

Most of these early feminists put their demands forward from the position of mothers and wives. These special roles, they claimed, deserved special protection. To that extent, they were not necessarily challenging accepted gender roles head on. Nevertheless, they did challenge the right of the state to demand that their husbands or sons give their lives as soldiers. The government condemned their activity as subversive. Facing constant police harassment, *Women of the World* was forced to close in 1909.[18] Nonetheless, feminist voices continued to be raised in following years.

The concern of feminists with women's labor conditions points to a third area of challenge to elite authority in the early twentieth century. Miners and factory workers, both women and men, challenged their bosses and company owners with increasing frequency. In Tokyo, just fifteen labor disputes took place from 1870 to 1896, but over the following twenty years, from 1897 to 1917, 151 such events occurred. Women in textile mills as well as men in coal mines, copper mines, arsenals, shipyards, and engineering works organized most of these strikes. Their demands often focused as much on dignity and decent food as on pay. For instance, in 1908 a group of workers at Japan's largest arsenal, in Tokyo, launched a protest described in an English-language column by socialist activist Katayama Sen. He had learned English during a sojourn in the United States:

> Government arsenal has been treating its employees in the most cruel manner. They cannot go to the W.C. without a permission ticket during recess. The number of the tickets is only 4 for a hundred workers, consequently some must wait five hours.... Every and all little mistakes are fined at least 5 hours' earnings. They are fined 10 to

20 hours' earnings if they forget any thing their personal belongings. They are now limited to drink hot water in the meal time. . . . Being unbearable at the treatment, they 15,000 in number in a body petitioned the authorities for the immediate remedy with a tactic threat of a strike.[19]

This event stopped short of an actual strike and did not achieve its demands. Over time, such protests became more effective. By the years of World War I, they typically lasted several days rather than a few hours, resulted from more careful advance planning, and drew in a larger proportion of the work force at any given factory.

Another sign of the increased coherence of labor protest was the appearance of relatively stable unions. In the 1890s, men in a few trades with preindustrial roots, such as ship carpenters, had organized effective labor unions. In addition, some heavy industrial workers in the 1880s and 1890s sporadically sought to create labor unions, but these efforts (described in Chapter 7) had collapsed by 1900. A successful unionizing effort began in late 1912. The founder was Suzuki Bunji, a Christian and graduate of Tokyo Imperial University. Looking to much older organizations in Britain as a model, he began by founding a tiny self-help group of artisans and factory workers called the Friendly Society (Yūaikai) in a church basement in central Tokyo with thirteen members. By 1915 he had built an organization of fifteen thousand dues-paying members. The Yūaikai boasted locals in factories large and small in the industrial areas of Japan's major cities.

The moderate spirit of this organization in its early years is captured in a play written by a member with literary ambitions, Hirasawa Keishichi. In it, a sympathetically portrayed worker refuses to join a strike. He addresses the issue of how workers were to secure their dignity:

> The Japanese blood is not fit for shouts of socialism. . . . The time has come for the Japanese people to take back their souls as Japanese. The enemy of Japan's worker is not the government or the capitalist. Japanese workers should not act as workers. We should act as humans and people of the country [*kokumin*].[20]

That is, Hirasawa and Suzuki believed that if working people appealed to their bosses in a moderate spirit as fellow Japanese, they could reasonably expect improved treatment in response.

A new political language of both propertied political activists and plebian protesters thus emerged in the early twentieth century. It was heard in new sites such as the Diet and the public park. It was presented in new forms of action, from elections and rallies to riots and strikes. One key word in this political language, which appeared in Hirasawa's play, was *kokumin*. It literally means "people of the country" and is usually translated as "the people" or "the nation." By the early twentieth century it was as common as the term *empire*. Both were watchwords of popular movements in Japan that pushed the government to open up the political process and rule with popular interests in mind. The irony is that the concepts of both nation and empire took root because of the government's own nation-building programs dating from the 1880s. The rulers of Meiji Japan had established an emperor-centered constitutional order. They had promoted a capitalist, industrializing economy. They had led Japan to imperial power in Asia. By doing this, they provoked movements that challenged their monopoly on political power.

ENGINEERING NATIONALISM

The years from the turn of the century through World War I were marked by contradictory political trends. Rulers and the populace alike delighted in the heady achievement of empire and an alliance with Britain, the greatest power of the day. But bureaucratic and military rulers simultaneously lamented the challenges from party politicians, as well as the protests and violence of working people, socialists, and feminists. From the turn of the century through the 'teens, three groups in particular—the Home Ministry, the army, and the Ministry of Education—responded with initiatives to generate greater nationalism and greater loyalty to the state and to authority more generally.

The Home Ministry took steps to dramatically reorganize the system of local government beginning in the 1890s. By the end of the Russo-Japanese War, it ordered the nation's seventy-six thousand small hamlets to merge into just twelve thousand larger villages. Fewer villages, the government believed, would be easier to control from the center. The Home Ministry for similar reasons ordered the merger of 190,000 Shinto shrines—often tiny sites maintained by villagers in the absence of a priest—to just twelve thousand officially recognized shrines, part of the state-administered Shinto network created in 1900. The ministry also sought to involve women as well as men in a variety of centrally controlled bodies, such as rural credit societies, to promote collective spirit under a central umbrella. The ministry had created a Ladies' Patriotic Association in 1901, and the group grew during the Russo-Japanese War to include five hundred thousand members nationwide. After the war, the Home Ministry drew together scattered local Gratitude Societies (Hōtokukai) into a national network with official sponsorship. These groups had been founded in the early Meiji era, usually by landlords hoping to improve technology and community cooperation. They honored the spirit of a famous agrarian moralist of Tokugawa times, Ninomiya Sontoku. A set of Women's Gratitude Societies was launched in 1907.[21]

The army, for its part, in 1910 founded the Imperial Military Reserve Association (Teikoku zaigō gunjinkai). Its members were volunteers, recruited from among young men who had passed the conscription exam. By 1918 the group had branches in virtually every village in Japan, boasting over two million members. Its founders wished to raise military preparedness among men who might be called to active duty in an emergency. They also had a more general goal of reinforcing social order in turbulent times. As one founder (General Tanaka Giichi) wrote in 1913, "If we think toward the future and correctly guide reservists . . . we can control completely the ideals of the populace and firm up the nation's foundation."[22]

The Ministry of Education joined the drive to promote nationalism and respect for authority by adding two years to compulsory education in 1907. It further stabilized school finances and changed the curriculum to emphasize nationalism and the emperor more heavily. The ministry also boosted the status of teachers by stressing their role as national servants and social and cultural leaders of local society.

The government thus reached far into local society to bolster social order. One final example is the effort of the Ministry of Education to remake the customary youth groups found in most Japanese villages since Tokugawa times. Such groups had consisted of separate bodies for young boys and girls. They were not unlike fraternities or sororities on college campuses. The groups typically gathered members together in the evenings for drinking and singing or gambling. The boys' group would seek out village girls. Government surveys from around 1910 hint at a lack of discipline or some delinquent behavior in these groups. They noted that members "demand a day off from farm work even if it rains a little" and that "if one member is arrested, others help him escape." The officials also lamented "licentious dancing from midnight till dawn at festival time, even 2 or 3 days before the festival, forcing young women of the village to join in, even physically dragging them to dance."[23]

The Ministry of Education tried to replace these groups in the years after the Russo-Japanese War with a nationally controlled network of officially sponsored and registered village youth groups. This project was similar in spirit to efforts in Britain to found the Boy Scouts around the same time, although the British initiative was nongovernmental while the Japanese push to reform came from the state. The new youth groups were designed to be carriers of government messages throughout the nation. Led by mayors and school principals, the groups sponsored festivals, sports events, and lectures on the virtue of good citizenship.

In the early twentieth century, this wide range of government campaigns, implemented through the leadership of local elites, aimed to reinforce social order and link it to the national government. They sought to transfer people's loyalties away from independent social groups on the hamlet level and link them instead to groups on the village and town level controlled by the state. By the time of World War I, many ties bound the Japanese people to the state. In theory, these included the ties of dutiful soldiers in reserve associations, obedient wives and daughters in women's groups, respectful tenant farmers in Gratitude Societies or credit associations, pious villagers supporting local shrines, and earnest students in youth groups.

Natsume Sōseki wickedly satirized these efforts when he lamented in 1914 the "horror" of encouraging the Japanese people to "eat for the nation, wash our faces for the nation, go to the toilet for the nation!"[24] But these links of people to the state were not always tight. Official reports complained of unreceptive coldness among the people. The Ministry of Education surveyed youths in 1915 and discovered with alarm that only 20 percent could identify the Shinto diety, the sun goddess Amaterasu. Only 30 percent knew of the Yasukuni Shrine to Japan's war dead. Rural youth, it seemed to many in the government, were looking to the city, not the countryside, for excitement and for models. The continued energy of a wide array of popular activity outside the purview of the state makes it clear that the impact of these varied efforts to engineer and coordinate a new degree of national loyalty was limited.

At the same time, the campaigns of the late Meiji years did put in place organizations that promoted nationalistic and patriotic ideals with new energies. They reinforced an orthodox view of Japanese-ness. This centered on a set of nested loyalties— of youths to adults, women to men, tenants to landlords, workers to bosses, soldiers and subjects to the emperor and the state. People had room to maneuver and even to challenge this system at times, but the political order of imperial Japan had a powerful constraining force as well.

IMPERIAL JAPAN FROM
ASCENDANCE TO ASHES

9

Economy and Society

Diversity and tension mark the economic and social history of the 1910s and 1920s in Japan. The economy experienced a great wartime boom followed by a prolonged postwar bust. Economic performance differed between industrial and agricultural sectors as well as between the technologically advanced zaibatsu firms and the mass of smaller, less productive enterprises. In social life the worlds of men and women differed greatly, as did those of city-dwellers and rural folk. Within the countryside, the lives of major landlords, owners with smallholdings, and landless tenants were vastly different in many ways. Within towns and cities, diverse groups of wage laborers, shopkeepers, and a "new middle class" of salaried employees of large corporations and state bureaus jostled in close proximity. The cityscape was also dotted with the grand compounds of a small elite of zaibatsu owners and top political leaders.

A newly booming publishing industry, including mass circulation magazines as well as books and newspapers, celebrated the modern lives of middle-class women and men. The press reported the anxieties of those striving to keep up or get ahead. It articulated themes that gave people a sense of participating in a common experience of modern Japanese life, including pride in the achievement of empire as well as economic transformation. It also provided a forum where all sorts of critics might lament the social and political tensions that were inevitable parts of a diverse modern society.

WARTIME BOOM AND POSTWAR BUST

World War I brought unprecedented human disaster to Europe. In Asia it brought some unexpected opportunities. The war cut European traders off from their Asian customers, and this gave a huge boost to Japan's newly industrializing economy. Between 1914 and 1918, Japan's industrial output rose from 1.4 billion to 6.8 billion yen. Exports surged with particular speed. Overseas sales of Japanese cotton cloth rose 185 percent during these years.[1] Industrial employment ballooned as well, and with workers suddenly in scarce supply, wages rose sharply. Unfortunately for most workers and consumers, prices rose even faster. Japan experienced its worst inflationary surge in modern times. Between 1914 and 1920 the retail price of rice increased

174 percent, and overall wholesale prices rose almost 150 percent.[2] The social emblem of this wartime boom was the so-called *narikin*, or *nouveau riche*. This figure was lampooned in cartoons—in Japan as elsewhere—in the form of an overfed businessman lighting a room with his money. The white-collar employees of such magnates prospered as well. They sometimes received bonuses that quadrupled their normal salaries.

The good times continued briefly for these men and their families after the war ended, but the boom came to an abrupt close in April 1920. The stock market plunged, as did the market in silk, Japan's major export commodity. Many banks failed. The value of production in key industries fell as much as 40 percent in one year. Major employers dismissed thousands of workers.

For the rest of the decade, the economy sputtered from crisis to crisis. One fundamental problem was that Japanese goods had climbed in cost during the war and remained overpriced in global markets. This placed exporters at a sharp disadvantage when European competitors returned to Asia after the war. One solution would have been to devalue the Japanese yen against other major currencies, thus lowering the cost of Japanese exports. But such a step went against the orthodox thinking of the day, which dictated that nations seek a stable and strong currency linked firmly to the gold standard. From this perspective, the solution for the Japanese economy was to restore competitivity by lowering domestic prices. The government thus consistently called for retrenchment and restraint as the harsh medicine needed to restore economic health, although its policies on occasion contradicted its own rhetoric.[3]

Manufacturing output showed some signs of recovery by 1922 and 1923. But then, on September 1, 1923, the Great Kantō Earthquake struck Tokyo and its environs with horrifying effects. The shocks came just at noontime. Lunch fires were burning in thousands of charcoal and gas stoves around the city. As wooden buildings collapsed and hibachi stoves tumbled over in neighborhoods crowded with rowhomes and narrow alleys, fire broke out all over the city. Particularly huge whirlwinds of fire swept through the eastern wards over the following two days. The city's distinctive mix of residential, commercial and industrial neighborhoods was devastated. Estimates of the dead and missing ranged from one hundred thousand to two hundred thousand. Tremors or fire destroyed 570,000 dwellings, roughly three-fourths of all those in the city.[4] For a time, economic activity in Japan's largest city came to a virtual standstill.

In the years after this disaster, tentative signs of recovery appeared. A "reconstruction boom" in the aftermath of the earthquake temporarily stimulated jobs and businesses in the Tokyo area. The government encouraged liberal bank lending as further stimulus—against the orthodox logic of retrenchment. Industrial production did increase steadily in key industries such as machine building and shipbuilding. But the basic problem of high international prices remained, and many producers stood on shaky grounds. Domestic textile mills, for example, were losing ground to lower-cost competitors in China, including Japanese producers with overseas investments.

In 1927 several long-standing weaknesses of the Japanese financial system converged to produce a major banking crisis. Japanese banks were numerous but quite small and quite vulnerable. Many of them were poorly diversified. Many were in far weaker condition than their balance sheets indicated because they had delayed writing off failed loans of the immediate postwar depression. In addition, many of the new

This drawing by the famous cartoon artist Wada Ikuo was titled "The Era of the Prosperous New Rich." It lampoons the lifestyles of wealthy businessmen of the World War I boom. As this captain of industry leaves a banquet, the geisha or waitress complains, "It's so dark I can't find your shoes." He lights a hundred-yen note and says, "How's that, it's brighter now isn't it?"

Courtesy of Kyuman Museum and Saitama Municipal Cartoon Art Museum.

loans banks made after the earthquake stood on shaky ground. Individual banks often concentrated their loans to a small number of large borrowers in a few industries in their region. The government offered no guaranteed protection to depositors.

Like matches dropped on this dry tinder, events at home and in the empire sparked a panic in the spring of 1927. Rumors spread that shaky loans made in 1923 and 1924 to promote earthquake recovery had placed numerous banks on the edge of collapse, just as news emerged that a Japanese colonial institution, the Bank of Taiwan, was going to fail. This semiofficial bank had been founded to promote development in Taiwan. It had aggressively expanded activities to include loans to speculative ventures of a Japanese major firm operating in Taiwan. When this borrower—the Suzuki Trading Company—was reported to be insolvent in early 1927, the Bank of Taiwan's investors pulled their short-term loans from the bank, forcing it to shut down. In a good example of the close links between imperial expansion and domestic economy and society, these events sparked a panicky chain reaction of depositor "runs" on domestic banks, followed by a three-week "banking moratorium" in April and May and the failure of dozens of small and medium-sized banks.

Over the next several years, the number of banks fell nearly in half because of failures and mergers. Although manufacturing output continued to rise through the end of the decade, the overall rate of economic growth in the 1920s was only half

Common scene of a run on a bank during the financial crisis of 1927, during which thirty-seven banks failed. Here, in April 1927, a crowd of women and men anxiously wait to withdraw their money from the Tokyo Savings Bank.
Courtesy of *Mainichi* newspaper.

that of the previous thirty years. Even before the world depression jolted Japan in 1929–30, the economy had been stumbling for the better part of a decade. Both popular and intellectual opinion blamed the nation's political leaders for lining their own pockets at the expense of the majority.

When critics parceled out blame, the zaibatsu combines came under particular fire. The major zaibatsu had been founded in the late nineteenth century and often had Tokugawa roots. But the term *zaibatsu* itself only came into widespread use around the time of World War I. A widespread belief that the zaibatsu wrongly dominated the economy—and politics as well—also dates from this time.

The Mitsubishi, Mitsui, Sumitomo, and Yasuda groups, and a handful of somewhat lesser combines, were indeed a dominating presence. In their mature form by the 1920s, each of the major zaibatsu was a sprawling business empire embracing dozens of corporations in finance, transport, trade, mining, and manufacturing. Each zaibatsu was held together at the apex by a holding company. Until the start of World War II, individual families (the Mitsui, Yasuda, and Sumitomo families and, in the case of the Mitsubishi combine, the Iwasaki family) were the exclusive owners of these holding companies. Through them, they controlled the overall affairs of the combine.

The zaibatsu were self-contained and exclusive in some respects. Mitsui manufacturing enterprises agreed to market their exports exclusively through the Mitsui Trading Company. Firms charged lower prices to businesses within the combine. One important exception to this exclusive behavior was the fact that zaibatsu banks made loans outside the combine, to spread risk and expand their power. Another exception was the policy of filling managerial positions by recruiting talented graduates from Tokyo Imperial University who were not members of the zaibatsu families. But even in these appointments, loyalty to the controlling family was valued highly alongside business skill and energy. Devotion was further reinforced when rising managerial stars on occasion married the daughters of zaibatsu families.

Through the economic troubles of the 1920s, the zaibatsu extended their reach. Already in 1918, the eight largest zaibatsu held more than 20 percent of all private capital in the manufacturing, mining, and trading sectors of the economy. The two largest combines, Mitsui and Mitsubishi, accounted for 12 percent of all capital in these sectors. The bank crisis of 1927 opened the way for the zaibatsu banks to dominate the financial world even more, and to take control of numerous smaller businesses as well. The reach of the Mitsui and Mitsubishi empires at their peak was extraordinary (see Table 9.1).

The zaibatsu were controversial at the time. In the late 1920s and early 1930s right-wing assassins targeted top executives, justifying their acts with the claim that "behind the political parties are the zaibatsu bosses."[5] The zaibatsu have remained controversial among historians ever since. On one hand, they played a central role in the industrialization of Japan. They mobilized resources and expertise—capital, labor, raw materials, and technology—in ways that smaller enterprises could not have duplicated. On the other hand, as they amassed extraordinary fortunes the zaibatsu generated and reinforced an extremely inegalitarian distribution of wealth and income. Although zaibatsu magnates opened their wallets to support the political parties in the imperial Diet, they hedged their bets by cultivating close ties to military and bureau-

TABLE 9.1 Core Subsidiaries in the Mitsui and Mitsubishi Combines at War's End

	Mitsui	Mitsubishi
First-line designated subsidiaries	Trading	Trading
	Mining	Mining
	Trust	Trust
	Real estate	Real estate
	Chemicals	Chemical process
	Shipbuilding	Oil
	Precision machinery	Steel fabricating
	Life insurance	Bank
	Agriculture and forestry	Electric
	Steamship	Warehouse
		Heavy industries
Second-line designated subsidiaries	Taisho Marine Fire Insurance	Tokyo Marine Fire Insurance
	Mitsui Warehouse	Japan Optical
	Mitsui Light Metal	Japan Steel Construction
	Tropical Produce	Japan Grain Products
	Mitsui Petrochemical	Mitsubishi Chemical
	Sanki Engineering	Machinery
	Toyo Cotton	Mitsubishi Steamship
	Japan Flour Milling	Japan Aluminum
	Toyo Rayon	Meiji Life Insurance
	Toyo Koatsu	

Source: From Eleanor M. Hadley, *Antitrust in Japan* (Princeton, N.J.: Princeton University Press, 1970), pp. 63–64.

cratic elites as well. The business elite wanted autonomy and stability above all. They offered no consistent or principled support for democratic or liberal politics.

LANDLORDS, TENANTS, AND RURAL LIFE

From the beginning of the twentieth century through the 1930s, rural life was stable in one regard. The relative proportion of landlords, owner-cultivators, and tenants barely changed. This contrasted sharply to the previous decades, during which tenant farmers had increased dramatically in numbers. If anything, conditions in the early twentieth century had improved somewhat for tenant farmers compared to the 1870s or 1880s. More tenants than before found that after setting aside a share of their produce for personal consumption and for rent, they had a modest surplus that they could sell on the market. Military statistics indicate that the height of average conscripts—primarily rural youths—rose as much as three centimeters (more than an inch) from the mid-1890s through 1905. This is a clear if crude indicator of improved standards of living and diets for the majority of the population.

Even so, by the 1920s the Japanese countryside was a troubled place. After several decades of increased total output, the overall productivity of Japanese farmers stopped growing. The gains from a series of relatively inexpensive improvements in tools and cultivation techniques had run their course in the more advanced central and western regions. These advances were slow to spread further north. As growth leveled off, social and political tensions began to increase. An immense gulf continued to distinguish the lives and lifestyles of the rural upper crust from others in the countryside. As a result, those in the middle and lower ends of the hierarchy protested more vigorously than before.

The wealthiest landlords—roughly 2 to 3 percent of all rural households—did no farming themselves.[6] They lived easily on rents collected from numerous tenant families who farmed their fields. They dwelt in large, comfortably furnished homes with many servants. In the decades since the Meiji restoration, such landlords had sometimes led the way toward improvements in agricultural practice that increased output and benefited tenants as well as themselves.[7] They continued in the vanguard in areas such as bringing electricity to their villages. The wives in such families often led newly founded organizations for women such as the Ladies' Patriotic Association, created in 1901. They would mobilize fellow villages to send "care packages" to Japanese troops overseas. They gathered with each other for tea and complained about their servants. They arranged marriages for their sons and daughters with children of similar backgrounds nearby. Their husbands, in addition to renting out their fields, invested in moneylending or small-scale manufacturing. They might spend their leisure time in traditional fashion, partying with geisha at hotspring inns. Or they might engage in newer pursuits such as politics, running for local or national office, or supporting the campaigns of fellow landlords. These men and women lived comfortable lives marked by ambition, confidence, and a belief that they were the local pillars of an emerging nation and an empire of consequence in the larger world.[8]

For the rest of those in the countryside, economic life ranged from modestly affluent to difficult to desperate. In good times, some tenant farmers could market a considerable surplus of their produce and use the profit to improve living standards. But they remained vulnerable to rent increases and fluctuating commodity prices. More fortunate farmers might own their fields, but their holdings were small. They were often just two or three bad harvests away from having to mortgage fields for cash to pay land taxes. After that, if conditions still did not improve, they faced foreclosure, loss of their land, and the more dependent life of a tenant farmer.

Such a life is dramatically evoked in a novel written in 1910 by Nagatsuka Takashi called *The Soil*. It tells the story of "poor farmers [who] spent long hours in their fields doing all they could to raise enough food. Then after the harvest, they had to part with most of what they had produced. Their crops were theirs only for as long as they stood rooted in the soil."[9] These tenant farmers lived in dark tiny homes with dirt floors in the kitchen and wooden boards but no tatami mats in the rest of the house. Their dwellings were drafty and bitter cold in winter. They subsisted on monotonous diets of barley gruel and pickles, with occasional treats of rice and some fresh vegetables. They depended on the benevolence of their betters to survive hard times.

This dependence was the most important source of resentment and conflict in rural Japan in the early twentieth century. Farmers lived in a world of great hierarchy. As social historian Ann Waswo explains:

> [T]enants were expected to step aside if they encountered anyone of superior status on a village road or footpath. They were at the beck and call of their landlords, to

Members of a tenant farmer family on the way to their fields in the 1920s. To diversify risk, farmers often rented small plots from several landlords, which could be quite far from each other and an arduous walk from their homes.
Courtesy of Akira Konishi.

perform chores in the landlords' fields or in the landlords homes, even if this meant delaying vital chores of their own. If they were given a meal at the end of their day's labor, they received it gratefully and consumed it in a dark corner of the landlord's kitchen.[10]

At such moments, a seething fury often lurked close below the surface. Consider the case of Kamimura Hideji, born in 1915. His memory of the humiliating interaction between the landlord and his father remained powerful when he was interviewed about his childhood at the age of seventy-five. In December each year in the 1920s, his father would take a day off from work in the fields to bring the rent rice to the landlord. His son sometimes joined him. Handing the rice over, Kamimura's father would bow low and thank the landlord. Kamimura remembered watching this ceremony and "thinking as a child 'what in the world is going on? Why thank the landlord? He should thank us!' "[11]

Such an inegalitarian system was sustained, however, by more than simple coercion. Hierarchies of status and power were buffered by customary gestures of benevolence. Landlords would customarily contribute the funds for festival celebrations. They were expected to reduce rents when times were particularly bad and to pay doctor's bills when a tenant farmer fell ill. It was in awareness that he offered such care that the landlord of Kamimura's father might have expected a thank-you together with the rent. The inequality of village life was also buffered by the presence of a substantial middling group of owner-cultivators. At the upper reaches, such families had a few extra fields to rent out to tenants. At the lower levels, a small-scale landowner would need to rent an additional plot or two from a landlord. Such farmers occupied a gradation of statuses. They played an important role in bridging the gap between the minorities of extremely rich landlords and extremely poor, landless tenants.

Even so, antagonism was not always contained. In the 1910s and 1920s, the paternalistic commitment of landlords to look after their dependent social and economic inferiors in the local community seems to have weakened. More landlords chose to live in the provincial capitals or in major cities, sites of greater cultural as well as economic or political opportunities. They delegated management of their lands to an estate overseer who might treat tenants in an impersonal fashion. Even wealthy farmers who stayed in the village often sent their children to provincial towns or major cities for middle school and higher education. Compared to resident elites, the absentee landlords provided fewer customary forms of benevolence to poorer villagers, and this became a source of social tension. In the late 1920s, leftist writer Kobayashi Takiji memorably described absentee landlords as "a strange breed of fish—like mermen. The upper part is a landlord, but the lower part is a capitalist, and the lower part is rapidly taking over the torso."[12]

From around the time of World War I, tenant farmers began joining together to demand that landlords reduce their rents. They used the effective tactic of divide and conquer. To minimize dependence on any single person, most tenant farmers rented fields from several landlords (just as most landlords rented to several tenants). A group of well-organized tenants could threaten to withhold all labor from the fields of just one landlord at harvest time. That landlord would face a total loss although each tenant faced only a partial one. Most landlords faced with such tactics settled by offering either a one-year or a permanent reduction in rent. Between 1923 and 1931, anywhere from fifteen hundred to twenty-seven hundred such tenant-landlord disputes took place each year. The most common demand, found in 70 percent of these disputes, was for lower rent. Participation varied from a handful of households in a single village to several hundred tenant households spread out over numerous villages. Tenants won at least some of their demands in three-fourths of all disputes.[13]

Many of these disputes were led by a new organization in rural Japan, the tenant farmer union. At their peak in the mid-1920s, such unions enrolled as many as one-tenth of all tenant farming families. Some local unions joined together into regional or national federations. The largest of these was the Japan Farmers Union, founded in 1922. These unions and their members lacked any legal recognition or protection. Village leaders exerted considerable social pressure and implied or explicit threats against joining. In such a context, to unionize 10 percent of tenant households in just a few years was an impressive achievement.

By the late 1920s, however, landlords began to counterorganize effectively. By pooling resources to hire lawyers and coordinate their responses through unions of their own, they had some success in fending off tenant demands. But in addition, a number of the wealthiest landlords in particular decided that managing a farm was simply too much trouble. Throughout the 1920s and increasingly toward the end of the decade, noncultivating landlords sold off fields and decreased their holdings. They turned instead to the stock market and industrial investments, which promised stronger returns with less onerous personal involvement.

The social upheaval in the countryside of the 1910s and 1920s did not stem primarily from the economic backwardness of abject poverty or traditional hierarchy. It was fundamentally the product of a more modern rural society. Landlord-tenant disputes in the 1920s were roughly twice as common in the more commercialized regions of central and western Japan than in the less productive and less commercialized northeast. Dispute leaders were not the poorest tenants, but those with some prospect to gain from producing cash crops for the market. Disputes were more common where modern, city-dwelling absentee landlords were more numerous. Such disputes are evidence of a gradual shift in the social relations of rural Japan away from personal forms of interdependence toward a more impersonal economic hierarchy.

Agrarian protesters were calling in part for better terms of access to the capitalist economy. At the same time, this modern world offered not only greater opportunities than in the past but also greater dangers and fewer customary social supports. Farmers facing this situation wanted the continued respect and support of their superiors together with a measure of personal control and security. Conservative observers viewed this changing landscape of rural society as one disturbing sign of social disintegration in the modern era.

CITY LIFE: MIDDLE AND WORKING CLASSES

Just as people in the countryside filled a complex array of statuses, so those in the cities of the early twentieth century consisted of more than the wage-earning masses and their wealthy employers. The homes and shops of a vast and diverse pool of middling classes gave urban life a measure of stability and community, and much vitality.

In Tokyo in 1908, for example, the category of "merchant and tradesmen" accounted for 41 percent of all employed people.[14] A stroll through any neighborhood in a major city presented a jumble of fishmongers, rice dealers, tofu or vegetable sellers, bath-house proprietors and booksellers, barbers and hairdressers, charcoal dealers, toystore and photo shop owners, all interspersed with tens of thousands of small restaurants. In alleys behind the retail lanes, one found tens of thousands of wholesalers who distributed goods to such retailers and comparable numbers of petty manufacturers who produced goods in the back of their homes: sandal or tatami or umbrella makers, as well as tiny producers of machine parts, cast metal objects, ceramics, or foodstuffs.

These small home-based businesses were invariably family operations. Wives would work alongside husbands.[15] The more successful of these people were anchors of the community. Local businessmen sought elected roles as representatives in the ward assembly or city council. They organized trade associations to press the state for various protections such as tax relief. Beginning in the years after World War I, municipal governments enlisted thousands of these men in cities, towns, and villages throughout Japan to carry out welfare services on behalf of the state. By 1920 around ten thousand such community leaders nationwide served in this role of "district com-

The lower end of the "old middle class" in towns and cities was made up of hundreds of thousands of small family businesses, both retail and wholesale trade and small-scale manufacturing, such as this store selling dolls, photographed in 1920. Sitting in the storefront opening out into the street, the owner and his daughter wait on two customers, a mother and her daughter.
Courtesy of *Mainichi* newspaper.

missioner," making home visits to impoverished neighbors and handing out modest welfare payments.[16]

Lower level office workers and even factory laborers in major corporations could earn better wages than many of those in the middle-to-lower levels of this vast group of small business owners. But the attraction of being one's own boss was considerable. The manager at one of Japan's premier engineering firms lamented in 1908 that factory workers were uppity and restless: "Teaching them anything is like trying to teach a cat to pray." At the same time, he admitted that these people were extremely resourceful when they worked for themselves. His company often lost contracts to "shrewd workers" who pulled up the floorboards of their homes, installed a machine or two, and started in business for themselves.[17]

These millions of shopkeepers, wholesalers, petty manufacturers, and their ill-paid employees made up what historians call the "old middle class" in Japan's modern cities. This was a group with some roots in the commoner society of the Tokugawa era, although their members in the early twentieth century included former samurai as well. Around the turn of the century, observers began to identify a smaller new group emerging beside them. This was the "new middle class" of educated salaried employees of corporations and government bureaus and their families.

Traces of this social class appeared in the late nineteenth century. Since about 1890 corporations such as Mitsui and Mitsubishi had recruited future managers from universities. Some graduates of the top private and public schools began to view private sector employment as an attractive option to positions in the government bureaucracy. The numbers of vocational middle schools also increased substantially in these years. A multitiered system of recruitment came to link such schools, as well as higher schools and universities, to corporate and government employers. Gradually but steadily, the proportion of private and public sector office workers in major cities increased. In Tokyo, their numbers rose from 6 percent of those employed in 1908 to 21 percent in 1920.[18] These employees were the primary breadwinners in the "new middle class" of the twentieth century. This was a group with some antecedents in the civilianized samurai administrators of Tokugawa times. But contestants for these more numerous jobs in the early 1900s included not only the children of former samurai. The offspring of the old middle class of urban shopkeepers or manufacturers, or middling farmers in the countryside, also sought entry into the ranks of the new urban middle class.[19]

Middle-class office workers included daughters as well as sons. The first well-known case of a major corporation hiring young women for clerical positions came in 1894. The manager of the Osaka branch of the Mitsui bank was inspired by a visit to the Wannamaker department store in Philadelphia to hire several teenage girls. They had recently graduated from higher elementary school, and he put them to work in the accounting section. The practice of hiring young women to work in offices and retail sales in department stores gradually spread over the next two decades.[20]

Only a minority of city-dwellers could take much advantage of these glamorous shopping emporiums with uniformed young women at the sales counter. The poorly paid clerk was a common figure of sympathy or ridicule in social commentary of the day. One observer in 1928 specified the lower range of income for the male office worker to be 20 to 30 yen per month. By contrast, the average wage of a skilled male machinist in 1927 was 2.6 yen per day, roughly double the clerical wage. Pay for a female textile worker stood at roughly 1 yen per day, similar to that of a female typist.[21] It is thus not surprising that schoolteachers and even employees at major trading houses at the height of the inflation of World War I formed impromptu struggle groups demanding wage increases. In Tokyo such groups converged by 1919 into the Tokyo Federation of Salary Earners. In March 1920, typists working in companies in Tokyo and Yokohama likewise formed Japan's first union of female office workers. They demanded higher pay and status on a par with regular male employees.[22]

These typists were following the example of increasingly assertive factory laborers, women as well as men, who clustered in and around the growing cities in the early decades of the century. Beginning in 1916, hundreds of female textile workers began to join the Friendly Society, founded in 1912 by social reformer Suzuki Bunji. The male union leaders assumed that husbands and fathers were the primary wage earners in families. They placed these women in a separate category of "auxiliary member." In textiles and other industries the average pay for women was under half that of men. While pay for men in this era tended to rise gradually over a lifetime of factory labor, women in their forties earned barely 10 percent more than those in their twenties. At first, the women were relatively quiet about such working conditions.

This situation began to change in the mid to late 1920s. For several reasons, Japanese women joined labor actions with unprecedented vigor.

First, as the industrial economy expanded, women began to work in a greater variety of sites. They labored not only in large textile mills but also in smaller factories especially in chemical and food-processing industries. Those in smaller workplaces typically commuted from home rather than live in a dormitory. Their greater freedom of action, and closer ties to men working side by side, allowed them to join labor disputes more easily than textile workers in large mills.

Second, even among textile workers, increased numbers had completed an elementary education and were able to read the pamphlets and leaflets of the organizers. A third factor was the government's decision, in 1922, to lift the ban on female attendance and speaking at political meetings. This made union organizing and demonstrating less perilous for women. Over the following years, women joined unions and launched disputes in unprecedented numbers.

Discontent over low wages and insecure jobs prompted these actions. But in addition, a profound sense of alienation from mainstream culture motivated women workers to seek greater respect in their working lives. The writer Sata Ineko nicely evoked this spirit in a story titled "From the Caramel Factory," set in a Tokyo neighborhood in the late 1920s. The heroine, Hiroko, reluctantly takes a job at a candy factory at the urging of her alcoholic father. As she works she gazes out of the window at billboard ads for soap mounted on the roofs of houses across the river. The ads reflect sunlight all day long, while her work room receives only shade: "The sunlight [shining on the ads] seemed happy." She and her coworkers complain that "we can't even afford to buy New Years gifts." On their once-daily break, the workers are allowed outside to buy snacks in pairs. In Hiroko's eyes, the poorly clothed factory girls appear somehow deformed walking along the main street. And at the end of the day, the employees line up at the gate for a body check. Waiting in a sharp, cold wind, each woman has her kimono sleeve pocket, breast pocket, and lunch box inspected for stolen candies, and Hiroko and her friends complain bitterly of the inspector's arrogance.[23]

In the words of a female union organizer who founded the Women's Labor Academy in Tokyo in 1929, which offered classes in "proletariat economics" as well as more typically female pursuits, the chance to learn to sew and to cook was the school's great attraction. She wrote that the women "all said they just wanted to do what human beings do."[24] Women in the textile mills of Osaka and Tokyo took the lead in seeking what they viewed as "human treatment." In addition to protesting wage cuts, they were especially concerned with changing the restrictive rules of dormitory residence. At most large companies, especially in the textile industry, women were still required to live in oppressively managed company-owned dormitories. They were allowed out only to go to work and for an occasional company-sponsored outing. In major strikes involving thousands of women in the late 1920s, they won better food and greater freedom to come and go from their dorms. This was part of a struggle among some women, which reached a prewar peak at this time, to live what they called "human" lives. At base, they sought minimal freedom and respect for themselves and their contributions to their families or to their nation.

Male laborers in factories and mines used a similar language of protest. They too called for improved treatment befitting a human being and a full-fledged member of the nation. Reflecting deeply rooted assumptions about proper gender roles, their working lives followed different patterns from those of women. For this reason, they defined "human" treatment in different ways and used different methods to seek it.

In the late nineteenth century, textiles dominated the industrial economy, and women outnumbered men in the industrial labor force. Over the next several decades, growth in heavy industries that hired primarily men—shipbuilding, iron and steel, machine engineering, and metalwork—outpaced that in light industries. In 1933 the number of male industrial workers nationwide reached about 968,000, just a shade more than the female wage labor force of 933,000.[25]

While close to 50 percent of female workers were teenagers in the 1910s and 1920s, more than 80 percent of male workers were adults over age twenty. Both men and women quit their jobs frequently, but the patterns of mobility differed. A typical female factory hand might change jobs once or twice and then exit the labor force for marriage. Male workers tended to move around as part of a strategy to advance over the long term in the working world.

Many aspired to eventual independence. An anonymous machinist in 1898 left a comment that remained the motto of the so-called travelers of the early twentieth century: "A worker is someone who enters society with his skills and who travels far and wide . . . finally becoming a worker deserving of the name.[26] Uchida Tōshichi was one man who exemplified this spirit over the following decades. At the age of twenty he began working at the huge naval arsenal in Tokyo in 1908, but he believed that in order to rise in the world he needed to polish his skills. He took a second evening job in a small metal-casting shop. After two years he could turn out hibachi grills on his own. He stayed at the arsenal, but "I felt that this hibachi work was a guarantee for the future, and I kept at it, all the while buying as many of the necessary tools as I could." Eventually, in 1939, age fifty-one, Uchida opened his own metalworking factory.[27] For men in Japanese factories, this was a common career path, and an even more common aspiration.

The simple act of quitting one job for another was one form of protest against unacceptable conditions. In addition, in the years during and after World War I, many of these same men protested by joining unions and organizing strikes for higher pay or better treatment. Uchida Tōshichi was one of them. He joined Suzuki Bunji's Friendly Society (Yūaikai) in 1913, just months after its founding. As he later recalled:

> I was psychologically on the verge of exploding. The arsenal was rigidly stratified. . . . Pay raises were given twice a year, but bribes had great influence, and since I believed in a world where one depended on one's skill and was rewarded for one's efforts, I was truly discontented.[28]

By 1919, the Friendly Society boasted a seven-year history and thirty thousand members.[29] It adopted a new name, the Greater Japan Federation of Labor (Dai Nihon Rōdō Sōdōmei), and a newly militant strategy. The group officially declared itself a labor union that would consider strike actions to win its demands. That year witnessed the largest number of organized labor disputes in Japan's history, 497 strikes and another 1,891 disputes settled short of a strike. Together these actions involved 335,000 working people, the great majority of whom were men.[30]

Over the next decade, many other unions formed as well. Some supported revolutionary politics and on occasion built ties to the fledgling Japan Communist Party. Others, including the Japan Federation of Labor, sought to raise the status of working people within the capitalist system. Strikes remained frequent throughout the decade, and they gradually spread to smaller workshops as well as large factories. At their prewar peak in 1931, labor unions enrolled roughly 8 percent of the industrial work force (369,000 members).[31]

At first glance, this is a modest proportion. But one must keep several points in mind while judging its significance. Unions had no legal protection. This meant that joining a union was a very risky decision. A worker fired for union activity had no legal recourse. In addition, because turnover among members was high and many strikes took place even in the absence of unions, the number of men and women who gained some experience of unions or strikes was far higher than the official membership at any one moment. Rates of union membership in most nations with similar legal contexts at similar stages of industrialization were comparable.[32]

Corporate owners and managers in the 1920s came to view the high mobility of skilled workers as a major cost. They were also alarmed at the spread of organizing and strikes. They responded with policies to both combat unions and retain valuable skilled men. Looking to Western models, they set up in-house "factory councils" as forums for the exchange of views, which might drain support away from independent unions. They began to offer in-house training programs for favored male workers. They made nonbinding promises of long-term job security to these trainees. They also began setting up health clinics and savings plans (sometimes these were compulsory savings programs). They started to offer bonuses and pay raises every six months on a regular basis to skilled loyal men.

Workers responded in a variety of ways. Facing a weak job market for much of the 1920s, some abandoned the ideal of the "traveler" and clung to a job at a single company. To win the favor of bosses, especially in larger factories that offered more generous new benefits, these men often turned their backs on unions and supported factory councils instead. But other workers were less impressed or reticent. They insisted that bosses match words with deeds. As one historian has noted, they demanded the "right to benevolence."[33] Even at times of business depression in the 1920s and early 1930s, some launched strategically dubious strikes to demand that a company honor its promise of paternal care by revoking dismissals. Others went on strike to insist on regular semiannual pay raises for all workers, and not just a favored few. Much like British workers who laid claim to "the rights of a freeborn Englishman," these Japanese workers insisted that "we are all equal before the emperor." They called for "human treatment" befitting a Japanese subject.

Some employers replied harshly that "while we sympathize with your plight, we cannot take responsibility for your poverty."[34] Others agreed to improve severance pay or implement a more systematic program of seniority-linked raises. By the end of the decade, although it was often betrayed in practice, the expectation had begun to take root that a good employer offered a long-term job and predictable pay increases to loyal male workers.

Two other social groups on the margins of urban society struggled to make a living and win some dignity in these years. Beginning around the turn of century, small numbers of Koreans migrated to Japan in search of jobs. By 1910, when Japan annexed Korea as a colony, about twenty-five hundred Koreans lived in Japan, mainly in Osaka and Tokyo. Migration increased sharply over the next decades. By 1930, the Korean population numbered around 419,000. The immigrants tended to live in run-down slums, taking dangerous and ill-paying jobs such as construction work, coal mining, and menial labor in rubber, glass, and dyed-goods production.

The Koreans, like ethnic immigrants the world over, were greeted with racism and discrimination. The Japanese tended to explain their poverty with stereotyped assumptions that the immigrants were lazy or stupid. Working-class Japanese who were themselves struggling to get by were especially resentful of job competition from these newcomers. These prejudices boiled over with tragic consequences in the wake of the 1923 Kantō earthquake. Within hours of the earthquake, rumors began to spread: Koreans and socialists had started the fires; they had poisoned the wells; they were planning rebellion. Encouraged by the authorities, residents throughout the region organized nearly three thousand vigilante groups. Their stated goal was to keep order in devastated neighborhoods and protect property from looters as well as rebellious Koreans or leftists. But some groups turned violent. They forced passers-by to speak a few simple phrases and then murdered those believed to have Korean or Chinese accents. The press, the police, and the military fueled the hysteria. One paper reported that "Koreans and socialists are planning a rebellious and treasonous plot. We urge the citizens to cooperate with the military and police to guard against the Koreans." Police and military troops themselves rounded up and murdered several hundred Koreans in at least two incidents in Tokyo. No precise death toll can be compiled, but the massacre took between three thousand and six thousand lives.[35]

The other important group that reacted with new militance to discrimination were the former outcastes, now called *burakumin*. These were the descendants of Edo era outcaste communities who had been officially liberated with the reforms of the 1870s. About half a million in number, they continued to face both official and unofficial discrimination. They clustered in urban and rural neighborhoods throughout Japan. The largest numbers lived in and around Kyoto and Osaka. As in the past, they worked in occupations associated with the slaughter of cattle and marked as polluted in Buddhist thinking: leatherwork, shoemaking, meatpacking, and meatselling.

But in a new departure, they began to organize to improve their lot. Around 1900 young male *burakumin* founded a number of moderate self-help organizations. They argued that by seeking education and working hard, *burakumin* could win acceptance by the mainstream society. Such efforts bore little fruit. In 1922 a more militant spirit led to the founding of the Levellers Association (Suiheisha). Members would confront and denounce those accused of discriminatory practices. They threatened and sometimes resorted to violence. The government responded with close surveillance and occasional crackdowns.

CULTURAL RESPONSES TO SOCIAL CHANGE

Few Japanese were much troubled by the plight of these minorities. Indeed, in a noteworthy contrast to the economic uncertainty of the era, a new exuberance marked cultural life not only in the booming 1910s but throughout the 1920s. New products

and possibilities for consumption sparked dreams of a modern life, whose bywords
were "rationality" "science" and "culture" and whose favored adjectives were "bright"
and "new." The department store, with its enticing array of consumer goods, emerged
in these years as one emblem of the "bright new life." Under one roof, together with
restaurants and exhibit halls for art or music shows, customers found the finest domestic and imported products: clothing and cosmetics, footwear, fancy foodstuffs,
furniture, lacquerware and ceramicware, and toys.[36] Many department stores were built
at major train terminals by new commuter rail companies that brought people into the
city from the expanding environs of Tokyo or Osaka. These department stores promoted and celebrated a new way to enjoy the fruits of one's labor, especially for
families whose husbands worked in salaried middle-class jobs.[37]

Such a family might take a commuter train to such a store from its home in a
newly founded "garden city" on the edge of Tokyo. Its dwelling would be called a
"cultural home" and typically boast a Western-style sitting room. A family excursion
to the Ginza shopping district on a Sunday would feature window shopping and perhaps the purchase of the latest style in ready-to-wear dress at Mitsui's pioneering
Mitsukoshi department store. Shoppers would take a break in a coffee shop or beer
hall, two other urban innovations of the early twentieth century. They might end the
day by dining in an elegant Western-style restaurant. A new term was coined for this
modern leisure, *Gin-bura*, loosely translatable as "Ginza cruising."

The flowering of new terminology for Japanese modern life reflects the excitement
of the era. An Edo era expression, *koshi-ben*, was one of the earliest labels for the
emerging middle class. The term literally refers to the lunch-box (*bentō*) that Edo
samurai would attach to their clothes at the waist (*koshi*). In the late nineteenth century,
it referred to an office worker in Western clothes making his way to work with his
lunch-box in hand. A new term, *sarariiman* (salary-man) then appeared in cartoons
of the 1910s titled "salary-man heaven" and "salary-man hell." These lampooned the
difficult life of the middle manager, whose workplace pressures and modest salary
undermined the promise of his social status as a modern city-dweller.[38] Through the
1920s "salary-man" coexisted with numerous other expressions such as "intellectual
class," "new middle class," the more colloquial "brain worker," and the familiar
"lunch-box class."[39] By the end of the decade, this jumble of terms had been sorted
out. *Sarariiman* became the most common label for a city-dwelling man of the middle
class. He had a middling to higher education, worked for the government or a private
company, and owed his job to these credentials.

Department stores, garden city suburbs, and a newly standardized terminology for
the middle class were part of a broader political, social, and cultural flowering of the
1910s and 1920s. Hollywood and Japanese movies began to draw huge audiences to
hundreds of theaters nationwide. The record player and jazz music enjoyed huge
popularity as well.

Some of the most interesting new cultural trends concerned women. In the 1910s
and early 1920s, an impassioned debate took place in the pages of magazines and
newspapers over the so-called new woman. Contributors included many women who
soon became prominent as writers of poetry, prose fiction, and essays. They addressed
serious topics such as women's education and political roles, their rights in the family
and workplace, and control over their sexuality. But in reporting this debate, the main-

Movie moguls entertain Charlie Chaplin with sushi and sake in Tokyo in May 1932. Chaplin is on the far right. Next to Chaplin is a famous Tokyo geisha, Ichimaru, holding the daughter of film producer Kido Shiro (third from right) in her lap. Chaplin had been a huge star in Japan for years. His visit drew attention, but it was overshadowed by the assassination of Japan's prime minister, Inukai Tsuyoshi, which took place during his stay.
Courtesy of Mrs. Kimie Sakomoto.

stream press devoted greatest attention to the private lives of these women, above all their reportedly scandalous, promiscuous sexual adventures.[40]

This treatment reflected uneasiness at challenges to prevailing ideas about gender roles. Unease continued in the excited discussion, mainly by male writers, of the figure identified as the "modern girl" (*modan gaaru*, sometimes abbreviated *moga*). She embodied the exhilaration of Japanese modern times and captured much popular attention from about 1925 through the early 1930s. The modern girl was said to be something new in Japan. She was a stylish follower of fashion, proud of her new slim look. One essay praising her liberated behavior ended with the exclamation "Onward! Dance! Legs! Legs! Legs!" Positive treatments of this figure praised her for puncturing the hypocrisy of a world where only men enjoyed economic independence and sexual as well as political freedom. Now, it was said, modern girls might enjoy all three, as they worked in urban offices, supported political rights for women, and sought out male companions.[41]

The modern girl was celebrated and feared mainly for her new sexuality. The modern boy was most notorious for a new political radicalism. In 1918, a small group of students in Tokyo University's Law Faculty organized the New Man Society (Shinjinkai). From this base in the citadel of the establishment, they built the most influential student political group of the prewar era. Similar groups were founded at many other universities as well. The student movement began with relatively moderate calls for democratic reforms. By the mid-1920s, the New Man Society had moved to a Marxist-Leninist stand that sought economic and social equality and a political revolution.[42] With a slogan of "To the People," inspired by the Russian Revolution, members joined organizing movements of wage laborers and tenant farmers.

Inseparable from the new enthusiasm for middle classes, cultural homes and de-

Stylish "modern girls" striding briskly along the streets of Tokyo in 1930. These women, and their flamboyant images in cartoons, literature, and photographs, exemplified a spirit of sexual liberation that was threatening to some, exhilarating to others.
Courtesy of *Mainichi* newspaper.

partment stores, movies and jazz, and modern girls and Marxist boys was a new anxiety. The other side of the glittering coin of modern life was a gloomy discourse of impoverishment, struggle, and social disorder. As the middle class expanded in the 1900s and 1910s, so did the number of schools offering promise of entry. Even an educated person's access to this world was not secure. Office workers were laid off en masse during periodic economic slumps. Even in good times such as the economic boom sparked by World War I, a new urgency marked discussions of middle-class life. Newspapers published laments such as this one, a 1918 letter to the editor by an elementary schoolteacher supporting a family of five. After listing monthly expenses that totaled 20.75 yen, the author asserts:

> [M]y monthly income after deductions . . . is 18 yen and change. Even 20 yen are not enough. How can we live on 18? There's no choice but to cut our rice costs a little by mixing in barley, more than 50 percent, and once a day making a meal of barley-rice gruel. Because charcoal is expensive, no one in the family has taken a bath for over a month, and we can hardly afford a cup of sake, or a few pieces of meat, or even a single potato. To buy a new kimono is out of the question. Is there anything so pitiful as the life of an elementary school teacher who cannot afford to dress his child in a New Year kimono or even eat *mochi*?[43]

Such a struggling schoolteacher would have been called "a Western-clothes pauper" (*yōfuku saimin*). This ironic and self-contradictory term came into widespread use in the early 1900s. Those who wore Western clothes (*yōfuku*) were supposed to be secure, educated members of the upper stratum of the new Japan. The slums of the urban paupers were supposed to be worlds removed. The expression signaled that even those with credentials to join middle-class society faced lives of uncertainty and insufficient earnings.[44] No less a figure than the Seiyūkai party president, Hara Kei, recorded a lament of his own in 1910 that "if people like teachers and policemen take even one false step, they might become socialists, so there is need to pay most attention to their treatment."[45]

Even more worrisome sources of potential unrest and radicalism were the increasingly militant organized factory workers. In the words of one leading bureaucrat in 1925, the state should not support unions because "just as a cart cannot stop rolling down a hill," a union would never stop at a moderate position.[46] A policeman sat on the side of the stage at every labor gathering. If a speaker crossed the boundaries of authorized discourse—by uttering words such as "revolution" or "capitalism" or "destroy"—he would first be warned and then halted, and perhaps arrested. These contests between police and speakers added some entertainment value to union rallies, but they imposed serious restrictions as well.

Youth in general, and young women in particular, were another lightning rod for the fears of modernity run rampant. Even as some celebrated the jaunty figure of the modern girl, others worried that she signaled the onset of far-reaching social decay. They feared that liberated women, perhaps even more than angry schoolteachers or militant laborers, might upset the established order of society and weaken the Japanese state. Anxious press reports described modern girls and boys as part of a communist conspiracy to weaken the nation by turning privileged youths into degenerate hedonists. They worried that the rise of divorces initiated by women would destroy the family system. In 1925 the press described a short-haired, Western-dressed woman accused of murdering a foreigner as a "vanguard *moga*."[47] Such labeling suggested that the modern girl, in particular, was un-Japanese and even criminal.

A surge of interest in so-called new religions is a further cultural manifestation of the strivings and fears of Japanese people in the early decades of the twentieth century. These religions tended to be offshoots of mainstream Shinto sects more than Buddhist groups. They were founded by charismatic men or women who typically presented themselves to believers as living gods. Some of them were brand new, others had been founded in the nineteenth century. At their peak in the mid-1930s, these "new religions" claimed several million adherents. They drew most support from people in cities and more commercialized or industrialized rural locales. Many believers were recent migrants to towns and cities who sought a new source of community and spiritual support. More than mainstream Buddhist sects or state-supported Shinto, these groups offered practical and concrete help. They promised to heal illness and help members overcome economic troubles and other personal problems. Records left by converts testify that these religions solved problems ranging from marital disputes to bedwetting.[48]

New religions might have offered spiritual and material support to members, but state officials viewed them as threats. Officials in the Home Ministry, the same body charged to oversee labor and other social problems, labeled them "pseudo-religions" or "evil cults." In the 1920s they suppressed several of these groups by arresting their leaders. They charged and convicted some of the serious crime of lèse-majesté (slandering the emperor).[49] But the religions themselves were not dissolved. They continued to thrive into the 1930s.

All these debates over the direction of social change and the character of modern Japanese life took place in burgeoning mass media. Magazines proliferated and circulation grew dramatically. The greatest of these was Kodansha's *Kingu* magazine. Based on the *Saturday Evening Post, Kingu* premiered in December 1924, selling 740,000 copies.[50] By November 1928, circulation had grown to 1.5 million. Magazines specifically aimed at women readers proved as popular as the general (male-oriented) publications. The start of radio broadcasting in 1925 gradually spread new cultural forms, jazz and dramas—as well as official government messages—to wider audiences throughout Japan. Between 1926 and 1930, the number of radios in Japan rose from 360,000 to 1.4 million.[51]

Works of literature, often serialized in magazines and newspapers, enjoyed growing audiences. Strongly influenced by Western literature since the Meiji period, Japanese authors had experimented with various schools of writing, including romanticism and naturalism. By the 1920s, most writers had moved beyond these schools to explore different styles. The predominant style of the time was the "I-novel," which tended to be a nearly autobiographical, confessional work that attempted to re-create the psyche of the author. Two new movements, however, moved away from this sort of fiction: the New Sensationalist school, which was the first clearly modernist writing in Japan, and the Proletarian school, which stressed the social role of writers.

The writers from this period whose work has proved most enduring, however, were not strict adherents to any school. Akutagawa Ryūnosuke (1892–1927) wrote powerful and sometimes fantastic works. He often turned to classical Japanese literature, rather than the latest European trends, for inspiration. "In a Grove," his refashioning of a twelfth-century story, became the basis for the famous film *Rashōmon*. Tanizaki Jun'ichirō (1886–1965) explored human sexuality unabashedly, while simultaneously undermining the narrative reliability that I-novels demanded.

The growing popularity of literature, both Japanese and translated works, was reflected in the spread of "one yen books," which ushered in the mass production of literature in Japan. In 1926 the publishing company Kaizōsha began publishing its sixty-three-volume series, *Collected Works of Contemporary Japanese Literature*. Overnight, writers whose works were included in these collections became wealthy. The profession of writing became more commercial as the rewards available to a successful writer grew tremendously. The series also made literature a cultural commodity available to a much larger segment of the Japanese population, including the diverse middle class, new and old.

Few of the social divisions and cultural trends of the early twentieth century were brand new. The Tokugawa era countryside had been filled with rich and poor farmers and many between. Tokugawa cities housed samurai clerks and constables, as well as commoner tradesmen, storekeepers, and back-alley manufacturers. Literature and the arts had flourished, and commercial publishing had appeared. Country folk and city-dwellers of the modern 1910s and 1920s sometimes made sense of their world with the language of this past. Footloose factory laborers described themselves with the Edo era term for "traveling artisans." Office clerks were rendered as Edo era *koshiben*.

But some things were new. In Japan as elsewhere, modern times differed from past eras. Both the economic opportunities and insecurities of life in a capitalist society were greater than in Tokugawa days. The market was less buffered than before by the "benevolence" of the state or local elites. Nearly universal literacy was achieved by the turn of the century. More people than ever could take some part in a larger public life and identify with a larger national and global community of imperialist powers. Expanded access to the modern media divided as well as united. Hand-wringing accounts of "modern girls" or Marxist students and chronic reports of labor or farmer protests raised awareness of tensions within the nation. Some of these social and cultural clashes reflected anxiety at the loss of an older community and a desire to recover it.[52] Farmers and workers pushed those with wealth and power to continue customary forms of benevolent care. But they had begun to claim benevolence as a "right." They were using a new, modern language of politics and culture. They were arguing less about sustaining old traditions than about defining new ones.

10

Democracy and Empire between the World Wars

The Taishō emperor, Yoshihito, took the throne in 1912 upon the death of his father, the Meiji emperor, at the age of thirty-three. He had suffered a childhood bout with meningitis. Although he recovered well enough to make numerous official tours around the country as Crown Prince, his health began to fail in 1918. By 1919 he was unable to perform his official duties. This was a time when European monarchs were falling from power one after another: the Russian czar in 1917 and the kings and emperors of Germany, Austria, and Turkey as well. This was also a time of political turbulence in Japan. Fearful palace officials felt a desperate need for a presentable imperial figure. They arranged, in essence, a forced retirement for Yoshihito. They elevated his son, the Crown Prince Hirohito, to the office of regent in 1921, and the Crown Prince presided at imperial functions in his father's place until the Taishō emperor died in 1926.

The era of rule by the Taishō emperor was thus briefer than the preceding Meiji reign, and the manner of Yoshihito's retirement spread a belief that the Taishō emperor had always been sickly and mentally disturbed. The brilliant intellectual historian Maruyama Masao recalled that he and his elementary schoolmates in 1921 would whisper about rumors of strange behavior. The emperor, it was said, had once rolled up the text of his proclamation to open a session of the Diet, and used it like a telescope to peer at the assembled dignitaries.[1] True or not, this story and the image of Taishō as a feeble monarch has persisted.

Despite these facts, his name has ironically come to refer to a spirit of liberalism associated with his reign. Historians conventionally speak of the years from 1905 through 1932 as the time of "Taishō democracy." The period begins with the political agitation of 1905 protesting the treaty that ended the Russo-Japanese War and ends with the fall of the Seiyūkai party cabinet in 1932. This era can also be described with a term that appears contradictory at first glance: "imperial democracy." Political rule by elected politicians who formed cabinets run by party members began to take hold in the Taishō era. This was a dramatic change in the direction of democracy. But one finds continuity as well in the fact that all prominent advocates of parliamentary rule, like the Meiji era oligarchs and their supporters in the military and the bureaucracy, were vociferous imperial loyalists. They were equally vociferous in their support for empire. In prewar Japan as in Britain or Holland, supporters of a more democratic political order believed that loyalty to a monarch, pursuit of empire, and popular participation in politics were mutually compatible, indeed reinforcing. Only in retrospect, and judged by the standards of a later age, do these goals appear contradictory.

THE EMERGENCE OF PARTY CABINETS

After the tumult of the Taishō political crisis of 1913 described in Chapter 8, Admiral Yamamoto Gonnohyōe ruled as prime minister in alliance with the Seiyūkai party for just one year. A major scandal forced him from office in early 1914. Top navy brass had taken kickbacks from Germany's Siemens corporation and bought German arms in exchange. In a replay of the upheavals one year before, rallies and riots greeted this revelation. One excited streetcorner orator got himself in trouble when he shouted to group assembled in the city center, "Yamamoto is a great thief! Overthrow Yamamomoto! We must sever Gonnohyōe's head from his body." This middle-aged tailor was a former popular rights activist. He was arrested and charged with incitement to riot, and he explained his motives to the judge this way: "Because it was the will of the people, I had no choice."[2]

The force of such popular indictments was powerful. Yamamoto resigned in disgrace over the scandal. From 1914 to 1916, the former government leader and popular rights activist Ōkuma Shigenobu made a political comeback. He served as prime minister with support from the recently formed Dōshikai party. But party men themselves only held five cabinet posts, and Ōkuma's policies deferred to the long-standing agenda of military men, especially Yamagata Aritomo and Katsura Tarō. They finally won funding for two new divisions, the very request that had sparked the Taishō political crisis. Ōkuma then came under attack from the oligarchs in 1916–17 for his handling of foreign policy, epitomized in the Twenty-One Demands addressed to China (discussed later). A Chōshū general, Terauchi Masatake, replaced him as prime minister. Terauchi's cabinet was nominally nonpartisan, but it actually worked closely with Hara Kei and the Seiyūkai.

In this fashion, between 1913 and 1918 the leaders of these two parties continued their political strategy of the previous decade, by which Diet representatives sought power through negotiations, compromise, and alliance with bureaucrats and military men. They were backed by considerable popular enthusiasm for parliamentary rule, which many observers now saw as the essence of constitutional government.

In 1918 Yamagata Aritomo was first among equals in the tiny clique of elder statesmen who made key political decisions in the emperor's name, including the designation of each prime minister. That summer, at the peak of the wartime inflation, the price of rice had doubled from the previous year. A wave of violent attacks on rice merchants and the government broke out nationwide. Yamagata was an austere man not given to displays of emotion or fear. But he was terribly upset by the riots. He decided he had to turn to the career party leader, Hara Kei, as the only man who could calm the situation.

In September 1918, Hara formed a cabinet composed almost entirely of party members (the exceptions were the army, navy, and foreign ministers). This was the first stable and effective party government in Japan's history. The Seiyūkai remained in power for nearly four years. When Hara acted swiftly and harshly to put down a steel strike with government troops in 1920, even Yamagata put his lifelong distaste for politicians aside and exclaimed: "Hara is truly remarkable! The streetcars and steel mills have settled down. Hara's policies are remarkable."[3] Hara himself fell victim to an assassin in November 1921, but the oligarchs agreed to install his finance minister, Takahashi Korekiyo, as the new Prime Minister, and Seiyūkai rule continued another six months.

The rise to power of Hara and his Seiyūkai party completed a two-decade process, marked by crisis and riot as well as backroom maneuvering, which now placed political parties and their elected representatives at the center and near the top of the political system. But it is important to note that the practice of selecting party leaders to form cabinets was still not firmly established. Takahashi proved unable to contain factional struggles within his party, and in 1922 he resigned as prime minister. Yamagata had just died. Over the following two years, the three surviving oligarchs returned to the practice of selecting nonparty prime ministers. In quick succession, they named two navy men and the president of the Privy Council to form suprapartisan, so-called transcendental cabinets with relatively weak ties to political parties. Katō Tomosaburō, who died in 1923, was followed by former Prime Minister Yamamoto Gonnohyōe, and then Kiyoura Keigo. Kiyoura filled his cabinet almost entirely with members of the House of Peers rather than the House of Representatives.

This challenge led most party leaders to put aside their factional bickering after a fashion, although one group of politicians split off from the Seiyūkai to form a third party that supported Kiyoura's actions. In 1924 the mainstream of the Seiyūkai joined the Kenseikai and another small party called the Reform Club to launch a series of rallies that called for a return to "normal constitutional government" (the Kenseikai had been formed in 1916 in a reorganization of the Dōshikai party). These parties together backed their campaign for "constitutional government" by threatening to refuse cooperation with a cabinet not comprised of elected parliamentarians.

The press and the public were not as enthusiastic in support of this drive for party rule as it had been in the 'teens, especially during the Taishō political crisis. Even so, the three parties calling for "constitutional government" won a firm majority in the Diet election of 1924. The Kenseikai party won a plurality of seats for the first time ever. As a result, Kiyoura stepped down, and in June 1924 a three-party coalition cabinet took office. The prime minister was Katō Kōmei, president of the Kenseikai party. His party dominated the coalition. Katō had impeccable elite credentials. He had briefly served in the Foreign Ministry after graduating from Tokyo Imperial University. His wife was the eldest daughter of Iwasaki Yatarō, the founder of the Mitsubishi zaibatsu. He had spent time in England as a youth and had come to see parliamentary government as the way to secure Japan's future power and stability.

The partners to this coalition were the Seiyūkai and Kenseikai (Constitutional Politics Association) and the Reform Club. In 1927 the Kenseikai absorbed some defectors from the Seiyūkai and changed its name to Minseitō (People's Politics Party). As the name suggests, by the mid-1920s the Kenseikai/Minseitō party had staked out a political position slightly to the liberal side of the Seiyūkai. It supported measures such as expanded suffrage as the best way to ensure social order. In 1925 a factional conflict broke up this brief coalition government, and Katō continued in office by forming a solely Kenseikai cabinet. Party cabinets then alternated in regular succession until 1932.

The ascendance of party government was remarkable. The elitist authors of the Meiji constitution had certainly not expected it. They had intended for the Diet to play a limited role on the sidelines of politics when they wrote that document in the late 1880s. Just thirty years later, in 1918, elected Diet politicians had moved from outsiders seeking to gain a share of power to insiders exercising executive power in consultation with bureaucrats. This unexpected outcome was a result of nation-building policies of the nineteenth century. The Meiji reforms had promoted a widespread belief that common people were members of the nation whose will should be respected. Such beliefs sparked men like the tailor who literally called for Prime Minister Yamamoto's head to speak on behalf of "the people's will." During the 'teens in particular, masses of Japanese people enthusiastically demanded "constitutional government." By this, they meant rule by a prime minister and cabinets comprised of elected parliamentary representatives.

By the mid-1920s, this demand was met. But considerable irony and uncertainty marked this political evolution. As the parties came to power, they compromised and

TABLE 10.1 Party Cabinets, 1918–32

Year	Prime Minister	Party in Power
1918–21	Hara Kei (Takashi) (9/29/18–11/13/21)	Seiyūkai
1921–22	Takahashi Korekiyo (11/13/21–6/12/22)	Seiyūkai
1922–23	Katō Tomosaburô (6/12/22–9/2/23)	Transcendental (nonparty) cabinet: Katō formed a cabinet composed mainly of bureaucrats and members of the House of Peers
1923–24	Yamamoto Gonnohyōe (9/2/23–1/7/24)	Transcendental cabinet
1924	Kiyoura Keigo (1/7/24–6/11/24)	Transcendental cabinet
1924–26	Katō Kōmei (Takaaki) (6/11/24–1/30/26)	Three-party coalition cabinet (Kenseikai, Seiyūkai, Reform Club)
1926–27	Wakatsuki Reijirō (1/30/26–4/20/27)	Kenseikai
1927–29	Tanaka Giichi (4/20/27–7/2/29)	Seiyūkai
1929–31	Hamaguchi Osachi (7/2/29–4/14/31)	Minseitō
1931	Wakatsuki Reijirō (4/14/31–12/13/31)	Minseitō
1931–32	Inukai Tsuyoshi (12/13/31–5/26/32)	Seiyūkai

cooperated with nonparty elites. Some idealistic politicians, many in the press and in universities, and many in the general population criticized the parties for betraying the people as they rose to power.

THE STRUCTURE OF PARLIAMENTARY GOVERNMENT

The political structure put in place by the Meiji constitution virtually assured that parliamentary government would be a hybrid product of willing compromise between party leaders and nonparty elites. First and foremost, the constitution enshrined the emperor as both sacred and sovereign. The emperor's precious body was literally untouchable—his aides and physicians used gloves whenever they came in contact with him.[4] The Meiji emperor (Mutsuhito), his son the Taishō emperor, and his grandson, Hirohito, all believed they had active roles to play as a monarch at the apex of the constitutional order. As Crown Prince, Hirohito had served an apprenticeship as de facto monarch, serving as imperial regent during the years of his father's illness from 1921 to 1926. After the Taishō emperor's death, he took office immediately, although the grand enthronement ceremony was held in 1928.

Emperor Hirohito's reign was given the era name of Shōwa. This reign name can be translated as Shining Peace, certainly ironic in retrospect since Hirohito was to reign through war as well as peace until his death in 1989. His carefully monitored education, undertaken in the awareness that he might ascend to the throne as a very young man, made him well aware of his duties as monarch under Japan's imperially centered constitution.[5] Following British practice, he was briefed regularly by his ministers throughout his life. He believed that the monarch had a responsibility to indicate his views to these ministers. His opinions could have major political consequences. In 1927–28, for example, Hirohito became upset with Prime Minister Tanaka's handling of several instances of Japanese military intervention in China. He personally reprimanded Tanaka, an act that forced the prime minister to resign his post.[6]

Another structural feature related to the emperor's powers was the fact that neither the military nor the bureaucracy bore any formal accountability to the parliament. The constitution set forth the emperor's direct right to supreme command of the military. Military leaders could take this clause as a license to act independently of the prime minister. Bureaucrats were also insulated from the parliament in an important formal sense. Although the laws they wrote and the budgets they designed had to be ratified by the Diet, they did not owe their jobs to the parliament. They served as appointees of the emperor.

Two other formal bodies bolstered the power of the imperial state in relation to the parliament and popular forces. The Privy Council was a body of fourteen members with extraordinary legal powers. It had been established in 1889 by imperial order as the group that would formally approve the Meiji constitution. It continued in existence under the new national charter. It met in secret session, sometimes with the emperor present, to advise the emperor on matters such as interpreting the constitution or other laws, analyzing the budget, or ratifying international treaties. Its very conservative members were appointed for life by the emperor and included former oligarchs such as Itō Hirobumi, Kuroda Kiyotaka, and Yamagata Aritomo. In the 1920s, in particular, the council often found itself at odds with decisions of party cabinets and successfully rejected some government decisions. In similar fashion, the House of Peers served as a bastion of emperor-centered authoritarian politics. Membership was either hereditary or derived from imperial appointment. On several occasions, the Peers proved able and anxious to obstruct major initiatives of party governments.

One key *informal* piece of the political structure of the era from the 1890s through World War II was that group of men called the oligarchs or elder statesmen (*genrō*). Like the Peers and the Privy Council (and overlapping in members with both), the oligarchs helped to ensure that party rulers did not contradict the wishes of nonparty elites. Their most important responsibility, which evolved by custom and not law from the 1890s onward, was to advise the emperor (and in essence decide) on the choice of prime minister. By 1918 the original group of seven Meiji oligarchs had dwindled to Yamagata Aritomo and Matsukata Masayoshi. They added two more men to their informal club: Saionji Kimmochi, the former prime minister of noble pedigree, and Makino Nobuaki, a veteran cabinet minister and diplomat with close ties to the imperial court. The final oligarch (Saionji Kimmochi) withdrew from an active political role in the early 1930s because of old age (he was eighty-one in 1930) and the increasing influence of the military. A group known as "senior statesmen" (*jūshin*) came to replace the oligarchs. Membership was routinized by custom to include all living former prime ministers.

Although the oligarchs and their successors regularly appointed party leaders as prime minister between 1924 and 1932, they did not necessarily appoint the head of the *majority* party. In fact, the oligarchs asked the leader of the Diet's largest party to form a new government on just two occasions. In 1918 the Seiyūkai already held a majority when Yamagata turned to its president, Hara Kei, to form a cabinet. In 1924 after the Kenseikai won a plurality at the polls, Prince Saionji tapped its president, Katō Kōmei, to form a coalition party government. But during the next eight years of uninterrupted party rule, power shifted between the Kenseikai/Minseitō and the Seiyūkai in the reverse fashion. On three occasions (1927, 1929, 1931) the senior statesmen led by Saionji appointed the leader of the *minority* opposition party as prime minister because of a perceived failure of the incumbent majority party. Each time, the new prime minister *then* called an election, and his party won a majority in the House of Representatives. He was helped by his control of the Home Ministry, the agency that ran the police and supervised elections. Japan's voters in this way ratified changes of government after the fact, but did not bring them about.

Another informal factor that compromised parliamentary government was the undercurrent of political terror that periodically erupted to the surface. One American journalist called this "government by assassination."[7] Its peak was to come in the 1930s. But even in the 1920s, Prime Minister Hara Kei was assassinated, and a failed attempt on the life of Hirohito himself took place in 1923 when he was Prince Regent. Hara's nineteen-year-old assassin acted out of anger at several political scandals involving Hara and his party. He claimed that Hara's cabinet ignored the good of the people while seeking only the party's well-being. Hirohito's attacker was a leftist seeking to avenge the 1911 execution of socialist Kōtoku Shusui. Such attacks intimidated future party leaders, and public opinion often praised the purity of the attacker's motives, which contrasted to the unseemly deal-making of party leaders. Political violence thus undermined the legitimacy of parliamentary rule.

IDEOLOGICAL CHALLENGES

Such acts grew in part from a political tradition in which righteous men hoping to spark revolutionary change would take violent steps to impose their vision of divine justice. This had been the ethos of the swashbuckling loyalists of the late Tokugawa years. In later decades such visions of change sparked by political violence were promoted by various secretive political groups such as the Black River Society, founded in 1901 by an extreme imperial loyalist named Uchida Ryōhei. For four decades Uchida pushed for expansion on the mainland and reform at home to bolster patriarchy and the glory of imperial rule. He attacked both the weakness of the oligarchs and the democratic ideas of party leaders and liberals.

Kita Ikki was probably the most influential intellectual to promote a radical nationalist vision that would later inspire political terror. In 1923 he articulated his stance in *An Outline Plan for the Reorganization of Japan*. He shared the imperial loyalism of Uchida, while supporting the goal of economic leveling of the political left. He called on a vanguard of young military officers and civilians to seize power, suspend the constitution, and remake the political structure to unite the emperor and the people. He expected these leaders to reorder the economy as well. They would respect private property but redistribute wealth and manage growth through a set of "production ministries." Kita would have returned land to tenant farmers and shared profit with factory workers, but he insisted that women remain "mothers and wives of the people." In the 1920s dozens of organizations sprung up devoted in some measure to Kita's program of emperor-centered, anti-party reform at home and expansion abroad.

Even more threatening in the eyes of both party rulers and nonparty elites were the varied, energetic left-wing movements that mushroomed from the time of the Russian Revolution through the early 1930s. Socialism, feminism, and labor protests had emerged to trouble Japan's rulers as early as the turn of the century (as described in Chapter 8). But the combination of the deepening reach of capitalism, the spread of education and political idealism, and in particular the rise to power of the communist regime in the Russian Revolution of 1917 inspired Japanese critics of inequality and poverty in their own society to undertake more forceful and widespread activities. They were moved by similar grievances and divided by similar tactical and ideological arguments as leftists the world over. Some, such as Ōsugi Sakae, had begun their activism in the socialist movement of the early 1900s. He survived the treason incident that led to the execution of several colleagues in 1911 because he was already in jail. By the early 1920s, Ōsugi had become a leading advocate of anarchism. He called for a freer, more egalitarian society to be brought about by direct actions such as strikes and attacks on the authorities.

Other activists of a new generation, such as Yamakawa Hitoshi and Arahata Kanson, envisioned a communist revolution that would be led by a vanguard party, following the example of the Russian Bolsheviks. They joined to found the Japan Communist Party (JCP) in 1922, with support from the Soviet Union's international arm, the Comintern. Yamakawa called for organizing of the masses through a united front with the noncommunist left. Rivals such as Fukumoto Kazuo stressed a more sectarian approach by which the JCP would act alone or work secretly through front organizations. The party was never legal before 1945, so a reliable count of members is not possible, but adherents perhaps numbered in the low thousands by the late 1920s.

The university graduates who dominated these small groups began to build bridges to labor unions in the 1920s and cultivate a larger base of support. Japan's first May Day celebration took place in 1920, replete with red flags and banners calling for the liberation of the working class. In the following years, it was common for thousands to attend union rallies during strikes or on May Day. Speakers not only demanded pay raises and better conditions but also quoted Lenin. They flamboyantly claimed "the labor movement must move to end the plunder of capitalists" and "destroy entirely the existing social order."[8] The police, who sat on the edge of the stage at every political meeting in prewar Japan, regularly halted speeches or broke up meetings when they heard such statements.

A new wave of feminist ideas was at least as threatening to the ruling elites of the 1910s and 1920s. In the feminist writing of this era, women in Japan were typ-

Speaker arrested at 1926 May Day rally. These annual celebrations of the labor movement were closely monitored by authorities. Those in attendance understood they were engaged in a risky activity on the margins of the law.
Courtesy of Ohara Institute of Social Research.

ically described as "caged birds" or "fragile flowers." How, then, to open the cage or protect the flower? Some feminists, such as Hiratsuka Raichō and Takamure Itsue, developed a line of thinking that has been called "woman-centered feminism." They continued the arguments of earlier women's advocates in calling for special protection for women because of their special role as mothers. Takamure was a particularly independent voice. She called for local institutions to provide community care for mothers. She condemned the institution of marriage as disastrous for women. She was quite distinctive in looking back to the ancient Japanese past as a time of a woman-centered society of respect and support for motherhood. Other feminists, such as the poet and essayist Yosano Akiko, called for women's liberation not only as mothers, and not solely as Japanese, but as human beings in a larger world. Yamakawa Kikue took the debate a step further by linking feminism with a call for socialism. She argued that working-class women suffered dual oppressions of gender and class. They therefore had to organize against both patriarchal authority and the exploitation of employers to bring about a "revolution in the economic system that brought about women's problems."[9] As in so many other areas of social thought, the divide in Japan between "woman-centered" and "humanist" versions of feminism was very similar to, and was informed by, similar debates in the West during the nineteenth and twentieth centuries.

Even those who accepted the modern capitalist order and initially welcomed parliamentary rule could be harsh critics of the reality of party government. The leading intellectual advocate of parliamentary liberalism was Yoshino Sakuzō, a Christian and professor of law at Tokyo Imperial University. In 1916 he published a famous essay that put forward his vision of a properly Japanese style of constitutional government. Yoshino held that the goal of the government should be to protect the welfare of the nation's people. Elections, and cabinets responsible to the parliament, would be the best guarantees of such a result. Such a political system would be "rooted in the people" (*minponshugi*), but it would simultaneously respect the emperor's sovereignty. But when Yoshino looked around him in the mid to late 1920s, he decided that the major political parties had been captured by selfish private "connections of interest," such as the zaibatsu. They had become morally decadent bodies, in his view, who did not properly serve the people.[10]

STRATEGIES OF IMPERIAL DEMOCRATIC RULE

Parliamentary government in prewar Japan was thus constrained by formal and informal institutions. It faced ideological challenge and organized attacks from emperor-centered radicals on the right and a wide range of activists on the left. By the late 1920s it commanded only tepid support from "natural" allies such as the press and many intellectuals. How, then, did political parties manage to share power and form cabinets from 1918 through the early 1930s to the extent that they did?

Parties joined the ruling elite in part because their leaders were extremely practical politicians who had come to see bureaucrats and military men more as allies than as opponents. In social terms, the party leaders were little different from elites in the bureaucracy and military. They included wealthy landlords and business leaders, some retired bureaucrats who sought a continued public role in politics, and some urban professionals such as lawyers and publishers or journalists. These men attended the same elite higher schools and imperial universities. Their families came from similar privileged economic backgrounds. They belonged to a handful of exclusive golf clubs founded in the early years of the twentieth century. Their children married each other.

Party rule had a practical economic foundation as well. It delivered important goods to significant numbers of people. When party cabinet ministers controlled public works or education budgets, small town mayors or business leaders or school principals had good reason to support the party in power. In exchange for delivering votes, or pledging to do so, they might see railway lines directed through their cities, harbors dredged in their ports, or schools built in their towns and villages. The promise of such favors, which were called "pork-barrel" benefits in the American political world of this era, was alluring in Japan as well. It was a key factor allowing the minority party, once in power, to consistently win the next election. On the other hand, press reports of such dealings, as well as outright vote-buying, turned more idealistic voters against the parties and undermined their legitimacy.

Parliamentary rule was also sustained from the 1910s through the early 1930s by shared political attitudes among party and nonparty elites. Few party leaders saw democracy as an end in itself. They considered it rather a means to ensure the position of emperor and empire, national power, and social order. To the extent that rulers and a wider public believed that party rule was achieving these goals, it gained legitimacy.

Party men, bureaucrats, and the mainstream of the military agreed on a basic politics of divide and rule. On one hand, voting rights would be extended, and men of substance and status would represent the will of the people in parliament. In the words of a leading Seiyūkai parliamentarian, politics in this new era were "rooted in the people (*minponshugi*) and tackle[d] social problems."[11] But all elites agreed as well that visions of economic democracy or political attacks on the imperial institution were beyond the pale. Under the Seiyūkai in 1920, Hara Kei moved harshly against a strike at the nation's largest steel mill. In the days following the September 1923 earthquake, as they tolerated and sometimes incited the massacre of thousands of Koreans, government forces also moved violently against those seen as political outlaws in a series of notorious acts of state violence. The police murdered the feminist writer Itō Noe, her famous anarchist lover Ōsugi Sakae, and their nephew. In a second attack, the police together with army troops rounded up and killed the union leader Hirasawa Keishichi and nine other labor activists. These figures hardly represented a major immediate threat to Japan's rulers, but many of those in the elite, especially in military and court circles, and some in the bureacracy, took a harsh "zero tolerance" approach to radical ideas. Political party leaders seem to have agreed. The parties scarcely murmured a word in protest at these acts. Under the Kenseikai in 1925, the Diet passed a repressive Peace Preservation Law. It made criticism of the emperor a capital offense and criticism of "the system of private property" punishable by up to ten years in jail. Under the Seiyūkai in 1928, police launched a massive crackdown on the JCP. They arrested sixteen hundred people and prosecuted five hundred. Police arrested another seven hundred accused as communists in a roundup the following year.

The parties thus ruled as partners of other elites. They shared social ties. They traded economic favors and political patronage. And they agreed in fundamental ways on their ideological commitments: They accepted some degree of democratic participation, but they supported empire and the emperor as foundations of the political order.

But through the 1920s, an important strategic division also emerged among parties and within the bureaucracy and the military. Some argued that imperial Japan should be a democracy for men of capital and landed property only. Others maintained that national power and social order would best be secured by making Japan a considerably more open, democratic society for all men, or even for women, as long as they stayed within the boundaries of acceptable thought and behavior.

Both these avenues were explored in the 1920s. The more conservative program of imperial democracy is associated with the Seiyūkai party and with bureaucrats in the Ministry of Agriculture and Commerce. It dominated national policy in the immediate wake of World War I. The Seiyūkai moved cautiously to broaden the scope of legal participation in politics. Hara supported a lowered property tax qualification for suffrage, which the Diet ratified in 1919. The change increased the size of the electorate to three million men, about 5 percent of the population. And the Seiyūkai did recognize at least an expanded role for women on the margins of politics in 1922 by amending the law of 1900 that denied all political rights to women. They were now given the right to attend political meetings, although not other rights such as joining political organizations. But Hara consistently opposed universal suffrage even for males in these years: "It is too soon. Abolition of property tax [voting] restrictions, with the intent to destroy class distinctions, is a dangerous idea. I cannot agree."[12] His home minister supported workplace councils to win employee loyalty, while refusing to recognize more autonomous union activity. In 1919 he played a key role in founding a think tank called the Harmonization Society with state and corporate financial support. The body's mission was to study social problems and promote harmony between labor and capital. The Seiyūkai also sought to bolster the position of small-scale landowners in the countryside. In 1920 it further set up a committee in the Ministry of Agriculture and Commerce to consider reform of tenant farming, but faced with landlord opposition, it shelved plans to write a law giving legal rights to tenant farmers.

The Seiyūkai administration of 1918–21, and the "transcendental" cabinets of 1922–24, also put in place a more elaborate set of social welfare programs of the local and national government. Hara's cabinet created a Social Affairs Bureau in the Home Ministry in 1920, charged to address issues such as unemployment, labor disputes, and tenant farmer protests. It pushed a health insurance law and a revised factory law through the Diet in 1922. The insurance law required all medium and large-scale companies to create health insurance unions for all employees, funded by a combination of worker and company premium payments, or to allow the employees to join a new government-administered insurance plan. The factory law raised minimum sums for death and injury benefits and sick pay.[13]

In addition, local governments beginning with Osaka in 1918 improvised a low-cost system to provide counseling and moral support to the poorest families in the nation. It drew community leaders into the administration of the system, giving them the unpaid position of "district commissioner." The commissioners made the rounds of indigent households in their neighborhood, counseling them on hygiene, offering job introductions, exhorting them to save, and introducing them to various sources of private charity or public relief. By the late 1920s, the Home Ministry had endorsed the district commissioner system as "the central institution of social work" in Japan.[14]

These various programs were significant. But they were clearly limited by the government's reluctance to spend its money on social problems. The Privy Council thwarted the will of the Diet by refusing to allocate funds to implement the new insurance and factory laws. The district commissioners by the late 1920s mounted strong campaigns calling on the government to provide more generous poor relief, with little immediate result.

Politicians in the Kenseikai/Minseitō did come forward with a more liberal version of imperial democracy, in an alliance with a new generation of Home Ministry bureaucrats. The latter were impressed that liberal reforms had brought a degree of social stability to postwar Europe, especially Britain. A more expansive social policy became the order of the day under the Kenseikai cabinet headed by Katō Kōmei in 1924. Katō won passage of the Tenant Farmer Dispute Mediation Law, which offered implicit legal recognition to tenant farmer unions. Over the next sixteen years, nearly two-thirds of all recorded tenant disputes were mediated under this law.[15] Katō also pushed to reform the Peerage and reduce its power, although without success. But he did push through the most famous reform of the era in 1925: universal male suffrage. All men over age twenty-five who were not on public assistance were granted the right to vote.

The Kenseikai in 1926 then called for a three-part program of "universal suffrage for industry": a law to give legal standing to labor unions, a labor disputes conciliation bill, and the repeal of the anti-union clause in the Public Order Police law of 1900. The union bill failed because of opposition from Ministry of Agriculture and Commerce bureaucrats, the Seiyūkai party, and most business federations, but the other measures became law. The Kenseikai also succeeded in allocating the funds to put into practice the changes approved in the factory law and health insurance laws of 1922. And the Home Ministry in 1926 directed prefectural authorities to respect the spirit of the labor union bill even though it had been defeated in the Diet. Taken together, these steps were very significant. They offered working people social support and the implicit right to organize and to strike.

The Kenseikai/Minseitō cabinets also broadened political and civil rights for women. After the modest political reform of 1922 that freed them to attend political events, women's groups continued pressing for rights still denied them: the right of political association, the right to vote, and the right to hold local public office. In 1929 Prime Minister Hamaguchi, his foreign minister, and his home minister held an unprecedented meeting with leading female suffragists to ask for their support for the government's policy of tight budgets and fiscal austerity. The prime minister in exchange promised to support female suffrage and civil rights. He was moved to take this step by the severity of the economic crisis as well as his liberal belief that expanded participation would bring stability in the long run. Women's groups optimistically interpreted this get-together as recognition that women were on their way to becoming full members of the body politic.

These Kenseikai/Minseitō policies sought to give excluded groups a voice and a stake in the system. Under universal manhood suffrage, new working-class parties formed immediately to challenge the so-called established parties, but they fared poorly in the first universal suffrage election in 1928. The Minseitō, on the other hand, gained new support in the industrial districts of major cities. The party's labor reforms bolstered the standing of relatively moderate unions whose leaders claimed it was possible to work within the existing political order. In these ways, the Minseitō's more inclusive version of imperial democracy seemed to be working to promote social order and win votes. The party maintained a working alliance with some in the bureaucracy, business world, and military.

But other elites were critical of these reforms. Many zaibatsu leaders, bureaucrats in the Ministry of Justice and Ministry of Agriculture Commerce, and many in the Seiyūkai party viewed these steps as dangerously radical. At the same time, intellectuals disillusioned with chronic party corruption gave tepid support, at best, to the Minseitō social liberalism. Some of these critics turned their discontent with the Minseitō into a broader attack on political party governments more generally. As long as a modicum of social order was maintained, the economy avoided a major collapse, and the empire appeared secure, one party or the other could pursue its agenda and keep the support of allies in the bureaucracy, the military, and the business community. But this hold on power was tentative.

JAPAN, ASIA, AND THE WESTERN POWERS

A similar mix of consensus on basic goals and strategic contention over how to achieve them marked Japanese foreign policy of the 1910s and 1920s. The mainstream parties, with other elites, fervently supported empire abroad. They sought equality with the imperialist powers of the West. In Asia, they wanted to make Japan more than the equal of the other powers, and they pushed the Western powers to recognize a special Japanese interest in Asia. They shared these general goals with military leaders as well as editorial writers in the press. But politicians as much as the military disagreed sharply among themselves on how to achieve these goals.

Several related issues proved most divisive. First, should Japan seek economic and military advantage in China by cooperating with the European powers and the United States, or should it take unilateral actions? Second, should Japan support and work with China's struggling young government, which had led the 1911 revolution against the Qing dynasty, or should it impose order in China by cutting deals with local warlords who were resisting the weak central government? Finally, should Japan recognize and work with the Soviet Union, or should it seek to destroy or contain it? In the years from World War I through the 1920s, all these alternatives were pursued.

The outbreak of World War I raised every one of these questions. It presented the Japanese government with golden opportunities to extend its power in Asia. The Anglo-Japanese alliance of 1902 (revised in 1911) led Japan quickly to join the war on the British side in August 1914. By year's end, Japanese troops had taken control of German possessions including railways and a military base in China's Shandong peninsula and several Pacific islands.

This course was more than acceptable to Japan's British ally. It did not particularly trouble the neutral Americans. But matters became more complex when the Japanese government followed by addressing the notorious Twenty-One Demands to China. In

January 1915, Prime Minister Ōkuma Shigenobu and his foreign minister, Katō Kō-mei, whose government was allied to the Dōshikai party, presented the young Chinese government led by Yuan Shikai with five sets of specific demands (twenty-one in all). The fifth group was especially offensive to the Chinese. It would have set up joint Chinese-Japanese police forces in China and required the Chinese government to accept the appointment of Japanese advisors in political and economic as well as military affairs. This would have sent China far along the road toward colonization by Japan.

The Chinese populace reacted with outrage. Anti-Japanese activists launched boycotts of Japanese goods and shipping. Yuan resisted the demands and sought international support. When the British and Americans objected to the more radical demands, the Japanese agreed to withdraw the claims put forth in group five. Yuan accepted the other demands. Among other things, China agreed to recognize Japan's control of the former German possessions. China also gave Japan rights to build railways in Shandong, and Yuan recognized that Japan had a special position in southern Manchuria.

Japanese military leaders supported the pursuit of economic and strategic power on the continent. But Yamagata Aritomo and others were troubled by the way Ōkuma and Katō stirred up anti-Japanese sentiment in pursuit of their goals in China. Of equal or greater concern to Yamagata was Katō's clear intent to increase civilian control of foreign policy and party control of the government. When Katō left his position and the Ōkuma cabinet resigned because of scandal, Yamagata was able to hold off party government by putting in place his ally, General Terauchi Masatake.[16]

With less diplomatic controversy, the new Japanese government continued to risk tensions with the West and press its advantage as the war continued. When the United States entered the war in 1917, it became Japan's ally. The two governments signed the Ishii-Lansing agreement. Japan agreed to respect China's independence and promised not to obstruct America's equal commercial access to China. In exchange, the Americans recognized Japan's "special interests" in China. In effect, the two countries agreed to recognize each other's colonial possessions in Asia. In 1918 Japan pushed ahead to secure its "special interests" with the so-called Nishihara Loans to China (named for Prime Minister Terauchi's representative who negotiated the terms). These were nominally loans from private Japanese banks for economic projects such as railway building. In fact, the Japanese government provided the funds to prop up one Chinese leader against warlord rivals in exchange for further economic privileges in Shandong and Manchuria.

Tensions over the Japanese stake in China carried over into the World War I peace negotiations at Versailles in 1919. Japan joined the peace conference as one of the victorious allies. Its delegates wanted above all to confirm Japanese control over the former German leasehold in Shandong. They also eagerly called for the principle of racial equality to be made part of the founding covenant of the League of Nations. The American president, Woodrow Wilson, and the other allied leaders allowed Japan to keep its foothold in Shandong, but they refused to include the racial equality clause. These decisions undermined the idealistic claims of the Western powers that principles of equality and self-determination should anchor the postwar international order. They fueled strong Japanese anger at the hypocrisy of the Western governments.

The Japanese rulers simultaneously provoked Western mistrust by the way it intervened against the Soviet Union in an episode known as the Siberian Intervention. When the Bolshevik movement triumphed in Russia in November 1917, the Japanese government began searching for some means to encourage a counterrevolution to topple Russia's new communist regime. At the very least, Japan hoped to support an anti-communist regime in the nearby regions of far eastern Russia, which were not yet securely under Bolshevik control. But General Terauchi's government was unwilling to move alone.

An opportunity to act presented itself in 1918. In March, the British, French, and American governments agreed to send troops to Siberia. Their goal was to protect allied war supplies and pro-czarist troops gathered in Vladivostok. President Wilson asked Japan to join the intervention. Prime Minister Terauchi was only too happy to oblige. Wilson requested the help of seven thousand troops. Japan promised to send twelve thousand and in fact dispatched no less than seventy thousand men! They were still in Siberia in 1922, two years after the other powers had decided the anti-Bolshevik movement was lost and had withdrawn their troops. The Japanese forces continued to support a small counterrevolutionary government in Vladivostok. This hopeless unilateral action came under mounting domestic and international criticism. Having gained nothing but the suspicion of the West and the distrust of the Soviet Union and having lost three thousand lives, Japan withdrew its troops and brought them home late in 1922.

The Treaty of Versailles and the Siberian Intervention marked a rocky start down the road of postwar cooperative imperialism. The major powers continued to seek ways to work together throughout the 1920s. As the Siberian venture drew to its close, the Hara government agreed to join an international peace conference in Washington. One goal of the meeting was to end an emerging naval arms race that set Japan, Britain, and the United States against each other. Hara was committed to an economic policy of reduced government expenditures, so he welcomed this effort. The treaty committed the British, American, and Japanese governments to keep their warship capacities (by tonnage) to a ratio of 5 : 5 : 3, respectively. The Japanese accepted the lower level because the British and Americans promised to build no naval fortifications in the western Pacific. The governments agreed that these ratios would ensure the security of each nation while preventing an arms race.

Throughout the 1920s, the Japanese government streamlined its military forces for strategic as well as economic reasons. Most military leaders supported these efforts. The government cut manpower and weapons. Military costs fell from a peak of 55 percent of the national budget in 1918 to just 29 percent by 1924. Troop reductions continued over the next several years. In 1925 Ugaki Kazushige, the minister of the army (who served in Kenseikai/Minseitō cabinets from 1924 to 1927 and again from 1930 to 1931), cut four divisions or thirty-four thousand troops. But much of the money saved was redirected to new commitments to buy modern weapons. Ugaki also implemented policies to build popular support for the military, such as required military education in middle and higher schools. This approach reflected the lesson learned by the Japanese high command from World War I: Any future war would require the total mobilization of the civilian population and resources.

Parallel to these policies to limit and modernize the Japanese military, the government for much of the 1920s pursued a more cautious policy toward China than it had during World War I.

At issue was the question of how best to protect the dramatically increasing Japanese presence and how to deal with the various contenders for political power in China itself. In 1900 no more than 4,000 Japanese civilians lived in China. By 1920, the expatriate community stood at 134,000. The Japanese resided mainly in Manchuria and North China, but by the mid-1920s Japanese businesses had made substantial investments in Shanghai as well, in textile production especially.

These men pursued their business goals in a constantly changing political environment. The Chinese Nationalist Party, or Kuomintang, had by now inherited the banner of the revolution that overthrew the Qing. But through the mid-1920s its hold on power was uncertain at best. It faced resistance from a growing communist movement in the cities and countryside, as well as from regional commanders called "warlords," who had mobilized substantial military forces. The warlords were especially powerful in northern China and Manchuria, where the Japanese laid claim to special economic and strategic privileges.

The Seiyūkai cabinet under Hara sought to safeguard Japan's interests by cooperating with the Western powers as well as the Chinese Nationalist regime. Hara discontinued the Nishihara Loans, which had facilitated Japanese intervention in Chinese politics. As part of the 1922 Washington agreements, he negotiated the return of Shandong to China, while keeping long-term rights over key railways. The Kenseikai/ Minseitō governments of 1924 through 1927, with the Western-oriented Shidehara Kijūrō as foreign minister, continued the conciliatory chorus. On three occasions from 1925 to early 1927, the British or the Americans called on Japan to join in the dispatch of troops to counter perceived threats to foreign interests. Each time, Shidehara refused to send troops.

At the same time, Shidehara was not willing to see Japanese businesses in China rely simply on free access to open markets. Following up on promises made at the Washington Conference, the major powers convened an international meeting on tariff reform in Peking in 1925. Its goal was to restore tariff controls to the Chinese, a power they had lost eighty years before in the Opium Wars. From the outset, Shidehara had reservations about supporting Chinese demands for tariff autonomy. He feared China would use its restored powers to impede Japanese textile exports, and he refused to make key concessions. No agreement was reached, and the meeting ended in failure.

Despite such hard-nosed economic bargaining, Shidehara was sharply criticized at home for "weak-kneed" diplomacy because of his reluctance to send troops to China to confront anti-Japanese agitation. The possibility of a different approach emerged in 1927 when General Tanaka Giichi took over as prime minister of a new Seiyūkai cabinet. Tanaka was a career military man, invited to join the Seiyūkai as party president in 1925. He did not directly repudiate cooperation with the West, but he promoted a considerably more assertive foreign policy than Shidehara. He sent troops to China on three occasions in 1927 and 1928, ostensibly to protect Japanese citizens and economic interests. In fact, the immediate threats were far less than reported back home. But the Nationalist army, now led by an ambitious leader named Chiang Kai-shek, had taken control of central China by 1927. The prospect loomed that he would extend his reach to North China and challenge Japanese privileges there and in Manchuria. The Seiyūkai and military leaders agreed that Japan should consider independent action and alliances with local warlords to protect these interests.[17]

Part of the passion moving people in Japan to oppose diplomatic cooperation with the West in China came from anger at the way America was treating Japanese immigrants. By the early 1900s, Japanese migrants to Hawaii and the American mainland were approaching one hundred thousand in number. Anti-immigrant rhetoric about the threat of this so-called Yellow Peril was particularly virulent on the West Coast. Local laws mandated that schools be segregated. President Theodore Roosevelt sought to calm the situation in 1908 by concluding the so-called Gentleman's Agreement with Prime Minister Saionji. This nonlegislative measure committed the Japanese government to limit drastically the flow of emigrants to the United States.

American discrimination against those Japanese already present was anything but gentlemanly. New legislation in California prohibited Japanese from owning land or leasing it long-term. The U.S. Supreme Court ruled in 1922 that no Japanese or other Asian immigrants could become naturalized American citizens. And a new Immigration Act in 1924 superseded the Gentleman's Agreement by prohibiting Japanese immigration entirely. Such steps not only contradicted the general spirit of postwar international cooperation but also specifically undermined American calls for Japan to support an Open Door policy to American interests in Asia. They aroused considerable anger in Japan. In a letter to the U.S. secretary of labor, Japanese ambassador Hanihara Masanao wrote,

> The important question is whether Japan as a nation is or is not entitled to the proper respect and consideration of other nations. . . . The manifest object of the [exclusion clause] is to single out Japanese as a nation, stigmatizing them as unworthy and undesirable in the eyes of the American people.[18]

But even more important in provoking domestic criticisms of the government's foreign policy was the trend of deepening resistance in Asia to Japanese colonial rule and imperialism. The great irony is that Japan's victory in the Russo-Japanese War had initially flamed anti-colonial passions from China and Vietnam to the Philippines, Burma, and India. People in all these lands viewed Japan as an anti-colonial force and took heart at what they viewed as the first modern victory of a "yellow" race over the "whites." From the turn of the century through the 1910s in particular, thousands of youths from China, hundreds from the Korean and Taiwanese colonies as well as Vietnam, and a handful from places such as India, Burma, and the Philippines sought education in Japan. These students won support for projects of reform in their own countries from many Japanese political figures, ranging from anti-Western nationalists to internationally minded socialists.

But Japanese support for these youthful Asian dreams of liberation evaporated in the face of imperialist realpolitik. When Japan concluded an alliance with France in 1907, for example, the two governments secretly agreed to respect each other's colonial possessions. As a result, the Japanese government forced Vietnamese students to leave the country. In the following years, in the eyes of vast numbers of Asians, Japan's aggressive policies from the annexation of Korea through the Twenty-One Demands turned the nation from a force for Asian liberation to one of oppression.

In particular, the year 1919 witnessed two momentous anti-Japanese outbursts. In Korea, patriots in exile were thrilled by Woodrow Wilson's 1918 call for national self-determination just prior to the Versailles peace conference. They tried to send delegates from Hawaii, but the Japanese refused them passports. In February 1919 hundreds of Korean students in Tokyo formed a Youth Independence Corps and ratified a call for immediate independence. Similar sentiments in Seoul crystallized around the funeral of the former king of Korea, Kojong, who died in January 1919. Anticipating a huge Japanese police presence at the funeral itself on March 3, nationalist organizers issued a Declaration of Independence on March 1. This sparked peaceful demonstrations of several hundred thousand students, laborers, and others in Seoul, which quickly spread nationwide. The Japanese authorities were stunned at the powerful sentiments and careful organization that obviously lay behind these widespread actions. They responded in a panic of violent suppression. Japanese forces killed thousands of Koreans. They arrested tens of thousands. By late April a brutal form of order had been restored.[19]

Immediately after this, similar massive demonstrations broke out in China. In late April, the great powers rejected China's appeal at Versailles to retake full control over Shandong from Japan. On May 4, several thousand students demonstrated in Tiananmen Square. As in Korea, this movement spread to other cities. It was directed in part at the weakness of China's own government, but fury at Japanese encroachment on China was the driving force. This May Fourth Movement marked a new stage in the power and breadth of popular nationalism in China. Anti-imperialist protests, including numerous boycotts of Japanese goods, recurred throughout the 1920s. In 1925, the May Thirtieth Movement began with strikes at Japanese-owned textile mills in Shanghai. When British police killed several demonstrators on May 30, a nationwide outburst of anti-Japanese demonstrations, strikes, and boycotts exceeded those of 1919.

Partly in response to these events in China, Japanese political leaders undertook relatively conciliatory efforts to protect economic interests in China for much of the 1920s. In similar fashion, Prime Minister Hara Kei decided that simple repression was the wrong way to sustain colonial rule in Korea. In the wake of the March 1 uprising, he appointed a new governor general, Admiral Saitō Makoto, with a mission to restore "harmony between Japan and Korea." Saitō's new departures came to be called "cultural rule." The essence of his program was a strategy of divide and rule. Colonial administrators were charged to support cooperative Korean leaders and organizations, while isolating and suppressing any sign of anti-Japanese activity.

"Cultural rule" has often been dismissed as cosmetic reform that masked unrelenting authoritarian control. After Saitō's arrival, the Japanese quickly and dramatically quadrupled the number of police stations and substations in just one year. The police developed a huge network of spies and informers throughout Korea. In the name of economic development, colonial administrators funded improved irrigation, and production did expand, but most of the increase was exported to Japan. Per capita rice consumption in Korea actually declined.

But Governor General Saitō's reforms were slightly more than window dressing. Saitō gradually expanded the number of public schools for Koreans. He recruited more Koreans into the colonial administration. He narrowed the inequality between their wages and those of the Japanese. Koreans were permitted to publish books, magazines, and newspapers more extensively than before. Colonial administrators allowed a much wider range of Korean organizations to carry on activities. Korean people founded thousands of new education and religious groups, youth groups, and organizations of farmers and laborers. A small number of Korean capitalists were given new economic opportunities.

Certainly, censorship and surveillance remained intensive. Those who challenged Japanese rule even slightly were jailed and tortured. Nonetheless, nationalist political activities continued, either openly in subtle disguise or in secret. As in Japan (although in a more tightly constrained fashion), a newly diverse and energetic modern cultural life—cinema, radio, and literature—flourished throughout the 1920s and into the early 1930s.

In Japan, one finds a wide variety of responses outside of government circles to the new postwar international environment. A few intellectuals such as Yoshino Sakuzō combined support for a more democratic system at home with support for a gradual move toward self-determination for colonial subjects, Koreans in particular. Such positions are noteworthy because Yoshino, among others, had previously opposed Korean independence without reservation. Yoshino and a number of others, such as the publisher and politician Shimada Saburō, also vigorously supported the program of arms reduction. By 1921, public opinion had turned sharply against the Siberian intervention, and newspapers called for Japan to withdraw its troops. Stories circulated in the early 1920s that soldiers were embarrassed to wear their uniforms in public. In a symbolic move against imperialism in 1920, Japan's largest union federation, the Greater Japan Federation of Labor, dropped the word "Greater" from its title. The group issued a call for self-determination in Korean and ran occasional articles on the plight of Korean workers. Working-class political organizations in the late 1920s endorsed the right of the Chinese people to self-determination. They uniformly criticized the military interventions of General Tanaka Giichi and the Seiyūkai.

Other civilian voices took a stand against *Western* imperialism, but portrayed Japan as a different sort of power. They actually called for a more aggressive Japanese foreign policy. Older ultranationalists such as Uchida Ryōhei (1874–1937) had supported Japanese imperialism in Asia since the 1880s, and they continued to demand expansion on the mainland to bolster the glory of imperial rule. But probably the most influential intellectual to promote such a vision was Kita Ikki (1883–1937). His famous manifesto, *An Outline Plan for the Reorganization of Japan* (1923), rejected class struggle at home but transposed it abroad. He called Japan an "international proletarian" and asked, "Does Japan not have the right to go to war and seize their [Anglo-American] monopolies in the name of justice?"[20]

Such ideas won some popular support. Kamino Shin'ichi, a machinist at a major shipyard, visited Shanghai in 1920 en route to Europe to study engineering. He later wrote of his shock at the signs that banned "Chinese and dogs" from using parks in their own city. He abandoned his internationalist socialism and began to espouse a vociferous self-styled "Japanism." He called on fellow workers to support emperor and empire against the West, and he won considerable support. In China, hundreds of Japanese adventurers called "China rōnin (*rōnin* were masterless samurai) combined profiteering with political maneuvers nominally in support of Asian liberation. By the late 1920s, a growing network of nationalistic political groups linked together these civilian expansionists at home and abroad with young, action-oriented military men. They won quiet (and sometimes open) support from top military brass including army ministers Ugaki Kazushige and Araki Sadao and the Korean governor general, Saitō Makoto. Their rhetoric was one of pan-Asian solidarity against the West, but they always saw Japan as the hegemonic leader of Asia.

In an era before widespread public opinion polling, it is impossible to judge the breadth of support for these various positions for and against imperialism. That an anti-military sentiment existed at all is worth noting. But it was certainly not the majority sentiment even at the peak of postwar internationalism. The mainstream of intellectual and popular voices in Japan supported the nation's empire, even as they complained of Western imperialism.

Inside and outside the government, the central line of contention in Japan's foreign policy over the 1910s and 1920s was not pro-imperialist versus anti-imperialist. Rather, it set "slow-track" versus "fast-track" imperialists. The former took a more cooperative approach to other powers, especially Britain, the United States and China. The latter stressed unilateral solutions to conflicts. This division did not always fall out neatly along party lines. Nor did it consistently set moderate "slow-track" civilians against an expansionist "fast-track" military. It was two politicians allied to the Dō-shikai party, after all, Ōkuma and Katō, who put forward the aggressive Twenty-one Demands during World War I. But by the end of the 1920s, some consistent patterns had emerged in the domestic debates over foreign policy. The Minseitō supported a more cooperative approach in negotiations with the British and Americans and in dealing with Chinese nationalism. The Seiyūkai supported more aggressive and uni-lateral diplomacy toward both China and the West. Both military leaders and many lower-level officers were impatient with cooperative diplomacy and increasingly scorn-ful of civilian politicians. The army saw the greatest threat to Japan's Asian hegemony—and the greatest opportunities to solve the problem—residing in China, especially North China and Manchuria. The navy focused its concerns on rival Western powers in the Pacific.

It is important to recognize that Japanese foreign policy differed little from that of other imperialist powers in its basic objectives. All of the powers continued projects of colonial or semicolonial domination in the 1920s. Some spoke of assimilation and others promised eventual independence and self-determination, but they all justified their rule with rhetoric of tutelage and advancement for colonized peoples. All powers spoke of cooperation among themselves even as each nation sought to safeguard its own imperialist hegemony in areas of special concern. The United States spoke of its unique rights and interests in Latin America in similar ways to the Japanese rhetoric of special interests in Asia.

But two differences would prove crucial. Beginning in the mid-1920s, the Western powers proved slightly more willing than Japan to pull back from their imperialism in China by restoring a measure of autonomy to the Chinese Nationalist leadership, and the clash between Japanese and Western approaches to China only widened from this point onward. And of greatest consequence, in the 1930s the political system created in Japan under the Meiji constitution made it difficult for leaders to mediate conflicts among powerful actors. It offered no institutional checks to control military officers who took unauthorized actions. Only the emperor had the theoretical power to rein in the military, and he proved unable and unwilling to use his power in this way.[21]

In sum, when the imperial democratic order came under fire at home and abroad at the end of the 1920s and the early 1930s, Japanese leaders chose emperor and empire over democracy. At a time of economic depression and international tension, they chose exclusive empire over cooperative imperialism. They abandoned the democratic path of parliamentary rule for a reinforced authoritarian politics.

11

The Depression Crisis and Responses

From the 1890s through the 1920s a hybrid politics of imperial democracy had emerged in Japan. The political order was anchored by a modernized imperial institution, which looked to the British monarchy as a model and anxiously offered space for a significant degree of pluralism. Organizations of landlords and businessmen, factory workers and tenant farmers, and women and men pursued their goals in a messy politics of confrontation and compromise.

Then, beginning with the years from 1929 to 1932, a combination of shocks—economic depression, intense social conflict, military expansion, and the assassination of prime ministers and leading capitalists—transformed Japan's political system. By the end of the 1930s, independent political parties, business associations, producer cooperatives, labor unions, and tenant unions were replaced by a series of state-controlled mass bodies intended to mobilize the nation for its "holy war" with China and bring harmony and order at home. A new political order that bore great similarity to the fascist systems of Germany and Italy had become ascendant and would plunge Japan and Asia into a disastrous war. At the same time, some of the changes initiated during the depression and in the name of mobilization for war proved enduring. It is possible to identify a transwar system in state policies toward economy and society and a transwar society in some of the characteristics of daily life.

ECONOMIC AND SOCIAL CRISIS

In October 1929 the New York stock market crashed. The global economic crisis that followed was a key incident in the conjuncture of events that brought about Japan's political shift. The world depression coincided in destructive fashion with a recent initiative in Japanese financial policy. A Minseitō government under Prime Minister Hamaguchi had come to power in July 1929. It resolved to implement two policies that had been pursued on and off throughout the 1920s to revive the stagnant economy. First, domestic prices would be forced down and exports encouraged by tightening the money supply and cutting government spending (i.e., retrenchment). Second, international trade and investment would be stabilized by returning to a fixed exchange rate. Japan would follow the lead of the Western powers by going back to the gold standard (which Japan and the other powers had left during World War I) at the prewar rate.

The fiscal retrenchment program came first. It appeared to be succeeding in the second half of 1929. Wholesale prices fell 6 percent. So, in January 1930, Japan returned to the gold standard as promised. At a moment of plunging prices worldwide, this move brought disaster. Deep global deflation erased the benefit of lower domestic prices. The fixed exchange rate prevented further devaluation that might have boosted Japanese exports.[1]

In addition, Japan's zaibatsu banks behaved in a way that was economically smart but politically damaging. Bankers quickly realized that the government would have no choice but to abandon this move to the gold standard and devalue the yen. They sold massive amounts of yen for dollars. When Japan indeed left the gold standard in 1931, the value of the yen quickly fell by half against the dollar. The banks happily doubled their money by repurchasing the cheaper Japanese currency with their dollars. This behavior reinforced the widespread belief that capitalists and their allies in the political parties were greedy and selfish: They were profiting handsomely by selling out the country during a depression that was impoverishing everyone else. Well beyond the small circle of Marxian intellectuals who first took this view, it became a commonplace idea that Japan stood at a systemic "dead end." The economy and political structure seemed paralyzed. Social disorder and immorality appeared rampant.

The crisis was especially acute among farmers. Between 1929 and 1931 the average price of basic agricultural commodities including rice and barley fell by 43 percent. As their incomes tumbled, small-scale landowners were unable to pay taxes. Many sought to raise their earnings by retaking land from tenants. They wanted to work these fields with family labor, including unemployed children returning from the cities. Tenant farmers resisted eviction. Land disputes surged in number.

The quality of disputes changed as well. Most tenant-landlord struggles in the 1920s saw the tenants on the offensive, demanding rent reductions. Now tenants were desperate and defensive. The proportion of disputes over contractual matters such as eviction rose from just 5 percent in the early 1920s to nearly 50 percent by the depression years. Tenant farmers often built crude fences around their fields and set up picket lines to protect them. More of these disputes than ever involved violence.

In the cities, the depression threatened shopkeepers and factory owners as well as their employees. Retail traders faced bankruptcy when wage cuts and job losses cut the buying power of their customers. Annual rates of failure among Tokyo retail stores nearly doubled from 1926 to 1930. The newspapers were filled with tales of small storeowners fleeing their creditors in the dead of night. Small-scale manufacturing businesses also failed by the thousands.

Disgusted with the ineffective response of the established political parties, thousands of small businessmen joined movements to found new ones. They lambasted the Seiyūkai as well as the ruling Minseitō as "running dogs of big capital." One such group, the Imperial Middle Class Federated Alliance, claimed "the established parties have betrayed us, becoming the political lackeys of the capitalist cliques and trampling the middle class of commercial, industrial, and agricultural producers." To save the long-suffering middle class, which had "supported the state financially and defended

*Tenant farmer dispute, 1930, in Niigata. Standing on a pile of rice stalks, a leader of the
farmers' union addresses the members. Such disputes surged in number and intensity during
the depression years.*
Courtesy of Shogakkan Publishers.

the country resolutely," Japan needed a "revolution in economic thought." These
groups demanded new policies to guarantee the "prosperity of the mainstay class" of
taxpayers, producers, and exporters. This class in turn would save Japan from "a
bloody war of labor and capital."[2]

The men who issued such fearful claims had reason to be worried. They faced
unprecedented hostility from employees who faced a dramatically increased threat of
unemployment. One historian's estimate of joblessness in 1930–32 places nationwide
unemployment at about 15 percent of the industrial work force. Jobless rates in the
city might have been double this, and they surely exceeded 20 percent.[3]

Unlike bankrupt shopkeepers, the men and women who lost their jobs did not
flee quietly into the night. Labor disputes, like agrarian struggles, took place in unprecedented numbers and with a new intensity. They took place in small factories as
well as large ones. More women than ever took part, especially in the embattled textile
industry. As a female speaker shouted at a rally during one such strike in Tokyo in
1930:

Even if we go back to the countryside, our parents and our brothers do not have enough to eat. Knowing this, how can we go back?[4]

Organized workers engaged in more prolonged disputes than in the past, and they turned violent more frequently. In part, the violence was calculated. When workers lost their jobs, they often camped outside the factory. They demanded rehiring or else a huge severance pay of six months' or one year's wages. They knew that the police valued order above all. When they drew in the authorities as mediators, for example by starting a fight with company guards, they often won a favorable compromise. They typically gained three or four months of severance pay instead of the minimum fourteen days pay dictated by Home Ministry regulations.

The escapade of the "chimney man" was one especially creative application of this tactic. When a group of textile workers at the Fuji Spinning Company near Tokyo walked out on strike in November 1930, one young man scaled the mill's smokestack. He refused to descend until the strike was settled. The genius of his move was that the emperor was scheduled to pass directly beneath this perch in his luxurious railroad car several days later. The police could not allow a militant unionist to look down on an imperial procession from such a height. They frantically mediated a compromise settlement, and the whole drama was widely reported in the press.

On other occasions, violence broke out that was less calculated and at least as shocking. During a dispute at the Tōyō Muslin textile mills in Tokyo that same autumn, launched to protest mass dismissals, hundreds of young women workers joined socialist organizers in a night-time march through darkened streets. They threw stones, smashed streetcar windows, and fought police. The newspapers immediately dubbed this a "street war." They wrote in dramatic fashion of the fighting spirit of the young women marchers, and the Muslin workers became famous.

Newly militant factory workers were not the only women who shocked the authorities and the public. The celebrated middle-class "modern girl" of the mid-1920s, who drew much attention at first for her audacious fashion, appeared to be taking her flamboyant ways in new directions by the decade's end. Most troubling to social reformers and state officials alike were the mushrooming numbers of waitresses in major cities. They worked in cafés and dance halls in all the major cities. The waitresses were not prostitutes, but they projected an erotic image. They earned their pay mainly from tips. Café managers encouraged them to flirt with customers, sell kisses, and have sex with favorite patrons. In 1929, the number of cafe waitresses nationwide passed 50,000, exceeding licensed prostitutes. By 1936, the police counted over 111,000 waitresses.

Bureaucrats and the public tolerated prostitution in part because they believed it offered a necessary outlet for the sexual desires of men, while protecting decent girls and women. In their view, the daughters of the rural poor worked as prostitutes out of economic need. Their filial piety in sending earnings home to their families was to be praised, not condemned. The surge of café waitressing undermined the social logic of this sexual and moral order. In the view of police and Home Ministry officials, the waitresses were pursuing their own desires rather than serving their families. The middle-class young women who were supposed to be insulated from sexuality by the separate world of licensed prostitutes instead were "abandoning themselves" to pleasure. They and their mates had become "delinquent modern boys and girls." Beginning in 1929 and continuing throughout the 1930s, officials launched various campaigns to suppress the "red lights and jazz world" of the cities. They arrested waitresses on charges of pursuing unlicensed prostitution, and they banned students from entering cafés or coffeehouses that employed women.[5]

The behavior of university students also contributed to the widespread sense of social crisis during the depression. Hundreds of students suspected of communist party membership had been arrested in the 1928 roundups, and the Ministry of Education dissolved the Tokyo University New Man Society (Shinjinkai). Nonetheless, a wave of student protests broke out at leading universities in 1930 and 1931. Although these protests concerned campus issues as much as national politics, government authorities feared that an underground communist movement and a more general attraction to Marxism and revolutionary ideas remained powerful. The Ministry of Education was convinced the nation faced a serious "student thought problem." It vigorously monitored and suppressed student activism, and by 1934, the student movement had lost its momentum.[6]

In a yearend essay in 1930, a well-known social critic, Ōya Sōichi, neatly summed up the belief that Japanese society faced unprecedented crisis. He referred in particular to the image of the textile women taking to the streets:

> The supervisor at X printer, largest in the Orient, claims he is always running out of two characters, no matter how many pieces he casts. These are the characters for "woman" and for "class." Demand for the former, especially, recently has risen suddenly, and if he stocks 10,000 pieces he runs out before he knows it. . . . Doesn't the fact of rising demand for these two characters give realistic color to the social face of 1930. . . . The bedroom has moved into the foyer, into the living room, and finally into the streets.[7]

Despite such rhetoric, and the wide-ranging social pain and turbulence that provoked it, Japan's experience of economic depression was actually less severe than that of the United States as measured in statistics for unemployment or industrial output. But the *perception* of crisis was profound and consequential, among the masses no less than the elites. Even before the depression, the practice of parliamentary rule enjoyed just lukewarm popular support. When combined with a simultaneous international crisis, the trauma of the depression era provoked new departures abroad and at home.

BREAKING THE IMPASSE: NEW DEPARTURES ABROAD

One impetus for change came from members of the officer corps in the military and their civilian right-wing allies. Through the 1920s, groups of young officers became increasingly frustrated with the Japan's foreign and domestic policies. They and their civilian comrades were unhappy with the perceived weakness of the cooperative diplomacy pursued by the political parties. They were angry at cutbacks in military budgets and force size. They feared the Chinese Nationalist Party's challenge to Japanese hegemony in Manchuria and North China. They resented the decline in the military's prestige at home. They viewed the cozy relations between zaibatsu and parties as emblems of a capitalist system that weakened the military by driving the families of young soldiers into poverty. They responded with acts of rebellion and independent military actions that dramatically changed the political landscape.

The Kwantung Army in Manchuria became one hotbed of such agitation. It had been created in 1906 to guard Japan's leased territory and rail lines in southern Manchuria (the province of Guandong, written Kwantung at the time) acquired in the 1905 settlement of the Russo-Japanese War. In the late 1920s, the army turned to insurgency and conspiracy to carry out its mission, which its leaders had redefined. No longer did they see their role as the simple defense of Japanese interests in Manchuria. They envisioned the army as a group in the vanguard of a coming war between Japan and the West, with a mission to build a model of a new society in the areas under its control. In June 1928 a Kwantung Army staff officer engineered a plot to blow up a train carrying the Chinese warlord, Zhang Zuolin, and blame the attack on his Chinese rivals. Zhang had long been friendly to Japanese efforts to bolster him as a buffer against the Chinese Nationalists to the south, led by Chiang Kai-shek. But as the Nationalists gained in strength, Zhang seemed to be shifting his allegiance in their direction. The Kwantung Army conspirators hoped that his assassination would lead Prime Minister Tanaka to support a more aggressive policy in Manchuria. Although Tanaka and the Seiyukai were more willing than the Minseitō to use military force to protect Japanese interests in China, the prime minister refused to take this radical step. But when he discovered that the Kwantung Army was actually responsible for killing Zhang, Tanaka's government came under pressure from the throne not to publicly embarrass the military. The government set an ominous precedent by taking no strong actions to discipline those responsible. Emperor Hirohito's displeasure at Tanaka's handling of the incident led the prime minister to resign.

Increasing antagonism between Japan and China over Manchuria was paralleled by heightened tensions between the Japanese, the British, and the Americans over naval issues. The Washington Conference of 1922 had stipulated that the powers reconvene in London in 1930 to extend or revise the 1922 limits on naval warships. The Minseitō government made a grave political error when it announced its goal to increase Japan's ratio from 60 to 70 percent of the British and American warship tonnages (that is, a $10:10:7$ rather than $5:5:3$ ratio). The Western negotiators bluntly refused to accept the full Japanese position. Hamaguchi's negotiators in London did achieve a compromise whereby Japan could increase its capacity in certain categories of warships but not others.

Back home, in the wake of these negotiations, the press and the navy condemned the agreement as a betrayal of the national interest as put forth by Hamaguchi himself just months earlier. The anti-treaty faction (called the "fleet wing") took control of the navy over the following three years. All told, the treaty controversy weakened the legitimacy of the Minseitō in particular and party rule in general.[8]

Rhetorical and physical attacks on the political establishment continued unabated. From late 1930 through 1932, young officers working in concert with civilian allies carried out a shocking series of assassinations and attempted assassinations. Minseitō Prime Minister Hamaguchi Osachi was the first victim, shot by a right-wing youth in November 1930. He died the following August. In February and March 1932, former Finance Minister Inoue Jun'nosuke and Mitsui zaibatsu chief Dan Takuma were murdered by members of an ultra-nationalist civilian organization called The League of

Blood. In addition, young military officers miscarried plots for coups d'état in March and October 1931, which had at least tacit approval from some top officers.

The men who carried out these acts were part of an empirewide network of clandestine study groups and associations linking military officers and civilian ideologues. They viewed the parties and the capitalist elite as enemies of a proper political system that would respect and unify the wills of emperor and people. In this, they echoed party leaders of the early twentieth century who had criticized the Meiji oligarchs and bureaucrats for the same sin. They offered no consensus on what new groups should speak instead for emperor and people. Some pinned hopes on the military, others on the agricultural mainstay class of owner-farmers, others on the urban mainstays in trade and industry.

The leaders of the Kwantung Army contributed powerfully to such thinking. They worked out a strategy to break the foreign and domestic impasse with bold action in Manchuria. One key figure was Colonel Ishiwara Kanji, the Kwantung Army's operations officer from 1929 to 1932. Ishiwara had developed an apocalyptic view of the international scene through his idiosyncratic studies of Buddhism and world history. He believed that a cataclysmic "final war" loomed inevitably between Japan and the United States. To prepare for a Japanese victory, he argued to his subordinates that Japan had to take over Manchuria. The region's rich mineral resources had strategic value. He saw its fertile plains as a friendly destination for emigrant farmers, which would relieve population pressures and agrarian poverty at home. In addition, Ishiwara and his supporters saw Manchuria as a laboratory to create a new social order based on principles of social equality and loyalty to the state, rather than selfish capitalistic profit-seeking. He believed that successful experiments in Manchuria would strengthen Japan as they were later implemented at home.

On September 18, 1931, Ishiwara's forces took bold clandestine action. They blew up some track of the southern Manchurian railway at the major crossroads of Mukden (now named Shenyang) and announced it as the work of Chinese military forces. The Kwantung Army used this as pretext for a runaway attack on Chinese regional armies in the area.

With this action, they achieved in 1931 what their assassination of Zhang Zuolin had failed to gain in 1928. By December the Japanese forces controlled most of southern Manchuria. The questions of whether the military leadership in Tokyo knew of the planning for these actions and, if so, whether it approved them, remain controversial to this day. Certainly the Manchurian Incident, as it came to be called, involved some degree of secret planning and insubordination by field officers. It is equally certain that both military and civilian leaders in Tokyo knew of the strong sentiment for direct action in the Kwantung Army ranks and knew something of the plans to act. They had no grounds to be surprised at the events that fall.

Whatever its prior knowledge, the Tokyo government of Prime Minister Inukai Tsuyoshi and the Seiyūkai responded weakly after the fact. Inukai had in any case been more sympathetic to a strong posture than his Minseitō predecessor, Prime Minister Hamaguchi. He resisted military pressure to annex Manchuria as a formal colony, but he allowed the Kwantung Army to install friendly Chinese leaders in a puppet regime. This was called Manchukuo, founded in March 1932. It was nominally an independent nation. The decision to create an "independent" state rather than an outright colony reflected the ideology of pan-Asian liberation and anti-(Western) imperialism that motivated the Japanese planners. But in practice the Japanese retained full control of the conquered territory. They placed the last emperor of China's Qing dynasty, Puyi, on a newly created throne as the Manchurian emperor. Many historians, especially those in Japan, regard this Manchurian Incident of 1931–32 as the start of what they call the Fifteen-Year War—essentially the start of World War II in Asia. Indeed, a strong case can be made that this act of aggression made further conflict inevitable.

Although unauthorized actions of field officers sparked the takeover of Manchuria, top leaders of the military establishment supported this shift toward unilateral imperialism in Asia. General Ugaki Kazushige, for example, was well known as a fairly moderate military figure. He had served as army minister in both Seiyūkai and Minseitō cabinets from 1927 to 1931. As the depression deepened in 1930–31, Ugaki came to believe that Japan faced a systemic crisis. He condemned the violence of left-wing and right-wing radicals, but like them he blamed Japan's weakness and disorder on capitalism and democracy run amok. Like many civilian bureaucrats, he and others in the military feared that Japanese society was about to split into a mass of impoverished proletarians and farmers and a handful of rich capitalists. Looking overseas, he feared that "defense limited to [Japanese] territory" was not enough. The world trading system was breaking down, he wrote in 1930, so that open competition in global markets was not possible. Only a more aggressive foreign policy would allow Japan to find markets so that it could raise productivity, diminish unemployment, and avoid "social tragedy."[9]

Immediately after the military action began, the police and military authorities intensified their surveillance and suppression of dissenting voices at home. But coercion was hardly needed to legitimate the Manchurian takeover. Most ordinary Japanese people, as well as elites, greeted the events of 1931–32 with unrestrained joy. Newspapers wrote exuberant accounts of Japanese advances. Newsreels and radio competed to broadcast the latest battlefield reports in sensational fashion. Former leftists changed their tune: The takeover of Manchuria was not an act of capitalist imperialism because it promised to benefit the entire nation by relieving unemployment. New popular songs, new Kabuki plays, and even new restaurant menus celebrated the acquisition of a rich "crown jewel" of the empire.[10]

Even the most nervous state officials relaxed a bit. The Justice Ministry's 1932 survey of "dangerous thought" called the Manchurian Incident a "divine wind" at a time of intense social ferment. In May 1932 the Army Ministry concluded that the incident had nurtured a new "spirit of solidarity" in place of social confrontation.

The takeover of Manchuria marked a watershed in the history of Japanese foreign and domestic policy. But far from stabilizing the borders of empire, it initiated a new era of expansionism. And far from stabilizing politics and society at home, it was followed by yet another outburst of violence. On May 15, 1932, a group of young naval officers assassinated Inukai Tsuyoshi, the seventy-six-year-old prime minister and Seiyūkai party president. Their actions would mark the end of parliamentary rule in imperial Japan.

These conspirators hoped to use violence to bring on martial law and policies of "national renovation." They simultaneously attacked the Mitsubishi Bank, the Seiyūkai party headquarters, the home minister's residence, and six power-generating stations. But their attacks did not spark a larger rebellion.

Even so, the impact of their actions was something close to a coup d'état. After the assassination, tense negotiations took place between the army and the leading "senior statesman," Prince Saionji, over the choice of a new prime minister and cabinet. The military leaders included officers who had been meeting regularly for several years to promote related programs of expansion in Manchuria and reform at home. They argued that "the fundamental causes [of such radical acts as assassinations] are political, economic, and other social problems, and a thorough renovation is needed [to solve these problems]."[11] To advance the cause of reform and to put in place leaders who might restrain insurgent young officers, they refused to allow the Seiyūkai party to form a new cabinet even though it retained its Diet majority. On May 26, Admiral Saitō Makoto took office as prime minister of a national unity cabinet with just five party men among the fifteen ministers. The remaining ten were top military men and bureaucrats.

Over the next several years, these leaders did little to restore discipline in the military and less to reverse the expansionist direction of Japan's foreign policy. An escalating logic drove Japanese strategy forward. Western and Chinese challenges to the new Japanese gains were presented to the public by government leaders as justification for further Japanese expansion in China. One example came in February 1933 when the League of Nations accepted the Lytton Report, a document prepared several months earlier that condemned Manchukuo as an illegitimate puppet state. The League called for a multilateral conference to demilitarize the region. Japanese diplomats responded with a defiant outcry. They portrayed Japan as a martyr on a hostile stage of world opinion. Japan withdrew from the League of Nations in March 1933.

Clashes with Chinese forces continued on the southern flank of Manchukuo, and the Kwantung Army pressed forward. By May 1933 it had annexed the province of Jehol (Rehe) and made it part of Manchukuo. Japan's virtual colony now extended as far as the Great Wall of China, a mere forty miles from Peking. Over the next two years, with the support of the cabinet in Tokyo, Japanese forces used border clashes and anti-Japanese activism as grounds to nibble away at Nationalist control of China's northern heartland. In June 1935 the Kwantung Army forced the Chinese Nationalist government to withdraw all troops from the region south of the Great Wall, including the key cities of Beijing and Tianjin. In November the Japanese further weakened Nationalist control by setting up a puppet government under a Chinese warlord to administer this strategic region. These actions set the stage for further conflicts in China.

They also increased tensions with the Western powers. Britain and the United States both supported the League of Nations in condemning the takeover. Although some American businesses hoped to work with Japan to invest in the region, the U.S. government continued to refuse to recognize Manchukuo. For its part, the Japanese navy became increasingly frustrated by the trilateral naval arms limitations renewed in 1930. The Japanese government abrogated this agreement in December 1934. An emergency three-power conference in London the following December failed to save it. The government authorized a major buildup of naval forces. It simultaneously decided to support a military capable of "defending in the north" (Soviet Union, the United States, and China) even while "advancing to the south" (Southeast Asia).

As they developed policies for the new Manchurian state, Japan's rulers also revised their strategies toward the older colonies of Korea and Taiwan. They no longer believed it enough to seek local stability and local profits. They redefined these colonies as places where human and material resources should be mobilized to support the expanding empire. In Korea beginning in 1931, Ugaki Kazushige took office as

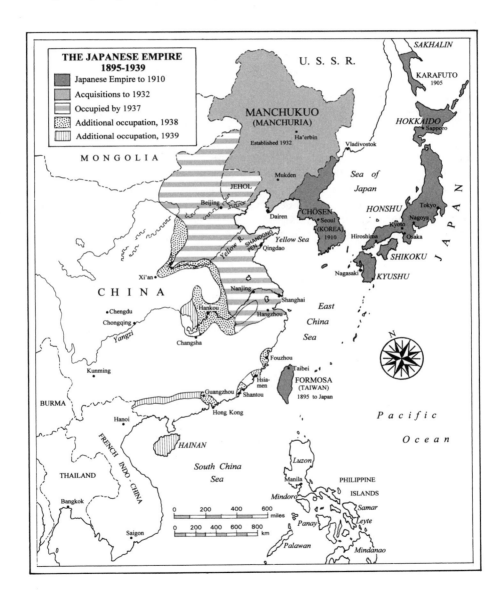

governor general. He launched ambitious and harsh economic and social policies. In the agrarian sector, the colonial regime pushed farmers to plant cotton and raise sheep to supply material for Japanese industry rather than food for the local population. Ugaki's regime also encouraged Japanese industrialists to invest in mining of strategic ore and metals, electric power generation, chemical (explosives) and fertilizer production, and the production of iron and steel. Some Korean entrepreneurs were able to found profitable industries as well. But regardless of the ownership, most industries drew on Korea's inexpensive labor supply to feed products and resources to Japan's own increasingly militarized economy. To mobilize human resources, Ugaki pushed forward an increasingly coercive program of ethnic assimilation in the schools. He expanded compulsory Japanese language instruction and sharply limited the teaching of Korean language in schools. By the late 1930s, Korean had been banned entirely.

Colonial rulers similarly shifted their strategic view of Taiwan. The governor general there had set up the semipublic Taiwan Development Company in 1936, mainly to promote sugar cane production on the island for export to Japan. In the late 1930s, the Development Company, already Taiwan's largest enterprise by far, redefined its mission to include industrial investment in nearby provinces along the coast of China proper, as well as islands toward the south. Authorities also cracked down on a political movement for home rule that had been tolerated in the 1920s.

Such projects of strategically focused, state-supported investment mirrored Japan's economic strategy in its new prize of Manchukuo. From 1932 through 1936 the Manchukuo government created one monopoly corporation in each of twenty-six key industries from mining and shipping to aircraft production. These were funded by a combination of state and private Japanese investment. The government in Tokyo was convinced that the world was breaking up into mutually hostile armed camps. It therefore treated the colonies in general, and Manchukuo in particular, as components of a self-sufficient trading bloc. Government bureaucrats and military leaders tended to see free-market capitalism as wasteful and immoral; they treated the Manchurian state above all as a laboratory in which to devise a new strategy of state-led economic development.

TOWARD A NEW SOCIAL AND ECONOMIC ORDER

The invasion of Manchuria coincided with, and partly caused, dramatic changes in Japan's domestic economy. From 1931 to 1934 industrial output rose 82 percent, as Japan recovered from the depression far faster than the Western economies. The volume of exports outside the empire nearly doubled from 1930 to 1936. Japan not only became the world's leading exporter of cotton goods. A newly diverse mix of products also made its way to American department stores and Asian marketplaces, ranging from toys and tires to bicycles and simple electrical machinery. All told, the economy grew by about 50 percent from 1930 to 1936. In 1937 one of the nation's most important economists, Arisawa Hiromi, described the 1930s as a time of "economic miracle." By 1938 employers were complaining of labor shortages and wages rose substantially.

The cause of this economic leap forward was twofold. First, the Japanese yen fell dramatically in value when the finance minister, Takahashi Korekiyo, took the nation off the gold standard. This allowed the yen to plummet in value: One dollar purchased

two yen in late 1931; a year later, the same dollar could buy five yen worth of goods. As a result, Japanese exports won new markets. They also won angry criticism. American and European competitors condemned what they called "social dumping." They blamed the export surge not on the exchange rate but on low wages paid to exploited workers, and numerous nations raised tariffs or imposed quotas on Japanese goods. In the eyes of many Japanese people, these objections validated the opinion of military leaders who had been arguing for some time that Japan needed to carve out a self-sufficient empire in a hostile world.

The second factor behind the 1930s boom was Japan's precocious discovery out of practical necessity of what came to be called Keynesian economic policy. In 1936 the famous British economist John Maynard Keynes published his *General Theory of Employment, Interest and Money*, which argued that deficit spending could "prime the pump" and spark renewed growth in a lagging economy. Four years before this, Finance Minister Takahashi Korekiyo undertook such a policy without benefit of Keynes's book.[12] He approved major deficit spending to finance the expanded cost of empire in Manchuria. His so-called red-ink bonds functioned, as Keynes would soon predict, to stimulate the economy. Government spending particularly benefited heavy and chemical industries that produced arms and supported major construction projects in Korea and Manchuria. These producer goods industries expanded even faster than the consumer goods manufacturing aided by the cheaper yen.[13] By 1937 the military budget accounted for an extraordinary three-fourths of all central government outlays, up from roughly one-third in 1930.

These economic advances took place under the shadow of what the authorities called the "time of emergency." With Westerners building tariff walls and condemning the Manchurian takeover and with the Chinese boycotting Japanese goods, the belief that the nation faced unprecedented crisis served to justify all sorts of new programs that changed the relationship of the state to the larger society.

In the economic sphere, the years of depression and recovery witnessed the birth in Japan of what later came to be called industrial policy. This heightened state involvement in orchestrating economic activity was a central component of the transwar political and economic system. Beginning in the late 1920s a group of bureaucrats in the Ministry of Commerce formulated plans to organize economic activity in what they expected to be a more rational fashion. This ministry had been created in 1925, split off from the existing Ministry of Agriculture and Commerce to encourage a more intensive government focus on the industrial economy. In 1930 the ministry set up the Industrial Rationalization Bureau. Its mission was to reduce what it considered the wasteful excesses of free competition by promoting trusts and cartels. The bureau took a major first step by writing the Important Industries Control Law, passed by the Diet in 1931. The measure legalized the creation of industry-wide cartels that could fix members' output, prices, market shares, and conditions of entry. Within several years, twenty-six cartels had been established in industries such as coal mining, electric power, shipbuilding, and textiles.

A deep-rooted distrust of the free market drove these reforms forward. Japan's state officials, both civilian and military, had long feared that unregulated profit-seeking would lead to investments that might serve the zaibatsu owners but not the national interest, as they defined it. The "nation," for example, might require electric

power stations to serve rural areas, but capitalists would not build these if the rural consumers were poor. The world depression seemed to confirm the bureaucracy's worst fears: Unreformed capitalism seemed both economically ineffective and socially damaging. At the same time, officials were neither willing nor able to replace the private sector with full state control. They were groping toward a mode of economic policy somewhere between the rigidly planned, state-run socialism of the Soviet Union and the laissez-faire economic liberalism of the United States or Britain, which would continue through the war and well into the postwar era.

With their new policies of the early 1930s, state officials sought to orchestrate economic decisions more carefully and centrally. But, by fostering cartels controlled by the largest corporations they ironically left the baton in the hands of the zaibatsu chiefs. The government then began to intervene more directly. In 1936, against intense business and political party opposition, the bureaucrats and generals who controlled the cabinet pushed through a law to nationalize the electric power industry. In 1937 the army and the bureaucracy began the practice of producing Five-Year Plans targeting certain industries for growth and channeling capital in their direction. Also in 1937, several existing bureaus were merged into a superagency called the Cabinet Planning Bureau. These bureaucrats comprised what one scholar has called Japan's "economic general staff." It was now working closely with the general staff of the military as well as the zaibatsu captains of industry, although the latter continued to resist intrusive state regulation of their firms.[14]

The military also supported several new business combines in hopes of nurturing sympathetic private sector allies, especially in the development of Manchuria. These were called the "new zaibatsu," a group of conglomerates centered in heavy and chemical industries. They benefited greatly from military demand, and some, such as Chisso Chemical Fertilizer and Shōwa Denkō, grew to be industry leaders and survived the war. The new zaibatsu were particularly dominant in Korea. But they did not have their own banks, and in fact the established old zaibatsu constituted the major source of direct investment in Manchuria throughout the 1930s. In this fashion, industrialists old and new followed the flag and moved into business in Manchuria in close collaboration with the military and civilian bureaucracy.

The state reached more closely than ever into agrarian society as well. As with industrial policy, the depression was a major catalyst of new approaches toward agriculture. In addition, the government's concern to reorganize agrarian as well as industrial society would continue through the war and into the postwar era. As prices crashed from 1929 through the early 1930s, both tenant farmers and small owners had to borrow funds to pay rent or tax bills. A government estimate in 1932 placed total farm debt at one-third the gross national product. The cabinet responded by dramatically boosting its outlays for rural public works to generate employment. The government also promoted debt relief with laws to provide emergency credit and help farmers refinance loans. These state programs were notable for their effort to aid middling farmers, including tenants, as well as the landlords whose political power and social prestige had long dominated village life.

Such measures were justified by a rhetoric of agrarian nationalism that equated Japanese national strength with harmonious, united villages. Farm-loving philosophers blamed the cities and unfettered capitalism for the crisis of the village. Such views

had motivated the young officers who had assassinated Prime Minister Inukai in 1932. They also stimulated a new effort of the Ministry of Agriculture to go beyond public works and debt relief. Beginning in 1932, the ministry threw its resources behind the Campaign for Economic Revitalization, which stressed the need to revive a spirit of cooperation in rural Japan and condemned Western-style individualism spreading from urban centers for eroding rural solidarity. Agrarianist rhetoric moved away from a focus on class conflicts to a focus on the city-country split. To strengthen the countryside, the revitalization campaign proposed a wide range of measures, such as industrial cooperatives, crop diversification, techniques for cost accounting, and long-range community planning. The campaign leaders, at both national and local levels, condemned farmers for making decisions based on superstitious belief in unlucky days or directions. They called instead for more rational and scientific farm management. Thousands of villages signed on to the campaign, and the government sought out and publicized model villages for the rest to follow.[15]

The combination of a traditionalist rhetoric of rural solidarity and modernizing strategies of better farm management was a striking feature of the drive to revitalize rural Japan. This mix echoed social reform projects of earlier decades. As in the 1920s, the rural reformers offered particular hopes to women and promised them new roles. Women were exhorted to improve kitchen design and hygiene and to organize everyday life more efficiently and scientifically. These responsibilities amounted to a significant public role in the community. Many responded to the campaigns with enthusiasm.

In both industrial and agrarian policy, the state appeared to be tightening its control of the larger society. But this appearance is somewhat deceiving. Bureaucrats left much authority in the hands of zaibatsu owners, and self-proclaimed leaders of the village retained great autonomy. The leaders of the revitalization campaign included small landholders as well as major landlords, men as well as women. The state had increased the range of its concerns and activity, but as of the mid-1930s it functioned mainly as an orchestrator of efforts by existing social organizations, rather than as dictator.

Some signs of a far more visible official hand in social matters were unmistakable, however. This is evident in the government's changed treatment of labor. The Home Ministry as well as the Minseitō had promoted unions as potential sources of stability in the 1920s. The ministry continued to tolerate them in the early 1930s, especially when the Sōdōmei federation adopted a new platform for the time of emergency, which repudiated strikes and promised cooperation to raise output and improve work conditions. But the government soon shifted its view of the best way to maintain order and mobilize working people to serve the state.

In late 1936 the army, fearing an "anti-fascist front" of unions and proletarian parties in military plants, forced eight thousand arsenal workers to withdraw from the Sōdōmei's union of government employees. Key military men and bureaucrats formulated a nonunion strategy for labor-management peace and stepped up production. By 1937 they decided to institute a nationwide network of "discussion councils" in all workplaces. These were to be composed of worker and manager representatives who would cooperate to prevent conflict. Such plans consciously drew on fascist models, such as the 1934 Nazi Law for the Organization of National Labor, which

had created advisory Councils of Trust in all German factories of twenty or more employees. Although the Japanese planners played down their debt to the German model, both programs sought a classless national community, and both replaced unions with advisory, universal plant councils. Both waxed eloquent on the organic harmony and unity of an industrial "shop community" based on mythic village, folk, or family models. The Japanese boosters of industrial peace repudiated liberalism and class struggle. They affirmed a literally "corporate" view of the enterprise, which would be echoed through the war and in the postwar era as well. Companies were communities in which all members, equal before the emperor, had equally valuable vocations. In a favorite metaphor of the times, labor and management were likened to the two wings of a bird. After several years of planning, in July 1938 the government created the Patriotic Industrial Service Federation to promote councils throughout Japan.

TOWARD A NEW POLITICAL ORDER

Parallel to its expanded role in the economy and society, the state moved to control political life more tightly. One sign of this shift was the nationwide Election Purification Campaign. Beginning in 1935 the Home Ministry spearheaded this drive to eliminate official corruption such as bureaucratic favoritism for a party's candidate and party corruption such as vote-buying. The movement combined a public relations campaign for "election purification" with closer police monitoring of elections. By 1937, the drive to "purify" elections had gone beyond these relatively neutral forms of supervision. The Home Ministry intervened more directly to make sure that candidates of all parties mobilized popular sentiment for state objectives. In the Home Minister's words, "under constitutional government the people bear an important responsibility to assist imperial rule . . . with the vote they cast."[16] Police interrupted election speeches regularly to prevent any utterance that set the people in opposition to either the military or the bureaucracy. Any speaker who criticized "fascism" or even mentioned a "gap between the military and the people" was sure to be given a warning or halted outright.

Purification campaigns did not lead Japan's voters to reject the mainstream parties at the polls. Women's organizations, for example, both strongly supported the campaigns while continuing to back the mainstream parties. Throughout the 1930s, the Minseitō and Seiyūkai never won less than a combined total 90 percent of the votes and seats in national elections. Even so, party influence was receding. Voting rates fell sharply by the mid-1930s. As few as 60 percent of eligible voters went to the polls in urban districts. Unlike the 1910s and 1920s, few voices defended "normal" constitutional government. No rallies were held to protest the fact that nonparty governments ruled, even when elections produced strong party majorities. Under five nonparty prime ministers between 1932 and 1937, cabinets were made up of increased numbers of bureaucrats and military men, and ever fewer professional politicians. Admiral Saitō's first nonparty cabinet of the "era of emergency" placed one-third of the ministries in the hands of party politicians. The cabinets of Admiral Okada Keisuke (1934–36) and the career diplomat Hirota Kōki (1936–37) included just five and four party men, respectively. By the time of the cabinets formed by General Hayashi Sen-

jūrō (1937) and Prince Konoe Fumimaro (1937–39), Diet representatives held just one and two portfolios.

As military men and bureaucrats consolidated power at the apex of the political order, they felt little need to intimidate party leaders with drastic steps such as arrests or violence. Most politicians supported the moves toward expansion abroad, either before the fact or afterward. They sought to protect their jobs and the interests of their constituents, the zaibatsu leaders and landlords in particular, by cooperating with the new rulers rather than resisting. They were fairly successful in these efforts. The parties managed to delay or weaken a number of military proposals—such as the nationali-zation of strategic industries—that would have compromised the autonomy of business leaders. The mainstream political parties were on the defensive, but they still won elections and mediated between bureaucrats and the military on one hand and their organized constituents on the other. They were out of power, but not powerless.

One new political trend of the 1930s was the emergence of a unified political party that spoke on behalf of the lower classes. In 1932 leading socialists such as Abe Isoo and Asō Hisashi founded the Social Masses Party (SMP). It united most of the small, competing "proletarian parties" that had emerged with universal male suffrage in 1925. By 1936–37, its candidates were winning considerable support in local and national elections. It sent eighteen men to the Diet in 1936 and won thirty-seven seats and 9 percent of the vote in the 1937 election. In a number of key races in multi-member, urban districts in 1937, the SMP candidates placed first with well over 20 percent of the vote.

When neither mainstream party won a Diet majority in the 1937 election, the SMP held a potentially decisive "swing bloc" that it might have used to build a coalition with one party or the other. Instead, it moved closer to the ruling military. The ground for this convergence was a shared distrust for capitalism and the "selfish" interest-seeking of the established parties. The SMP sought to ride the tiger of au-thoritarian rule to win support for its programs to defend the masses. It called for local reforms such as rent controls and lower utility prices and national measures such as health insurance, pensions, and protective laws for workers. It styled this as a platform for "a prosperous populace to perfect national defense."[17] The SMP accepted the proposition that Japanese control of Manchuria, and later of China itself, served the cause of ethnic self-determination against the West.

The most crucial features of politics in the 1930s were continued turbulence within the military and the rising power of the army over the bureaucracy, the court, and the parties. The two trends were related. One reason for the move away from party cabinets was the belief among the senior statesmen that only military leaders could control the hotheads in the ranks. From the late 1920s through 1936, many of the most radical military men clustered in the Imperial Way faction (*kōdō-ha*). These officers and some civilian sympathizers wanted to eliminate the influence not only of parties and zaibatsu but also of status quo–minded senior statesmen and court figures. They stressed the importance of spiritual education and loyalty to the emperor as foundations of national strength. Younger activists in this group enjoyed support at the very top from people such as Araki Sadao, especially during Araki's term as army minister from 1932 to 1934.

Imperial Way sympathizers were responsible for numerous acts of terror, from the assassinations of political and business leaders in 1930–32 to the assassination of opponents within the military itself. With supporters in high places, the assassins occasionally were allowed to use the witness stand as a platform to advertise their pure motives and high ideals. These showcase trials won favorable press and popular sympathy. One notorious example was the 1935 trial of Aizawa Saburō, a young officer in the Imperial Way group who shot a top-ranked army planner, Nagata Tetsuzan. Aizawa was enraged that his leader, General Araki, had been recently pushed aside by officers more committed to economic and material modernization than spiritual education.

Nagata was identified with the nemesis of the Imperial Way officers, a group dubbed the Control Faction (*tōsei-ha*). These were usually more senior officers, including General Tōjō Hideki. They preferred to collaborate with existing elites. They rejected terrorist violence, but they were hardly moderate in other ways. They wanted to concentrate power in military hands and mobilize society for an impending total war.

Conflict between the two groups came to a final head in the most shocking political upheaval of the prewar era. On the snowy morning of February 26, 1936, about fifteen hundred army troops loyal to Imperial Way leaders such as Araki took over central Tokyo. They sent squads to murder most of the cabinet, and former Prime Minister Saitō, as well as opponents in the military and among high court advisors. They demanded that the senior statesmen appoint a sympathetic prime minister and other new leaders. Their vague plans called for a Shōwa restoration—a phrase chosen to suggest comparable ambitions to the Meiji restoration. They wanted to restore Japan's glory by honoring the emperor, defending the empire, and improving the lot of common people.

Prime Minister Okada survived the coup by hiding in a storage shed in his home. The rebels killed his brother-in-law, thinking it was Okada. They also murdered Saitō and Takahashi Korekiyo, the venerable party politician and incumbent finance minister, and the army's inspector general of military education. But their larger plan collapsed, despite some high-level support, when the emperor sharply condemned their action and issued an order for them to surrender. This time there were no show trials. Nineteen leaders of the conspiracy were tried and executed swiftly and secretly. Although the coup failed, the army emerged stronger than ever. Its leaders finally mustered the determination to purge the ranks of assassination-minded radicals. Bureaucrats and civilian politicians were terrified by the coup. They welcomed the promise of a more disciplined military.

In the context of this shifting domestic power balance and the escalating tensions with China and the West, the military and bureaucratic rulers of the 1930s imposed ever harsher restrictions on acceptable beliefs. Communism and Marxism had long been anathema to Japanese elites. In addition to the roundup of communist political activists in the late 1920s, left-wing literary figures were targeted. Kobayashi Takiji, an eloquent writer of proletarian fiction who held potential to transcend the limitations of this often heavy-handed genre, was murdered in jail in 1933.[18]

By the mid-1930s, even rather conservative ideas that had previously commanded wide support came under fire. The most famous such attack came in 1935. It was

directed at Minobe Tatsukichi, a well-respected legal scholar at Tokyo Imperial University. His so-called organ theory held that because the emperor's role was defined in the constitution, he was an organ *within* the state structure, rather than a sacred source of legitimacy that stood outside and above the state. For several decades, this interpretation had been taught to students at the elite imperial universities with little serious dissent. But in the hypercharged atmosphere of the 1930s "time of crisis," a number of scholars and military figures associated with the Imperial Way group condemned Minobe as the author of "treasonous works" for expressing this opinion. The affair peaked in 1935 with virulent attacks on Minobe in the House of Peers (where he was an appointed member). One member condemned him as "an academic tramp."[19] Both houses of the Diet censured Minobe. He was accused of slandering the emperor (lèse-majesté). Although Minobe was never convicted of this crime, several of his works were banned for "being contrary to the true meaning of the national polity," and he was harassed into resigning from the House of Peers.

Other far from radical victims of the increasingly intolerant political climate included Takikawa Yukitoki and Kawai Eijirō. Like Minobe, both were university professors. Takikawa was attacked for his liberal views by right-wing ideologues in 1932. The minister of education bent to this pressure and forced him to resign his Kyoto University position the next year. Kawai was a student of British liberal philosophy. He was indicted in 1938 for violating publication laws and importing "dangerous" Western ideas. In addition, the new religions, which had already come under fire in the 1920s, suffered greater persecution than ever. A number of groups, including the Ōmoto religion in 1934, the Tenri religion in 1938, and the Jehovah's Witnesses in 1940, were charged with various crimes and disbanded.[20]

The ambivalent democratic ideas of the 1920s had justified constitutional government and popular participation as the means to uphold emperor and empire. The narrower orthodoxy of the 1930s exalted the emperor as transcendent. In 1937 the Ministry of Education promulgated a famous manifesto throughout the school system. It was titled "The Cardinal Principles of the National Polity" (*Kokutai no hongi*). It blamed Japan's social and ideological crisis on Western beliefs ranging from individualism to communism. In place of such ideas, it asserted that "serving the Emperor and accepting the Emperor's august will as one's own" should be the basic principles of social life and morality. It exalted loyalty and military spirit as the nation's core values and the hierarchical family system as its core institution.

In these varied ways, the shadows of censorship and rigid orthodoxy overspread political life. So-called traditional Japanese virtues were celebrated to an extreme degree. But it is important to recognize that the social and material life of ordinary Japanese people remained essentially modern in many respects, and quite receptive to Western influence even after the outbreak of full-scale war with China in 1937. In some cases the state collaborated with existing organizations, such as the zaibatsu-dominated business federations or rural mutual aid societies. In other cases it sponsored new organizations such as patriotic labor associations and the Women for National Defense. In all cases it continued the modern effort to organize society into discrete functional groups.

The mechanization of material culture likewise proceeded apace, especially in middle-class homes. Hair salons spread throughout Japanese cities, offering perma-

A 1933 Tokyo street scene conveys a sense of the continued modernization of the cityscape: taller new office buildings and streets filled with cars, streetcars, and pedestrians. The Tokyo subway system also began service in these years.
Courtesy of *Mainichi* newspaper.

nents (*paamonentu*) to thousands of middle-class women. By 1939 there were about 850 such hair salons in Tokyo alone. Many businesses and a fair number of private homes signed up for telephone service; nationwide, the number of subscribers nearly doubled from 550,000 in 1926 to 982,000 in 1937. City streets began to fill with buses and taxis, and a few private autos competed with bicycles, streetcars, and pedestrians. The nation's first subway line opened in Tokyo in 1927 to great fanfare, and the first Osaka subway began service in 1933. By 1939 three lines curved beneath the main commercial and shopping districts of the capital.

A varied popular culture continued to flourish. Radios became a fixture of middle-class life. In 1932 as many as 26 percent of urban households owned radios, although less than 5 percent of rural homes could receive broadcasts. By 1941, 6.6 million radio receivers brought news and entertainment over the airwaves to over 45 percent of all households in Japan.[21] Radio broadcasts as well as victrolas boosted the popularity of jazz and Western classical music as well as Japanese popular songs and military marches. Brilliant filmmakers, such as Ozu Yasujirō, began to produce hit movies featuring stories of the lives of ordinary people, while others turned out ever-popular samurai battle epics. Hollywood productions drew equal if not greater crowds. Charlie Chaplin's May 1932 visit to Japan was the focus of huge popular interest, even though it coincided with the assassination of Prime Minister Inukai. Japan's first professional baseball teams began to compete in 1934. That same year, thousands of people thronged to see the great Babe Ruth play with an American team in eighteen exhibition games in twelve major cities during a monthlong tour. A capacity crowd of sixty-five thousand jammed Jingu Stadium in Tokyo for the first game. Such behavior makes it clear that many people responded to moralistic condemnations of Western culture with lukewarm enthusiasm or frosty disregard.

In sum, the 1930s in Japan witnessed a rise of "traditionalism." One can define this as the loudly propagated belief that time-honored, quintessentially Japanese practices and ideals should be touchstones for morality and action. Yet these years did not see an actual return to an earlier, traditional society. Popular culture remained cos-

The February 1936 cover of Japan's best-known magazine of satirical art and commentary, Tokyo Puck. *Published just before the February 26 attempted coup d'état, the cover makes fun of military influence in everyday life. The object of the cartoonist's pen appears to be two European, probably British, women who treat militarism as just another fashion trend. But the tone of the articles inside reveals a critical view that also extends to the militarization of Japanese society.*
Courtesy of Mr. Ono Kosei and Kawasaki Municipal Museum.

*American major league baseball players came to Japan for a round of exhibition games with
Japanese teams in 1934. Here Babe Ruth stands with Japanese star pitcher Date Masao.
Baseball remained extremely popular throughout the 1930s and during the Pacific War, de-
spite official efforts to restrict the sport.*
Courtesy of Mainichi newspaper.

mopolitan and lively. Material culture incorporated new global trends. Even the newly
dominant political forces of the 1930s had been put in place as part of Japan's Meiji
revolution. A renovated imperial institution, a meritocratic and proud bureaucracy with
high aspirations to manage society, and a technically advanced and efficient military
had been emblems of the modern nation since the 1880s.

To recognize such continuities is not to deny change. The cumulative weight of
a politics of assassination, repression, and military-bureaucratic rule, a shrill cultural
orthodoxy, and unilateral expansionism on the continent amounted to a sharp change
in the character of Japan's modern experience. This change would have tragic consequence for millions.

Should we sum this up by calling the 1930s the era of an emerging Japanese
fascism? I would say yes, although other historians disagree. But in thinking about
the history of these times, we should not be snarled by a definitional tangle. It is not
that important whether one labels the Japanese political order of the 1930s "fascist"
or "militarist." It is more important to note that the dynamics and outcomes of political
and cultural life in Japan shared much with the experience of the fascist states of
Europe.

One can identify in the German, Italian, and Japanese experiences a common
response of a second generation of modernizing nations. European fascist models

inspired the men who came to rule Japan in the 1930s. Rulers in all three nations shared the objective of funneling the energies of a glorified national body (whether the "Volk" or the Yamato race) into a quest for military hegemony, a closed economic empire, and an anti-democratic, hierarchic domestic politics, culture, and economy. The Japanese and Italian rulers, and even Hitler to a lesser extent, also shared the inability finally to dissolve all existing plural bases of political and economic power into a totalitarian system.

Certainly there were important differences between these nations as well. A fascist party never came to power in Japan. No figure emerged with charisma or longevity comparable to that of Hitler or Mussolini. But the process that produced these regimes shared a great deal. They all experienced economic crisis, sharp polarization of left versus right, intense conflicts in industrial workplaces and rural society, and murderous right-wing terror. In each case a perception took root among intellectuals and the political elite that a cultural malaise gripped the nation. Fear spread that established gender roles were breaking down. Elite and popular opinion in each case held that Anglo-American power blocked the nation's legitimate international aspirations to empire. The problems facing Japan in the 1930s ultimately were not those of monolithic homogeneity or a feudalistic society and beliefs. They were the problems of coping with modern diversity and tension. The nation's response to these problems led to the catastrophe of war and sparked a postwar revulsion for fascism and militarism. But programs of political and economic reform and mobilization also set in motion enduring transwar changes in industrial, agrarian, and social policy.

12

Japan in Wartime

On the night of July 7, 1937, Japanese troops engaged in a minor skirmish with Chinese soldiers in the vicinity of the Marco Polo Bridge just south of Beijing. On July 11 a local cease-fire took effect. Even so, the Japanese government sent additional troops from Korea and Manchuria. The Chinese challenged the Japanese positions, and further skirmishes took place. In late July Japanese forces attacked and occupied Beijing and Tianjin. Within a month of the Marco Polo Bridge incident a full-scale war was underway.

WIDER WAR IN CHINA

It is not clear who fired the first shots at Marco Polo Bridge. But in contrast to the events of the Mukden incident six years earlier, which sparked the takeover of Manchuria, it is clear that the Japanese cabinet under Prime Minister Konoe Fumimaro authorized the decision to launch a major offensive. The army itself was divided between expansionists and a minority who feared a protracted war and wished to negotiate a cease-fire. Konoe sided with the expansionists. They wanted to control the iron and coal resources in North China. They also believed that Chiang Kai-shek's Nationalist government would always remain a threat to Japan's control of Manchuria and North China. The expansionist faction hoped to destroy the Nationalist regime and replace it with a friendly government.

Although he widened the war, Konoe initially sought to use military pressure to negotiate a settlement with the Nationalists. In the fall of 1937, Japanese forces extended their control south from Beijing. They occupied the Shandong peninsula and a large portion of the Yellow River. Aided by the navy, Japanese troops also took Shanghai. They then moved swiftly to occupy Nanjing by mid-December. But negotiations stalled. By early 1938, it was clear that the Nationalists would not recognize the Japanese conquests. Despite the loss of China's three major cities, Chiang Kai-shek decided to withdraw to the west and continue a defensive war of resistance. In response, Prime Minister Konoe announced a new goal in January 1938. He issued a chilling call for a war to "annihiliate" the Nationalist regime.

Even as he spoke, one of the worst massacres in a century of horrific acts of

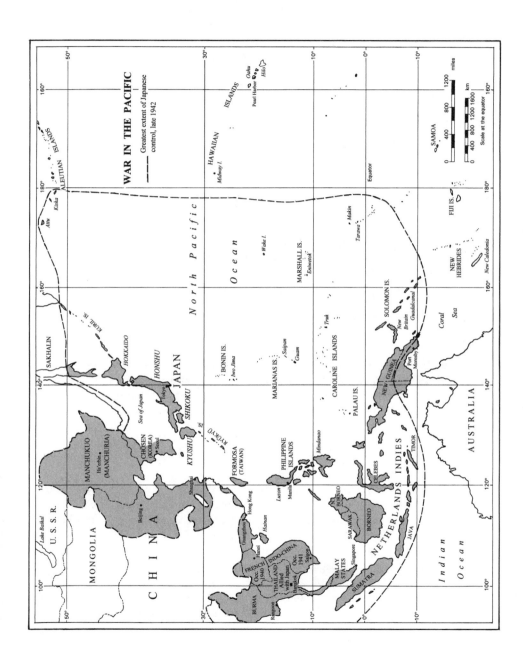

WAR IN THE PACIFIC

- - - - Greatest extent of Japanese
control, late 1942

U.S.S.R.

MONGOLIA

C H I N A

Lake Baikal

Beijing

Shanghai

MANCHUKUO
(MANCHURIA)
Ha'rbin

CHOSEN
(KOREA)
Seoul

Sea of Japan

SAKHALIN

HOKKAIDO

HONSHU

JAPAN

Tokyo

SHIKOKU

KYUSHU

RYUKYU IS.

FORMOSA
(TAIWAN)

Hong Kong

Guangzhou

Hainan

Hanoi

FRENCH
INDO-CHINA
Occ.
1940

THAILAND
Allied
with Japan
Bangkok

Saigon

Occ.
1941

BURMA

Rangoon

MALAY
STATES

Singapore

SUMATRA

NETHERLANDS INDIES

JAVA

BORNEO

SARAWAK

BORNEO

CELEBES

Indian
Ocean

AUSTRALIA

TIMOR

PHILIPPINE
ISLANDS

Lazon

Manila

Mindanao

PALAU IS.

CAROLINE ISLANDS

NEW GUINEA

Port
Moresby

SOLOMON IS.

New
Britain

Guadalcanal

Coral
Sea

NEW
HEBRIDES

New Caledonia

FIJI IS.

SAMOA

Equator

North Pacific

Ocean

MARIANAS IS.

Saipan

Guam

Truk

BONIN IS.

Iwo Jima

KURIL IS.

ALEUTIAN ISLANDS

Attu

Kiska

MARSHALL IS.

Eniwetok

Wake I.

Tarawa

Makin

HAWAIIAN
ISLANDS

Midway I.

Oahu
Pearl Harbor

Hilo

miles
0   400   800   1200

km
0   400   800   1200 1600
Scale at the equator

205

mass murder was underway in Nanjing. As Japanese troops entered the city in mid-December 1937, they began to round up civilians as well as surrendered soldiers. For seven weeks, through the end of January, they murdered tens of thousands of these people and raped countless women of all ages. The scope of the Nanjing Massacre remains controversial. Some Japanese historians insist on "low" estimates of perhaps forty thousand killed, while the Chinese government stands by a figure of three hundred thousand murders. A broadly accepted body count may never be reached, but there is no denying that Japanese soldiers carried out massive acts of atrocity.

Explaining why this massacre took place is as difficult as agreeing on a count of the victims. Frontline soldiers were certainly embittered by tough fighting en route to Nanjing. They were frustrated at the blurred line between Chinese soldiers and civilians, and they feared guerrilla attacks. They were also subject to harsh discipline. Like soldiers everywhere, they were taught to hate a dehumanized enemy. That soldiers in such circumstances might run amok and vent aggressive rage on civilians or disarmed troops is sad but not surprising. One finds too many such examples in the modern history of warfare.

The greater puzzle, and the greater crime, is that the Japanese high command in Nanjing allowed the roundups, rapes, and killings to proceed for weeks on end. Authorities in Tokyo were probably informed as well, but they took no decisive steps to rein in the troops. It may be that high-level Japanese in both Nanjing and Tokyo, frustrated at the inability to negotiate favorable terms, hoped that the example of these murders would destroy the Chinese will to resist. If so, they were as mistaken as they were brutal.

Over the following months the Japanese army expanded its control by seizing further key cities and railway lines. The military situation then reached a stalemate in the fall of 1938. Japan had committed six hundred thousand troops to the field, but they were barely able to defend the cities and railway lines in the occupied regions. The occupiers had little control over the countryside, and troops faced constant threat of guerrilla attack. Japanese forces murdered civilians as well as soldiers in numerous other incidents throughout the course of the war, especially in North China. Terrorizing the population in this way appears to have been part of a broader, ultimately failed military strategy to "pacify" the Chinese people.

The Nationalist government eventually retreated to the far western city of Chongqing, where it was protected from Japanese attack by mountains and sheer distance. In addition, tensions with the Soviet Union erupted in a major—although little reported—series of battles in the summer of 1939 along the border of China and Mongolia, a region called Nomonhan. The better equipped Soviet forces overwhelmed the proud Kwantung Army. The Japanese lost about twenty thousand soldiers to battlefield death or illness, out of a total of slightly over sixty thousand troops.[1]

In the effort to better control the three hundred million Chinese in the occupied areas, Japan created and recognized a new Chinese government to administer these regions in March 1940. It was led by Wang Jingwei, a rival to Chiang in the Nationalist movement. He shared with the Japanese a distrust of both the Soviet Union and the Western powers. He justified collaboration with Japan's military forces by claiming that the two sides shared a vision of pan-Asian unity against these outside forces. But the Japanese forced him to accept a humiliating "treaty" that undermined any claims he might make to popular support. Wang's regime remained weak. It depended on Japanese military backing for its survival.

Since the mid-1930s, a minority of strategists had warned that Japan should not overextend its forces. It was Ishiwara Kanji, the planner of the Manchuria takeover, who argued most forcefully at the highest levels that Japan lacked the resources to control China. He feared the Soviet Union and the West above all. He consistently urged the government to focus on building Manchuria while conserving strength to deal with these potential enemies. These views were not in favor. In the fall of 1937, Ishiwara was shoved aside and relegated to a succession of minor posts. But his worst fears came to pass. Japan's rulers trapped their soldiers in the swamp of a continental war. They were unwilling to retreat, but unable to overcome their foes.

TOWARD PEARL HARBOR

Having failed to break the deadlock in China, Prime Minister Konoe resigned his position in January 1939. Over the next eighteen months, three men in quick succession served as prime minister: the ultra-nationalistic career bureaucrat Hiranuma Kiichirō, followed by two military men, General Abe Nobuyuki and Admiral Yonai Mitsumasa. They pursued a combination of strategies to break the China stalemate by isolating Chiang and destroying his will or ability to survive. With the West, they tried diplomacy to induce the United States and Britain to recognize their position in China. To the north their diplomats sought to neutralize the threat of the Soviet Union, thus freeing the Kwantung Army forces for action in China. To the south, they considered both diplomatic and military steps to neutralize or eliminate the hold of the British in Malaysia, the French in Indochina, and the Dutch in Indonesia. This was desirable for two reasons. Japanese control of Southeast Asia would deliver strategic natural resources such as oil, rubber, and tin to the military. It would also provide a base to encircle and attack the Chinese Nationalists.

As Hitler's regime moved toward war in Europe, the Hiranuma government was attracted to the idea of an alliance with Nazi Germany to counter both Soviet and Western power in Asia. The ground had been prepared by the Anti-Comintern Pact of 1936. This committed Japan and Germany (Italy joined in 1937) to cooperate to oppose communism. Each state agreed to reach no agreements with the Soviet Union without the other's consent. Hitler violated this pact in August 1939 when he suddenly announced a nonaggression treaty with Stalin. With the failure of his strategy of cooperation with Germany, Hiranuma's credibility collapsed. Furious at Hitler's betrayal, he resigned as prime minister.

When Hitler invaded Poland and France the following month, the Abe and Yonai cabinets pursued a course of neutrality in the European war and slightly shifted the aim of their diplomacy. They made tentative efforts to engage American and British help to negotiate a settlement in China. But the army continued to press for an Axis alliance. It forced Prime Minister Yonai to resign because he preferred to seek accommodation with the British and Americans.

At this point, in the summer of 1940, Prince Konoe Fumimaro returned to power amid great elite and popular hope that he would provide strong leadership and construct a "New Order" abroad and at home. His lineage as an aristocrat close to the imperial family gave him particular legitimacy at this time of crisis. His first major initiative came in September when he concluded the Tripartite Pact with Germany and Italy. It committed the Axis powers to support each other against the United States, should it enter the war. By this move, Japanese leaders hoped that the path to a southern advance had been cleared. In June 1940 Hitler's troops had entered Paris, and the Germans set up the collaborationist Vichy regime to rule over occupied France. The Vichy government administered French colonies as well. The Tripartite Pact enabled the Japanese to negotiate an agreement with the Vichy authorities to station troops in the northern region of the French colony of Indochina (Vietnam). It is doubtful that an independent French government would have accepted the presence of Japanese troops.

The response of the United States would determine whether Japan's southern advance might succeed. Tensions between the United States and Japan had been building for some time. Throughout the 1930s, the Americans supported Chinese self-determination with strong words, but they had committed no significant resources to the Nationalists. Some business interests hoped to cooperate with Japan in the economic development of Manchuria. But in July 1939, hoping to send a signal of resolve that would deter Japanese expansion, Roosevelt broke off the Japanese-American commercial treaty. This step freed the United States to place an embargo on exports to Japan, if deemed necessary.

When Japan moved into northern Indochina, the Americans indeed countered with a gradually expanding export embargo. This further provoked Japan's war hawks. They began to argue for a preemptive strike against the United States and its allies. Hitler complicated these calculations when he broke his peace with Stalin and attacked the Soviet Union in June 1941. Japan chose not to join Hitler's new war. Its goals in the south required peace in the north, and two months earlier, in April 1941, Konoe had concluded a neutrality agreement with the Russians. He followed this by extending Japan's hold over Indochina, gaining Vichy permission to occupy the entire peninsula in July 1941. The agreement left Japan as the virtual ruler of the former French colony.

The Americans countered this advance with a strong and threatening move. Roosevelt immediately pulled together an international embargo that cut off all foreign oil supplies to Japan. He also offered below-cost military supplies to the Chinese. Without oil the Japanese government could not sustain its military or economy. It faced a difficult choice. It could agree to American conditions for lifting the embargo by retreating completely from China. Or it could follow the hawks and attack the United States and British, taking control of the Southeast Asian oil fields by force and hoping to negotiate for a cease-fire from that strengthened position.

For a time, it pursued both courses. Japanese diplomats sought in vain to negotiate a formula for a partial retreat in China that might satisfy both their own reluctant army and the United States. The Japanese military, meanwhile, drew up plans for a bold attack that might force the Western powers to recognize its hegemony in Asia. Diplomacy continued late into the fall of 1941, even as Konoe was replaced by General Tōjō Hideki. In the event of all-out war, the senior statesmen wanted a military leader at the helm. In an unusual concentration of power, Tōjō simultaneously held positions as army minister and prime minister.

By November it became clear to the key figures in the cabinet that a satisfactory diplomatic agreement was impossible. Japan was willing to withdraw only from Indochina. The United States would accept no less than withdrawal from all of China, except for Japan's pre-1931 holdings in southern Manchuria. In a meeting before the emperor on November 5, the inner cabinet agreed that if a final round of negotiations did not win American acceptance of Japan's position in Asia, the army would launch a major offensive to conquer the British and Dutch colonies of Southeast Asia and the American possessions in the Philippines. The navy would carry out a simultaneous attack on the American fleet at Pearl Harbor. Last-minute negotiations indeed produced no agreements. The Foreign Ministry intended to hand over a long memorandum notifying the Americans that negotiations were terminated—in essence a declaration of war—just before the Pearl Harbor attack. It took Japan's embassy staff in Washington so long to decode, translate, and type the memorandum that it was in fact delivered just after the attack on Pearl Harbor on December 7, 1941 (December 8 in Japan).

Thus ended a complex set of diplomatic and military maneuvers. Japan had plunged into a war that proved devastating for people throughout Asia. At key moments Japanese leaders grievously miscalculated the consequences of their actions. In 1937 the majority of the Japanese military, as well as civilian bureaucrats, politicians, intellectuals, and the press, failed to understand the force of nationalism in China, which fueled Chinese resistance. Likewise, in 1940–41 prior to the Pearl Harbor attack, Japan's leaders did not realize that the United States would be willing to cut off trade with Japan to defend the British and Dutch colonies. In the fall of 1941, as they made the decision for war, they understood well enough that American industrial power made a prolonged war with the United States unwinnable, but they naively convinced themselves that the Americans lacked the will to pursue such a war in distant lands.

It is true that the American moves to block Japan's advances in 1940 and 1941 confirmed the views of those in Japan who saw war as inevitable. For this reason, some historians blame the Americans for taking steps that led to the war. But it is difficult to argue that a different American response would have avoided a war. If the Americans had responded in conciliatory fashion, the logic of expansionism would almost surely have led the Japanese military to view this as weakness and take further aggressive steps. Japanese rulers were blind to the possibility that others would not bend to their will. Begining in 1931, they consistently responded to tension on the borders of the empire by pushing forward rather than standing in place or stepping back. Insofar as such tensions were virtually inevitable, the invasion of Manchuria set in motion a chain of events that led inexorably to war.

THE PACIFIC WAR

The Pacific War began with swift dramatic victories for the Japanese army and navy. The attack on Pearl Harbor destroyed the heart of America's Pacific fleet. Of its nine battleships, six were destroyed entirely and two damaged seriously. A daring drive down the Malay peninsula drove out the British and delivered Singapore to Japanese control in February 1942. The campaign for the Philippines ended in victory by May. American general Douglas MacArthur was forced to retreat to Australia. In these first six months of the war, the Japanese also took Burma from the British. They secured control of the sprawling possessions of the Dutch East Indies from Indonesia to Borneo and the Celebes. They occupied the islands of the Central and South Pacific (see map on p. 205).

The Pearl Harbor attack has become enshrined in American memory as an immoral "sneak attack." The Japanese apparently intended to provide minimal advance notice, although not enough to allow the United States to prepare defenses in Hawaii. In any case, American policymakers by late 1941 had ample evidence that the Japanese were considering war and were likely to launch an attack soon, someplace in Asia. In addition, at the time of the Russo-Japanese War in 1905, Japan had made good use of a surprise attack at Port Arthur. American military strategists in 1941 might have anticipated a similar tactic, but the United States commanders in the Pacific were complacent and ill prepared. Ironically enough, Western observers in 1905 praised the Japanese military for its brilliant strategy.

For all these reasons, condemnation of the mode of Japan's attack rings rather hollow today. At the time, however, anger at the tactic, and the devastating toll of thirty-seven hundred Americans killed or wounded in a single day, sparked a fierce desire for revenge in the United States. "Remember Pearl Harbor" became the watchwords of the war, and reverberations echoed well into the postwar era in the form of a stereotypical view of the Japanese as untrustworthy. At the time, anger at the attack also allowed President Roosevelt to bring the United States into the war against the Axis powers in Europe, something he had hesitated to do until that time in the face of reluctant public opinion.

People in Japan greeted these victories with jubilation. The government and media justified the campaign with grand claims that Japan was pursuing a war to return Asia to Asian control. But a huge practical task faced the Japanese government. It suddenly possessed a vastly expanded empire, roughly four thousand miles from north to south and six thousand miles from west to east. In what manner, and by what logic, would it be ruled? In 1938 Prime Minister Konoe had proclaimed Japan's intent to create a New East Asian Order as an equal partnership of China and Japan. In 1940, as a prelude to the move into Indochina, the government expanded its vision to call for creation of a Greater East Asia Coprosperity Sphere that included Southeast Asia. But neither the military nor the bureaucracy had made extensive plans for consolidating control of these new possessions.

Officials improvised their strategy as they went along. They ruled the older colonies more harshly than ever. In Korea the government-general mobilized students into factories and imposed a massive migration on as many as four million adults. They were forced to work as mine workers in Japan and as prison guards and laborers building airstrips in China. Thousands of young women were sent throughout Asia and forced to serve the sexual needs of soldiers. Taiwanese males were recruited into a "volunteer corps" to provide military and support services operations in various parts of Asia and the Pacific. They in fact had little choice in the matter. Many of those who remained on the island were mobilized into "public service brigades" to work in fields and factories.

The manner of rule varied in the newly conquered regions of Southeast Asia. In a gesture toward anti-colonialism, Japan sponsored nominally independent states in

Burma, Thailand, and the Philippines, while Japanese occupying forces ruled Indochina and Indonesia more directly. The government did not begin planning for a Greater East Asia Ministry until the spring of 1942, and it founded the ministry in November of that year. The ministry never became a powerful agency of integrated control. Representatives of the five states that constituted the Coprosperity Sphere (Burma, Thailand, China under Wang Jingwei, the Philippines, and Manchukuo) held just one Greater East Asia Conference, in Tokyo in November 1943. It was marked by praise for pan-Asian solidarity and condemnation of Western imperialism, but few practical plans to integrate or develop the region economically.

In practice, local Japanese military commanders dictated policy. They suppressed independence movements directed at the Japanese themselves while nurturing anti-Western independence fighters who pledged allegiance to Japan. The army sponsored the Burma Independence Army, led by anti-British Burmese nationalists. They joined forces with the Japanese troops that conquered Burma in early 1942, but by 1944 they had turned against the Japanese colonial rulers with an underground resistance movement. In similar fashion, the Japanese army recruited captured Indian soldiers in Singapore into the India National Army. With grand promises to help him oust the British from India, the Japanese army convinced a fervent Indian nationalist, Subhas Chandra Bose, to lead this force. In the spring of 1944 his army of about ten thousand men joined a Japanese force of more than eighty thousand for the disastrous Imphal Campaign, a drive from Burma across the border into India. The Japanese could not deliver logistical support to these forces, and an estimated seventy-five thousand Japanese and Indian troops died of disease or in battle. In Vietnam, in contrast, the Japanese harshly suppressed the Vietminh nationalist movement until the very end of the war. The army also confiscated much of the Vietnamese rice harvest in 1944 for use by its troops in the Philippines. This led directly to a famine that took almost one million lives.

Throughout the empire such cruel episodes squandered the goodwill that the Japanese initially won by ousting the Western overlords on behalf of a grand vision of Asian solidarity. Initial hopes among Indonesians, Filipinos, and Vietnamese that Japan would forcefully promote national liberation were betrayed. Even so, the brief interlude of Japanese control had an important long-run impact. Independence movements organized during the war, whether with inconsistent Japanese aid or in the face of Japanese repression, survived into the postwar era. They ultimately doomed the continuing hopes of the French, Dutch, and British for a return to the prewar system of colonial control.

The Greater East Asia Coprosperity Sphere amounted to little in part because the tide of war turned quickly against Japan. The failure of Japanese forces to take the Coral Islands in May 1942 was followed by a major defeat in the battle for Midway Island in June, just six months after Pearl Harbor. The Japanese navy lost four aircraft carriers that were the core of its fleet. The Americans and their allies then began a long, grinding drive toward the Japanese home islands. Submarine and air attacks devastated the Japanese merchant fleet. This cut off the homeland from the empire and crippled the domestic economy. The Americans largely ignored the huge land forces entrenched in China, Indochina, and Indonesia. They concentrated on a two-pronged drive across the Pacific. General Douglas MacArthur pushed to retake the Philippines from New Guinea, while the American navy under Chester Nimitz attacked strategic Japanese-held islands in the central Pacific. The capture of Saipan in July 1944 placed the main islands in range of American bombers. Japan's air defenses were helpless against high-flying B-29s, which rained down fire-bombs on civilian homes as well as factories. The war was essentially lost at this point, a full year before the Japanese surrender.

MOBILIZING FOR TOTAL WAR

Parallel to their push for a New Order in East Asia, bureaucrats, military men, political activists, and intellectuals issued loud calls for a New Order at home. A diverse assortment of men—and a few politicized women—looked above all to Prince Konoe Fumimaro to unite varied actors and remake Japan. The New Order slogan came into widespread use in 1938 during the time of Konoe's first cabinet. It pulled together strands of thinking that had been emerging since the 1920s. Self-styled advocates of "renovation" sought to remake the economic, political, and social order. They wanted to restructure industrial workplaces and agriculture and transform cultural life as well.

Advocates of a new order envisioned a flowering of indigenous practices that would transcend those of the decadent West. Yet they pursued a path—sometimes wittingly and sometimes not—with clear parallels to that of the Nazis in Germany and the Fascisti in Italy. They sought to replace messy pluralism with central planning and control of the economy, authoritarian rule grounded in a single unified political party, and firmer social discipline. Like Western fascists, they glorified mobilization for war as the "mother of creation." The pursuit of war was both catalyst of change and the result of these changes.

The Economic New Order was the brainchild of "economic bureaucrats" and military men centered in the Ministry of Commerce and the Cabinet Planning Board. They worked together with intellectuals in the Shōwa Research Association—a think tank close to Prince Konoe. One leading architect was the Ministry of Commerce bureaucrat Kishi Nobusuke, who came to head the Munitions Ministry at the height of the war (and would serve as prime minister in the late 1950s). Such people wanted to replace messy competition and profit-seeking with "rational" control of industry. They believed industry should serve "public" goals of the state, not private goals of capital. They argued that depression and social conflicts were inevitable in free market economies and undermined national strength. Only a state-controlled form of capitalism could resolve chronic conflict and crisis.

Economic controls were strengthened most dramatically under the Konoe cabinets of June 1937 to January 1939 and July 1940 to October 1941. A key step came in 1938 when the Diet ratified a National General Mobilization Law. It stipulated that once a "time of national emergency" was declared, the bureaucracy could issue any orders necessary—without Diet approval—"to control material and human resources." To win passage of the law, Konoe promised that the China war did not constitute such an emergency. But within one month of Diet approval, he nonetheless activated the law. The state had gained vast new authority to mobilize "material and human resources." Few areas of social or economic activity remained outside the reach of this order.

The Konoe government used the Mobilization Law in 1941 to create one capstone of the Economic New Order. This was the system of Control Associations brought into being by the Important Industries Control Order. The order allowed the Ministry of Commerce to create supercartels called "control associations" in each industry. These bodies were given power to allocate raw materials and capital, set prices, and decide output and market share quotas. In practice, the presidents of zaibatsu firms sat on the boards of each control association together with bureaucrats. By collaborating with the state, big business managed to retain significant authority over the cartels and control associations.

Smaller businesses, too, retained some autonomy for several years after the Economic New Order was proclaimed, but in early 1943, the government created a uniform national system of industrial associations (called "unions") with mandatory membership. Thousands of small manufacturers were forced to pool resources into these groups and dissolve themselves as independent firms. These industrial unions usually shifted to military production. Small-scale textile manufacturers, for example, were ordered to put their machines in mothballs and produce parts for airplanes as subcontractors for the giant industrial firms.

Advocates of top-down mobilization for economic efficiency and social order pushed for a Labor New Order parallel to these economic reforms. Beginning in the mid-1930s Home Ministry bureaucrats and police officials had been planning to set up factory-based councils of worker and management representatives. These were to feed into a pyramidlike structure of regional and national federations.

In July 1938 the Home and Welfare ministries launched the nominally independent and voluntary Federation for Patriotic Industrial Service (Sangyō hōkoku renmei, or Sanpō). The few remaining unions almost all supported the war and cooperated with managers already. They quietly coexisted with the federation. Many large companies joined the federation by renaming existing factory councils—founded in the 1920s as alternatives to unions—as Sanpō units. Owners of smaller factories, where neither unions nor councils were previously in place, were reluctant to join the federation. It appeared a distraction at best and a threatening form of outside interference at worst. The local police typically stepped in to force these factories to form Sanpō units. By the end of 1939, nineteen thousand enterprise level units had been formed, covering three million employees.

In 1940 under the second Konoe cabinet, the government took full control of the Patriotic Industrial Service Federation. It forced Japan's five hundred remaining unions (360,000 members) to dissolve. It mandated that all workplaces in the nation were to form factory councils. By 1942 Sanpō consisted of some eighty-seven thousand factory level units that enrolled about six million employees.

Federation supporters hoped the councils would build morale and solidarity among employers and employees as well as help expand production for the "holy war" in Asia. The model for this effort was the Nazi Labor Front put in place several years earlier in Germany. In practice, the councils were greeted with apathy by employees. One man reported that "we basically slept through meetings" while another called the councils "a complete waste of time." Owners and managers similarly held low expectations of the groups and gave them no authority. Sanpō was ultimately of little value to wartime mobilization.[2] It did, however, establish the precedent of including white-collar as well as blue-collar employees in workplace organizations. It offered official and high-profile lip service to the belief that all employees were valued members of the nation and the corporation. The postwar union movement would build on—as well as transform—these wartime precedents.

Wartime mobilization severely restricted the autonomy of managers and employees in several respects. Under the Mobilization Law after 1938, bureaucrats in the Home and Welfare ministries worked with school principals to assign new graduates to war industries. In 1941 as the war intensified and adult male employees were drafted into the army, the government put a labor draft in place to replace these workers. It authorized the conscription of adult males ages sixteen to forty and unmarried women ages sixteen to twenty-five. Over the following years roughly one million men and another million adult women were drafted into workplaces. The women were typically moved from domestic labor into the workplace, while the men were usually shifted from a "peacetime" job into a munitions plant or other strategic industry. Between 1943 and 1945, three million Japanese schoolboys and schoolgirls were drafted into plants producing for the war effort. Another one million Koreans and Chinese were sent from the continent to Japan and put to work in factories and mines under harsh supervision and dismal conditions.

Once on the job, employees had less and less freedom as the war progressed. Between 1939 and 1941 the government—also under authority of the Mobilization Law—issued a complex system of job registration and work passports that outlawed job changes. Simultaneously, the state restricted wages with increasingly severe regulations. Officials wanted to help employers and slow inflation by stabilizing labor costs.

The bureaucrats who devised these controls were moved in part by suspicion of the free market. Their regulations declared that the employment relation was no longer a contract between private parties. Rather, the primary obligation of managers and workers alike was to the state. Bureaucrats hoped to improve morale and productivity by forcing employers to offer a "living wage" that would rise with seniority to meet the increased needs of older workers with families. By 1943 Welfare Ministry officials had forced managers at thousands of companies to rewrite their personnel rules. All employees were to receive pay raises twice a year. Employers were given only limited discretion to reward talented producers or penalize poor performers. By these rules, the existing informal practice of giving seniority-linked raises to valued workers was systematized and extended to millions of employees. The postwar union movement would build on this reform.

The state also exercised more authority than ever in wartime agriculture, acting with a similar bias against the free market. In 1939 the Ministry of Agriculture put in place controls on rice prices and on the rents landlords could charge to tenants. As with wage controls, the goals were to stop inflation and to encourage production, in this case by protecting tenant cultivators. The state took virtually full control over the purchase and sale of rice and other foodstuffs with the Food Control Law of 1942. The government not only set the price of wholesale rice. It also took over distribution and retail sales, buying crops from rural producers and selling them to consumers in towns and cities.

Agricultural controls offered incentives to the actual cultivators at the expense of landlords. The Food Control Law set up a two-tiered pricing system. The government purchased "landlord rice" collected by landowners from their tenants at one price. It bought the remainder of "producer rice" directly from tenants or small-scale owner-cultivators at a higher price. The government at first paid a 20 percent premium for producer rice. By the end of the war it offered producers double what it paid to landlords. By this time, two-thirds of the rice crop was covered by the control apparatus. The government had bolstered the fortunes of cultivators and weakened the social prestige as well as the economic base of landlords.

The projects to mobilize for war by transforming industrial work and farming were riddled with contradictions. Labor regulations sought the goal of a secure "living wage," but government inspectors on the spot allowed companies to give large incentive premiums to fast young producers. Agrarianist rhetoric exalted village harmony, while incentives set tenants and cultivators against landlords. Such contradictions were most glaring in the state's approach to the economic role of women. With millions of men taken from the workplace to the military, the logic for drawing women into the work force was compelling. Yet deeply held beliefs about proper gender roles were equally compelling to many. The Home Ministry in 1942 refused to draft women into workplaces "out of consideration for the family system." Prime Minister Tōjō put it most grandly:

> That warm fountainhead which protects the household, assumes responsibility for rearing children, and causes women, children, brothers, and sisters to act as support for the front lines is based on the family system. This is the natural mission of the women in our empire and must be preserved far into the future.[3]

By late 1943, government officials recognized the need to somehow square the circle and, in the words of one bureaucrat, "simultaneously mobilize Japanese women while giving rise to their special qualities associated with the household." They put in place a virtually mandatory program to bring at least unmarried women into the workplace. All single women between twelve and thirty-nine were ordered to register as potential workers in the so-called Women's Volunteer Labor Corps. Pressures from neighborhood associations made it virtually mandatory to join. Between 1943 and 1945, some 470,000 women had gone to work in this program. This accounted for about one-third of the total increase in wartime female employment.

Yet even at the peak of the mobilization effort in 1943 Prime Minister Tōjō noted that "there is no need for our nation to draft women just because America and Britain are doing so. . . . [T]he weakening of the family system would be the weakening of the nation. . . . [W]e are able to do our duties here in the Diet only because we have wives and mothers at home."[4] Influenced by such views at the top, the overall mobilization of women's labor power proceeded in a comparatively halting fashion. Between 1941 and 1944, as many as 1.5 million young and adult women entered the labor force, producing a total of 14 million women working outside the home at the peak of the wartime economy. They made up 42 percent of the civilian labor force. The increase reflected market demand as well as state coercion. Women and their families needed money, and factories needed workers. Although the increase was significant, it contrasts sharply to the 50 percent rise in the United States and the even larger increases in the numbers of women workers in the wartime Soviet Union, Germany, or Britain.

Just as the economic reforms of the war years often fell short of the ambitious goals of planners, or foundered on internal contradictions, so did a parallel drive for a Political New Order produce mixed results. It began as a drive of some bureaucrats and officers to replace the existing political parties with a single mass party along the lines of Hitler's Nazis. It ended halfway to that goal. No energetic mass party was created, but in 1940 all existing parties were dissolved. A sort of political cheerleading squad called the Imperial Rule Assistance Association (IRAA) replaced them.

Advocates of a new mass party coalesced around Prime Minister Konoe in 1937 and urged him to head a mass campaign against the established parties. They were principally concerned with muzzling the Minseitō and Seiyūkai, which were still vigorous enough in the Diet session of 1937–38 to force the government to delay or slightly modify its legislative agenda. They also viewed low voter turnout as a form of resistance. In the view of New Order supporters, individualism or socialism had poisoned the masses, rendering them insufficiently committed to the agenda of the emperor's ministers. The campaign for a Political New Order was intended to transform apathy into enthusiastic support for the state.

During his first cabinet, Konoe focused on building consensus among opposed elite factions, so he shrank from the confrontational effort to lead a new party. The next two years witnessed a complicated series of struggles between advocates and opponents of the New Order. Key figures in the military, the bureaucracy, the Social Masses Party, and the civilian right, who supported a relatively pure fascist regime, placed their hopes in Prince Konoe. They saw a need for a powerful organ of mass mobilization to channel the economic and spiritual energies of the population in support of state goals. Against them stood most party politicians and their supporters, particularly the zaibatsu leaders.

At the outset of his second term as prime minister in July 1940, Konoe finally moved to proclaim a Political New Order by creating the IRAA. All political parties were required to dissolve themselves, and elected politicians were told to join the new association as individuals. But just as the zaibatsu accepted but co-opted the system of economic controls, the Minseitō and Seiyūkai parties preserved some prerogatives within the new structure.

The Diet election of 1942 nicely demonstrates this halfway result. About 1,000 candidates contested for 466 seats. The IRAA put forward a government-approved slate of precisely 466 men. This included 247 incumbents and 20 former Diet representatives, a significant continuity from the previous decades of party politics. Roughly 550 independent candidates ran for office as well. These included another 150 party politicians. The official IRAA candidates won 82 percent of the seats (381 of 466). All the incumbents on the IRAA slate were reelected.[5] Many party men, whether those serving in the IRAA or those elected as independents, continued to command the local loyalty of their constituents. To a considerable extent, the individual members of established political parties remained a part of the ruling system.

Yet they were certainly a far meeker group of people than in the past. A total of 199 newcomers were elected to the Diet, a higher turnover than in previous elections. And all the Diet members were now acting less as representatives of popular interests than as transmitters of state interests to the people. They no longer constituted an organized or independent political force. The vast majority supported Prime Minister Tōjō. Those who did not kept their doubts private or faced arrest and prison.

Taken as a whole, state mobilization programs fell short of their more ambitious, even totalitarian goals to "renovate" the nation. Significant though limited pluralism remained. Neither the Economic New Order nor the Industrial Patriotic Federation nor the IRAA brought the state total control over Japanese subjects. Yet the drive to mobilize society for war, and remake it in the process, did change the relation between state, society, and the individual. The Diet became a peripheral institution. Relatively independent organizations of socialists or feminists, of factory workers or tenant farmers, of businessmen or party politicians were dissolved or transformed. The state became more intrusive than ever. Political expression was tightly and harshly monitored.

This new order was promoted using the latest technologies, from radio to newsreels and cinema. It linked people to the state and the emperor through a vast network of organizations that had been created in the modernizing endeavors of previous decades. These bodies were now more closely managed by the state: youth groups, women's groups, village and neighborhood associations, workplace councils, agricultural and industrial producers' unions. The wartime order was cloaked in a traditionalistic rhetoric that glorified ancient loyalty to the emperor, but in many ways it was exceedingly modern.

LIVING IN THE SHADOW OF WAR

Through most of the 1930s, despite the costly and escalating war in China, most Japanese enjoyed economic good times. Industrial production increased by a total of 15 percent from 1937 through 1941, with particular gains in heavy and chemical industries producing for the military. Censorship constrained public discourse, but cultural life remained rather upbeat and lively. In the immediate circumstances of their lives, most people saw little reason to doubt the basic wisdom of their leaders' new departures in foreign and domestic policies.

But signs of trouble gradually were becoming visible toward the end of the decade, well before the tide of the Pacific War turned against Japan in 1942. Economic growth after 1937 was considerably slower than in the previous several years. After the war in China broke out in 1937, inflation jumped from worrisome but manageable levels of about 6 percent annually to double-digit annual levels. Taxes rose sharply from the late 1930s onward. By 1938 military spending accounted for a full three-fourths of the government's budget and 30 percent of gross national product. This was already an extraordinary imbalance, comparable to that of the Soviet Union's economy in the 1970s and 1980s. It only got worse in the next several years. The consumer economy was virtually shut down by the early 1940s. Controls on resource allocation denied raw materials and capital to textiles and other consumer industries, and mobilization plans forced these producers to retool for war production. Price and wage controls had unintended adverse effects. They pushed consumers, employers, and laborers to create black markets in goods and jobs. Standards of living collapsed. The real wages of Japanese people fell by 60 percent from 1934 to 1945. By contrast, real wages rose more than 20 percent in the United States and Britain over this span and remained constant in Germany. By early 1944, even before fire-bombing devasted the major cities, civilian life had been a dismal grind of scarcity and restriction for several years.

The gradual descent into deprivation can be glimpsed in the plain but compelling recollection of a relatively fortunate Tokyo woman who ran a bakery with her husband:

> For a while we had a supply of Shanghai eggs. . . . They didn't get frothy like real eggs, and the [cakes] wouldn't rise either. Eventually they became unavailable, so we had to change our business to sandwiches. There was no more sugar. We'd buy ten loaves of bread, slice them as thin as possible, fill them with whale ham. There wasn't any real pork ham anymore. . . . Soon enough bread disappeared for us ordinary people. Even whale ham. We had to give up the sandwich business. . . . Eventually we had to deliver our baking machinery to the military because it was made of iron. . . . Finally we decided to evacuate from Tokyo, since we had little left and the air raids were coming more often. . . . My house in Monzen Nakachō burned down in the March 9 air raid. . . . But we were lucky. We didn't have anybody killed by that war.[6]

As mobilization and war came to dominate the lives of such ordinary people, Japan's cultural leaders played a variety of roles. Some turned to aesthetic projects and nonpolitical endeavors out of self-protection or disgust. The brilliant writer Tanizaki Jun'ichirō devoted himself to a modern "translation" of the great Heian era work of prose fiction, *The Tale of Genji*, which he completed in 1938. Some left-wing scholars withdrew from activism to produce translations of classics of European social science. Kuruma Samezō began work on his extraordinary complete "concordance" of the work of Karl Marx, a precomputer equivalent of what the Internet generation would call a Marxism search engine.[7]

A small and scattered number of dissenters tried to slip their critical views past the censors. The following poem was published in 1944, apparently because the authorities did not catch its pacifist implication:

A Mouse

Throwing away his life
as if he were a cardboard statue,
one mouse
marched out into a busy street
and was squashed.
Many wheels rolled over the mouse
and ironed him out flat,
spreading him thinner and thinner on the pavement.
Soon he was unrecognizable—
as a mouse,
as an animal,
even as something that had died.
One day someone crossed the street
and saw a flattened object
battered and warped in the sunlight.[8]

Unlike this poet, the majority of intellectuals supported the war with enthusiasm. They joined government-sponsored associations of artists or writers. They produced important essays and speeches that justified wartime mobilization and reform as a grand mission to "overcome modernity."

An attack on modernity and Western culture was the most important intellectual reaction to the war. It reached a peak in July 1942 in a famous conference on "overcoming modernity" held at Kyoto University. Some of the nation's most prominent intellectuals gathered, convinced there was a link between their academic musings and geopolitics. They sought to identify "the world historical meaning" of the wars in China and the Pacific. They saw their intellectual battle as a complement to the "glorious war" underway, a struggle between "the blood of the Japanese that truly motivates our intellectual life and Western knowledge that has been superimposed on Japan in modern times." Just as a war to liberate Asia was preferable to accepting Western hegemony, so was a cultural war against modernity and the West better than "cultural submission" to Western ideals.[9]

Advocates of "overcoming the modern" argued that the cultural enemy was the rational "science" that had grown out of Western traditions variously traced back to the Greeks, Jews, or Christians. Such traditions set men in struggle against God. In Japan, to the contrary, there was no conflict or tension between gods and men. Japanese spirituality, such as that seen in Shinto practices, was said to be a source of "unified knowledge" stressing the "wholeness" of beings, creatures, and things.[10]

The anti-modernists saw the decades from the 1880s onward as a long era of betrayal. The true potential of the Meiji restoration, they claimed, had been the promise of the East asserting itself against the West. On one level this restoration succeeded: Where India was overwhelmed and China dismembered by the West, Japan withstood the Western onslaught. But then what happened? Japan's Meiji "modernization" inundated the nation with Western materialism. Japanese people became selfish seekers of advantage. They lost sight of their true essence as a classless community living in harmony under a benevolent emperor. By the 1920s, this argument went, the nation was marked by crass profit-seeking and hedonism, emblematized in "modern girls" and American movies, in fast living (*supiido*) and eroticism. Remarkably enough, given the commercialism and ribald character of so much of Tokugawa popular culture, these trends were usually described simply as Western cultural invasions, in particular the poisonous output of the United States. American democracy was condemned as a sleight of hand that satisfied the ignorant masses with trivial goods.

A poem published in the *Yomiuri* newspaper just after Pearl Harbor summed up the spirit of such critiques:

We are standing for justice and life
While they are standing for profits
We are defending justice
While they are attacking for profits
They raise their heads in arrogance,
While we are constructing the great East Asia family.[11]

The war was glorified as a quest to liberate all of Asia from Western-dominated modernism, thus restoring an Asian social harmony. As one essayist put it in early 1942: "[T]he races of East Asia are going to establish a united cultural sphere, like the ones the Europeans have created since the medieval age. As the first step . . . the influences of the occidental peoples in East Asia must be driven away."[12]

The government's cultural policies during the war closely reflected this spirit. The state quite literally sought to expel Anglo-American cultural influences. American and British films were banned. German and French movies were allowed, but to preserve the martial atmosphere, the love scenes were cut. All "enemy music" was banned, especially decadent jazz. In January 1943, the Nippon Music Culture Association, a government creation with a large membership of musicians and teachers, announced it would "weed Japan of the influence of American jazz," which had permeated Japan's daily life. Every third Friday was set aside to discuss ways of "ousting degenerate jazz music." Beauty parlors, which had surged in number since the 1920s, were condemned for corrupting the purity of women, and permanents were banned. Baseball, popular since the 1890s, was banned in 1943. And the state launched a drive to purify the language, which had been permeated with English and other Western language expressions for decades. Japanized pronounciations of "strike" and "out" (sutoraiki and a-u-to) were ordered to be replaced by native words. The "Japan Alps" were likewise renamed indigenously, and the popular Westernisms for parents ("mama" and "papa") were discouraged.[13]

The calls to replace profligate Western ways with a spirit of sacrifice appropriate to the pure Japanese spirit were loud and consistent. They came from both intellectuals and the state and were addressed to the entire population. Shortages of consumer goods made austerity and sacrifice unavoidable. Western luxury items disappeared from stores. City women gave up stylish dresses for baggy workclothes called monpe. Hairdryers were recycled for war production.

But cultural restrictions that were not reinforced by material scarcity or direct military necessity had rather limited effect. Baseball continued after the ban. When the military started drafting university students in the fall of 1943, six months after the ban took effect, the best farewell present the administrators of Keio and Waseda universities could think of was a baseball match between the two schools. It attracted a huge crowd. Similarly, cafés turned off Victrolas for a few days after jazz was outlawed. But owners soon started playing old favorites again, softly at first, more boldly over time. One kamikaze pilot wrote in his diary, "[H]ow funny [it is] to listen to jazz music the night before going out to kill the jazzy Americans."[14]

The effort to overcome modern culture—like the various projects to construct a new political and socioeconomic order—was full of contradictions. It did not generate consistent or well-enforced policies. At the intellectual level, anti-modernism actually drew on a Western conceptual language articulated in Europe by figures such as Nietzsche and Heidegger. Indeed, the centrality of calls to "overcome modernity" was an indication of how fully modern Japan had become. At the popular level, trends, tastes, and hobbies of Western origin had been so deeply rooted that they could not be cast out easily. Despite slogans to the contrary, the war did require the use of "rational science" to manufacture planes and in all other aspects of production and battle. Indeed, Japanese engineers excelled in the design of the Zero fighter plane. Likewise, the scientists of the notorious "unit 731" used coldly "modern" rationality in biological warfare experiments on Chinese subjects. Finally, it is important to recognize that unease about modernity and losing one's traditional essence was not limited to Japan

One part of the government policy to encourage Japanese values and a return to a "traditional" culture was a restriction on Western cultural influences, from music and sports to fashion. Here, a military inspector on a sidewalk in the fashionable Ginza shopping district of Tokyo admonishes women with permanents to conform to policy and adopt "Japanese" hairstyles in 1940.
Courtesy of *Mainichi* newspaper.

or to the Axis powers. Indeed, such unease has been a defining feature of modern life itself, all around the world. In an extreme way, and with unusually devastating consequences, wartime Japanese were grappling with quintessential modern dilemmas.

ENDING THE WAR

People in Japan lived through most of the war with remarkable public perseverance, despite mounting private doubts. But toward the end, signs of social breakdown increased. Chronic absenteeism in urban workplaces throughout Japan reached 20 per-

Toward the very end of the war, the rhetoric and preparation for a "decisive battle" to the death, in defense of the homeland and throne, reached unprecedented intensity. Here members of the Women's Defense Association in Nagasaki train with bamboo poles for the expected final battle in 1945.
Courtesy of *Mainichi* newspaper.

cent daily even before air raids forced workers to flee the cities. After the raids began in 1944 and 1945, absentee rates often came to a full 50 percent of the work force. Wildcat disputes over wages and work conditions rose in number. The military police also noted an alarming rise in passive resistance such as anti-government graffiti. One imperial household aide recorded in his diary in December 1943 the fearful spectacle of a drunken gentlemen singing the following ditty on the streetcar:

> They started a war
> they were bound to lose
> saying we'll win, we'll win,
> the big fools. Look, we're sure to lose.
> The war is lost
> and Europe's turned Red.
> Turning Asia Red can be done before breakfast.
> And when that time comes, out I'll come.[15]

As they observed these trends, and as they realized that the war had turned decisively against Japan, some leaders in court, diplomatic, and business circles and a few military brass concluded that even a nearly total surrender would be preferable to the consequences of a doomed last battle. Most prominent among them was Prince Konoe Fumimaro, the former prime minister upon whom the more radical reformers had pinned great hopes several years back. Konoe and others were terrified at the prospect that the Soviet Union might enter the war against Japan (the 1941 Neutrality Treaty between Japan and the Soviets had remained in effect throughout the war). The group around Konoe feared above all that a prolonged war would crush the imperial institution. They came to identify a three-pronged threat: Foreign attack might combine with unrest from below and revolutionary plans from above to destroy the spiritual and cultural heart of their world.

These fears—especially the fear of a domestic revolution initiated by high-level military and bureaucratic radicals—were exaggerated. Factional conflict near the war's end indeed set Konoe and his allies against the army leadership in particular. But this was not a fight setting pro-emperor conservatives around the throne versus anti-emperor revolutionaries in the military. The dispute centered on the question of who posed the greater threat to the imperial institution: the United States or the Soviet Union. Army officers who feared the Americans even entertained desperate plans to evacuate the emperor to the Asian continent with Soviet protection during a final battle for the homeland. Their opponents preferred to take their chances by accepting the American conditions for peace.

The army strategy prevailed in the first stage of the war's endgame. Prime Minister Tōjō resigned in July 1944. He had lost the support of the court, the navy, and his own cabinet ministers. But these elites believed they could not control the military, so another army man, General Koiso Kuniaki, succeeded him. In February 1945 Konoe made a desperate attempt to take the initiative from army hardliners. He presented a plea, known as the Konoe Memorial, to the emperor in person. He urged Hirohito to make peace with the United States, even at the cost of unconditional surrender. This, he argued, was the only way to "extricate the people from the miserable ravages of war, preserve the *kokutai*, and plan for the security of the imperial house."[16] The emperor appeared intrigued, but did not follow his advice to replace the prime minister with someone willing to take this course. Several of the men who helped Konoe formulate his proposal were briefly jailed, including the diplomat and postwar prime minister, Yoshida Shigeru. Koiso continued his public stance of confidence in the aggressive pursuit of the war, but he secretly made overtures to the Soviet Union seeking its help in working out a peace agreement.

This approach had clearly failed by the spring of 1945. Facing strong American pressure to join the war, the Soviets announced they would not renew their neutrality pact with Japan. Koiso resigned in April 1945. In an atmosphere of grave crisis, he was succeeded by Admiral Suzuki Kantarō. As Suzuki was forming his cabinet, American forces launched the fierce battle for Okinawa. By the time the United States took the island in June, the fighting had taken 12,500 American lives and left a stunning toll of 250,000 Japanese dead (including 150,000 civilians). By this time Germany had surrendered, and fire-bombing had turned Japan's cities to rubble.

Those with access to accurate reports were well aware that continued fighting was hopeless. But Suzuki and the others in the inner circle of senior statesmen around the throne feared the uncertainty of a peace that might bring down the imperial institution more than the certainty of a war that would yield nothing but continued death and destruction. Through July and the first days of August, they continued to make diplomatic maneuvers based on the fantasy that the Soviet Union might mediate a surrender that would guarantee the emperor's survival.

Only the combination of the two atomic bombs, dropped on Hiroshima (August 6) and Nagasaki (August 9), the declaration of war by the Soviet Union (August 8), and, a Soviet invasion of Manchuria (August 9), led the emperor himself to end the war. Even in the face of these blows, it took nearly a week to reach the point of surrender. At midnight on August 9, after a daylong conference in his presence, the army and navy chiefs of staff and the army minister were still holding out. They wanted Japan to negotiate a surrender without an Allied occupation or any Allied war crime trials. Siding with the prime minister and two other members of the Supreme Council of State, the emperor cast the deciding vote to surrender with the sole condition that the imperial institution be preserved. The Americans offered the unsettling reply that the Japanese people would be allowed to decided the emperor's fate, despite the fact that top-level planners in Washington intended to keep the emperor in place and use him to facilitate a smooth occupation. On August 14, perhaps believing that he would fare better under American than Soviet control, the emperor broke another deadlocked conference to accept the American surrender terms. The following day, he broadcast this news directly via radio to the entire nation. On September 2, the surrender document was signed aboard the battleship *Missouri* in Tokyo Bay.

BURDENS AND LEGACIES OF WAR

The war bequeathed a complex legacy. It left deep physical and emotional scars both inside and outside Japan. More than fifty years later, these wounds are not yet healed. At the same time, the war laid the groundwork for a very different postwar world.

By temporarily ousting the British, Dutch, French, and American rulers from Southeast Asia and the Philippines, the Japanese rulers both intentionally and unwittingly hastened the demise of colonialism in Asia. By developing modern industries in colonies from Korea to Manchuria to Taiwan, they fostered postwar industrialization. But the superintendents of the Greater East Asia Coprosperity Sphere won little thanks and much enduring hatred for their repressive practices of colonial and wartime rule, in Korea and China above all. Millions of people suffered from the unrelenting pursuit of empire and war. The roll call of devastation included the Nanjing Massacre, uncountable further atrocities in China, the Vietnamese famine, and the hopeless campaign of the Indian National Army. In addition, nearly thirty-six thousand British and American prisoners of war died in captivity. This represented more than one-fourth of all captured soldiers.[17] The survivors nursed intense anger for decades.

Another group of war victims received much less public attention at the time or immediately after the war. These were the many thousands of young girls or women who were forced to work in euphemistically named "comfort stations" near the front lines of battle. About 80 percent were Koreans, and the remainder included Chinese, Japanese, and a small number of European women. Recruiters told some women they were hired as waitresses or servants. They simply captured others at gunpoint. Once at the front, all the women were forced to serve as prostitutes for Japanese troops. The soldiers were typically required to pay for the services of these women. From their perspective, the comfort stations appeared little different from the licensed brothels throughout Japan proper. But many of the women received no pay. Others received "pay" in the form of military tickets whose only use was to purchase daily necessities such as soap or food. The women thus worked in conditions closer to slavery than to prostitution. What further distinguished the plight of the "comfort women" from the common wartime phenomenon of prostitutes selling themselves to soldiers was the hands-on role of Japanese authorities. From cabinet ministers to local commanders, state officials authorized, regulated, and in some cases directly managed the comfort stations.[18] As with the death toll in massacres, the precise number of women forced into sexual slavery will never be known. Estimates range from one hundred thousand to two hundred thousand.

The war was also traumatic for the Japanese people. About 1.7 million soldiers died between 1937 and 1945. As many as three hundred thousand prisoners of war perished in Soviet detention camps after the war. Air raids left nine million homeless and killed nearly two hundred thousand civilians. The two atomic bombs killed an additional two hundred thousand people immediately. All human beings within a two-mile radius of the epicenter were incinerated in an instant. Hiroshima and Nagasaki became hellish zones of fire, death, and total destruction. Another one hundred thousand or more bomb victims died in the following months and years because of the lingering effects of radiation sickness. The overall Japanese death toll of close to 2.5 million, and above all the unprecedented experience of atomic bombing, left to survivors a powerful sense of themselves as victims—and not perpetrators—of war. The experience of defeat sparked a deeply felt revulsion toward all wars among millions of Japanese people.

Policies of the war years also consolidated what has been called "the 1940s system," although it is more accurately described as a "transwar" set of programs.[19] The famous postwar practice of industrial policy was rooted in the years of trial-and-error efforts from the depression era through 1945. During this time bureaucrats constructed enduring institutions to guide and control the private economy. They also nurtured complex ongoing networks of major manufacturers and subcontracting suppliers, which would continue into the postwar era. The effort to mobilize for war likewise sparked changes in systems of landholding, work organization, and gender roles. Landlords lost power. Blue-collar workers were given materially empty but ideologically potent promises of equality with managers. Women were pulled into workplaces in record numbers. Certainly Japan's surrender marked a great divide in modern history. But the dramatic new postwar departures in every area, from social and cultural life to politics and international relations, would build upon such wartime experiences in subtle and surprising ways.

13

Occupied Japan
New Departures and Durable Structures

On August 15, 1945, the emperor of Japan announced the nation's surrender to the Allied powers with his first radio broadcast ever. Some of his stunned listeners would later recall that August noon as an instant of "rebirth." For these people, the surrender was a moment when past experience and values were rendered illegitimate. They decided to chart a totally new course, whether personal, on behalf of a national community, or both. Other listeners, already struggling to find food and shelter in bombed-out cities, fell into a condition of despair and passivity. Still others—especially those in positions of power—resolved to defend the world they knew. Despite the shared national experience of defeat, individual experience varied greatly.

Even before the war ended, many court figures, as well as some politicians, businesspeople, and bureaucratic leaders, feared that defeat might bring a revolution that would sweep away the imperial institution and replace it with state socialism on a Soviet model. After surrender, these fears only intensified, although the United States came to be seen as the agent of revolution. These apocalyptic visions of revolution—for some fearful visions, for others hopeful ones—were not realized. Profound tensions and conflict *have* remained constant features of Japanese life. But, as one examines the history of the second half of the twentieth century, a central task must be to explain a process of stabilization that somehow contained these tensions. How and why did a conservative political and social order emerge and endure in the decades after 1945?

BEARING THE UNBEARABLE

Hardly any of the millions of people who listened to the surrender announcement had ever heard their sovereign's voice. Their surprise at the sound of his high-pitched words fighting through the radio static compounded their shock at the content of the message. For eight years Japan's rulers had exhorted the Japanese people endlessly to sacrifice in the emperor's name for the sake of a great and certain victory to liberate Asia from the tyranny of the "British and American devils." Japanese soldiers had killed millions of soldiers and civilians throughout Asia, and about 2.5 million out of 70 million Japanese subjects had perished. Now, suddenly, in stilted and deliberately ambiguous language, the emperor was telling them that the war was over, and Japan was defeated.

Hirohito explained the decision to surrender with one of history's most remarkable understatements: "The war has not turned in Japan's favor." He stressed the destructive power of the enemy's new "cruel bombs," which threatened "not only the extermination of our race, but the destruction of all human civilization." He offered words of regret for other peoples who had worked with Japan "for the liberation of East Asia." The emperor then announced his intent "to open the way for a great peace for thousands of generations to come." He ended by urging his subjects "to endure the unendurable, bear the unbearable" and unite "to keep pace with the progress of the world."[1]

This announcement was a noteworthy first effort of the emperor and his closest advisors to justify the past as a selfless war of liberation and defend their continued authority in a world about to turn upside down. It presented the Japanese people and even the state as victims of the war and cruel weapons. Although Hirohito ended by invoking Meiji era rhetoric in which Japan sought to emulate the progress of the Western world, his overall thrust was a call for endurance more than great change. He was urging his subjects to "sacrifice as usual."[2]

For a few, the prospect of defeat was literally unbearable. About 350 military officers committed suicide soon after this announcement. But when measured against the strident calls by military rulers for soldiers to give their lives for the state in a battle to the death, this was not a large proportion of the roughly six million men in arms at the war's end. Most civilians and soldiers responded more practically or passively, and far less dramatically.

One of the most practical immediate steps took place in bureaucratic, military, and corporate offices. During the two weeks that elapsed between the end of the fighting on August 15 and the arrival of General MacArthur and the occupation army in early September, hundreds of bonfires flared all around Tokyo. To erase evidence of their wartime activities, which might bring on retribution from the occupiers, officials and managers by the thousands destroyed all manner of documents.

In another swift and practical step, the government took a page from its wartime policy book by recruiting women to work as prostitutes and thereby "defend and nurture the purity of our race." Planning for official comfort stations began on August 18. By year's end, thousands of women, most with no previous experience as prostitutes, were serving Allied soldiers in dozens of "Recreation and Amusement Centers" in cities throughout Japan. In January 1946, the occupation authorities condemned and outlawed this official prostitution. They called it a violation of the human rights of the women. But the occupiers accepted the decision of the Japanese government to continue the prewar system of licensed, privately run brothels. The soldiers of the occupation army provided a steady source of customers. The women who worked as prostitutes, and sometimes developed long-term relationships with particular men, faced a double-bind of discrimination. Although American officials allowed brothels to function, they strongly discouraged GIs from marrying Japanese women. Yet mixed-race children born to these women faced considerable discrimination in Japan.

Energetic entrepreneurship, legal or not, was another notable practical response to defeat. Within hours of the emperor's broadcast, an editor named Ogawa Kikumatsu was inspired with the realization that English conversation books would soon be in huge demand. He hastily produced a language manual that sold 3.5 million copies by the year's end. It remained the all-time bestseller in Japan until 1981.[3] More typical was the turn to the black market. As wartime rationing and price controls continued after the war, many men, and a few women, including numerous Koreans and Taiwanese, made fortunes selling scarce food and household items to desperate buyers. Gangsters ran these illegal, but openly tolerated, outdoor markets. They battled violently to protect their turf. By October 1945, approximately seventeen thousand "blue-sky markets" had sprung up in cities and towns nationwide. Sellers procured their goods wherever they could: from farmers, from caches of Japanese war supplies, from prostitutes and GIs with access to the abundant stores on American bases. Some clothing and blankets for sale had even been lifted from corpses.[4]

For several years, millions of people faced starvation. Thousands actually starved to death.[5] By the spring of 1946 poor harvests and a paralyzed rationing system had produced a serious urban food crisis. The average household spent 68 percent of its income on food in 1946. The average height and weight of elementary school children decreased until 1948.[6] Newsreels recorded tragic scenes of emaciated youths with distended bellies being examined by anxious officials from the Ministry of Welfare. Adults and children, women and men, crowded onto trains bound for the countryside to barter kimonos for cabbage. One memoir notes that "shedding clothes to buy food

One of the most common scenes of the desperate first two years after the war was the crush of city-dwellers in search of food crowding onto trains bound for the countryside. They carried bags of personal belongings, such as kimonos, which they planned to barter for vegetables or rice.
Courtesy of *Mainichi* newspaper.

was first compared to the snake's shedding of its skin, then to the peeling of an onion, because it was accompanied by tears."[7]

The clinical word for exhaustion—*kyōdatsu*—was one defining term for the state of mind of Japanese people in these early postwar years. Alcohol and drug abuse were identified in the media as major social problems. Newspapers published numerous reports of deaths from homemade liquor. Rates of armed robbery and theft rose sharply from levels of the 1920s or 1930s. On the other hand, murder rates did not increase. The perception of social disorder as recorded by anxious observers in the government and press was probably exaggerated.

Another byword of the era was *kasutori* culture. The term referred to a popular cheap wine brewed from sake dregs (*kasu*). It suggested a psychological world of sentimental self-pity balanced by a defiant resolve to live for the day at a time when the future seemed hopeless. As one black marketeer put it, "I drank trying to forget a life that hung suspended like a floating weed." In both their writing and their own lives, several famous writers, most notably Dazai Osamu and Sakaguchi Ango, celebrated the humanity of peacetime decadence in contrast to the inhumanity of wartime loyalty. In a brilliant essay "On Decadence," Sakaguchi wrote:

> Could we not say that the kamikaze hero was a mere illusion, and that human history begins from the point where he takes to black-marketeering? We have only returned to being human. Humans become decadent—loyal retainers and saintly women become decadent.[8]

THE AMERICAN AGENDA: DEMILITARIZE AND DEMOCRATIZE

In sharp contrast to people in Japan, the American occupiers who began to arrive in September 1945 were well fed, well equipped, and overflowing with confidence. They brought a vision of far-reaching reform. For nearly seven years the Japanese people faced the unprecedented experience of occupation by a foreign power wielding the authority to rewrite laws, restructure the economic and political system, and even seek to redefine culture and values.

The occupation in theory was a collective endeavor of the Allied powers. A four-nation Allied Council for Japan was created in early 1946 to advise the Supreme Commander for the Allied Powers (SCAP). An eleven-member Far Eastern Commission was charged to formulate occupation policy and review SCAP actions.[9] In fact, the supreme commander, in the imposing person of General Douglas MacArthur and a mostly American staff, took orders from the U.S. government and paid scant attention to these bodies. As a matter of convenience, the acronym SCAP quickly came to refer both to MacArthur himself and to his extensive administrative bureaucracy.[10]

The initial American strategy in Japan was encapsulated in two words: demilitarize and democratize. To achieve the first goal, SCAP dissolved the army and navy immediately: Japan's armed forces were officially disbanded on November 30. To follow up on this order was a daunting task. It meant demobilizing the gigantic Japanese military, and repatriating to the home islands a total of 6.9 million people. When the war ended, nearly ten percent of the population of Japan was overseas: 3.7 million soldiers and 3.2 million civilians in Korea, Manchuria, Taiwan and the Chinese mainland, as well as the far-flung wartime empire to the south. With the exception of about 400,000 people who remained prisoners in the Soviet Union, and smaller numbers left behind in Manchuria, demobilization and repatriation were completed by the end of 1948. While this was a relatively swift and smooth process, to absorb such a vast number of people was a complex undertaking which left a legacy that has not yet been fully studied or understood. Repatriates, both civilian and military, often felt out of place back "home," regarded with a mixture of pity for their poverty and scorn for their role in pursuing what now appeared to have been a hopeless war. Returned veterans were prominent among those who organized politically in the 1950s and thereafter to pressure the government to rearm and revise the American-imposed reforms of the occupation era.

Other demilitarizing steps focused on those outside the military who had supported the war machine In October 1945 the Americans disbanded the oppressive Special Higher Police (dubbed "thought police" by Western critics). Between 1945 and 1948, the occupiers purged over two hundred thousand men from positions in the government and business world who were judged responsible for leading the war effort. They disestablished the official state Shinto religion. During and immediately after the war, the allies tried some six thousand military men for conventional war crimes, such as abuse of prisoners. They convicted and executed over nine hundred. They also set in motion an ambitious plan for war reparations. Significant portions of Japan's industrial plant were to be loaded onto ships and given to the wartime victims of Japanese expansion in Asia.

The most significant arena of retribution was the International Military Tribunal for the Far East, also called simply the Tokyo Trial. It dragged on from May 1946 to November 1948 and put Japan's wartime rulers on trial. Beginning with General Tōjō Hideki, twenty-eight men were charged with both conventional war crimes and the newly minted crime of engaging in conspiracy to wage war. All were found guilty of some charges. Tōjō and six others were executed. Another seventeen defendants were sentenced to life in prison.[11]

The United States in 1945 sought to do far more than demilitarize Japan and punish the nation's leaders. It was striving to reconstruct the entire world in its image, Japan included. In this spirit, SCAP imposed a rush of reforms in the fall of 1945 and 1946. They were based on a simple logic: Militarism stemmed from monopoly, tyranny, and poverty. To construct a peaceful, nonmilitaristic Japan required more than just disbanding the military. It required vast reforms to smash authoritarian political rule, equalize political rights and even wealth, and transform values.

SCAP announced the first major reforms in October 1945, with declarations that guaranteed freedoms of speech, press, and assembly and the right to organize labor or farmer unions. SCAP also ordered the Japanese government to extend civil and political rights to women. A bit later, in December, the occupiers told the Japanese government to undertake land reform that would allow tenant farmers to purchase their fields.

With these steps, the Americans sent a clear message that democracy should be the cornerstone of a new Japan. The capstone of this effort was the rewriting of the constitution. This was drafted by a committee of occupation officials in the winter of 1946. It was vigorously discussed and ratified that spring in the imperial Diet (still in existence until the new constitution replaced it). It was promulgated in November 1946 and took effect in May 1947.

The postwar constitution downgraded the emperor from absolute monarch to a "symbol of the State and of the unity of the people." It granted to the people of Japan an array of "fundamental human rights," including the civil liberties of the American Bill of Rights such as freedoms of speech, assembly, and religion. It also boldly extended the concept of rights into the social realm. The new constitution guaranteed rights to education "correspondent to ability" and to "minimum standards of wholesome and cultured living." It assured the right (and obligation) to work, to organize, and to bargain collectively. It outlawed discrimination based on sex, race, creed, social status, or family origin. It gave women explicit guarantees of equality in marriage, divorce, property, inheritance, and "other matters pertaining to marriage and the family." Finally, its article 9 committed the Japanese people to "forever renounce war as a sovereign right of the nation and the threat or use of force as means of settling international disputes."

Japanese elites were stunned by these sweeping guarantees, especially when the Americans insisted that the Japanese government present them to the people as the government's own recommendation. But the draft document met an enthusiastic popular response. As officially sanctioned goals or ideals, its ambitious provisions have framed the discourse and institutions of contemporary Japanese life ever since.

From 1945 through 1947 occupation officials imposed important additional changes. SCAP freed Communist Party members from jail as early as October 4, 1945. It outlawed Japanese institutions of censorship and arguably allowed a greater range of political expression than was possible in the United States at the time. At the same time, with little sense of irony, SCAP put in place its own program to censor the newly "liberated" Japanese cultural world to prevent continued support of the military or war regime.

The occupation reformers attacked the sprawling business empires of the zaibatsu. They took away ownership and control from holding companies dominated by the zaibatsu families (Mitsui, Sumitomo, Yasuda, Iwasaki [who owned Mitsubishi], Asano, and others). They broke up some of the larger firms within each zaibatsu network. They encouraged and advised labor unions, and at first SCAP officials welcomed the extraordinary drive of organizing and strikes. The program of land reform enacted under SCAP order revolutionized the distribution of social and economic power in rural Japan. It essentially expropriated the holdings of landlords, gave them to former tenants, and created a countryside of small family farms.

The schools were also subject to reform. SCAP ordered the Ministry of Education to replace lessons for war and loyalty to the state with teachings of peace and democracy. Wartime textbooks were quickly rewritten, although for the first year or so students had to cross out offending phrases about tanks and battleships and use the old books. Some of them were little more than a mass of inked-over paragraphs. In 1947 compulsory education was extended through the ninth grade. The university system was dramatically enlarged. The "imperial" label was removed from the handful of elite state-funded prewar universities, renamed simply as Tokyo University or Kyoto University. These were joined by dozens of newly founded or expanded four-year colleges throughout Japan. In 1947 women were granted access to private and public universities. SCAP also sought to implement an American-style system of local school boards and local control.

These sweeping measures changed the climate of ideas and the distribution of

Until new books were produced, wartime textbooks full of references to the glory of the Japanese nation and military were the only ones available for use in schools. Occupation authorities had teachers and students themselves cross out offending passages, sometimes producing essentially useless pages of black ink. The irony, if not hypocrisy, of this American program to democratize Japan was a lesson that many young students learned and remembered.
Courtesy of Shogakkan Publishers.

economic and social power. A fever of "democratization" swept Japan. The projects of democracy and equality were understood in extremely expansive terms by their advocates; they meant far more than voting and land reform. They implied to many—and this was both promise and threat—a remaking of the human soul. Intellectuals engaged in searching and sophisticated debate over how to nurture the autonomous subjectivity of a truly democratic person. Many looked to Marxism for inspiration and the Japan Communist Party for leadership, and the political parties and philosophies of the left enjoyed unprecedented support. Crowds of people as hungry for ideas as for food rummaged through used book stalls. Others camped overnight outside major bookstores to purchase the latest installment of major works of political philosophy. Talk of renovating and remaking and transforming echoed throughout Japan.

General Douglas MacArthur stood as the human symbol of the American power that was imposing these massive reforms. He was a charismatic leader of extraordinary confidence. A master of the sparing and symbolic use of his own image, MacArthur kept himself hidden from direct contact with ordinary Japanese people but still released

General MacArthur meets Emperor Hirohito for the first time, at the U.S. Embassy in Tokyo on September 27, 1945. This photograph was published in all major papers the next day. Showing the two leaders' contrast in height, and the general's casual dress compared to Hirohito's formal wear, this image had a huge impact in bringing home the fact of defeat and the subservient relationship between the Japanese nation and its occupiers.
Courtesy of *Mainichi* newspaper.

to the public one of the most remarkable political photographs in Japanese or world history. The picture, taken on the occasion of his first meeting with Emperor Hirohito—in MacArthur's headquarters and not in the palace—on September 27, 1945, was published in all the major newspapers. It conveyed the subordinate position of the Japanese state and people with shocking force to the entire population.

It is important to note that despite the supreme commander's strong personality and emperorlike image, he was not an independent ruler imposing policies of his own design. SCAP policies had been designed by planners in Washington, DC, during the war and approved by President Harry Truman. Both the initial reforms, and the shifts in American policy that became visible in 1947, generally reflected the thinking of the mainstream of American policymakers.

One exceptional area where MacArthur clung to a very personal agenda was religion. He was a devout Christian and he wanted to use his prestige and power to spiritually transform the Japanese people by Christianizing them. He encouraged Western missionaries to come back to Japan. He requested that ten million translated copies of the Bible be distributed to the Japanese people.[12] In the end, his efforts bore little fruit. Some people did turn to Christianity for explanations or comfort in the face of the disaster of the war. But the overall proportion of Japanese Christians remained relatively constant at approximately 1 percent of the population.

Of greater long-term consequence, MacArthur's personal views did shape American policy toward the imperial institution. A significant group of "soft peace" advocates in Washington favored preserving the emperor and using his prestige to legitimize occupation reforms. But this issue was not firmly settled as the occupation began. In the fall of 1945, MacArthur emerged as a decisive supporter of the throne. He sent home alarming reports of the threat to social order and American policies that would ensue should Hirohito be forced to stand trial for war crimes or even simply abdicate. His lobbying ensured that Japan's postwar political system would be a hybrid form that some have called "imperial democracy."[13]

JAPANESE RESPONSES

Despite the surface appearance of overwhelming American power in occupied Japan, both elites and ordinary citizens retained space to interpret the reforms of the occupiers. SCAP ruled indirectly, implementing changes through the existing Japanese bureaucracy. This choice was probably inevitable. The occupiers simply did not have sufficient personnel or language ability to staff a full government to put the vast changes into practice. Instead SCAP's General Headquarters (GHQ) consisted of a shadow government of smaller offices parallel to the Japanese government bureaucracy. SCAP/GHQ passed orders to its Japanese counterparts through a liaison office staffed by bilingual Japanese officials. This structure offered government officials and other wartime elites some important room to maneuver, whether to resist or reshape the occupation directives.

Ordinary citizens likewise enjoyed considerable freedom to improvise upon the American agenda. In such a context, the fate of reforms was only determined in part by the extent to which the occupiers consistently promoted them. Even more importantly, it was determined by a transwar legacy of prewar and wartime history. Individuals and groups in Japanese society and government who had long been concerned with shaping their modern institutions continued their efforts, in conflict with each other as much as with the occupation forces.

Land reform, for example, proved to be one of the most thoroughgoing and long-lived changes of the occupation era. Landlords had been on the defensive in the 1920s and early 1930s. Organized groups of tenants had frequently confronted them with successful demands for rent reductions or more secure tenancy rights. Many landlords had responded by selling off holdings. During the war, the government had stepped in, less to promote social reform than to spur food production. Its program of subsidized purchases of tenant rice further weakened the economic power of landlords. In addition, bureaucrats within the Ministry of Agriculture had been calling for land reform since the 1930s as a way to bring social stability to the countryside. And of course, the tenants wanted to own their fields.

Land reform was thus a transwar endeavor, and this historical context explains the deep, enduring impact of reforms initiated by SCAP. At the same time, SCAP certainly pushed for reforms that went beyond the intentions of Japanese officials themselves. The Japanese government enacted its own land reform law in December 1945. SCAP judged this to be too weak and demanded that the government draft a second reform measure. A stronger law was approved in October 1946. It forced each landlord to sell all but a small, family-sized plot of farmland to tenants at 1945 prices. Observers joked—with justification—that by the time the payments were actually made, inflation had reduced the real cost of a tenant's field to the price of a carton of cigarettes.

In the realm of social policy, transwar continuities were important as well. Several key Home Ministry bureaucrats had pushed for a labor union law in the late 1920s. They were still at their jobs in 1945. The Home Ministry, seen by SCAP as a bastion of domestic repression, was the only bureau outside the military to be dissolved during the occupation. But these officials shifted to the new Labor Ministry (founded in 1947). From this perch they oversaw the occupation labor reforms. They called for cooperation between management and labor, sometimes echoing the wartime rhetoric of the Industrial Patriotic Association. But they returned to their position of the 1920s that a regulated system of unions and collective bargaining would bring the greatest social stability, and most productive economy, in the long run.

Of equal importance, a minority of industrial workers had prewar experience in labor unions. These people helped lead a great rush to embrace unions, collective bargaining, and strikes. The labor movement also quickly drew in millions of newly active men and women discontent with their low wages, poor job security, and lack of power in their working lives. Union membership surged from zero to nearly five million by the end of 1946. The proportion of wage workers in unions reached a peak of more than 56 percent of the work force by 1949.

Business leaders had no choice in the immediate postwar years of 1945–47 but to give way to this powerful labor movement. They conceded large wage increases in collective bargaining. They concluded thousands of contracts that gave real power to new labor-management councils including union representatives. In the face of strikes, despite dire business circumstances, some of the nation's leading employers revoked plans to dismiss workers.

But in contrast to the land reform, countervailing forces remained powerful in the case of labor reform. Even as they made concessions, business leaders and many in the government feared that militant unionism was leading straight to communism. They were determined to change the balance of power and the character of unions. Beginning in 1947 and 1948, as the Americans shifted their focus from democratization to promoting economic recovery, these managers were able to regain the upper hand and cultivate enduring alliances with more cooperatively inclined union leaders.

In the case of women's rights, important political reforms took root thanks to an alliance between reformers in SCAP's headquarters and a small band of Japanese women who had been seeking the vote and other civil rights since the 1920s. In 1945, even before revising the constitution, the Americans ordered the Japanese government to give women the vote. In the first postwar elections, thirty-nine women were elected to the Diet, accounting for just under 10 percent of the seats. Women's suffrage was a wildly popular reform.

Beyond political reform, SCAP put a powerful statement of social and legal equality for women in the constitution. These clauses were the work of a remarkable young woman, Beate Sirota, who had lived in Japan as a child in the 1930s and become fluent in Japanese. She returned in 1945 as a recent college graduate working as a researcher in SCAP offices. In the winter of 1946 Sirota suddenly found herself appointed to the SCAP committee to draft the new Japanese constitution. She seized the opportunity to author the provisions that guaranteed "the essential equality of the sexes" in marriage and all other legal matters pertaining to inheritance and the family.

In this instance, the existing balance of power and ideas was not congenial to radical change. Despite the presence of some Japanese feminists who supported basic change in gender roles and power relations, the dominant position of males in the family and in society at large was not overturned by constitutional reform. Nonetheless, Sirota's constitutional provisions remained on the books. They provided a new context in which women and men would debate the merits of changed gender relations for decades.

In some areas, the occupation reforms found little domestic support. The Americans came to Japan convinced that the zaibatsu trusts bore major responsibility for expansionism and the war. Initial SCAP policy called for the zaibatsu owners to sell off their assets and for the constituent corporations to be dissolved into independent, smaller companies. But the bureaucrats charged with responsibility for postwar economic affairs were the same men who had forged close ties with the zaibatsu from the depression through the drive for wartime mobilization. They saw collaboration between state bureaucrats and big business as the best strategy for economic recovery. They viewed American policies to dissolve the zaibatsu as utterly naive. The postwar political leadership agreed. At the same time, although the parties of the left opposed capitalist monopolies, they did not oppose large-scale economic organizations in themselves. They rather wanted a strong state to nationalize industries to serve workers and the people. There was little intellectual or popular support for thoroughgoing free markets and economic deconcentration.

The program of zaibatsu dissolution therefore proceeded slowly. When the American commitment shifted from reform to recovery, pressure on the zaibatsu diminished. In the end, the power of the privately owned holding companies was destroyed, but the zaibatsu enterprises regrouped around the banks of the dissolved combines. They also proved willing to cooperate with state bureaucrats. This set in place a pattern of bank-centered capitalism and bureaucratic guidance of the economy that persisted for decades.

Likewise, American initiatives to decentralize the police and education systems did not last. The projects reflected peculiar American ideas about the importance of local self-government, which had no natural constituency in Japan. SCAP dictated that cities, towns, and villages were to fund and control their own police departments. Conservative politicians feared these forces would be ineffective at monitoring left-wing challenges. Local taxpayers, especially in small communities, were not enthusiastic about paying for their police forces. As the occupation ended, the government gave communities the power to end support for local police. Most did so immediately, and by 1954 a national police agency had been created. In similar fashion, a 1948 reform provided for elected local school boards throughout Japan, but the Japanese government delayed implementation. After the occupation ended, a revised education law replaced elected with appointed school boards. Fierce debate raged over the *content* of education for decades, but neither conservative nor liberal or radical voices were particularly concerned with carrying out the debate in autonomous local units.

The political context for such debates was a sharp division between parties of the left and right. This divide also had prewar roots. After the five year hiatus of the Imperial Rule Assistance Association, the two major prewar parties regrouped under new names. The remnants of the Seiyūkai came together into the Liberal Party (Jiyūtō), while the Minseitō politicians for the most part joined in a new Progressive Party (Shinpotō), which later evolved into the Democratic Party (Minshutō). Although these parties managed to cling to power through most of the occupation era, they got off to a rough start when the majority of their founding members were purged for their role as part of the wartime political elite. They were far less dominant than they had been before the war.

The non-communist parties of the left, which had spoken on behalf of wage laborers and tenant farmers before the war, had actually supported the wartime government with great enthusiasm. A number of their leaders were purged as well. Nonetheless, the surviving leaders of the prewar socialist camp formed the Japan Socialist Party in late 1945. They won much support by criticizing the wartime regime and the postwar successor elites of businessmen, bureaucrats, and "established" politicians. And for the first time, the Japan Communist Party was able to function openly and legally. The communists were the one group with a consistent (underground) record opposing the imperialism and expansionism of the prewar and war years, and they gained much moral support for these stands.

In elections of the 1920s and 1930s, the Seiyūkai and Minseitō had together controlled roughly 80 to 90 percent of the votes. The proletarian parties had grown from as little as 3 or 4 percent of the vote in the first elections under universal male suffrage to almost 10 percent by the mid-1930s. After the war, the socialists and communists continued this upward trend. The socialists won 92 seats and 18 percent of the vote in the first postwar election of 1946. They surged to 143 seats and 28 percent of the vote in a general election the following April 1947. The Communist Party had greater strength in labor unions and among intellectuals than among the populace at large; they managed just 3 to 4 percent of the vote and 4 or 5 seats in these early postwar ballots. In addition, significant numbers of independent candidates won votes and seats, as many as 20 percent in the first postwar election of April 1946. As the left and these independents gained ground, the combined votes of the established parties fell to roughly 50 percent. (See Appendix B for detailed election results.)

Despite these opposition gains, the Liberal Party, led by Yoshida Shigeru, managed to form a cabinet after the 1946 election, working together with the other conservative party. Yoshida was a former diplomat. He had served as Japan's ambassador to Great Britain in the late 1930s. He was a strong supporter of the Japanese empire who energetically pushed the British to accept Japan's hegemony in China. But Yoshida kept some distance from the military during the war. He was the key supporter of Prince Konoe's direct appeal to Hirohito in 1945 seeking to bring about an early surrender. For this effort, Yoshida had been briefly put in jail in April 1945. The episode gave him postwar legitimacy as a liberal who had opposed the military.

But his hold on power was tenuous. The socialists and communists rode a surge of unionizing, strikes, and protest demonstrations over the next twelve months. They criticized in particular the government's corruption and mismanaging of the economy. A broad coalition of unions planned a national "general strike" on February 1, 1947. The stated goal was to overthrow the Yoshida cabinet. In dramatic fashion, SCAP forbade this strike late on the night of January 31. This delivered a severe blow to the revolutionary hopes of the communists and left-wing socialists. Even so, just two months later in April 1947, when the first election was held under the new constitution, the Japan Socialist Party won a plurality. They formed a government in coalition with the Democratic Party, headed by the socialist leader Katayama Tetsu as prime minister. In March 1948, Katayama was forced to step down after just eight months in office. The cabinet fell in part because his agenda to nationalize major industries was rejected, although factional strife between the left and right wings of the party was the fundamental cause. Even so the socialists continued as partners in a governing coalition, this time led by the Democrats, which continued until the end of 1948. Japan appeared to be on a political course in which socialist rule was a real possibility.

In fact, the Katayama cabinet proved to be a brief interlude of socialist power-sharing. The liberals under Yoshida staged a major comeback in the elections of 1949. They won over half the seats in the House of Representatives and were able to rule on their own. The fact that this "established party" of prewar vintage managed such a strong comeback is as impressive as the earlier gains of the socialist opposition. The Liberal Party returned to power despite the fact that its Seiyūkai predecessor had controlled the cabinet at the outset of Japan's expansionist adventures in 1931–32. And of course, despite his wartime call for an early surrender, the Liberal Party's prime minister, Yoshida Shigeru, had served as a loyal diplomat in the 1930s. One could imagine many people condemning such politicians as responsible members of the wartime elite that brought death and ruin to millions.

Despite this, the staying power of the prewar parties was substantial. It was probably rooted in fear of the unknown and a deep desire for the return of some sort of familiar "normalcy." Having been pushed to the margins of government in the 1930s and 1940s, the Liberal and Democratic parties could present themselves as reluctant wartime collaborators. They could claim to be champions of modest reform, determined to rebuild a peaceful Japan but determined not to change too much. In addition, and perhaps even more important, it was this old guard that could deliver the goods of state subsidies or protections to many of their prewar supporters, from small and large businesses to farmers, including the new owners of formerly tenanted fields.

Thus, through the era of American occupation and beyond, the old guard parties returned to power based on their *prewar* experience and promises of normalcy and political spoils. The socialists and communists emerged as leaders of a combative opposition, but they were to remain more or less permanently in the minority.

THE REVERSE COURSE

The peak years of reform in Japan were also the years when tension in American-Soviet relations reached a peak. The Cold War came to the fore of international politics in 1946 when Winston Churchill gave his famous speech about the Iron Curtain descending in Europe. In 1947 American Secretary of State George Marshall announced his famous plan to offer massive economic aid to promote European recovery. In Asia, the Nationalists in China had been seen by the United States as the anchor to a postwar Asian order. By 1947 they were losing ground to the communists. In Japan the Socialist Party was gaining ground at the polls, huge crowds were marching in the streets, and the communists were dominating labor unions that planned strikes with explicitly political goals.

These trends led to an important shift in the balance of power and views among American government officials. Even during the presurrender planning, some policymakers in Washington had questioned the assumption that far-reaching reform was the best way to ensure a stable new Japan. These were members of the so-called Japan crowd, led in Washington by Joseph Grew, the former ambassador to Japan. They called for quite modest reforms. In Tokyo, key aides to MacArthur, in particular the chief of his intelligence staff General Charles Willoughby (referred to by MacArthur as "my pet fascist"), took a similar position.

In their view, the war was a slight misstep in which a few militarists had hijacked a relatively sound and well-run ship of state. Simply dismantling the military and putting in place the basic laws of political democracy would be enough. Other reforms went too far, they argued, toward a dangerous socially based democracy of the masses. They advocated handing power back to the "responsible elements" of the prewar elite: business leaders and relatively pro-Western Foreign Ministry veterans such as Shidehara Kijūrō and Yoshida Shigeru. They supported using the emperor as an anchor to keep Japan socially conservative and cohesive.

Beginning in 1947, such attitudes began to shape policies in Washington and Tokyo. These new departures have come to be known as the occupation's "reverse course." In 1948 the Americans sharply scaled back plans to dissolve the former subsidiaries of the zaibatsu combines, and in 1949 they relinquished all claims to war reparations. In 1948 SCAP encouraged the Japanese government to revise the new postwar labor laws to outlaw strikes by public employees and weaken protective labor standards. They encouraged the Japanese to create a national police force beginning as early as 1947 and promoted Japanese rearmament (within limits) thereafter.

The Americans also promoted a crackdown on the Japan Communist Party. In 1950, the Japanese government launched the so-called Red Purge with SCAP encouragement. Roughly thirteen thousand people alleged to be Communist Party members were ousted from their public or private sector jobs, on the grounds that their political activities were impeding the goals of the occupation. This was the same justification for the 1945–46 SCAP purge of wartime leaders. The Red Purge coincided with the de-purging of some of these men, who quickly returned to prominent positions in the political world. It was perhaps the most dramatic example of the "reverse course."

The shift in American policy was very controversial at the time. It remains a topic of debate among historians, especially those in Japan. Some condemn the reverse course as an American betrayal of an immediate postwar promise to build a true democracy, which then enabled the Japanese elite to continue a program of reaction and reversal after the occupation ended. Others praise the new direction as a prudent step, necessary to ensure stability and the long-run success of earlier reforms.

Coupled with the initial decision to retain the imperial institution, the shifting American policy did make Japan's postwar transformation less thoroughgoing than it would have been. The Red Purge surely changed the political balance in many labor and cultural organizations. But the reverse course left some crucial early reforms untouched, including the new constitution and the land reform. It did not rig elections or shut down newspapers or prevent defenders of the peace clause (article 9) in the constitution from continuing their activity. It changed the political environment, but it did not simply determine the outcome of ongoing contention among vigorous actors in political or cultural life. The shifting course of American reforms was part of an improvised recipe for stabilization that first opened politics to an unprecedented degree and then shored up the many surviving elements of the old order.

TOWARD RECOVERY AND INDEPENDENCE: ANOTHER UNEQUAL TREATY?

Economic recovery was also a basic ingredient of postwar stabilization. At the outset of the occupation, SCAP rejected any responsibility for helping Japan's economy to revive. Left to their own devices in an uncertain context, business leaders combined fear with greed in disastrous ways. The early postwar government offered reconstruction subsidies to major firms in hopes the funds would be used to revive production. Rather than processing them into finished goods, businesses found it more profitable to use these funds to buy and resell raw materials to black market brokers. Many of the industrial plants that had survived stood idle. From 1945 to 1949, inflation surged out of control. As one American on the scene recalled: "For four years after the war, the great inflation hung over Japan like some immense, brooding presence . . . By 1949, when inflation was finally contained, the price level had risen 150 *times* in four years."

The first glimmer of hope in the effort to revive confidence and restart production came in 1947. Economic policymakers observed a vicious cycle of coal shortages that inhibited the recovery of other industries, especially the crucial iron and steel industry, in turn keeping coal demand low. Their answer was the Priority Production program. Drawing on wartime experience, bureaucrats in the Ministry of Commerce allocated both coal and imported fuel on a preferential basis to steelmakers. This allowed steel companies to revive production and feed steel back to the coal industry, which in turn could rebuild the mining infrastructure and raise productivity. The program succeeded modestly in reviving both industries and generating coal supplies for other customers.

But throughout 1948 the economy remained relatively stagnant, and inflation continued to surge. The Americans were now committed to Japan as Asia's "bulwark against communism," in the words of Secretary of the Army Kenneth Royall.

They were now anxious to promote economic recovery. George Kennan, among the most important American strategists of the postwar era, put it bluntly in October 1949:

[T]he terrific problem [is] how then the Japanese are going to get along unless they reopen some sort of Empire toward the South. Clearly we have got . . . to achieve opening up of trade possibilities, commercial possibilities for Japan on a scale very far greater than anything Japan knew before. It is a formidable task.[14]

As a step in this direction, the United States in February 1949 sent a special financial advisor to Tokyo, a Detroit banker named Joseph Dodge. He was an orthodox economist who detested government support or regulation of the economy. SCAP took his advice and imposed a harsh medicine in three doses: a balanced budget, the suspending of all state loans to industry, and the abolition of all state subsidies. SCAP also followed the advice to set a favorable exchange rate of 360 yen to the dollar to encourage Japanese exports. This "Dodge line" program indeed halted inflation, but industry found itself starved for capital. In the spring of 1950, a year after this deflationary program had been implemented, Japan appeared on the brink not of recovery but of a deepening depression.

In June 1950, just as it appeared SCAP's medication might kill the patient, the Korean War began. This tragedy across the straits conferred great fortune on Japan. With the war came a surge of American military procurement orders placed with Japanese industries, which were located conveniently close to the front. In the years 1951–53, war procurements amounted to about two billion dollars, or roughly 60 percent of all Japan's exports.[15] Japanese leaders tastelessly celebrated what Prime Minister Yoshida called a "gift of the gods" and businessmen dubbed "blessed rain from heaven."[16] From 1949 to 1951 exports nearly tripled, and production rose nearly 70 percent. Corporations began to show profits for the first time since the surrender, and they responded with a surge of investment in new plants and equipment. The gross national product began to increase at double-digit rates. Japan's recovery was underway.

With reforms in place and the economy on the mend, and with the Korean War placing great demands on American military resources, pressures in Washington mounted to end the occupation. The end came sooner than many had anticipated; in 1945, some top officials in the United States had spoken of the need to occupy Japan for two decades, or even a century. As it turned out, the era of formal occupation lasted just under seven years.

Some of America's wartime allies were reluctant to sign a treaty so quickly that would bring the occupation to a close. The British, the Chinese, and Southeast Asian governments wanted a harsh peace with reparations paid and with strong guarantees against a revival of the Japanese military. Led by Secretary of State John Foster Dulles, the United States negotiated vigorously on multiple fronts to hasten a settlement. It concluded defense agreements with the Philippines, Australia, and New Zealand that assuaged the fears of these nations. Asian nations were also given the right to follow the treaty by negotiating bilateral reparations agreements with Japan. In September 1951, representatives of forty-eight nations met in San Francisco and signed a treaty to end the state of war that still formally existed with Japan. The occupation officially ended in April 1952.

Several key issues remained unresolved. The United States retained control of Okinawa indefinitely, although most Japanese saw the island as part of their nation. Both the Republic of China (Taiwan) and the mainland People's Republic of China wanted to sign the treaty as the sole Chinese government. Neither was invited to the peace conference, and Japan was instructed to reach agreements on its own. And the Soviet Union and other European communist states walked out of the conference. They were particularly angry that a large force of American troops was going to remain in Japan after the occupation ended. The Soviets retained control of several disputed islands just north of Hokkaido.

Two hours after the San Francisco treaty was signed, the United States and Japan ratified the controversial U.S.–Japan Security Treaty. It granted the United States the right to keep bases and troops in Japan. The official mission of the troops was to protect Japan from attack and guarantee international peace and security. From the perspective of the Americans and many in Asia, the function of the American troops was to contain Japan as much as to protect it. Not surprisingly, the security treaty faced much opposition in Japan. Some on the political left quite logically saw it as a violation of Japanese neutrality and the principle of unarmed peace enshrined in the constitution. They feared that U.S. troops made Japan a lightning rod for an attack by America's enemies. Others on the left, together with many in the conservative camp, saw the treaty—again with considerable justification—less as a violation of Japanese neutrality than as a betrayal of its sovereignty. They scorned Prime Minister Yoshida for accepting a "subordinate independence." Yoshida indeed had been convinced for several years that an American military presence and a secure, if subordinate, place in a *Pax Americana* was the best Japan could hope to achieve. He got his way. But the agreement that some labeled a "second unequal treaty" would be subject to fierce debate and political struggle for decades.

The occupation forces arrived in 1945 determined to engineer a root-and-branch transformation of Japan. They did change a great deal, but a considerable portion of the old order of imperial Japan, and the revised order of wartime mobilization, remained in place when the Americans packed their bags in 1952.

The occupiers had intended to destroy the zaibatsu, seen as the moneybags of militarism. They had intended to destroy the centralized control held by the bureaucracy over key realms such as education and policing. They had intended to purge from public life, forever, the militarists in the army and navy and their supporters in civilian life, politicians and businessmen as well as intellectuals.

Japan's American rulers made attempts in each of these areas. But by the early 1950s, the subsidiaries of the prewar zaibatsu were on the way toward regrouping around banks instead of holding companies, the prewar political parties had survived to dominate the Diet and cabinet, and the civilian bureaucracy was as strong as ever, or perhaps even stronger. These enduring features of political and economic life are what one historian has called the "passage through" of the old guard, from prewar, through war, to postwar.[17]

The relative stability of postwar Japan, however, rested on more than continuity in the power of the old guard, even though various transwar continuities noted earlier were important. The postwar order also was rooted in great changes that would endure: in civil rights granted under the constitution as well as in land reform, labor reform, and legal changes for women that went well beyond what Japan's rulers would have enacted on their own. These gave more people than ever a stake in the system. The postwar stabilization of Japan was far from a static process involving little change. It was precisely the result of massive change. Reforms accelerated changes underway and set renewed struggles in motion. The political and social realm ultimately settled into a sort of isometric stability: Important, and occasionally explosive, tensions remained at the center of society, culture, and politics, but these were ultimately contained.

Over the next several decades, as the economy boomed, the three interlocking institutions of big business, establishment political parties, and the bureaucracy achieved a remarkably durable hegemony. This postwar stability was importantly rooted in the "passage through" of the old guard. But one also sees great social stability anchored in large and growing middle classes focusing their energies on gaining a stake in the system through education and employment in factories as well as office buildings. This was the legacy of the reforms.

POSTWAR AND
CONTEMPORARY JAPAN

1952–2000

14

Economic and Social Transformations

The Japanese economy expanded at a stunning pace from 1950 through the early 1970s. These two decades, beginning with the Korean War boom, have come to be called the "era of high speed growth" by historians. At unprecedented speed, Japan changed from a site of destruction and poverty to a place of prosperity. How did this happen? The so-called economic miracle was in part produced through the transforming magic of the market. But in important and distinctive ways, it was a managed miracle guided by the Japanese state. The experience of high growth was also a costly one. Jobs were often grinding, with long hours and tight discipline. Benefits were unevenly distributed between cities and country, between men and women, and between employees at large and small workplaces. Environmental damage was immense. The political struggles over these costs and contradictions of growth will be covered in the following chapter.

Change came more slowly in the realm of social experience. But several years after the postwar economy took off—from roughly the late 1950s into the 1960s—a *postwar* society took shape that differed greatly from the *transwar* Japan of the wartime or immediate postwar era. A way of life identified with what people called the "new middle class" rose to prominence. The middle class in Japan presented a powerful set of standardized images of a typical life. More people than ever came to share in experiences understood as those of middle-class or "mainstream" society. Nonetheless, some important social divisions persisted, and others were reshaped but not erased.

Japanese leaders in the bureaucracy and ruling political party, working in tandem with corporate executives, actively sought to manage these trends toward more standardized patterns of middle-class social life. A variety of programs supported particular versions of family and domestic life, schooling, and the workplace. Like its economic history, the social history of postwar Japan was shaped by numerous state programs to influence the thought and behavior of ordinary citizens.

THE POSTWAR "ECONOMIC MIRACLE"

Over the twenty-three years from 1950 to 1973, Japan's gross national product (GNP; the total value of goods and services produced in a year) expanded by an average annual rate of more than 10 percent. Such a record of growth over such a long period of time had never been seen in world economic history (the People's Republic of China since the 1980s has grown with comparable speed). Only a few minor downturns, such as that in 1954 caused by the end of the Korean War, show up as slight dips on a growth chart that runs smoothly and sharply upward (see Figure 14.1). Measured in U.S. dollars, the Japanese GNP totaled just $11 billion in 1950. By 1955 it had more than doubled to about $25 billion. By 1973 it had increased an additional thirteen-fold, to $320 billion. Measured comparatively, the Japanese economy stood at 7 percent of the American in 1955 and ranked below all the major European economies. By 1973, Japan's GNP had climbed to nearly one-third of the American total. Its economy was the third largest in the world, after the United States and Soviet Union (see Table 14.1).

Equally remarkable was the sustained and massive investment in new technology and manufacturing plants. The standard measure for such basic investment is gross capital formation. During the heart of Japan's high-growth era, from 1955 to 1973, rates of capital formation averaged more than 22 percent per year. As with GNP, these rates are historically and comparatively without parallel.

While such growth had no precedent, the change in economic structure had historical roots. At the cutting edge of the postwar surge stood producers in iron and steel, shipbuilding, automobiles, and electronics. Most of these same heavy industries—and many of the same companies—had led the economic surge of the militarized economy of the 1930s. They now proved able to prosper through peacetime as they had during wartime. The overall weight of heavy industrial production increased from 45 percent in 1955 to 62 percent by 1970, and the prominence of light industries such as textiles fell sharply.

As early as 1962, the British magazine *Economist* ran a feature story on what it called Japan's postwar "economic miracle."[1] The term stuck. It has come to be a shorthand description of the postwar decades of high growth. Historians and economists have produced a growth industry of their own trying to offer logical, this-worldly explanations for this seemingly astounding development.

One important part of the postwar story was the unusually favorable international environment. Economies boomed in other countries as well—observers used the term "economic miracle" for Germany as well as for Japan. The global economy overall grew unusually fast in the 1950s and 1960s, at a rate of 5 percent per year. The United States led the way in negotiating a more open trading system through treaties such as the General Agreement on Trade and Tariffs in (GATT) in 1947. As a result, the total volume of international trade more than tripled over these two decades. In addition, cheap and reliable energy supplies in the form of oil from the Middle East and elsewhere fueled industrial expansion at relatively low costs. Finally, in this more open world economy, relatively affordable licensing agreements gave Japanese (and other) businesses unusually open access to a host of new technologies from transistors to steel furnaces. These allowed productivity to rise quickly and consistently.

But this conjuncture of international fortune smiled on the entire capitalist world. Why did Japan's economy grow with particular speed? A few of the international

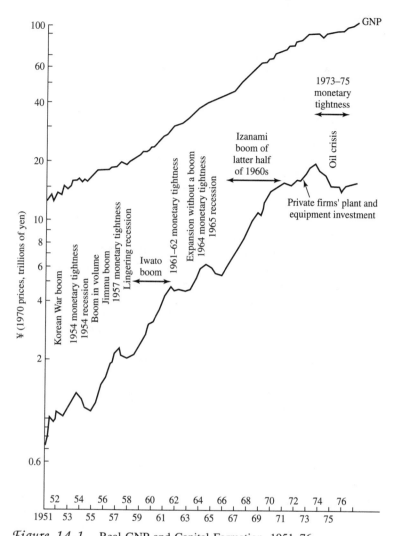

Figure 14.1   Real GNP and Capital Formation, 1951–76

Source: Economic Planning Agency, *Kokumin shotoku tōkei nenpō*, adapted in Nakamura Takafusa, *The Postwar Japanese Economy* (Tokyo: Tokyo University Press, 1981), p. 35. Reprinted with permission.

factors favored Japan more than others. America's continued military presence and the constitutional limitation on Japan's own military spared the government from high defense costs. The Korean War stimulated exports at a key moment. And a favorable exchange rate from 1949 through the early 1970s functioned as a sort of export subsidy.

TABLE 14.1 **Nominal GNP of Five Major Nations, 1951–80 (amounts in $U.S. billion)**

	Japan	United States	West Germany	France	Great Britain
1951	14.2	328.4	28.5	35.1	41.4
1955	22.7	398.0	43.0	49.2	53.9
1960	39.1	503.8	70.7	60.0	71.9
1965	88.8	688.1	115.1	99.2	100.2
1970	203.1	992.7	184.6	145.5	124.0
1975	498.2	1,549.2	418.2	339.0	234.5
1980	1,040.1	2,633.1	816.5	657.1	525.5

Source: Keizai Kōhō Sentaa, *Japan: An International Comparison* (Tokyo: Keizai Kōhō Sentaa, (1983), p. 5.

But a full explanation of economic growth must look in addition to domestic factors. Entrepreneurship is one of them. A new generation of daring younger managers took charge of established companies and founded new ones. They were helped in part by the occupation era purges, which forced many top managers of the wartime economy into early retirement. In several famous cases, they defied the cautious warnings of government bureaucrats to invest in new fields and new technologies, despite the presence of experienced global competitors.

The government advised automakers, for example, to consolidate via mergers, the better to compete with Detroit's Big Three. Instead, Toyota, Nissan, Isuzu, Tōyō Kōgyō (Mazda), and Mitsubishi all decided to produce full lines. Even more remarkably, an upstart motorcycle company founded by Honda Sōichiro defied bureaucratic warnings and entered the auto market in 1963 with great long-run success. In similar fashion, a bold executive in Kawasaki Heavy Industries, Nishiyama Yatarō, spun off his company's metal division to found a new iron-and steelmaker in 1950. He proposed a massive investment in a fully integrated, state-of-the-art iron and steel plant. When state bureaucrats denied access to domestic capital, he obtained funding outside Japan, from the World Bank. By 1961, the Kawasaki Steel Company had established itself as the fourth largest producer in the nation. And in 1953, two young mavericks, Morita Akio and Ibuka Masaru, struggled for months with reluctant state officials before winning permission to purchase a license to make transistors. Beginning with the radio in the 1950s, their infant company, Sony, soon emerged as the global leader in quality and innovation in consumer electronic goods.

In general, Japanese private companies expanded quickly and fearlessly. They borrowed massive amounts from banks and took on large debts. Private banks, as well as public institutions such as the Industrial Development Bank, drew on individual savings to channel capital to businesses large and small. The typical ratio of debt to equity for a Japanese company in the high growth era stood at 75 : 25, far different from the prewar economy, where a typical debt level was closer to 40 percent. Because output and revenue (aided by inflation) grew so quickly, corporations were able to repay these loans without major trouble.

The high quality of human capital was another important domestic factor that boosted the postwar economy. As compulsory education was extended through middle school under the occupation, young working people in Japan were increasingly well educated. Employees of all ages were delighted at the prospect of a return to normalcy and a chance to work for themselves, instead of sacrificing for the military. An unprecedented proportion of the work force joined labor unions—over 50 percent at the peak in the late 1940s and early 1950s. Organized workers were often militant in their actions and demands. But they were also energetic and committed on the job, willing to work long hours and master new skills. As new technologies came on line and were used effectively, productivity increased substantially. Labor productivity in manufacturing rose 88 percent in the decade from 1955 through 1964.

In addition to working hard as producers, ordinary Japanese played important roles as both savers and spenders. In sharp contrast to the prewar era, but continuing trends from the war years, ordinary Japanese wage earners saved unusually high proportions of their income. The average household saved under 10 percent of its income in the early 1950s, but savings rates soared steadily as the economy grew. They reached 15 percent by 1960 and topped 20 percent by 1970. Households have continued to save in excess of 20 percent of income since then. These funds, deposited in savings accounts of commercial banks or in the government-run postal savings system, made up a vast pool of capital available for investment in industry.

But even as they saved, ordinary citizens happily spent their growing salaries on a wide range of consumer goods. To be sure, export markets were crucial to the economy; exports earned dollars that were vital to finance continued investment in foreign technology. But from the 1950s through the early 1970s, exports accounted for just 11 percent of GNP. Over the same time span, the capitalist economies of Western European nations exported an average of 21 percent of their GNP.[2] Domestic demand, including the retail consumer market, was therefore a significant engine of growth. Consumers, like industrial producers, continued trends of the 1920s and 1930s that were interrupted by the war. They flocked to stores to buy a widening array of household and leisure goods: washing machines and electric rice cookers, radios, record players, and then televisions. These were costly purchases. In 1957, a typical new TV sold for eighty-five thousand yen, roughly two and one-half months' income for an average urban family. Nonetheless, by 1963, more than four of every five households in the nation owned a television. Overall, real per capita domestic consumption rose at an annual rate of 7.5 percent between 1955 and 1973.[3]

The most controversial domestic element in postwar economic history is the role of the Japanese state. The government did not run a "command economy" on the Soviet model. Private businesses took significant initiatives, sometimes against official advice. But even so, Japan's postwar economic story is not a simple tale of a free market miracle. State management, which grew out of practices improvised in the prewar and war years, was extensive. These practices are summed up by the term *industrial policy*, and they made a difference.

The Japanese government (assisted by SCAP during the occupation era) retained important wartime powers over access to key resources such as foreign exchange and technology licenses. It used these powers as levers to support some business ventures and discourage others. In the immediate postwar years, this formal authority played a major role. Over time, the weight of state intervention shifted to more informal practices not written into law, called "administrative guidance." The most important guiding agency was the Ministry of International Trade and Industry (MITI). It was the successor to the prewar Ministry of Commerce, which became the Munitions Ministry at the height of the war. This agency was renamed the Ministry of Commerce and Industry in 1945 and was once more relabeled, as MITI, in 1949. Other government bureaus that played important roles included the ministries of Finance, Transport, Construction, and Post and Telecommunications and the Economic Planning Agency.

At the most general level, the government fostered a climate of confidence by acting as economic cheerleader and sign-painter. A series of "five-year plans" issued by the Economic Planning Agency beginning in 1948 had no binding force. But they signaled to private investors that the state was interested in the success of certain industries and stood ready to step in as lender; as facilitator of access to foreign exchange, raw materials, or technology licenses; and as rescuer should problems arise. The government role as business booster brought a certain (perhaps jealous) scorn from foreigners. In one famous incident in 1962, the French president Charles Degaulle referred to visiting Prime Minister Ikeda Hayato as "that transistor salesman."

In more hands-on fashion, state bureaus protected and nurtured nascent industries. Through the 1960s, they used old-fashioned tariffs as one tool to limit imports. In addition, a Japanese company needed to convert yen to dollars in order to import and required government permission to buy dollars. The government could use this power to obstruct imports and protect Japanese firms from foreign competitors in domestic markets. The state also nurtured favored Japanese companies with all manner of benefits. Government lending agencies offered low-interest loans to targeted industries. Bureaucrats arranged technology licenses and gave tax breaks to firms in sectors designated for growth. A rush to invest in such firms often resulted in excess capacity. In such cases, MITI might broker a "depression cartel." These were industrywide agreements by which major firms coordinated their cuts in output to ensure that all were able to survive.

The benefits of such practices could be substantial, and they were not necessarily limited to privileged insiders. In the 1950s, to give one example, MITI pressured the major iron and steel producers to share the costs, and the benefits, of a single license for the cutting-edge technology of the basic oxygen furnace. The free market alternative would have been for each interested producer to pay the Austrian inventor for its own separate license. Japanese producers in this way obtained a critical technology for a small fraction of the cost borne by American steelmakers.[4] They were then able to forge ahead of their global competitors by more swiftly building a new generation of production facilities.

This informal mechanism of state intervention in the economy came to be called *administrative guidance*. It was a cornerstone of the transwar political economy. It drew on relationships and practices first improvised in programs from the 1920s and 1930s to rationalize industrial production by encouraging or compelling cartels in major industries. Bureaucrats in the postwar era further developed these practices of managed capitalism, but they used less coercive forms of persuasion than during the war. They left more room for the market to reward those who used government help effectively, and their interaction with businessmen proved considerably more constructive.

TRANSWAR PATTERNS OF COMMUNITY, FAMILY, SCHOOL, AND WORK

The concept of a transwar system can be used to describe *political* and *economic* arrangements improvised from the depression through the war and into the postwar era: industrial policy and the reorganization of business combines, labor-management relations, women's changing roles in the labor force, or agrarian land reform. It is also possible to speak of a set of transwar *social* patterns. For the first decade or so after World War II, the social structure and the texture of people's lives shared much with a transwar era that stretched from roughly the 1920s to the 1950s. A heterogeneous society was marked by enduring diversity and division in community and family life, in schools, and in workplaces.

Wartime scarcity, bombing, and evacuation had briefly devastated urban society in the early 1940s. But a vibrant city life revived even before the economy recovered. The flow of migrants to major cities, underway since the nineteenth century, resumed as well. In the 1950s and 1960s, roughly one million people left the countryside for cities each year. The gradual spread of suburban living had started with the construction of commuter rail lines and new residential neighborhoods in the 1910s and 1920s. Cities such as Tokyo and Osaka continued to sprawl in the 1950s and 1960s. They served as magnets for those looking for a bright, new, modern life. Japan's urban population rose from 38 percent of the nation in 1950 to 75 percent by 1975.

Migration to the cities did not deplete the countryside. After the war, millions of soldiers came home to rejoin their families or start new ones. The result, in Japan as elsewhere, was a dramatic baby boom. At the peak from 1947 to 1949, births numbered nearly 2.7 million per year. Overall, between 1945 and 1955 the population of Japan increased by 18.6 million. This sharp rise kept the rural population high even while millions moved to the cities. Japan's agricultural population at the end of World War II accounted for roughly 50 percent of the populace, or 36 million people. A decade later in 1955 this absolute number of people stood unchanged, although the proportion of the population in rural areas had fallen. Dynamic urban *and* rural societies were part of the heterogeneity of transwar Japanese life.

The transwar social world was also notable for the diversity in the way people came to be educated and earn their livings. Despite occupation era reforms, the school system through the 1950s remained a hierarchy with three very different, and quite respectable, exit points: the end of middle school, the end of high school, and graduation from college or university. From the late 1940s through the 1950s increased numbers of youths advanced to high school, but even in 1955 roughly half of all youths ended their education when they graduated middle school. Another third completed high school, and approximately 15 percent went on to college.

This education-based hierarchy with roots in the prewar and wartime eras connected neatly to the workplaces of the 1950s. Middle-school graduates, both male and female, took jobs as blue-collar operatives with relatively limited future prospects. Boys leaving high school could enter skilled production or clerical positions with a reasonable expectation of rising at least to foreman, in some cases beyond. Girls with high school degrees could move into secretarial jobs in the offices of prestigious companies. Male university graduates entered elite managerial positions in corporate and bureaucratic offices. But, as in most of the industrial capitalist world of the early postwar decades, women graduating from universities faced tremendous barriers to such careers, with occasional exceptions such as teaching in public schools. Gender and education in these ways combined to channel people into jobs with sharply different levels of responsibility and pay.

As in the prewar era, the world of work was extraordinarily diverse. While a significant minority followed their education by working for wages outside the home—whether in factories or mines, in government offices, or at companies large and small—the majority of adults in the city as well as the countryside continued to work in small, home-based family businesses or farms. In the 1950s, as before the war, more than half of the nation's labor force consisted of family members working on a family farm or fishing boat or in a small family-owned retail, wholesale, or manufacturing shop. The husband would be counted as the business owner. The wife, on a farm or in a vegetable market or a barber shop, would work alongside, counted as "family labor." Government statisticians did not classify these women as "employees." Typically they shared the overall revenues as a family member but received no wages. From the 1930s through the 1950s, well over two-thirds of women workers fell into this category of family labor. These women and their families were the core of Japan's "old middle class" of the prewar and transwar era: shopkeepers, small traders, and small manufacturers. They remained a dominant presence in the neighborhoods of postwar Japanese towns and cities.

Variety in family type was part of the transwar social pattern as well. Nuclear families had already accounted for 54 percent of all families in the 1920s. Most of the remainder were extended families of three generations under one roof. Transwar society was marked by the coexistence of these two forms of family life.

The material conditions of daily life of the 1950s also retained qualities that were part of an old transwar world more than a new postwar one. Photographs of the 1950s resemble those of the 1930s more than the 1970s. People in the countryside wore sandals and kimono-style everyday clothing. Houses still had thatched roofs, roads were unpaved, and oxen plowed fields. Labor on farms was scarcely mechanized. A photograph of a young woman's hands taken in 1963 could just as well have been taken from the early days of the century. Farmwork was arduous and literally left scars. Some exciting consumer innovations were spreading in cities and in the countryside. But until the late 1950s, these consumer goods were not basically different from those of the 1920s and 1930s: electric lighting, radios, record players, and telephones.

The routines of daily life were similarly enduring from prewar days through the 1950s, with a similar mix of the cosmopolitan and the local. A social survey of "laboring households" in the Tokyo region in 1950 revealed that more than two hours of a woman's average day—every day—were devoted to sewing. Some of this domestic work was done with sewing machines, following store-bought patterns. It was part of a commercial world of fashion that had been celebrated flamboyantly in department stores since early in the twentieth century. But much sewing, whether by

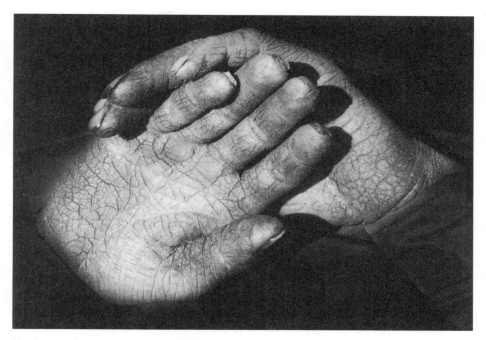

The hands of a twenty-one-year-old farm daughter in 1963. One can easily imagine the diffi-cult work, both in the home and in the fields, that is etched in these lines. The photo attests to the continuity in rural society and farming technology from the early twentieth century through the 1950s. Not until the fruits of high growth allowed farmers to mechanize their operations in the 1960s and afterward did the work routines of rural society change fundamentally.
Courtesy of Mr. Minami Yoshikazu.

hand or machine, consisted of mending old clothing. The role of homemaker thus remained a time-consuming occupation demanding considerable skill. The modern consumer realm of ready-to-wear clothing coexisted with a significant realm of home-based, noncommercial reproductive activity.

In other ways, as well, a local world of home-based, partially commercialized activity coexisted with a world of mass, bureaucratized, profit-seeking institutions. Cultural and leisure activity through the 1950s, as before the war, remained tied to community events such as festivals at Shinto shrines or Buddhist temples or holiday visits to nearby sites or ancestral villages. The great milestones of individual and family life—birth, marriage, death—were commemorated in relatively intimate set-tings. The vast majority of people in Japan until the late 1950s were born at home, not in hospitals. They were attended by midwives, not doctors. Most people died at home. Funerals and weddings usually took place at large rural homes or at temples and shrines, rather than at commercial establishments dedicated to providing these services.[5]

SHARED EXPERIENCES AND STANDARDIZED LIFEWAYS OF THE POSTWAR ERA

Profound social changes then took place across the decades of rapid growth. To an important extent, the economic ground had been equalized by events of the war and immediate postwar years, ranging from the fire-bombings and SCAP's land and labor reforms to the massive inflation that destroyed much of the wealth of the prewar elites. Against this background, trends toward standardized ways of life accelerated sharply as the economy grew. The gap between rural and urban life shrank. A greater majority than before came to grow up in nuclear, rather than extended, families. The gap between those with higher and basic education diminished. The extent of hierarchy within many workplaces also decreased. It would be a mistake to overstate this decline in social division and produce a false stereotype of Japan since the 1970s as a paradise of homogeneity. But it is undeniable that from the 1950s through the 1970s the realm of shared experience among people in Japan expanded, as transwar gave way to post-war society.

The spread of shared experience was accelerated by physical changes in the land-scape that brought people more easily and quickly in contact with each other. In 1946 barely more than 1 percent of Japan's 900,000 kilometers of roads were paved. By 1970, 15 percent of roads had been covered with pavement, including a modest 640 kilometers of toll expressways. By 1980 the paved total had tripled to 46 percent of all roads. The high-speed "bullet train" began service between Osaka and Tokyo in 1964. This cut travel time between the two cities from eight to three hours. Known as the bullet train outside Japan, it was more prosaically called the "new trunk line" (*shinkansen*) in Japanese. But the train was anything but ordinary. It both transformed the sense of distance between Japan's greatest urban centers and stood as a proud symbol of technological achievement in the forefront of global progress.

As the landscape was literally bulldozed at a rapid pace, the countryside began to shrink in a figurative sense as well. Both the number as well as the proportion of full-time farmers declined sharply and steadily, from 2.1 million full-time farm house-holds in 1955 to well under half that number (830,000) in 1970. The proportion of the labor force employed in agriculture fell below 20 percent by 1970. But part-time farming expanded simultaneously. Mechanization—and the small size of the average landholding—made this possible, as did the movement of new forms of employment to the countryside. Using better roads, and able to afford motorcycles and cars, working-age people began commuting from villages to jobs at factories or offices in nearby towns or cities. At home, grandparents took care of grandchildren and tended vegetable or rice fields. The adult children would help on the weekends. Farm villages came to resemble suburban communities, emptied of adult men and women on week-days. By the 1970s this transformation of the countryside had diminished the gap in lifestyles between people in rural, urban, and suburban Japan. In extreme cases the demographic shift to the cities had created empty ghost villages. More typically, rural villages survived in this new form.

At the heart of the standardization of social experience across the landscape was a process in which large-scale, bureaucratic, and commercial institutions touched peo-ple's lives to an unprecedented degree. Public schooling and military service had defined the modern social experience since the nineteenth century, but other institutions expanded their reach dramatically in the postwar era. Hospitals became the almost universal sites for birth and death: In 1955 82 percent of childbirths took place at home; in 1975 the proportion was a mere 1.2 percent.[6] Weddings were transformed into lavish and costly spectacles, aggressively marketed and expertly performed in thousands of hotels and wedding halls nationwide.[7] Funerals and the various anniversary memorial services of Buddhist observance were also increasingly provided by such enterprises. As bullet trains, automobiles, and jet travel came within reach of the middle class, standard commercial packages of mass tourism at home and abroad surged in popularity. In 1960, just 120,000 people traveled overseas. By 1970, the number was nearly one million, and by 1980 nearly four million Japanese citizens traveled outside the country.

Two key sites for this standardization of social experience were schools and workplaces. Education changed greatly from the end of the 1950s through the 1960s. The high school entry rate soared. From about 50 percent in 1955, it reached 82 percent of the potential cohort in 1970 and 94 percent by 1980. Large proportions of students also went on to two- or four-year colleges. By 1975, 35 percent of high school graduates entered college each year, a rate exceeding most European societies and approaching that of the United States. Only a tiny minority ended their schooling before high school. The education hierarchy had been compressed from three tiers to two.

As before, public universities were the most prestigious ports of entry to elite positions. But one important feature of mass higher education sets this era off sharply from the transwar years (and later decades): Access was remarkably equal. In the 1960s, the children of the poorest families in the nation won admission in precise proportion to their numbers in the overall population (see Table 14.2).[8] This was a stunningly egalitarian profile of student backgrounds. It resulted not from affirmative action, but from the high level and the standardized quality of teaching in public schools across the nation. It also reflected the fact that merit-based exams denied wealthy parents the chance to "buy" entrance with a donation to a favorite university.

TABLE 14.2 **Equality of Access to Japanese Higher Education, 1961–74 (percentage of students from each of five income levels, among all students entering national universities)**

National Universities	1961	1965	1970	1974
I (lowest income)	19.7	16.3	17.3	14.4
II	20.2	15.1	13.9	11.2
III	15.4	18.6	17.7	16.0
IV	18.5	22.5	21.2	24.3
V (highest income)	26.2	27.6	29.2	34.1

Note: Each group, from lowest (I) to highest (V) represents 20 percent of households based on income level.
Source: Adapted from Thomas Rohlen, "Is Japanese Education Becoming Less Egalitarian?" *Journal of Japanese Studies* (Winter, 1977), Vol. 3, No. 1, p. 41.

An additional factor was perhaps the devastation of the war and early postwar inflation, which had eroded the position of old elites and equalized the distribution of wealth.

The newly egalitarian schools became a sorting machine for the middle-class masses. The result was the notorious experience called "examination hell." To enter top high schools and then the best colleges, the only measure that mattered was performance on the entrance examination. Students spent long hours and years cramming for these tests. If they failed to win a place at a coveted elite school, they often took a postgraduate year (or two) to study more and try again. These youths, floating between high school and college, were dubbed *rōnin,* a premodern term for "masterless samurai." The examination-centered school curriculum offended many teachers who wanted to emphasize other modes of learning. It was designed both to sort young people and to discipline them. Vast experience at repetitive cramming for dull exams prepared young boys, especially, for a demanding, competitive working routine as an adult.

Japanese workplaces also took on new standardized "postwar" characteristics. The majority of workers no longer held family-based jobs; they worked for wages outside the home. The proportion of family workers in the labor force dropped from two-thirds of all in the late 1950s to under half by the end of 1960s. This change affected women as well as men. Between 1960 and 1970, the proportion of women workers who were employed outside the family sector rose from 42 to 53 percent.[9]

A second key postwar change in the workplace ran parallel to that in the schools. Hierarchy was compressed, and a more egalitarian spirit spread. As almost everyone went on to high school in the 1960s and 1970s, the high school diploma came to define a floor rather than a privileged middle point of entry. A better educated and better disciplined work force was one result. Another result was a much smaller gap between white-and blue-collar work, especially among men. When prewar managers with college degrees and technicians with high school diplomas had supervised production workers with a middle school or grade school education, the differences in experience and expectations were great. By the 1970s, when virtually all employees had gone to school through age eighteen and college education itself imparted relatively little new knowledge or skills, the gap between the skills brought to the job by blue-collar high school recruits and white-collar college grads was much smaller.

In the new social order of the high growth era, the experience of family life was also standardized to a significant extent. The proportion of nuclear families rose through the 1960s, reaching a plateau of just under two-thirds of all families by 1975. At the same time, single-member households—typically young unmarried wage earners living in company dorms or apartments—increased from 3 percent in 1955 to 14 percent by 1975. Extended families fell from one-third of all to one-fifth. The definition of "extended" is ambiguous. Most elderly parents who did not live with their children resided within a short walk or drive to their children and grandchildren.[10] One might call these "extended nuclear families." But the rise of one-person households and the decline in extended ones gave two-generation families greater prominence than before as the normative state of family life.

Nuclear families comprised the heart of what commentators in the late 1950s began to call Japan's "new middle class."[11] The adjective "new" marks a contrast to the older middle class of family farmers in the countryside and traders and small manufacturers in the cities. The expanding new middle class took up residence in the growing suburbs of Tokyo, Yokohama, Nagoya, Osaka, and other cities. In the booming decades of the 1960s through the 1980s, huge apartment blocks called *danchi* sprouted up in what had been rice or vegetable fields. Over one million units were built by public housing authorities. Private developers also put up single-family homes sprawling in all directions out of these cities for the more successful middle-class citizens.

New architecture drew on innovations of the prewar era to promote a "modern" living space. Bedrooms were separated from the dining/kitchen area. Tables with chairs replaced floor-level seating. Children often had their own separate bedrooms. In the typical nuclear families of the high-growth years, the husband commuted by train from such a home to a demanding full-time job in an office or a factory. The wife often took on a part-time job, but she devoted herself primarily to the care of their children, rarely more than two in number.

As people yearned for this new sort of home, they yearned for each other in new ways as well. In upper-class and middle-class Japan of the early twentieth century, marriages were typically arranged, although a minority and somewhat subversive ideal of love as the basis of marriage had appeared. In the 1950s, the arranged marriage was still quite common in the new middle class of white-collar salaried workers.

Government investment in public housing and private investment of hard-earned savings by the parents of the baby boom generation combined to fuel a postwar housing boom. Apartment complexes such as this one in an Osaka suburb, Hirakata City, in 1961, sprung up all over Japan.

Courtesy of *Mainichi* newspaper.

Partners were introduced by parents, relatives, friends, or a professional marriage arranger. They would meet several times for a brief "look-see" (the *omiai*) before deciding whether to wed.[12] But the custom of dating became popular among college youths and young workers in these years, and the word for *date* (*deeto*) was imported from English. Gradually but steadily, the ideal of the "love marriage" won the day. Increasingly extravagant weddings to celebrate such marriages came to define the founding moment of the standard family of postwar Japan.

At the same time, the worlds of work and family remained quite separate for many middle-class men and women. A man's commitment to his company—especially for white-collar employees—generally required him to join the after-hours life of drinking and socializing with workmates or customers, often in the company of female bar hostesses. The so-called water trades of the female companion (referring to the mixed drinks poured by the hostesses) combined elements of the café culture of the 1920s and the elite world of the highly cultivated female entertainers known as geisha, generally stopping short of prostitution but not ruling out occasional liaisons with customers. The water trades flourished in Japan from the 1960s onward, generating billions of dollars in revenues for thousands of bar owners (often older women who had worked as hostesses) and their employees.[13]

Dating and the pursuit of "love marriages" became increasingly popular from the late 1950s onward. In this photo from the 1960s, couples neatly spaced along the Wadakura Bridge in Tokyo demonstrate their affection for each other.
Courtesy of Tomiyama Haru.

DIFFERENCES ENDURING AND REALIGNED

It is important to recognize these substantial increases in the realm of shared experience in postwar society. It is equally important to understand that crucial social differences persisted nonetheless, while others emerged in new forms: between the old and new middle class, between those entering college prep high schools and those in the vocational track of "overflow" schools, between men and women, and between the Japanese majority and the ethnically "other" minorities of Koreans and *burakumin,* as well as Ainu aborigines to the north and Okinawans to the south.

One enduring division was that between the lives of the old and new middle class in towns and cities. Just as village life was transformed but not destroyed in the high-growth era, the large population of self-employed urban families did not disappear. The old middle class remained numerous while the new middle class grew. Local retailers and traders strove to fill their homes with the same consumer goods as the families of the "salaryman." Their children had similar basic education and reasonably similar chances to enter well-regarded higher schools. The dense local networks of shopkeepers and small manufacturers provided a social glue for urban neighborhoods that made them safe and vibrant places to live and shop and a source of the vitality of city life.[14] But despite some convergence of their lifestyles toward a common middle-class pattern, the old middle class faced less certain economic prospects than employees of large companies. Small businesses went bankrupt in significant numbers: Throughout the high-growth decades, between 3 and 5 percent of all small businesses failed each year.[15]

In education, key axes of difference emerged in new form. As high school education became nearly universal, the gap *between* those with basic and higher levels of schooling diminished. But new divisions emerged *among* high schools and *among* colleges. Merit-based exams for high school and college, and the relatively even quality of elementary and middle-school public education, created far more even competition for higher education than ever before. But this equality of opportunity went hand in hand with inequality of result, both individually and collectively. Certain public high schools in all the major cities developed well-deserved reputations as top-flight "prep" schools. Those who passed the demanding entrance exams for these schools were then groomed for three years to pass the entrance tests for elite universities. Other high schools developed equally accurate reputations as mediocre "overflow" schools for those who proved less motivated or successful in cramming for exams.

A related realignment of division marked Japan's burgeoning manufacturing industries. Thanks to changes in the education system, the power of labor unions, and new management policies, equality in the treatment of blue- and white-collar male employees of large companies increased substantially. But inequality persisted between these fortunate persons—perhaps one-fourth to one-third of working people—and the rest of the working population. Wages of men in smaller and medium-sized workplaces in the 1960s stood at 50 to 60 percent of the pay given to workers at large companies.[16] Their job security was considerably less as well.

Perhaps the most important social differences across the postwar decades could be found in the realm of gender relations. In the workplaces of the high-growth era, for example, the division between the labor of women and men changed surprisingly little. In manufacturing in the prewar era, the great majority of heavy industrial workers had been men, while roughly two-thirds of female workers had been textile operatives. In the early 1950s, as many as 55 percent of women in manufacturing jobs still worked in textile factories. At this point, the mass production factories of electronic equipment makers began to grow at extraordinary rates. They hired many thousands of young women. From the mid-1950s into the 1960s, women at assembly lines producing transistor radios, and then TVs, became international symbols of the emerging Japanese economic miracle. The proportion of women employed in textiles plummeted from over half in 1955 to just 18 percent of female manufacturing labor by 1965. But the characteristics of the electronic workers were precisely those of the textile operatives of years past: teenage girls hired directly upon completing the compulsory middle schools, living in company housing, and enjoying the very constraining benefits of paternalistic management policies. And the labor-intensive substance of work on a television assembly line was not very different from that of a textile operative.

In the expanding offices of corporate Japan, women were hired in the role of "office flowers" intended to brighten the workplace for their male coworkers on career tracks. They were taught to keep a cheery demeanor as they performed low-level clerical jobs with little prospects of advancement. They were typically required by

Women working on the assembly line of the Seiko Watch Company in 1958. Hundreds of thousands of young women, just out of middle school, took such jobs in the booming high-tech industries of electronics and precision machine manufacturing, as well as in established industries such as textiles.
Courtesy of *Mainichi* newspaper.

their employment contracts to quit their jobs at marriage. Some women challenged this sort of job discrimination, both through collective bargaining and, most importantly, through lawsuits. Beginning with a 1966 decision in a famous case brought against Sumitomo Cement, the courts typically ruled to uphold the right of women workers to keep their jobs after marriage. But many employers were committed to sustaining a gender division in the workplace. They kept a step ahead of the law by revising their recruiting policies. They began to avoid women, such as graduates of four-year colleges, likely to exercise this new right to a job. Instead they hired graduates of two-year junior colleges, who experience had shown were more likely to quit upon marriage even if not required to do so.[17]

Religious behavior also differentiated the lives of Japanese people in the postwar era. Some of those left behind in the race for success and affluence turned to a dizzying array of new religions for spiritual and social support. Many of these religions had been founded in the nineteenth or early twentieth century. Others were newly established in the immediate postwar years. Some were small and ephemeral. To secular observers they appeared very eccentric. They might offer faith healing through the laying on of hands or channeling of divine power through a charismatic leader's body.

A few of these religions won millions of adherents. The largest was Sōka Gakkai (Value Creation Society). Beginning in the late 1930s as a tiny offshoot of the Nichiren Buddhist sect, it took off in the 1950s and grew to claim seven million adherents by the late 1960s. Other thriving new religions, each with millions of members in the postwar era, included the Risshō Kōsei kai, also a Nichiren offshoot, and Tenrikyō. In contrast to the established Buddhist temples and Shinto shrines, which maintained the passive allegiance of the majority of people, these new religions cultivated a far more active commitment, both in prayer and financial support. They typically offered solace in this world as well as salvation in the next. Sōka Gakkai was notorious for its aggressive proselytizing. Its ritual practice consisted of thirty minutes daily of chanting before a Buddhist altar. This devotion, it was promised, would solve immediate problems, whether economic or emotional. New recruits were told that the religion was akin to a credit card. Instead of "buy now, pay later," one could "pray now, believe later." That is, one could pray in a skeptical spirit and come to believe when good things eventually came to pass. As a strong network of supportive believers helped new converts to find jobs or friendship, many prayers indeed were answered and the religion thrived.

Ethnic and racial minorities marked another realm of continued division in postwar society. Roughly two million Koreans had migrated to Japan or had been brought by force by the end of the war. The majority returned to Korea, but some 540,000 remained in Japan when the American occupation ended. Their legal status had changed from subjects of the Japanese emperor to resident aliens. They maintained strong communities and their own network of private schools, but they faced economic hardship and discrimination. Few of them won significant shares in the growing affluence of the society as a whole. They generally had little choice but to work in difficult, low-paying jobs such as day-labor on construction sites.

A second "ethnic" minority were the *burakumin*. Their outcaste status had been nominally eliminated in the Meiji era, but discrimination persisted even a century later. In the 1950s and 1960s, employers at prestigious workplaces would typically check the household register of job applicants to screen out *buraku* applicants. This was possible because the *burakumin* were chiefly identified by their traditional villages or neighborhoods (the term *burakumin* literally means "village person"), and the system of household registration in place since the Meiji era provided an official record of these social origins. The Buraku Liberation League, an extremely well-organized and militant advocacy group, exerted much political pressure to prevent the use of this information as a means to discriminate. The government in response enacted legal reforms in the late 1960s that restricted outsider access to a person's household register. But several private agencies responded to a continued discriminatory ethos by compiling unofficial lists of buraku addresses. They sold these lists to private companies. The government condemned this practice but did not outlaw it. By the late 1970s, as many as eight separate lists were in circulation.

In the face of this discrimination, the Buraku Liberation League supported a "separate but equal" sort of reform movement. They mobilized to win better collective treatment for *buraku* neighborhoods through subsidies, construction projects, or improvements in schools. These programs of support were codified in 1969 in a Buraku Special Measures Law. Over time, the standard of living in buraku neighborhoods rose significantly and approached that of mainstream society. But discrimination persisted, and *buraku* residents found it extremely difficult to enter mainstream corporate jobs and careers.[18]

MANAGING SOCIAL STABILITY AND CHANGE

The Japanese state bureaucracy and the ruling political party, often working in tandem with the business elite, were actively concerned with reducing social tensions and managing processes of social change. Numerous programs and campaigns to manage society ran parallel to those to manage the economy. For example, in addition to rebuilding the *burakumin* ghettos, government housing policy (as in the United States) provided middle-class families with low-cost mortgages. The government also founded a public corporation to build large numbers of high-rise "new towns." By the early 1970s, the public housing corporation had constructed nearly two million units, including apartments and single-family homes. Middle-class citizens applied in huge numbers and were selected via lotteries—sometimes with 100 : 1 odds—for these low-rent, subsidized dwellings.

One drive at the intersection of social and economic policy was the effort to encourage people to increase their rates of saving. Building on prewar and wartime programs, the Ministry of Finance launched a major effort to encourage savings in the 1950s. It built powerful alliances with women's organizations and focused its persuasive powers on housewives, who typically kept charge of household finances. By the 1960s, Japanese families were saving an average of about 15 percent of household income. This was the highest rate in the world and was also considerably higher than prewar levels of saving. Japanese banks were able to invest these funds in the booming economy. The causes of higher rates of saving are complex and included the need to save for old age as life expectancy increased, but the ubiquitous exhortations to save were probably a significant factor.[19]

Education was an important arena of social policy endeavor. Advisory committees of businessmen in the early 1960s joined education bureaucrats to call for exam-focused public schooling that would impart basic skills to an expanded pool of new workers. They wanted blue-and white-collar employees who could adapt to rapidly changing production and office technologies. They wanted schooling to allocate a hierarchy of credentials from high school to junior college to college degrees, so as to slot young men and women into appropriate levels and roles in the workplace. They generally got what they asked for. As their operations expanded, corporations recruited long-term employees directly from school more systematically than ever before. Magazines began publishing detailed lists that ranked both schools and companies in terms of difficulty of entry and popularity. The media thus further standardized popular images of mainstream and successful pathways through life.

Powerful institutions of the state, and the business world as well, acted with particular concern to define and manage "proper" gender roles. The Ministry of Education and the leaders of corporate Japan designed the school curriculum to reinforce a gendered vision of standard family and working life. In middle schools and high schools, gender-tracking placed young girls, but not boys, in courses in home economics and health. Here they learned the skills of good wives and mothers. In higher education in the high-growth era, about 90 percent of students at two-year junior colleges were women. They typically majored in subjects considered suited to women, such as home economics, education, or literature. Three-fourths of students at four-year colleges, in contrast, were men. The great majority majored in engineering and social sciences.

Some policies to uphold gender divisions in the workplace and at home took the form of state-imposed economic incentives. An expanded social security system was put into place from the 1950s through the 1970s. It supported the gender-based division of labor of a "standard" nuclear family because its benefit structure assumed that a husband was the primary wage earner. Also, a spouse's income under about $10,000 per year was not taxed at all, but earnings above this level were taxed at the much higher rate of the primary earner. This strongly discouraged married women from working more than part time.

Some state and corporate programs more directly encouraged women to define their primary role as that of homemaker rather than worker. Beginning in the late 1940s, government ministries worked with women's organizations on a number of loosely connected initiatives that evolved into a campaign called the New Life Movement. The movement got its postwar start in farm villages. Its activities built on various prewar and wartime campaigns to "improve daily life" aimed first at urban women in the 1920s and extending to villages by the 1930s. The prominent concern with kitchen design and hygienic handling of garbage prompted critics to joke that the movement consisted mainly of women swatting flies. Lectures, pamphlets, and most notably thousands of local study groups promoted new practices of hygiene (protecting food from insects, promptly disposing of garbage), kitchen design (bringing more light into kitchens), and household accounting (keeping careful records). In this way, bureaucrats in the ministries of agriculture, welfare, and education worked with local women's organizations in the countryside to push for their version of "enlightened" and "modern" household management. Beginning in 1955 the prime minister's office funded an association to coordinate the various New Life activities. Major corporations jumped on this New Life bandwagon as well. In the 1950s and 1960s over fifty of Japan's leading companies, with more than one million employees, organized New Life groups for the wives of their workers. The idea was, as one steel company's personnel manager put it:

> Life in the home is the barometer for the next day's life [at work]. In principle the housewife is in charge of home life, and we can say that the husband both takes his rest and builds his energy under her initiative. Thus, we wished to elevate the house-wives who played this role and thereby establish the foundation for a bright, cheerful home, a bright society, and beyond that, a bright, cheerful workplace.[20]

Birth control was a particular concern of both corporate and government New Life programs. Bureaucrats and business leaders from the early postwar days had feared that the surging population would literally eat up the economic gains of the postwar recovery. As one response, abortion had been legalized in 1948. At the peak in the late 1950s over one million abortions were performed each year. Many people criticized this use of abortion as a first-resort form of birth control. Some objected on moral grounds. Others were concerned at the unnecessary health risk to women. One practical response was to promote condom use and to distribute them not to the husbands, but to the wives in New Life groups. Although the New Life movement was organized from above, it empowered its participants in this and other ways. It gave them new forms of practical knowledge and a new voice in their families. Many women who later joined citizens' movements concerned with causes ranging from the environment to nuclear nonproliferation had their first taste of civic activity in these New Life groups.

IMAGES AND IDEOLOGIES OF SOCIAL STABILITY AND CHANGE

In the 1920s and 1930s social tensions—between landlords and tenants, zaibatsu owners and impoverished workers, city and country—were part of a volatile mix that pushed Japan toward a disastrous war. In the high-growth era after World War II, social divisions old and new proved somewhat less explosive. Ongoing and refigured differences were managed by government policies. They were also dampened by powerful cultural images of Japan as a land of a homogeneous people, where virtually everyone could share to some degree in the growing bounty and security of a modern, middle-class life.

The mass media played a key role in postwar social history by amplifying this sense of shared experience among Japanese people. This role was not new. The newspaper and book publishing industry from the late nineteenth century, and then newsreels, movies, and radio from the 1920s, had provided people with a powerful sense of belonging to a common national community. Government-controlled media in the 1930s and wartime—and then under American occupation—had defined national missions of mobilizing for war and then of embracing democracy. Although the forms of media became more varied in the high-growth era, the images of "the Japanese people" spread by the media were remarkably standardized.

The publishing industry flourished. Beginning with just a handful of magazines at the end of the war, the genre of the news and entertainment weekly grew explosively in the postwar decades. New publications targeted particular audience segments such as young women, young men, housewives, and adult men. By 1960, the circulation for these magazines averaged 11.5 million copies per week. In addition, Japan's newspapers published a total of 24 million issues per day. That year, book publishers came out with about twenty-four thousand new titles, and they sold 125 million books. By these measures, the reading public in Japan was among the most word-hungry in the world. On a per capita basis the only comparable or slightly larger publishing industries were found in Britain, Germany, the Soviet Union, and the United States.

At the same time, television broadcasting took off together with the surge of television ownership. The publically regulated NHK (Nippon Hōsō Kyōkai, or Japan Broadcast Association) network began broadcasting in early 1953. The first commercial competitors took to the air later that same year. By the 1960s, television was a constant presence in Japanese homes. Opinion polls concluded that the average viewer watched 2.5 hours of television each day.

In this media-saturated environment, standardized images of normal middle-class life spread widely. Coverage of exceptional events helped define the dreams of ordinary people. This was the case with the 1959 marriage of the Crown Prince Akihito (Emperor Hirohito's son). He broke tradition by choosing his own mate, a woman from outside the old aristocracy named Shōda Michiko. She was the daughter of a wealthy industrialist but nonetheless a commoner. A desire to watch the event reportedly sparked a huge boom in television sales, and the mass media provided the means to share this experience.[21] As described by announcers, their union symbolized a modern postwar ideal of marrying for love and forming a new nuclear family, in close contact with a larger family circle.

The ordinary run of media productions similarly defined the lives of middle-class, educated urban Japanese families as the typical experience of all Japanese people. One of the most important fictional families to play this role was that of "Sazae-san," created immediately after the war by a pioneering female cartoonist, Hasegawa Machiko. In comic strip form through the 1950s and 1960s, and as a long-running television show from 1969 through the 1990s, "Sazae-san" captured and shaped popular imagination. It offered an affectionately humorous look at three generations of a middle-class family. The fathers commuted to generic office jobs and stopped off for a few drinks before the homeward evening commute. The mothers cooked and ran the household, kept up with the neighbors, and nagged at boisterous children to keep at their studies.

Both ordinary programs and coverage of big events made it clear that Japan's postwar modern life was part of a global modern culture common to the advanced capitalist world. Several spectacles of the 1960s and 1970s were promoted as signs that Japan had reentered international society as a full member in good standing. Authorities used these occasions to boost social order and patriotism. They included a world exposition at Osaka in 1970 and the Winter Olympics in Sapporo in 1972. But the first and most significant was the Eighteenth Summer Olympiad, held in Tokyo in 1964.

In some ways the event did not meet expectations. Controversy marked plans to finance the Olympics, and the numbers of foreign tourists fell far short of predictions. In another example of its impulse to manage society, the government used the event

The Japanese women's volleyball team celebrates its victory in clinching a gold medal in the 1964 Tokyo Olympics. The players secured a place for themselves as national heroes. The Olympics sparked a global recognition of Japan's extraordinary recovery from the ruins of war as well as domestic pride in achievements such as the high-speed bullet train, which opened just before the games began.
Courtesy of *Mainichi* newspaper.

as an occasion for a variety of social reform campaigns. It called on citizens to improve public hygiene and sanitation and exhorted shopkeepers to curtail shady retail sales tactics. The Ministry of Education seized the moment to expand coverage of "patriotism" and increase the compulsory character of "moral education" or "civics" courses in the schools.

But it was the mass media, television above all, that made the Olympics a high-impact cultural event. The games won unprecedented ratings: an 84 percent share for the opening ceremony and an 85 percent share for the women's volleyball finals. The Japanese team won the gold medal and became national heroes. The presence of seventy-five hundred athletes from ninety-four countries, Kenzō Tange's monumental architecture of the stadium and pool, the opening of the bullet train to Osaka and a parallel network of expressways, and the success of Japanese athletes, who won an unprecedented sixteen gold medals (twenty-nine overall), sparked a media-induced surge of national pride in peaceful collective achievements in economy, technology, sports, and culture.

A huge advertising industry helped to reinforce the notion that "the Japanese people" shared a common sociocultural world. Industry revenues rose ninefold over the 1950s. By the end of the decade, advertising outlays accounted for roughly 1.5 percent of the Japanese GNP. Consumers were exhorted in print, on radio, and on TV to partake of the "bright new life" of the modern era by purchasing products flooding from Japanese factories, electrical appliances above all. By the 1970s, the consumeristic commercial culture that had emerged in the early twentieth century—at first mainly limited to middle-class city-dwellers—embraced the vast majority of people. Japanese society was no longer a place where the majority worked to satisfy basic needs for food, clothing, and shelter. The proportion of household budgets devoted to food fell from about half in the early 1950s to just under one-fourth by the late 1970s.[22]

As people were "liberated" to pursue their wants and desires under the spell of mass advertising, a succession of consumer durables moved from undreamt luxury to possible dreams. In the mid-1950s, pundits played on the three sacred imperial regalia (jewels, mirror, sword) and spoke of the "three sacred regalia" of modern life: television (black and white), washing machine, refrigerator. By the mid-1960s, upward of 90 percent of the population possessed these items. Observers then began to talk of the "three new regalia," also referred to as the "three Cs": car, cooler (air conditioner), and color TV.

As more and more people were able to afford the "typical" modern life symbolized by these possessions, or at least could reasonably hope to obtain this life for themselves or their children, a large majority of people in Japan came to identify themselves as members of mainstream or middle-class society. This change in social consciousness is neatly reflected in social surveys beginning in the 1950s. These reveal the sharp climb in the proportion of people who felt they belonged to either the upper, middle, or lower level of "the middle class." By the mid-1970s this proportion topped 75 percent in one authoritative social survey (see Figure 14.2). This self-identified middle-class actually exceeded 90 percent in other polls, including some by the prime minister's office. Perhaps most notable was a significant decline over these years in the self-identified "lower-middle class," matched by a sharp rise, from about 35 to 60 percent, in those who placed themselves squarely in the middle of the middle class. Observers read these and similar surveys and marveled at the advent of a nearly universal middle-class consciousness in what recently had been a society marked by sharp divisions of social status, wealth, and power.[23]

Some writers and intellectuals celebrated these postwar social changes. They wrote of the advent of a bright new life of possibility for individuals, liberated to pursue and fulfill personal desire. Yoshimoto Takaaki, an unorthodox philosopher on the left wing of the political spectrum, wrote in 1960 of "a private sense of interest [which] forms the basis of postwar 'democracy' (bourgeois democracy). If we do not recognize something positive at the root of this development, we can recognize no progressive developments whatsoever in Japanese society since World War II. Such a privatized consciousness neither idolizes the organization nor exalts state authority." Writing at the time of the massive protests against the security treaty linking Japan and the United States, Yoshimoto was objecting to a view put forward by liberal thinkers such as Maruyama Masao that the pursuit of material desires generated a "privatized" spirit of "indifference" that proved "very convenient for the governing elites who wish to 'contain' " political activism.[24]

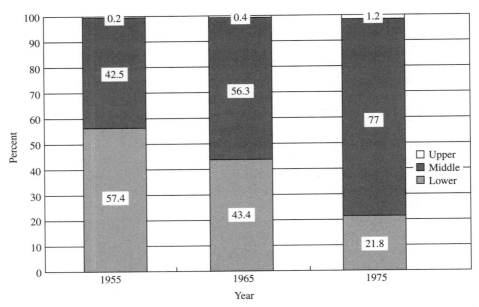

Figure 14.2   Rise of Middle-Class Consciousness. Respondents' definition of their social class in nationwide social surveys.

Source: 1975 nen SSM zenkoku chōsa hōkoku iinkai, ed., *Shakai kaisō to shakai idō 1975 nen SSM zenkoku chōsa hōkoku* (Tokyo: 1978), p. 310.

Other cultural critics, on both the left and right of the political spectrum, echoed Maruyama in criticizing the status quo and expressing fear for the future. One stream of thought on the Japanese left drew on European social theorists of the Frankfurt school. It sharply attacked the Japanese version of an "administered society" and lamented the ways in which the mass media, together with corporate employers and state institutions such as the schools, prescribed the normal course of a proper citizen's life, crushing individual impulses and diversity. They criticized the exaltation of GNP growth at the expense of building social solidarity, protecting the environment, or cultivating local culture and the self. The expression "escape from salary" (*datsu-sara*) became popular from around 1970. It referred to a dissenting ideal of those seeking to escape the oppressive grind of the organization-oriented salaryman. Yoshimoto himself seems to have been torn between a desire to respect the private strivings of ordinary people and a belief that they must feel a "continually increasing burden of a sensibility gripped with an amorphous sense of boredom, enjoying a bloated material life and a relatively improved standard of living, but an absolute impoverishment."[25]

On the right, even as critics celebrated the growing power of the economy, they lamented the way affluence threatened to undermine what they described as traditional Japanese values of endurance and sacrifice to a larger collective. Such sentiments could be ironic or even laughable, as when automotive industry executives reportedly complained that their spoiled children wanted their own cars. Many observers on the left and right, in fact, could share a lament over the way materialism and consumerism overwhelmed any commitment to political values, whether those of a revived nationalism or a humanized capitalism.

One early episode that served to focus debate on the cultural changes of the postwar years was the royal wedding of 1959. It illustrates the complexity of crosscurrents of criticism and celebration of postwar social change. Some on the left criticized the "Michiko boom" as an ominous revival of reverence for the throne. But others welcomed it as a healthy sign that the "emperor system of the masses" had been democratized. They stressed that the imperial household was now viewed with playful affection rather than awe or fear.[26]

A decade later, the dramatic suicide of the writer Mishima Yukio once more drew attention to a radical critique of Japan's modernizing, materialistic postwar culture. His fiction written from the 1940s through 1970 explored diverse themes of love, obsession, masculinity, and homosexual longing. He also sought to define and defend "traditional" Japanese aesthetic values, and he came to link these to a militaristic veneration of the emperor and nation. In the late 1960s Mishima formed a small rightwing militia devoted to body-building and training in martial arts. Then, in November 1970 he ended his life in spectacular fashion by invading a Tokyo headquarter of the Self-Defense Forces and making a speech calling on the troops to launch an uprising to restore the prewar political order. The audience responded with indifference, and Mishima sliced open his belly in the ritualized suicide know as *harakiri* or *seppuku*. The Japanese public was shocked but not sympathetic to this theatrical call for a return to old values.

Although few wished to follow Mishima's reactionary cultural politics, two episodes in the 1970s served as a focal point for ongoing unease and debate over the changes of postwar decades. Remarkably enough, more than twenty-five years after the surrender, two "last soldiers" of the imperial army were discovered fighting on in sad isolation, convinced the war was still going. Yokoi Shōichi returned from Guam in 1972. Onoda Hiroo came home from the Philippines in 1974. Each man had been cut off from his unit when the war ended and remained hidden in remote hills or jungles ever since, occasionally raiding local villages or somehow living off the land. These media dramas sparked a mini-boom of nostalgic commentary on the contrast between the determination and selfless commitment of these men and the individualism and materialistic consumerism of the youth of postwar Japan. Such debates were often framed as arguments over the quality of a generalized Japanese character, and its postwar transformation and decline. But they in fact were addressing global issues of modernity more than issues peculiar to Japan. How should the gains of affluence be enjoyed and shared? What sort of social values and commitments should link people together in an era of growing abundance yet ongoing division?

15

Political Struggles and Settlements of the High-Growth Era

The histories of politics and economy in postwar Japan offer a study in contrasts. Across three decades, the economy grew so quickly and consistently that even the United States began to study "the Japanese model" for lessons of success. The political world, in contrast, witnessed numerous sharp struggles. People argued over how to distribute the fruits of economic gain. They fought over the divisive question of Japan's international alignment. From the 1960s into the 1970s, the intensity of political confrontation seen in the previous decade diminished somewhat. But some new issues came to the fore, centered on the costs and dilemmas of affluence. Domestically, the nation confronted the problem of protecting people from pollution, as extraordinary growth incurred extraordinary environmental costs. Internationally, Japan's place in the Cold War struggle *between* the capitalist and communist worlds became less controversial, while tension over trade imbalances and economic friction *within* the capitalist world grew more intense. The story of the postwar economy is thus inseparable from the turbulent postwar history of political struggle and settlement.

POLITICAL STRUGGLES

As the occupation ended, the national political map remained divided into two major camps, referred to at the time as "conservative" and "progressive." They opposed each other bitterly, and their all-out clashes were the most important political events of the 1950s. But these groups were also divided sharply within themselves. One cannot understand the outcome of these political struggles and later settlements without recognizing the major schisms within.

At the head of the conservative forces, with close links to the bureaucratic and business elites, stood the Liberal Party. Its leader, Yoshida Shigeru, was prime minister when the treaty was signed. In the first post-occupation general election, of October 1952, the Liberals won 48 percent of the vote and 52 percent of the Diet seats. But the party was divided internally over both personality and policy. Hatoyama Ichirō led the opposition within the party. Like many of his opponents on the left, he objected especially to Yoshida's willingness to accept "subordinate independence" under American hegemony.

ate; it put him above political battles but still made him a symbol of national identity and order. They tended to agree that the prohibition on the military was an idealistic excess. But they concluded that the political cost of revision would be even more excessive. Gradually in the 1960s, the drive to revise the constitution lost momentum, although it long remained a back-burner issue capable of sparking heated debate.

The Socialist Party's outright boycott of the constitutional commission is one key instance of the fierce struggles between the political left and right throughout the 1950s. Outside the Diet, several overlapping political constituencies on the political left led the charge to defend and deepen the postwar reforms at home while repudiating the United States–Japan alliance.

The largest was the labor movement. In 1949 at the postwar peak, 6.7 million men and women, 56 percent of the employed work force, were union members. The unions were divided on key issues. A significant minority heeded managerial pleas to moderate their wage demands and accept flexible job assignments and new technologies. They agreed that such cooperation was the only way to improve productivity and profits, and thus defend jobs and wages over the long run. These unionists were also reluctant to see their groups actively join political struggles against the security treaty. In several showcase disputes in the 1950s, such workers formed dissenting second unions at particular companies. These linked up with management to undermine strike actions over wages or job security. In the wake of failed strikes, these breakaway unions typically won the day. They gradually consolidated a new cooperative union majority.

But this contest was far from decided at the end of the decade. The majority of unions took more militant and politically engaged positions. They were federated under the umbrella of the General Council of Trade Unions of Japan. Abbreviated in Japanese as Sōhyō, this group formed in 1950 through a merger of various anticommunist unions. American occupation officials had supported Sōhyō at its founding, and the union did keep some distance from the JCP. But contrary to American expectations, Sōhyō quickly emerged as a vociferous foe of the United States–Japan Security Treaty, an ally of the leftist Socialist Party, and a supporter of militant demands and tactics in the workplace.

In steel mills, shipyards, public and private railways, chemical processors, auto plants, and coal mines Sōhyō pursued a program called "workplace struggle" throughout the decade. Union activists encouraged members to seek a voice at the production site over matters such as job safety and allocation of job assignments or overtime. In many leading enterprises they built vigorous unions through such grassroots tactics. They were pointing toward a political order in which unions would share in the control of the workplace.

These unions simultaneously raised demands for large wage increases. Strikes were frequent and hotly contested. In 1955 Sōhyō began to organize loosely coordinated nationwide wage campaigns of unions in diverse companies and industries. Although managers successfully refused to engage in formal industrywide bargaining, these annual Spring Offensives took root. By the end of the decade they were able to set effective targets for company-specific wage bargaining.

The peace movement was a second core component of the "progressive" drive of the 1950s. In addition to unions and the Socialist and Communist parties, a huge variety of citizens', women's, and student organizations carried the banner of the postwar peace movement. Two galvanizing issues were the United States–Japan treaty and the American military bases that were authorized in the treaty agreement. In 1960, the year of the most intense anti-treaty protests, the American presence amounted to forty-six thousand troops stationed on several hundred military installations on Japan's four main islands, and another thirty-seven thousand soldiers on Okinawa.

Local residents detested the noise of these bases and the chronic instances of violence or rape perpetrated by the soldiers. In addition to tens of thousands of traffic accidents, over one hundred thousand crimes involving off-duty personnel and Japanese citizens took place from 1952 through the 1970s. The majority were incidents of assault, including rape and murder. Some five hundred Japanese were killed in accidents or assaults over these years. Critics were particularly upset because such crimes fell under the jurisdiction of American military justice. The bases were thus a symbol of extraterritoriality that evoked memories stretching back to the unequal treaties of the nineteenth century. The bases were surrounded by bars and massage parlors, and protesters invoked powerful images of the violation of Japanese women by foreigners. They also saw the American bases as military targets that could make Japan once again an atomic victim if a war erupted between the Soviet Union and the United States.

A second cause addressed by the peace movement was nuclear disarmament. The devastation of Hiroshima and Nagasaki, and the ongoing suffering of tens of thousands of atomic bomb survivors, called *hibakusha*, gave a particular force to Japan's antinuclear movement. In 1954 a Japanese fishing boat, the *Lucky Dragon*, was showered with radioactive fallout from an American thermonuclear test on Bikini Island in the central Pacific. This catalyzed a surge of organizing against nuclear arms and bomb testing. The most prominent anti-nuclear organization to emerge in the 1950s was the Japan Council Against Atomic and Hydrogen Bombs (Gensuikyō). It came to lead a large annual anti-bomb conference, convened on the anniversary of the Hiroshima and Nagasaki bombings. Divisions among the left-wing political parties led to splits and conflicts in the ranks of the peace movement. But well beyond the formal membership of various contending organizations, anti-war, anti-base, and anti-nuclear sentiment remained powerful among masses of Japanese people. In the wake of the *Lucky Dragon* incident, more than thirty million people signed petitions opposing nuclear bomb tests.

Women and students formed a wide array of their own political organizations. These took up issues at the core of the political agenda of the left, including the movement against bases and nuclear weapons. Both women and students had been active in politics since Meiji times. Some important women's groups had been founded as early as the turn of the century, such as the Christian Women's Reform Society. Important new groups included the Housewives Association (Shufuren), founded in 1948, and the Mothers Conference, an umbrella organization founded in 1955. Its affiliated groups covered a vast range of concerns, from labor rights, pacifism, and education to drug use, sanitation, and consumer safety.[3]

Like feminists the world over, the women in these groups differed on the key issue of whether to frame their demands in terms of universal human rights or the particular concerns and traits of women. Should they demand wage equality and the right of women to perform any job, or should they stress special protection for women workers, which might in fact exclude them from certain arduous jobs? Japanese feminists in some cases anchored calls for women's rights in concepts of universal human rights. But even such activists tended to combine their appeals with "maternalist" positions based on women's unique role as mothers. Anti-war groups, in particular, tended to speak of the special desire of mothers "to safeguard the happiness of our children" when they issued statements opposing nuclear testing or the security treaty.[4] Such appeals drew on the prewar state's rhetoric of "good wife, wise mother." They forcefully turned the phrase on its head to promote new roles and rights for women.

Women were also active in labor unions. They enjoyed some notable successes in the 1950s, at a time when militant actions of male unionists often failed to achieve their goals. In 1954, fifteen hundred women at the Ōmi Silk Reeling Company organized a strike demanding recognition of their union, an end to restrictive dormitory rules and company inspection of letters and personal belongings, and the right to work after marriage. Their action focused on what many had come to see as the basic human rights of Japanese people, women as well as men, under postwar democracy. The silk workers won wide attention and support, and they ultimately prevailed. In 1959 and 1960, a comparable success came to unionized nurses and hospital workers in Tokyo and elsewhere. In addition to better wages, they demanded and won similar basic freedoms, especially the right to work after marriage. As a result, the proportion of married nurses rose from a mere 2 percent in 1958 to 69 percent by the 1980s. This action transformed nursing from a short-term job for young women who "retired" at marriage to an adult career.

The student movement was another key element in the progressive drive. The core organization was the All-Japan Federation of Student Self-Governing Associations, abbreviated Zengakuren and founded in 1948. Much like a union with a closed shop that automatically enrolled all employees, these "self-governing associations" were found on virtually all college campuses, and they enrolled all students as members. Student members of the Japan Communist Party dominated the Zengakuren at first. It suffered a blow in the early 1950s when the JCP came under fire and lost popular support. But the *Lucky Dragon* incident revitalized the student as well as the anti-war movement. By the end of the 1950s, students were a major force in political causes and demonstrations ranging well beyond the campus.

Toward the end of the 1950s, these various "progressive" forces were confident and energetic. They appeared to be on the rise. Despite some setbacks, many unions remained quite militant. Student and women's groups had enthusiastic followings. The peace movement had a broad base of millions of sympathizers. The Socialist Party had reunited. Small groups of citizens in towns and villages as well as cities were organizing all sorts of "circles." These engaged in cultural pursuits such as music appreciation or poetry writing but often also organized into larger networks with ties to unions or political parties.

Out of this energy came a surge of popular protest in the late 1950s that erupted in a major crisis in 1960. The first act in the drama was protest in 1958 at the proposed new Police Duties Law. The LDP intended this law to bolster the "emergency powers" of the police to contain demonstrations and monitor the left. The bill ironically provoked what it sought to curb. Unions and political parties led a vigorous round of demonstrations. Public support and a united opposition in the Diet led the LDP to back down. The party never brought the bill to a vote.

Then, in 1960, two massive streams of protest converged to make this the most tumultuous year in postwar history. The conflict began with the United States–Japan Security Treaty, or Anpo. To extend the treaty past its original term of eight years, it was necessary for the United States Congress and the Japanese Diet to ratify a renewed treaty by June 1960. After several years of negotiation, the two governments agreed on a revised security treaty early in 1960. The fundamental structure remained in place. American bases would protect Japan, and the Japanese would accept the bases, help pay for them, and help protect them in an emergency. Some minor changes sought to head off key objections. The Americans promised to offer advance notice of plans to bring nuclear weapons onto Japanese soil. But the treaty also made future renewal automatic, unless one or the other side asked for a change or an end to the treaty.

As the June 1960 deadline approached, a powerful groundswell emerged to oppose the renewed treaty. Socialists, student groups, women's groups, and even some in the LDP objected to the prospect of a nearly permanent "subordinate independence" under American hegemony. They objected as well to the ongoing risk that Japan would be drawn into a larger war. Beginning in April, dozens of demonstrations brought protesters into the streets of Tokyo. Amid growing public uproar, late at night on May 19 Kishi's government literally shoved the law through the Diet. Like a human ramrod, the speaker of the lower house was carried to the podium sideways by Diet police through a crowd of opposition party politicians. He called the Diet into session and passed the law with a snap vote.

In reaction to this maneuver, the demonstrations grew dramatically in size and intensity. For several weeks, huge protests took place daily in the vicinity of the Diet. The largest drew well over one hundred thousand people by conservative estimates, and perhaps over two hundred thousand. President Eisenhower had accepted an invitation to attend a grand signing in Tokyo on June 19. This was to be the first visit to Japan by a sitting American president. On June 10, Eisenhower's press secretary, James Hagerty, arrived in Japan to work out the details of this trip. An angry crowd surrounded his car and threatened to overturn it as he left the airport and headed for the American embassy. Hagerty was rescued by an American military helicopter. In another demonstration on June 15, a young woman was killed. Protestors blamed her death on police brutality. The police claimed she was crushed to death in a stampede of retreating demonstrators. Fearful that security could not be guaranteed, Eisenhower called off his visit at the last minute. Kishi's credibility stood in tatters, and he resigned. But he had achieved his goal. The treaty had been passed, securing the United States–Japan military alliance for the long term.

Once the new treaty took effect on June 19, the demonstrations gradually petered out. But the opposition's political energy quickly shifted to a battle over jobs underway in the Mitsui Corporation's Miike Coal Mine far to the south, in Kyushu.

Japan's mining industry had begun a slow painful decline several years before. As the economy surged ahead, so did demand for energy. By the end of the 1950s, oil had proved itself decisively cheaper than coal, and the foreign supplies seemed reasonably reliable. Mining companies, Mitsui included, sought to survive by raising productivity with new equipment and cutting back on jobs. The Miike union, in the

Police officers help the Liberal Democratic Party literally ram through the renewal of the United States–Japan Security Treaty, as they carry the speaker of the House of Representatives to the podium to force a vote, over the resistance of the Japan Socialist Party, on May 19, 1960. The battle over treaty revision was the most intense political struggle of the postwar era.
Courtesy of *Mainichi* newspaper.

face of this daunting environment, stood at the forefront of the shopfloor struggles waged by the militant unions in the Sōhyō federation. Through several disputes in the 1950s, the miners had built a powerful union upon the solidarity of their isolated, relatively homogeneous community. The union's "workplace committees" had come to control job and overtime allocations as well as safety standards. Their grassroots activism stood as a model to other unions and a major threat to industrialists nationwide. This gave the Miike strike of 1960 a broader significance. Transposing the wartime political vocabulary, observers dubbed it a "total war between labor and capital."

A company plan to dismiss two thousand of roughly thirteen thousand union members precipitated the dispute. Mitsui was determined not only to "rationalize" the mines by introducing new equipment and reducing the work force. It was intent upon dismissing activists and breaking the union, so as to regain workplace authority. In October 1959, the union called the first of several time-limited strikes in opposition to the rationalization plan. In December the company announced the dismissals, which indeed targeted union leaders in particular, and in January 1960, the company imposed a lockout. The union replied by declaring a strike. Some four thousand miners, with company assistance, immediately launched a second union with a pro-company plat-form and tried to return to work.

But a strong majority of the miners stood by the original union. With remarkable discipline and tenacity, members survived for ten months on union allowances of roughly one-third their normal wages. In June and July, after the security treaty was renewed, some ten thousand to twenty thousand treaty protesters and union sympa-thizers converged on Miike to support the strikers. For months, picketers kept the second union members from going to work. Numerous tense confrontations threatened to spill over into major violence. One miner was killed by gangsterlike enforcers hired by the company, and over seventeen hundred miners were injured during the course of the dispute.

To keep order, the government sent in fifteen thousand police troopers, 10 percent of the nation's entire police force. Other mines remained open and temporarily sup-plied coal to Miike's customers, even if this meant shortchanging their own regular customers. Bolstered by this managerial solidarity and tacit state support, the mine company outlasted the union. In the fall of 1960, the original union was forced to

The peak of the confrontations between militant labor unions and managers determined to break the unions came with the Miike Mine dispute of 1959–60. The yearlong struggle be-tween union and company focused on job security and control of the workplace and mobi-lized the entire community. Here members of the Miike Mine Union Wives Association con-front executives of the Mitsui Mining Company in April 1960.

Courtesy of *Asahi* newspaper.

accept a government-mediated settlement. After a 313-day strike, the company won the right to impose the entire rationalization plan.

That same October, a youth who belonged to an extreme right-wing organization stabbed and killed the chairman of the Japan Socialist Party, Asanuma Inejirō. This popular politician had aroused controversy the previous year by denouncing American imperialism as the common enemy of the people of China and Japan. The shock was intensified because of wide exposure: The assassination came during a televised speech at a political rally. Just as the Miike strike was drawing to a close, this act of terror only heightened the atmosphere of political crisis.

THE POLITICS OF ACCOMMODATION

In the wake of these dramas and traumas of 1960, the political climate calmed. On the right, key voices in the LDP, the bureaucracy, and the business elite deemphasized the drive for constitutional revision and confrontation with unions. They sought to win support from at least a portion of the political opposition by stressing policies to grow the economy and improve popular welfare. They changed their tactics in the Diet by conferring informally with the opposition parties on numerous bills and making token changes to win their support. On the left, a cooperative (or co-opted) minority in the union movement and the conservative wing in the Japan Socialist Party responded by repudiating the politics of confrontation on workplace as well as international issues. The result was a new politics of high growth marked by accommodation and compromise.

The centerpiece of the new LDP approach was Prime Minister Ikeda Hayato's "income doubling plan." Announced in September 1960, the plan set forth the goal of rapidly "achieving full employment and radically raising people's living standard by doubling the gross national product" by 1970.[5] It exemplified the philosophy of state guidance of the market economy that scholars have seen as the central idea of what they call the "developmental state."[6] The plan set forth specific targets for investment in priority industries, called for mergers and cooperation among companies, and committed the government to an active role in guiding the private sector toward these goals. Ikeda further stimulated the economy by lowering taxes and interest rates. Roughly three years ahead of schedule, the economy indeed doubled in size.

The income doubling plan was part of a conservative political strategy that had been worked out beneath the turbulent political surface for about a decade. In the 1950s the LDP sought alliances with a variety of social constituencies beyond its prewar base of landlords and the business elite. The LDP concluded the first of several implicit social contracts with the millions of farmers who had taken ownership of their fields under the land reform. The government regulated rice prices to protect farmers from market fluctuations throughout the 1950s. Then, in 1961, the new Agricultural Basic Law put in place a system of even more generous price supports. In exchange, the LDP won the solid support of rural voters. And farm districts accounted for a disproportionately large share of seats in the Diet because LDP leaders moved slowly to redraw electoral district boundaries as the population shifted to cities.

A second core constituency of the LDP was the huge population of small-scale business owners and their dependents. Throughout the postwar era, businesses with fewer than thirty employees in manufacturing, retail, and wholesale trade accounted for well over half of the nonfarm labor force. Building on prewar organizations, these businesses organized a powerful set of lobbies. The LDP responded from the early 1950s with a variety of helpful measures. The government taxed small businesses lightly, and it did not enforce these taxes aggressively. The LDP also passed the Department Store Law in 1956. This bill made it virtually impossible for large retailers or supermarkets to locate in the thousands of urban and suburban shopping districts dominated by tiny "mom-and-pop" stores of every description. These stores gave the sprawling Japanese cityscape of the high-growth era a small-town feel. Their owners and employees also gave the LDP crucial electoral support in urban districts.[7]

A third party to the social foundation of LDP rule came from a less likely source: salaried workers, both white and blue collar, in the highly unionized segment of the labor force in large corporations. The United States played a role in promoting positive ties between the LDP, business managers, and organized labor. Beginning in 1953 it helped the Japanese government to found and fund a semi-independent institution called the Japan Productivity Center (JPC). Proclaiming that increased productivity would "expand markets, increase employment, raise real wages and standards of living, and advance the common interests of labor, management and consumers," the center quickly reached out to factories across the country.[8] In its first two years, the center sent fifty-three small groups of managers and union leaders on missions to learn the art of productivity from the Americans. The pace of exchange increased thereafter.

Some important unions endorsed the productivity drive, and these labor groups gradually became an informal part of the governing establishment. The two more conservative federations, Sōdōmei and Zenrō, agreed to accept new technologies in exchange for a promise that jobs would be protected and productivity gains shared in the form of higher wages. The Sōhyō federation, in contrast, vigorously opposed the JPC. It claimed that without a stronger union voice in setting conditions at work, new productive technologies would actually cost jobs and erode working conditions. But the overall union response led the Labor Ministry in 1957 to note happily "the birth of a practical, rather than an abstract, response to the productivity movement" at major manufacturers.[9]

This cooperative spirit did not win the day immediately. Intense industrywide struggles brought production to a halt in the iron and steel industry in 1957 and 1959, and of course in the Miike mines in 1960. The militant tactics and progressive political agenda of the Sōhyō federation continued to retain considerable support among public sector employees. Unions of national railway employees, postal workers, prefectural and municipal government employees, and public school teachers sought higher wages and greater voice over the pace and conditions of work. They chafed at the fact that, since 1949, they had been denied the right to strike. As part of the annual spring wage offensives of the 1950s and 1960s, they improvised an effective array of slow-down tactics short of outright strikes. Public railway unions sought to "democratize" the workplace by gaining some control over the the authority of supervisors and the relative weight of merit and seniority in setting wages. By 1967, the union had forced the railway to create "workplace discussion councils" that gave the union control of job assignments and promotions. By the early 1970s this union had forced railway managers to reinstate seniority as a major factor in promotions and raises.[10]

But in the private sector from the late 1950s through the 1960s, the militant force of the labor movement faded in the face of the appeal of the productivity movement.[11] In the wake of bitter struggles, cooperative leaders won control of most all private sector unions. They argued that in the face of tough domestic and global competion, long-run job and wage security demanded short-run moderation in wage demands and flexibility over work conditions and technology. Public sector workers, whose jobs were insulated from the global economy, generally resisted such appeals. Faced with incentives both positive and negative, private sector employees were often convinced to go along. Labor managers in large corporations wooed their workers in various ways. They expanded a wide array of corporate welfare programs. This was a conscious effort to preempt the appeal of similar welfare activities sponsored by unions and to build a sense of belonging and obligation toward the company. Some welfare programs dated from before or during the war; others were new. By the 1960s an employee of any large corporation enjoyed an impressive array of cradle-to-grave benefits: company hospitals, health clinics, and stores; dorms for single workers; apartments for married employees with families; company-owned vacation retreats; company-sponsored trips, sports teams, and music festivals; commuter-train social clubs; social organizations for employee wives; and more. At the same time, militant dissenters faced the daunting prospect of management discrimination in promotions and pay raises.

Managers also extended implicit guarantees of job security. With rare exceptions over the high-growth era (and beyond), they did not lay off workers outright even if business slumped. In consultation with unions, they made substantial efforts to transfer excess employees to other divisions or to subsidiaries. These policies have often been summed up by the misleading term *permanent employment*. One problem with the notion that men in Japan's large companies had come to enjoy "lifetime" or "permanent" jobs is that many so-called "permanent" employees decided on their own to look elsewhere for work. In the 1960s in manufacturing industries, between one-third to two-thirds of young male recruits typically quit their first job within five years. The other problem is that companies developed tactics such as the call for "voluntary retirements" to oust unneeded or unwanted employees without resorting to outright dismissal.

As these corporate policies were gradually implemented, the level of antagonism receded between managers and employees in the workplace. In a related shift on the national, political level, supporters of a more cooperative order provoked a major realignment. In January 1960, the "right-wing" faction of the Japan Socialist Party (JSP) once again bolted, this time to form the Democratic Socialist Party (DSP). At the moment of founding, it claimed 41 seats in the House of Representatives, although the socialist mainstream retained a strong majority in the progressive camp of 125 representatives. The two federations in the conservative wing of the labor movement (Sōdōmei and Zenrō) supported this move. In 1962, they joined in a new federation called Dōmei Kaigi with 1.4 million members. Again, this was significantly smaller than the 4.1 million members in the Sōhyō federation.[12] In both party and union organization, the "progressive" political forces were now divided into a left-wing majority and a right-wing minority. But even so, as a potential partner with the LDP, this conservative-leaning minority had a significance beyond its numbers.

This move toward an informal centrist coalition was furthered decisively in 1964. Some of the private sector unions *within* the Sōhyō camp pulled together a coalition of cooperative unions in the automobile, shipbuilding, electronic, and iron and steel industries that cut across the opposed national federations. This group was called the Japan Council of the International Metal Workers Union (abbreviated IMF-JC). Aligned with the anti-communist IMF federation centered in North America and Western Europe, it called for wage moderation and more restrained use of strikes as a bargaining tactic.

LDP strategists intensified their efforts to cultivate these allies. They were well aware of the demographic shift of population from rural districts to cities and from farm work to the manufacturing and service sectors. They argued that the Socialist Party was the natural, but not the inevitable, beneficiary of such trends. They urged the LDP to offer a "labor compact" that would build bridges to "cooperative" unions and offer security and improved livelihoods to the majority of working people.[13] In 1964, encouraged by the formation of the IMF-JC, Prime Minister Ikeda took the unprecedented step of meeting the head of the Sōhyō federation, Ōta Kaoru, to discuss wages. They agreed to peg the public sector employees' increases to those won by private sector unions. Ikeda was anxious to use the more cooperative private sector unions as a lever to moderate public sector demands. Ōta hoped to parlay this seat at the table into a stronger future voice. The Liberal Democrats were becoming a big tent party. The political world was shifting from a politics of confrontation to one of accommodation.

Even so, significant tensions remained. Sōhyō was still much larger than Dōmei. The Japan Socialist Party was still much larger than the Democratic Socialist Party. In fact the DSP did not fare well at the polls. In 1962 the party lost ground to the socialists in the first general election after its founding. The DSP fell sharply from 41 to 17 seats, while the JSP jumped to 145, and the DSP never matched its initial strength in subsequent elections. Militant unions continued to organize energetic spring wage offensives and to support political causes.

And in addition, major new conflicts emerged and significant new forms of political action developed. Observers labeled this the politics of "citizen movements." It was a form of activism distinguished by a nonpartisan spirit and relatively decentralized grassroots organizing. The wave of citizen activism peaked in the late 1960s and early 1970s, but some groups remained important in later years as well.

Pacifist sentiment and anger at Japan's compromised sovereignty, which had fueled the 1950s protests against the security treaty, energized the new citizen movements as well. This spirit coalesced in the mid-1960s into a creative new form of protest, part of the drive against Japan's role as an American staging ground for the Vietnam War. Protestors feared that Japan might be drawn into a wider war. They also believed that the United States was intervening in cruel, imperialist fashion in a civil war. In 1965 grassroots citizens' groups came together in a loose, non-hierarchical network called Citizen's Federation: Peace to Vietnam! (abbreviated in Japanese as Beheiren).[14] Several Tokyo-based publications knit together the local groups, which numbered almost five hundred at the peak in the late 1960s. Beheiren was remarkable for maintaining no formal membership lists, bylaws, or dues. One estimate is that over eighteen million people participated in some form of anti-war protest during the peak years from 1967 to 1970. The largest single demonstration drew 770,000 people into the streets to denounce the automatic extension of the United States–Japan Security Treaty in June 1970. Less publically but of no less importance, Beheiren supporters offered aid to runaway American soldiers and helped organize anti-war activities of soldiers on the bases.[15]

Beheiren dissolved in 1974 as the war came to an end. One disappointment for many of its adherents was the failure to generate a successful movement in 1970 against the second renewal of the United States–Japan Security Treaty. In 1960 a vote was required to extend the treaty, which put the political burden to act on treaty supporters. The 1970 extension was automatic unless the Japanese Diet (or American Congress) decided to cancel it. This procedural difference put the burden of parliamentary action on opponents. It largely explains why the 1970 protests were relatively ineffective, despite some massive public demonstrations. But many of the students and adults who took part in these anti-war, anti-base activities later turned to other issues and forms of citizen protest.

Parallel to the Beheiren protests, in the late 1960s Japanese university students, like their counterparts the world over, undertook intense, often violent protests. For over a decade the core of the student movement in the Zengakuren organization had been riddled with factional conflicts setting communist-linked groups against a non-communist "new left." Even so, in 1968–69 at the peak of the anti-war protests, student radicals at more than half of all Japanese college campuses came together to launch unprecedented strikes and boycotts. They protested increased tuition and demanded curriculum reform and a greater role in university governance. In the spring of 1969, many college campuses were virtually shut down. Zengakuren turned to a tactic of armed struggle called *geba* (from the German word for "force," *gewalt*, pronounced *gebaruto* in Japanese). Helmeted snake-dancing demonstrators took over classroom buildings and dormitories. That spring, for the first time in its history, Tokyo University took in no entering class. The movement collapsed in the summer of 1969, as public sentiment turned against the student tactics. The government sent riot police onto campuses throughout the nation to retake control.

Until the time of these violent protests and their suppression, it had been common for student activists at major universities to move into positions with business or government organizations after graduation. Mainstream employers were said to have valued "leadership" skills, even if demonstrated in political protests against the establishment. This attitude seems to have changed after the crisis of 1969. Reports circulated of corporate blacklisting of student activists. The force and reach of the student movement declined sharply from the 1970s onward.

Perhaps the most effective new area of citizen activism focused on the environment. As industry expanded relentlessly and sometimes recklessly, air and water quality deteriorated sharply. The cost of a damaged environment, and the damaged health of workers and residents, was neither imposed on producers nor borne by the government. Nor was it subtracted from the soaring totals of the GNP. Indeed, if environmental destruction led to further economic activity in the building of water-purification plants or treatment of pollution victims in hospitals, these goods and services were simply added to the "growing" economic numbers.

Already in the 1950s, symptoms of a devastating array of pollution-related dis-

Demonstration during the student strike at Tokyo University in 1968 that paralyzed the university for more than a year. Students supporting the Revolutionary Marxist faction assemble in front of the Yasuda Hall at the center of campus.
Courtesy of *Mainichi* newspaper.

eases had appeared. Mercury poisoning struck and killed residents in the vicinity of chemical plants in southern Japan (Minamata) and northern Japan (Niigata). Cadmium poisoning caused intense pain to residents of Fuchū city along the Jinzu River in Toyama prefecture, in central Japan. Their affliction was dubbed the "it hurts disease" (*itai-itai byō*). Air pollution around oil refineries in Mie along the industrialized coastline of central Japan generated a rash of serious asthma outbreaks. Similar illness struck residents of the heavily industrialized cities of Yokohama and Kawasaki (near Tokyo) and Amagasaki (near Osaka). In these cases and others, victims sought redress immediately, but efforts of the 1950s and early 1960s were ineffective. The polluters typically denied responsibility and obstructed investigations. Local and national governments were relatively passive.

Then, from the mid-1960s through the early 1970s, in similar fashion to the antiwar protesters, local groups of pollution victims reached out to build strong networks of support nationwide. They improvised tactics such as sit-ins and boycotts. They bought token shares in offending companies and used these as a foothold to disrupt annual meetings. And they turned to the courts with lawsuits to demand compensation. A series of landmark decisions were handed down in the "big four" pollution cases from 1971 to 1973: Minamata and Niigata mercury poisoning, cadmium poisoning, and asthma from air pollution. In all cases, the victims won the right to compensation.

They established important precedents that forced the government and corporations to take preventive as well as remedial steps in the future.

One particularly intense episode of protest linked elements of the student movement with normally conservative farming families. This was the long struggle against construction of a new international airport near the town of Narita in Chiba prefecture, about forty miles east of Tokyo. Plans for this airport began in 1966, when it became clear that the capacity of the existing Haneda airport could not accommodate fast-growing traffic. The government chose the site because it could easily get hold of half the needed land, which was owned by the imperial family as a hunting preserve. But it moved in high-handed, clumsy fashion and tried to force farmers in the area to sell the remaining land. A powerful alliance quickly formed between student activists and these farmers. The former saw the conflict as a chance to attack the arrogance of the oppressive bureaucratic state at the heart of the postwar capitalist system. The latter began with simple goals of keeping their land and defending their community. In time, many came to support the broader political critique of the students. Protesters literally dug in for a long struggle. They built a complex system of tunnels under the disputed land and refused to move. Construction of the airport began in 1969. But the protesters delayed completion of the runways from 1971 to 1975 and prevented authorities from actually opening the airport for another three years, until 1978. It was only after highly publicized pitched battles between heavily armored police and the fiercely opposed farmers and students that the airport finally opened. Although most citizens repudiated the violent tactics of some activists, the Narita struggle did force the government to respond to citizen concerns and take a more conciliatory approach in future projects of this sort.[16]

Other important forms of citizen activism also developed in the 1960s and 1970s.[17] These included movements to monitor product safety and popular networks of consumer cooperatives that sought to deliver fresh foodstuffs at reasonable prices. Women as well as men were active in all forms of citizen protest, from the anti-war and student movements to environmental organizations. They played an especially prominent role in areas linked to domestic life. Consumer advocates did not support an uncritical, materialist "consumerism." They stressed high quality and product purity over low price. They also built close links to farmer cooperatives and government agencies concerned with protecting domestic products. In fact, their concern with safety standards was sometimes criticized from abroad, with much justification, as a disguised form of protectionism.

From the late 1960s through the 1970s, this new politics of citizens' movements joined forces with an older partisan politics. In large and small cities nationwide, residents organized around environmental issues, calls for better public housing, or anti-base struggles to bring socialist or communist politicians to power. At the peak in 1975, as many as 147 cities, towns, or prefectures—including the seven major cities of Tokyo, Osaka, Kyoto, Yokohama, Nagoya, Kawasaki, and Kobe—were headed by mayors or governors of left-wing parties.

This trend was dubbed the era of "progressive local government." It was an unusual moment in Japan's modern history when local governments ran ahead of the national government. They took the initiative in areas ranging from environmental

Farmers and students forged an unusual and unusually effective alliance during the pro-longed struggle to oppose construction of a new international airport at Narita, serving To-kyo. Here the protesters have barricaded farmers' fields to prevent the government from tak-ing their land as part of the new airport.
Courtesy of *Mainichi* newspaper.

legislation to social welfare benefits. Perhaps the most famous progressive leader was Minobe Ryōkichi, a professor turned politician who served as governor of Tokyo from 1967 to 1980.[18] He won strong support and wide attention for pioneering programs such as free health insurance for Tokyo residents.

The central bureaucracy and the Liberal Democratic Party responded to these unprecedented gains for the opposition by joining rather than fighting. The LDP put the local government initiatives on the national agenda. In 1973 it announced "Year One of Welfare," and it greatly expanded pensions and health insurance programs. That same year, it strengthened environmental laws, passing a Pollution Related Disease Compensation Law. This made it much easier for victims to gain some measure of economic support and medical care. These steps helped the conservative forces regain support in urban areas, even though government ministries and the LDP cut back on the more generous new programs by raising premiums or reducing benefits when the economy slowed down in the late 1970s.

Another new element on the political scene that promoted a centrist politics was the religiously based Kōmeitō party (Clean Government Party, CGP). It drew support from the hugely popular new religion called Sōka Gakkai (Value Creation Society). Some leaders in this religion began to seek political offices in the 1950s with a platform of "clean government." Sōka Gakkai formally launched the affiliated Kōmeitō party in 1964. By the end of the decade, the CGP was the third largest political force in the Diet, after the Liberal Democratic Party and the Japan Socialists Party. At this point criticism mounted that the party was violating the postwar constitution's separation of church and state. The CGP responded by cutting all official ties to the Sōka Gakkai religion, although in fact many candidates and most electoral support for the party still came from Sōka Gakkai believers. The CGP labeled itself a "centrist party." It supported stronger welfare programs and defended the postwar constitution, but it accepted the basic structures of the capitalist system. It often supported the progressive candidates of the JSP in local elections. It also pulled both JSP and LDP toward the political center, as they competed for the votes of Kōmeitō supporters.

The flourishing of grassroots activism in the 1960s was not limited to the political left or center. One of the most prominent efforts on the right was the drive to reestablish a holiday to celebrate the "birth" of the Japanese nation. In the 1870s, the Meiji state had rather arbitrarily designated February 11 as Origin Day (Kigensetsu). This was said to be the anniversary of the founding of the imperial state in 660 B.C.E. under the legendary Emperor Jimmu. The holiday was abolished by the occupation forces in 1948. From the 1950s into the 1960s, a campaign unfolded to revive the holiday. The movement was noteworthy not only for its support from conservative political leaders beginning with Yoshida Shigeru in 1951. It also echoed the tactics of the "citizen movements" by mobilizing masses of supporters through widely dispersed networks. The association of Shinto shrine priests played a crucial role in this campaign, as did conservative politicians such as mayors and assemblymen in towns and villages nationwide. The movement achieved apparent success in 1966, when a law passed the Diet to establish February 11 as National Foundation Day. But contrary to the hopes of more ideological supporters, the holiday did not establish a strong religious tone of emperor worship along prewar lines.

GLOBAL CONNECTIONS: OIL CRISIS AND THE END OF HIGH GROWTH

Japan's extraordinary era of double-digit economic growth ended abruptly in the fall of 1973. The major Arab oil producers restricted output toward countries, including Japan, that were aligned with Israel in the Middle East War, which broke out that October. Oil prices quadrupled in a matter of weeks. The Japanese government quickly—some said cravenly—distanced itself from Israel. It suddenly found reason to support the rights of Palestinians to a homeland. This solved the immediate crisis by convincing the Arab exporters to reopen the flow of oil. But the huge cost of oil imports led to a deficit in international payments. Higher energy prices sparked a major recession. They also sparked the worst inflation since the 1940s. In 1974, consumer prices increased by 25 percent. And for the first time since the 1940s, GNP actually declined in 1974, by 1.4 percent.

The "oil shock," as it came to be called, had important social and cultural impacts. The threat of disruption in Japan's energy lifeblood confirmed the worst fears of the advocates of a self-sufficient economy. It highlighted the vulnerability of a resource-poor economy in an interdependent world and powerfully recalled the scarcity of the wartime and early postwar years, which were still a living memory for the millions of adults in their forties or older. Consumers suddenly began to hoard all manner of goods, beginning with petrochemical derivatives such as laundry detergent. Pundits

dubbed it the "toilet paper panic" when thousands of housewives crowded into supermarkets and emptied the shelves with panic-buying of this crucial necessity of daily
life.

The crisis also spurred the government to develop a long-range plan to reduce
Japan's dependence on oil in general, and Middle East sources in particular. Bureaucrats accelerated plans to build nuclear power plants and more hydroelectic plants and
funded projects to develop alternative sources from shale oil and solar energy to plat-
forms that might harness the movement of ocean waves. They simultaneously put
forward a call for "energy conservation" that harked back to the wartime rhetoric of
frugality. MITI ministers turned down their heaters in winter and their air conditioners
in summer. They required schools and government buildings to do likewise, and they
urged all others to comply. In summer they came to work sporting a new look for
office employees: no neckties and short sleeves. The combination of conservation and
diversification succeeded to some extent. Dependence on oil from the Middle East fell
from 85 percent of Japan's total oil supply in 1970 to 73 percent in 1980.

Double-digit inflation briefly spurred a resurgence of militant labor protests. Organized workers had become relatively moderate in their demands and tactics through
the 1960s, but in the spring wage offensive of 1974 they mounted a credible threat
of strikes in many industries. They won the largest wage increases in history: an
average hike in starting salaries of 33 percent.

Public employees were particularly vociferous. In contrast to unions in the private
sector, the militance of their organizations had grown through the 1960s and reached
a peak in the early 1970s. But union leaders ignored clear signs that the broader public
had turned hostile. When railway workers caused rush hour delays and extraordinary
crowding by using work-to-rule tactics during the 1973 spring wage offensive, angry
commuters rioted. At twenty-seven stations they beat drivers and smashed trains.

A turning point came in late 1975. Over one million public sector workers participated in the Strike for the Right to Strike.[19] This general strike of public sector
employees failed. The labor movement could not mobilize on a broad front; private
company railway workers, for example, did not join. The public response was cool.
In contrast to the Miike strike fifteen years earlier, few students rallied in support.
After one week, the unions called off their strike, having made no significant gains.
The government took disciplinary action against roughly one million employees. It
fired 1,015 leaders of the illegal strike. A long, slow decline of public sector unions
then began.[20]

Simultaneously, the leading private sector unions pulled back sharply from their
aggressive demands of the previous year. Managers and government leaders pleaded
that wage moderation was needed to control inflation, restore corporate profits, and
guarantee long-run job security. Union officials in the major export industries, centered on the IMF-JC federation, now set the pace of annual wage demands in the
private sector. They agreed with this logic. In 1975, they accepted wage increases
that averaged only 13 percent—one-third the level of the previous year. In hard-hit
industries such as shipbuilding, they also accepted major cutbacks in the work force;
thousands of long-time employees were forced to take early retirement. Unions imposed this sacrifice on a portion of their members for the sake of long-run promises
of security and shared benefits for the rest. Members often questioned the wisdom

of such ready cooperation, but dissenters were unable to alter the decisions made by union leaders. In fields ranging from environmental and welfare policies to labor-management relations, a political system marked by compromise and accommodation had taken root.

The Japanese trajectories of the 1950s through the 1970s, from poverty to prosperity and from confrontation to accommodation, were very much part of a global history of the postwar era. The devastated economies of Europe, Germany and Italy in particular, experienced their own "miraculous" recoveries in these decades. American aid in the early days was crucial in all cases, as was the United States' role in promoting a more open world trading system. In Europe as in Japan, American television and movies promoted dreams of affluence and the bright new life of middle-class consumers. American exports of technology, and Cold War projects to promote non-communist political forces, influenced economic and political history around the world.

Some of America's outreach to Japan was covert. The CIA provided funding to anti-communist allies in the Liberal Democratic Party in the 1950s.[21] Intelligence operatives worked to promote pro-business unionists and obstruct those with radical visions and militant tactics. The full scope of this covert American role in postwar Japan, and in much of the world, is unknowable. But it seems safe to say that it weighted the scales in favor of political accommodations that were gradually evolving in any case.

Other forms of political outreach at the height of the Cold War were more open. In 1961, newly elected President John Kennedy appointed Edwin O. Reischauer to the position of ambassador to Japan. As a university professor and a historian of Japan, he was an unusual choice. But he had caught Kennedy's attention with a 1960 article calling for the repair of a "broken dialogue" with Japan in the wake of the riots and canceled presidential visit during the security treaty crisis.[22] He served as ambassador until 1966. Reischauer worked vigorously to blunt the sharp edge of anti-American sentiment on the political left and right. He also sought to influence cultural and intellectual life. He countered critical Marxist appraisals of Japanese history and society with a far more upbeat view of Japan as a successful model of non-communist modernization.

The strong opposition of many Japanese to the American role in the Vietnam War limited Reischauer's immediate impact on United States–Japan relations. In addition, the ongoing presence of American bases, and in particular the continued American control of Okinawa, angered many Japanese across the political spectrum. In 1968, U.S. President Lyndon Johnson promised to return Okinawa to Japanese control. In 1972, twenty years after the end of the occupation, the reversion took place. This event marked an important halfway step toward a more amicable relationship. But the American military continued to maintain a huge presence on the island. To this day, its bases cover about 20 percent of the best agricultural land in central and southern Okinawa.[23] This has remained a sore spot in United States–Japan relations both in Okinawa and on the mainland.

People in Japan thus chafed at their uneasy position of subordinate independence under the American strategic umbrella. At the same time, in an American-dominated economic environment they prospered from the ability to process goods and sell them throughout the non-communist world. Part of the international significance of Japan's high-growth era lies in the force of these politically constraining and economically liberating alignments.

But it is important to recognize that people in Japan were taking part in a shared modern experience that was not simply orchestrated in Washington or on Wall Street. They were grappling with issues common throughout the newly interdependent—but still divided—world order from the 1950s through the 1970s. Student protests, women's movements, and environmental movements came to the fore around the globe more or less simultaneously. Many labor unions worldwide shifted from a stance as rebels to legitimate bargaining powers, sometimes part of governing coalitions. At roughly the same time governments in the advanced capitalist world—of which Japan had become a part—developed more extensive programs to extend social welfare benefits to the middle classes. The Japanese state and its citizens, like those elsewhere, sought to work out a balance between the drive for profits and the desire for stable, healthy, meaningful lives.

16

Global Power in a Polarized World

Japan in the 1980s

The emergence of Japan as a prosperous, confident, and peaceful nation was a striking development of postwar global history. At home, from the 1970s through the 1980s, some people swelled with pride bordering on arrogance at national achievements. They chafed at the jealous criticism of foreigners. Some spoke nostalgically of the vanishing of older ways of life. They worried that the younger generation had lost the focused commitment of their seniors. Others argued for a greater openness to the world, more tolerance of variety, or more equality in the worlds of men and women. They protested that ordinary Japanese, working long hours and commuting long distances from cramped homes, were not fully sharing the fruits of affluence.

Views from outside mixed attitudes of envy with admiration. In the eyes of some, the image of Japan turned sharply from economic miracle to economic menace. Others looked to a "Japanese model" as an alternative form of capitalism more successful than the Western or American version. In this regard, the decade of the 1980s, in particular, was a remarkable moment of satisfaction and congratulation, unimaginable in the early postwar era and premature in retrospect.

NEW ROLES IN THE WORLD AND NEW TENSIONS

The reversion of Okinawa to Japanese control in 1972 eliminated a major legal remnant of the American occupation. Although U.S. troops and bases remained on the island, the long-awaited return of sovereignty offered the possibility of a new equality in the relationship of the United States to Japan. But two events of the previous year, the so-called "Nixon shocks," undercut this promise. In July 1971, U.S. president Richard Nixon announced the stunning news of his plan to visit the People's Republic of China (PRC). In short order the United States and the PRC established normal diplomatic relations. Then, in August, Nixon announced that the United States would abandon the gold standard and allow the cost of the dollar to fluctuate against other currencies. The value of the yen rose sharply, reflecting Japanese economic power but also making Japanese exports considerably more expensive.

Both of these announcements had major consequences for Japan. The fact that Nixon made them without consultation or even prior notice angered the Japanese government and public. They concluded—with much justification—that the American government did not fully trust the Japanese state or regard it as an equal partner. Most galling was that for two decades, despite considerable domestic opposition, the Japanese government loyally had followed the American policy of isolating and "containing" the communist regime in China. When the American policy turned on a dime, the Japanese were left embarrassed and scrambling to catch up. They did so by opening diplomatic ties with the PRC in 1972. China-Japan economic links slowly developed in the 1970s. They took off in the 1980s with the Chinese turn to de facto capitalism, and China became one of Japan's leading trading partners.

Thus, despite the Okinawa reversion, the Nixon shocks marked a new era of chronic tension in the partnership between Japan and the United States, in economic matters especially. Beginning in 1965, Japan's balance of trade with America had shifted from chronic deficit to a slight surplus of exports over imports, and in the 1970s, a flood of Japanese products to the United States began to overwhelm the flow of American exports to Japan (see Figure 16.1). By the mid-1980s, Japanese exports to the United States were valued at more than double the amount of American exports to Japan. Annual U.S. trade deficits with Japan stood at roughly fifty billion dollars.

The basic pattern was consistent. Japan imported huge amounts of oil, raw ma-

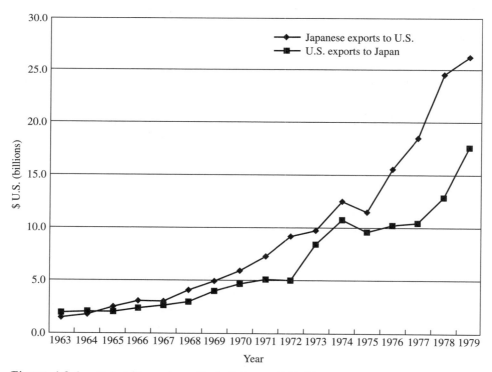

Figure 16.1   United States–Japan Trade Balance, 1963–79

Source: U.S. Department of Commerce, *Statistical Abstract of the United States* (Washington, D.C.: US Government Printing Office, 1963–1979).

terials, and food, while it exported finished manufactured goods of increasing value and quality. The result was not only a chronic export surplus with the advanced capitalist world, but also chronic political tension, with the United States above all. America's most famous manufacturers were unable to match the price and quality of competitive Japanese goods. In electronics, for example, twenty-seven U.S. firms produced televisions at American factories in 1955. By the 1980s, only one, Zenith, continued to manufacture TV sets in the United States.

Faced with this tough competition, American executives and labor unions from as early as the 1960s began to complain vociferously about what they viewed as unfair trade. They accused Japanese producers, with considerable justification, of charging high prices in protected domestic markets while "dumping" products overseas below cost to win market share. Japanese firms, they said, could make up for losses at the initial stage of market entry by raising prices later, when American competitors had retreated or folded. Whether such tactics (remarkably similar to aspects of Microsoft's strategy in the 1990s) were unethical or simply smart business strategy depended greatly on the interests of the observer.

In any case, the Americans used their political leverage to contain Japan's trade advances. A series of acrimonious negotiations produced agreements in which Japanese exporters "voluntarily" agreed to limit their sales to the United States, most notably in textiles (1972), steel (1969 and 1978), color TVs (1977), and then automobiles (1981 through 1993). In 1988, the U.S. Congress passed a trade bill whose "Super 301" clause granted the government the power to unilaterally decide that the domestic markets of Japan or other foreign countries were unfairly closed to imports and unilaterally impose penalties on exporters of those countries in retaliation. The likelihood that this law would be invoked against Japan provoked harsh Japanese criticism that it revived the gunboat diplomacy of the nineteenth century, when American or British warships dictated the terms of trade to weaker states all around the world. Indeed, soon after the law was passed, the Americans used the threat of Super 301 sanctions to enforce access to Japanese markets in supercomputers, satellites, and wood products.

Above all, the automobile quotas dramatically brought into focus the turnabout in Japanese and American fortunes. General Motors and Ford had long been the pride of the American industrial heartland and the engine of postwar prosperity. Their products had symbolized the good life of the American Dream for decades. Now, unless the government helped them with trade quotas, these humbled giants could not convince Americans to choose their vehicles. Consumers by the millions were turning to economical, increasingly reliable cars from Toyota or Nissan, Mazda or Subaru.[1] Trade tensions sometimes erupted in nasty symbolic displays, as when American autoworkers protested by smashing to bits a Japanese car in front of TV cameras. They led to at least one tragic instance of racial violence. In 1982, two autoworkers beat a young Chinese-American man in Detroit to death with a baseball bat. It appears that they attacked him in the belief that he was Japanese. Their trial produced the extraordinarily light sentence of three years' probation and a modest fine.[2]

The American government also pressed a case for a more general restructuring of United States–Japan trade and economic relations through the 1970s and 1980s. In 1979, the two governments agreed to appoint a small group of so-called wise men to offer advice on long-range steps to reduce trade friction. A decade later, from 1989 to 1990, American and Japanese trade negotiators were still focused on broad structural issues in the so-called Structural Impediments Initiative (SII). The idea was to change the underlying structure that produced economic imbalance, such as American budget deficits and low savings rates, and Japanese import barriers, such as the cumbersome distribution system that inhibited price competition. The talks produced various sensible ideas, but few were politically feasible.

As Japanese banks and corporations accumulated huge reservoirs of foreign exchange, investment followed the trade routes. Japanese institutions began to invest in American treasury bills. These purchases financed the ballooning U.S. budget deficits of the 1980s. In addition, Japanese corporations committed large sums to building manufacturing plants in the United States, Europe, and Asia. Japan's global foreign direct investments (FDI) stood at barely one billion (U.S.) dollars in the mid-1960s. By 1975, total Japanese FDI topped fifteen billion dollars, and by the end of the 1980s cumulative FDI came to roughly fifty billion dollars. North America was the site of about 40 percent of these investments, followed by Europe, Asia, and Latin America. As Japan's economy—and land prices—soared, Japanese investors made some particularly high-profile purchases of famous American properties that struck them as relative bargains, such as the Pebble Beach golf course (1990) and the venerable Rockefeller Center in the heart of Manhattan (1989). These deals sparked headlines in the United States of Japanese "takeovers" and "invasions." The tone of some criticism harkened back to the racist anti-immigrant rhetoric that had targeted the Japanese from the early twentieth century through World War II. In one famous example, the well-known journalist Theodore White wrote a front page story for the *New York Times* magazine in 1985 titled "The Danger from Japan." The photo spread contrasted a gleaming new Japanese steel mill with a rusted and vacated American facility. White's article accused Japan of "dismantling American industry." He claimed that Japan's economic gains resulted from a sinister long-term program to dominate the global economy.[3]

Despite such denunciations, the economies of the United and Japan were more interdependent than ever. Policymakers understood this. Even while government negotiators continually argued about trade, state officials also cooperated in multilateral as well as bilateral economic policy. In 1964, Japan had joined the Organization for Economic Cooperation and Development, a body that primarily addressed common issues of the advanced industrial economies and their relations to the rest of the world. Then, beginning in 1975, the heads of state of the seven leading capitalist economies, including Japan, began a regular series of annual "summit" meetings.[4] The role of host nation rotated among the members, who came to be called the "group of seven" or "G-7 nations." They discussed coordination of macroeconomic policies to control inflation and encourage growth and trade. In addition, the finance officials of the G-7 nations, and a core "G-5" group that also included Japan, began to meet on a regular basis in the 1980s. Japan's participation in these meetings was a sign of the nation's central role in the global economy. This was a source of pride. It was also, however, a source of pressure on Japan to design economic policies to serve international as well as national interests.

Among the most important decisions of the G-5 was the Plaza Accord of 1985 (named after New York's Plaza Hotel, where the ministers met). To help their own industries, the finance ministers sought to boost Japanese imports by coordinating currency purchases to strengthen the yen. They also asked the Japanese government to stimulate domestic demand. The Finance Ministry obliged with a policy of low interest rates and fiscal expansion. To boost domestic spending it doled out huge grants to local governments to invest in all manner of projects from roads and bridges to amusement parks and museums. Easy money had complex effects. It helped companies to invest in state-of-the-art technology that could lower production costs and sustain global competitivity despite the rise in the yen. It also provoked the dramatic asset inflation of the late 1980s, Japan's so-called bubble economy.

Japan's relations with Asia and the rest of the world also involved a complex mix of tension and cooperation. Postwar economic relations with Asian nations developed slowly. In the 1950s the Japanese government had restored economic ties to Southeast Asia with reparations agreements. In four separate treaties with Burma, the Philippines, Indonesia, and South Vietnam Japanese companies gave $1.5 billion worth of manufactured goods to the governments of these countries. The Japanese government paid the bill. Building on the connections created by these reparations deals, trade gradually expanded. By the 1980s, the United States accounted for roughly one-third of Japan's export trade. But China, South Korea, Taiwan, and the Southeast Asian nations together stood a close second as trading partners, well ahead of Europe.

Considerable historical irony attended this development. As the Allied occupation drew to a close, American strategists had supported a revival of Japan's "empire to the south." They had expected Southeast Asia to be Japan's most important economic partner, playing a semicolonial role as customer for Japanese manufactured goods and source of raw materials. As it turned out, Japan indeed built solid economic ties in Asia. Yet, despite the imperial presence of its troops on Japanese soil, from the 1950s through the 1980s it was the United States that played an even greater role in a semicolonial pattern as seller of raw materials to Japan and buyer of manufactured goods.

Unsettled issues of the wartime era marked and marred Japan's postwar, postcolonial relationship with the governments and people of other Asian nations. Although the Soviet Union and Japan normalized diplomatic ties in 1956 and opened trade relations, the two countries did not conclude a treaty of peace. A dispute over territory stood in the way. Both governments claimed sovereignty over what Japanese called their "northern islands" (located at the southern end of the Kuril chain. The disagreement remains unresolved to this day. Despite the reparations agreements and expanding economic ties, Southeast Asians often criticized Japanese businesses for what they considered to be predatory trading and investment practices that left no benefit to the host nations. In 1974, the Japanese public was shocked when major anti-Japanese riots greeted Prime Minister Tanaka Kakuei during a visit to Bangkok and Jakarta.

The most complex postcolonial relationship was that with Korea. Facing opposition from the Japanese left, from North Korea, and from many within South Korea, the Japanese and South Korean governments could not negotiate the Treaty on Basic Relations until 1965. As finally concluded, this agreement recognized the Republic of Korea (South Korea) as the sole legitimate Korean government. It negated the validity of the 1910 Japanese annexation of Korea and all prior treaties. South Korea waived

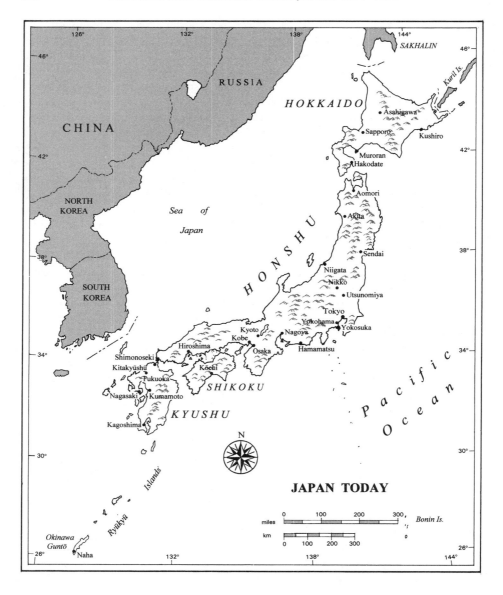

JAPAN TODAY

future reparations claims, but Japan extended $800 million dollars (U.S.) in economic aid. Economic ties flourished through the 1970s, and in the 1980s especially. By 1990 South Korea was Japan's third largest trading partner.

But serious tensions persisted. In 1973 agents of the Korean CIA kidnapped Kim Dae Jung, a prominent Korean opponent to the authoritarian regime of President Park Chung Hee, from a hotel in Tokyo. They took him by force to Seoul. These actions clearly violated Japanese sovereignty and infuriated public opinion in Japan. Koreans, on their part, remained deeply enraged at their treatment by the Japanese during the decades of colonial occupation and war. Thus, when a Korean resident of Japan attempted to assassinate President Park Chung Hee in 1974, the assassin's long-term residence in Japan painted the Japanese with a sort of guilt by association in this context of historical animosity.

From this low point in the mid-1970s, the Japanese government made substantial efforts to improve its relations with Asian countries. At a meeting of the Association of Southeast Asian Nations (ASEAN) in 1977, Prime Minister Fukuda Takeo expressed a strong desire to strengthen Japanese cooperation with Southeast Asia. Following this, Japanese and ASEAN officials began to meet regularly. Japan greatly increased its foreign aid spending (official development assistance, or ODA) in the 1980s. In 1991, it became the world's largest donor, surpassing the United States. Japan has remained the world's leader in the annual dollar value of development aid since then. The largest share of Japanese ODA (roughly 60 percent) went to Asia. Direct investments offering employment opportunities increased substantially as well.

Prime Minister Nakasone Yasuhiro took the lead in promoting stronger ties with Korea in the early 1980s. He promised substantial economic aid ($4 billion). In an important symbolic step during Nakasone's term as prime minister, the Shōwa emperor (Hirohito) gingerly apologized to the visiting South Korean President Chun Doo Hwan for the brutality of the colonial era. He noted his "sincere regret" for the "unfortunate past."

But it remained difficult for the Japanese government and people to erase the distrust held by many Asians. In 1982 Japan's Ministry of Education sparked a huge outcry from China and South Korea when it suggested that the authors of public school history textbooks make revisions that minimized Japan's aggression. The ministry's textbook office, for example, recommended relabeling the "invasion" of China in 1937 as an "incursion." Japanese and world media generally described these as required changes. In fact, the government had made nonbinding "suggestions," and the textbooks were not changed. But understandably, for the Japanese government to suggest that treatment of the war be toned down in this way was sufficient to infuriate Koreans and Chinese, in particular. The governments of South Korea and the PRC made formal protest to the Japanese state over the incident. In 1986 the minister of education further enraged Koreans with a claim that the Koreans were in part responsible for the Japanese annexation of Korea in 1910. He was forced to resign.

From the 1980s through the 1990s, major political figures made a succession of such volatile comments on Japan's recent history, on one occasion minimizing the scope of the massacres in Nanjing, on another asserting that Korea was colonized willingly rather than by force. Each such pronouncement sparked outrage abroad and usually cost the speaker his job. These controversies originated in the sharply polarized view of Japan's responsibility for World War II. Significant differences remained alive not only between Japanese people and others but also within Japan.

Those on the Japanese left blamed military and bureaucratic elites together with corrupt, illiberal politicians and monopoly capitalists for pursuing expansionism and military conquest without regard to the human costs. They contended that the war was both strategically unwise and morally unacceptable, although they generally questioned the morality of the leaders and not ordinary people. They saw popular support for the war as the result of censorship, manipulation of the education system and mass media, and outright suppression of dissent.[5]

In contrast, many government officials and conservative intellectuals developed a very different understanding of the recent past. The first major statement of this position was *In Affirmation of the Great East Asia War*, written in 1963 by Hayashi Fusao, a writer of proletarian fiction in the 1920s who converted to an ultra-nationalist position in later years. Hayashi and others defended Japan's wartime motives as pure. They claimed that the nation led a war to liberate Asia from the grip of Western imperialism. They pointed to the fact that the Japanese occupation of Southeast Asia ended Dutch and British colonial rule and began the process by which the French were ousted from Indochina. They gave less attention to the inconvenient facts of Japan's own colonial rule in Korea or Taiwan, or later in Manchuria and China.

If anything, arguments over "war responsibility" increased in their intensity as the war receded into the past. The effort to deny responsibility fell on increasingly receptive ears at times of economic friction, when many Japanese felt they were unfairly criticized for simply working hard and succeeding in the global economy. Thus, through the 1980s, Asian hostility to Japan was kept alive not simply by old memories of the past. It was fueled anew by the unwillingness or inability of many Japanese people, including cabinet ministers, to look back on that past with sympathy for the experience of others.

ECONOMY: THRIVING THROUGH THE OIL CRISES

Through the 1970s and 1980s tensions with Asia and the West were chronic but contained. They did not provoke a major crisis at home in part because of the soothing effect of continued economic growth and the spreading fruits of affluence. After a brief recession during the first oil crisis, the Japanese economy recovered quite smartly. From 1975 through the end of the 1980s, it grew at remarkably consistent pace, with average annual rates of GNP growth ranging from 4 to 5 percent.

The contrast with the performance of other advanced capitalist economies, not to mention the Soviet Union, was striking. In Western Europe in the 1970s and 1980s, economic growth was anemic, inflation and unemployment were high, and labor protests were widespread. The major European economies grew at half the Japanese pace, or less. In the United States the late 1970s were years of so-called stagflation: stagnant growth rates and double-digit inflation. In the early years of Ronald Reagan's presidency, from 1980 through 1983, the industrial heartland—now dubbed the "rust belt"—experienced a deep recession. Unemployment in major midwestern states climbed to the range of 10 to 13 percent in these years.

In Japan, not only was the economy growing, but inflation was modest and unemployment remained below 2 percent. In addition, through the 1970s and 1980s, Japan's industrial productivity increased at the fastest rates in the world.[6] In the late 1980s, corporate Japan turned particularly exuberant in its behavior, at home as well as abroad. Businesses embarked on a record surge of investment in new plants and equipment. Rates of gross fixed capital formation were close to 30 percent of GNP annually between 1985 and 1989, numbers comparable to the pace of investment in the peak years of high growth in the 1960s. It is no wonder that people in Japan looked around the world with increasing confidence at their success and good fortune (see Table 16.1).

Many looked with particular pride at what had come to be called "the Japanese management system." Japanese manufacturers in the 1960s had proved able to produce quality goods in an era of expansion and global growth. Now they showed the ability to adjust and prosper in tough times. In the 1970s they faced soaring energy costs and weak foreign demand. In the 1980s they faced soaring export costs because of the expensive yen. They adjusted with a drive toward what pundits dubbed "stream-lined management."[7]

Firms facing excess capacity, slack demand, or high costs eased out thousands of workers with the cooperation of their unions. The shipbuilding industry, for example, eliminated 115,000 jobs between 1974 and 1979. This cut overall employment in that industry by roughly one-third. Facing tough competition from new Korean mills in the late 1980s, the top five iron and steel producers likewise cut employment by one-third. Few workers were fired outright in either case. Those targeted for streamlining were reassigned to subcontractors or offered inducements to take "voluntary" early retirement. Large companies expanded flexibility by hiring increased numbers of women as part-time workers who were easily let go when business slackened. For similar reasons they contracted numerous auxiliary functions to outside firms. They spurred on the remaining workers by increasing the weight of annual merit ratings in decisions about promotions and raises.

Even as they streamlined work forces, corporate managers carried on a famous drive to increase quality and contain costs through innovation in the workplace. The emblem of this was the movement for quality control (QC). This campaign began in the 1950s as something called "statistical quality control (SQC)." It was an American import. In first the United States and then Japan in the 1950s, expert staff used charts

TABLE 16.1 **Real GNP Growth of Major Economies in the 1980s (change in percent over prior year)**

	Japan	United Kingdom	United States	France	West Germany
1980	4.3	−2.6	0.2	1.6	1.5
1981	3.7	−0.5	1.9	1.2	0.0
1982	3.1	1.4	2.5	2.5	−1.0
1983	3.2	4.1	3.6	0.7	1.9
1984	5.1	2.2	6.8	1.3	3.3
1985	4.9	3.1	3.4	1.9	1.9
1986	2.5	4.3	2.7	2.5	2.3
1987	4.6	4.4	3.7	2.2	1.7
1988	5.7	4.3	4.4	3.9	3.6
1989	4.9	1.5	3.0	3.8	4.0
Average, 1980–89	4.5	3.5	3.4	2.8	2.7

Source: Foreign Press Center, Japan, ed. *Facts and Figures of Japan, 1991* (Tokyo: Foreign Press Center, 1991), p. 31.

and sophisticated analysis to examine work processes and impose changes that would raise productivity or quality.

The Japanese innovation in production management that attracted global attention was to draw the entire work force into the QC movement. From the 1960s through the 1970s, first supervisors such as foremen and then rank-and-file operatives and clerical staff formed thousands of study groups called QC Circles. Roughly eight to ten men and women would meet regularly, sometimes on their own time, to learn basic problem-solving and statistical techniques. They would then analyze their jobs and come up with strategies to make work more productive or efficient, or in some cases safer and less taxing.

The movement was made possible by high levels of employee education. It was also enabled by managerial commitments to job security, since QC groups often came up with changes that reduced the need for employees in a given work group. The "extra" personnel were usually reassigned to other jobs. By the late 1980s over two million working men and women in Japan had been registered at one time or another in over 260,000 quality circles.[8] Critics noted, with justification, that participation was hardly voluntary as management claimed. Those who did not join faced retribution in promotions or raises. Polls showed that a substantial portion of the participants considered the circles "burdensome" or "stressful." But many of these groups did offer workers a welcome chance to apply their own rich knowledge of their jobs to upgrade their skills as well as to raise productivity or improve quality.

By the affluent 1980s, the once loud dissenting voices of militant unionists on the inside of the corporation, or citizen activists on the outside, were scarely audible. Foreigners flocked to Japanese factories to study the secrets of the managerial system. Highly paid Japanese consultants reexported the revised "total quality control" (TQC) program to the United States.

Japan had become an extraordinarily corporate-centered society. The majority of people believed that what was good for the company was good for the larger society. Pundits grandly celebrated the success of the Japanese system. In 1986, the eminent promoter of Japanese-style quality control, Karatsu Hajime, offered this claim: "I believe that the results of Japan's experimentation [in industrial management] should be disseminated throughout the world. . . . More fundamentally, Japan should offer a positive challenge to the Cartesian assumptions underlying Western business methods."[9]

Karatsu's analysis was typical of a genre of writing called "theories of the Japanese," or *Nihonjinron*. Such work typically stresses the particular uniqueness of Japan in realms ranging from traditions of thought, aesthetics, social or economic organization, and political culture to neurobiological traits such as the tendency to use one side of the brain more than the other. *Nihonjinron* has a long history, going back at least to mid-Meiji thinkers such as Miyake Setsurei and Okakura Tenshin and foreign observers of that time such as Ernest Fenellosa. As Japan's economy flourished through the 1980s, so did the cultural industry producing "theories of the Japanese." As before, they stressed the unified cohesiveness of the whole of the Japanese people, obscuring important differences and tensions within. Bookstores would typically devote a special section to works of *Nihonjinron*.

Some of this writing was superficial and silly. Writers pointed to traits ranging from toilet functions and nose picking to Japan's version of pinball, called *pachinko*, as emblematic aspects of a unique Japanese culture.[10] This sort of thinking emboldened Japanese trade negotiators to make some remarkable claims. One defended import restrictions on beef on the grounds that the unique structure of Japanese intestines could not tolerate imported sirloin. Another defended the domestic sporting goods industry by claiming that the special character of Japanese snow ruled out importing foreign skis.

One of the more interesting "theories of the Japanese" was put forth in *The Anatomy of Dependence* (*Amae on kōzō*). This book identified a psychological trait of "dependence" (*amae*) as a defining feature of Japanese culture. The author, a noted psychiatrist, Doi Takeo, took care not to portray "the Japanese" as unique; he suggested that this psychological dynamic, although very prominent in Japan, could be found in societies around the world.[11] The best-selling foreign work of this era on the particularity of Japan was titled *Japan as Number One*.[12] Its author, Harvard professor Ezra Vogel, reflected—and furthered—the confident spirit of this time. He claimed that the Japanese had synthesized a remarkably successful social and economic system, from which Americans and others might take lessons. The book sold well in the United States but found its true audience in translation among Japanese readers proud to be told of their special positive achievements.

POLITICS: THE CONSERVATIVE HEYDAY

In such a buoyant context, it is no great surprise that the Liberal Democratic Party continued in power. Two sorts of men dominated the ruling party. Career politicians built power upon strong local bases, usually in rural Japan. They protected the interests of powerfully organized constituents such as farmers or the construction industry and profited from their support. The archetype of this sort of ruler was Tanaka Kakuei, a self-made dynamo dubbed "the computerized bulldozer." He built his political fortune as king of the construction industry first in his native Niigata and then throughout Japan. He served as prime minister from 1972 to 1974. He also used his personal wealth and access to corporate generosity to consolidate the most powerful faction within the party. His main tactic was simple: He bankrolled the campaigns of his grateful followers. For nearly two decades after he resigned as prime minister in the face of scandal, the Tanaka faction dominated Japanese politics behind the scenes. Two of his own faction members served as prime minister, Takeshita Noboru (1987–89) and Hashimoto Ryūtarō (1996–98), while several other prime ministers, most notably Nakasone Yasuhiro, owed their jobs to the support of Tanaka's faction. When the LDP voted him into office as prime minister in 1982, Nakasone noted with some awe that "the might of the Tanaka army has been brought home to me as never before."[13] (See Appendixes A and B for details of prime ministers and election results.)

Career bureaucrats-turned-politicians were the second source of LDP leadership. They built power on their elite credentials and close ties to their powerful ministries of origin, Finance and MITI in particular. The leading politicians of the 1950s and 1960s, each of whom served as prime minister, were Kishi Nobusuke (1957–60), Ikeda Hayato (1960–63), and Satō Eisaku (1963–72). All three began their careers as elite bureaucrats in these ministries or their wartime predecessors. The two most prominent such ministry men in the 1970s, who led the party through the oil crises and recovery, were Fukuda Takeo (1976–78) and Ōhira Masayoshi (1978–80). The bureaucratic politicians needed the financial and electoral clout of the career pols, while the latter needed the expertise of the bureaucrats. The two groups often viewed each other with scorn. The struggles between the Fukuda and Tanaka factions, in particular, were famous. On the eve of Tanaka's election as prime minister in 1972 the so-called Fuku-Kaku War nearly split the party in two.

But LDP unity held. Through the end of the 1980s, the opposition parties were unable to break the LDP's Diet majority or shake its control of the prime ministership and the cabinet. The opposition seemed to have a demographic advantage. Socialists, communists, and the CGP (Clean Government Party) all gained support from the increased numbers of urban "floating" voters not part of the organized conservative base. As a result, in 1967 total LDP votes fell below 50 percent in a lower house election for the first time. The party has not won an outright majority of votes in a lower house election since then. But it kept a majority of Diet seats by drawing district lines to give disproportionate weight to its solid rural base. Observers by the 1970s were describing Japan as a country with a "one and one-half party system." Bureaucrats with close ties to the party wrote laws and designed budgets. The party made sure these were approved by the Diet. Big business funded LDP election campaigns and reaped benefit from its policies. The "iron triangle" seemed virtually rust-proof.

Two sources of corrosion led to the only slight cracks in the unity and power of the ruling triad in these years. The first was corruption. Perhaps inevitably, given its long years in power and its practice of trading favors to funders, scandals sometimes broke to the surface. In 1974 a maverick reporter published a scathing exposé in a major monthly magazine. It detailed the massive shady deals, in the construction business above all, that financed Tanaka Kakuei's political empire. The mainstream media jumped on the bandwagon. Later that year, Tanaka resigned as prime minister in the face of fierce scrutiny and public criticism. Two years later, Tanaka's political troubles took on an extraordinary international dimension. A witness who spoke to a United States Senate committee accused Tanaka of pocketing several million dollars in bribes from America's Lockheed corporation in 1972. In return, Tanaka had allegedly directed civilian and military aircraft purchases to Lockheed, whose executives were allies of President Nixon. In 1983 Tanaka was convicted of bribe-taking, although he never served time in jail.

Later in the 1980s, political scandal became a chronic factor on the political scene. The Recruit incident of 1988 implicated former Prime Minister Nakasone and most of his cabinet. The scandal touched dozens of politicians, including some in the opposition parties. They were accused of taking illegal contributions and stock options from the head of the upstart Recruit publishing company. A similar scandal involving the hugely successful Sagawa Express Delivery company tainted some of Tanaka Kakuei's closest followers in 1992. Top politicians were never actually convicted of crimes in these cases, but the continuing run of scandal bred deepening public cynicism toward the LDP and politicians in general.

The other source of corrosion of conservative hegemony was discontent that the fruits of affluence were not shared equally and that the rush to affluence had destroyed the environment and ignored social welfare. In the elections of 1976 and again in 1983, such discontent combined with the fallout from the Tanaka scandals to swing votes away from the LDP. On both occasions the party fell just a few seats short of a parliamentary majority, but each time the LDP drew in a handful of independent Diet members to secure scant majorities. The opposition parties together nearly equaled the LDP in the number of seats, and Diet rules gave them control of a few parliamentary committees. The press called this a new era of "parity politics."

The greater bargaining power of the opposition produced little significant shift in policy. In the move toward political accommodation of the 1970s, the LDP had already co-opted key opposition demands for expanded social welfare. The emergence of centrist parties had likewise blunted the sharp edge of political contention. The Japan Socialist Party, still the largest opposition force, grew increasingly tepid in its criticism. In a sense, its greatest contribution was now a conservative one. It defended the status quo of the postwar democratic constitution against occasional talk of revision. The leadership of all parties was increasingly entrenched, and rarely inclined to take bold initiatives. By 1980, as many as 140 of the 512 Diet seats in the House of Representatives were occupied by so-called hereditary representatives. These were sons, daughters, grandchildren, or even great-grandchildren of veteran parliamentarians. Nearly 90 percent of these "legacy" politicians were in the LDP. Another 7 percent were in the JSP.

The key policy initiatives of these years came from the conservative side of the aisle. Politics in Japan was moving in tandem with trends in Britain and America in particular. British Prime Minister Margaret Thatcher and U.S. President Ronald Reagan cut back welfare programs while deregulating and privatizing major industries. The Japanese government of the mid-1980s, in particular the Nakasone administration, launched a similar campaign for "financial and administrative reform." By 1987, Nakasone cut the annual budget deficit roughly in half. His policies won considerable support, and the LDP regained a solid Diet majority in the lower house election of 1986. By 1990, further helped by increased revenue thanks to a new consumption tax and a booming economy, the Japanese budget stood roughly in balance.

Nakasone's government also privatized several huge public corporations, in particular the debt-ridden Japan National Railway (JNR) and the Public Telephone Company. A key goal of these moves, beyond saving money by forcing the new corporations to operate without subsidy, was to break the back of the JNR union, the one large remaining site of labor militance. The Socialist Party and the JNR union resisted privatization vigorously, the former with political pressure in the Diet, the latter with various protests in the workplace. Thousands of union leaders lost their jobs, accused of illegal labor dispute tactics. The opponents of privatization claimed that it was justified for the government to operate and subsidize such a crucial public service, but Nakasone prevailed. The government railway and telephone service were reorganized as private corporations, called Japan Railway (JR) and Nippon Telephone and Telegraph (NTT). The management of JR took a number of significant steps such as closing down money-losing rural lines and focusing on profitable interurban routes. The new private telephone company, NTT, in contrast, continued to act as a rather complacent near-monopoly. For years it was notorious for high rates and its molasseslike pace of moving to provide new forms of telecommunication service.

The cost of welfare services to an aging society emerged as another crucial political issue in the 1980s. As health care improved, the average Japanese life expectancy rose steadily. Already by 1977 it had reached the highest levels in the world, surpassing that of Sweden. At this point, men in Japan lived to an average of 73 years, women 78 years. These numbers continued to slowly improve through the 1980s and 1990s. The birthrate (the number of children the average woman would bear in a lifetime) also declined steadily. By 1990 it hit an all-time low of 1.6, sparking worried talk of a looming "baby bust." Many commentators lamented the trend toward later age of marriage and smaller families. Men in the government tended to blame selfish young women. Feminist observers noted persuasively that many women were probably postponing marriage and childbirth to avoid the double burden of caring for children and aging parents simultaneously, while their husbands commuted to distant jobs and worked long hours.

These two trends of longevity and a baby drought combined to increase Japan's ratio of elderly to young more rapidly than anywhere in the world. Nakasone called for a more "efficient" social welfare system that would rely on family and neighborhood services—especially the services of women in the home—as well as state-funded programs to care for the elderly. This policy of relying on community and family was consistent with the overall pattern of social welfare programs in Japan reaching back to the prewar era.[14] In the mid-1980s, medical premiums were raised and other costs of the welfare system were shifted from government to citizens.

Another high-profile political reform of the 1980s followed closely the 1970s pattern of conservative co-optation of the progressive agenda. Demands for increased equality of the sexes rose globally in the 1970s, leading the United Nations to adopt a convention to eliminate discrimination against women. Japan's own constitution was clearly committed to equality of women and men, so the Japanese government had little choice but to sign this convention in 1980. It also had little enthusiasm for major reform. Prodded by a growing feminist movement in Japan and committed to take some action, the government took various steps. It changed the citizenship law so that Japanese women married to foreign men could claim Japanese citizenship for their children. Until this point only Japanese men married to foreigners could confer citizenship on their children. The government also drew up the Equal Employment Opportunity Law for Men and Women (EEOL), which passed the Diet in 1985. It called for employers to provide equal hiring, training, and career opportunities for women. It provided the government with no significant enforcement powers and specified no sanctions against violators. But as a symbolic statement of a desirable social goal, it had some impact on employer policies. Most leading companies redefined their jobs into nominally gender-neutral categories of "comprehensive work" (the formerly men-only career track) and "general work" (the formerly women-only clerical track). Women and men were in theory now eligible for both sorts of jobs. Small numbers of women began to enter the comprehensive track and seek private sector careers comparable to those of men.

SOCIETY AND CULTURE IN THE EXUBERANT EIGHTIES

In the era of postwar growth and recovery, millions of Japanese people had understood their efforts as part of a purposeful drive for national economic power and a better life for themselves and their families. By the affluent 1980s, a rather different spirit reigned. Young people and city-dwellers in particular launched into a frenzy of getting and spending. Single young women emerged as a significant force in the consumer economy. They typically worked in dead-end, modestly paid jobs as "office ladies" (abbreviated with a slight pejorative sense as OL), but they often lived rent-free at home. The media described the lives of these women with the same mixture of exuberance and scorn that characterized treatment of the "modern girl" of the 1920s. The "office ladies" of the 1980s enjoyed significant disposable income. In their free time they crowded the stores of the major cities in search of the latest fashions. With their boyfriends they searched out gourmet restaurants, which competed to offer exotic and extravagant choices, even sushi wrapped in gold leaf. They snapped up the latest gadgets of consumer electronics, from fax machines to Walkmans.

Together with people of all ages, they traveled overseas in record numbers. In 1965, only three hundred thousand Japanese had traveled abroad. The majority went on business trips. By 1980, the Japanese took as many as three million trips abroad annually. The number shot up to ten million by the end of the decade.[15] The great majority were now leisure travelers. Roughly 40 percent were women, young and old. Group package tours remained popular, but increased numbers ventured off on their own. Trips were short, averaging just eight days and reflecting the stingy vacation policies of most employers. But Japanese tourists were welcomed by merchants and hotels around the world for their generous spending. Japanese language ability became a job requirement in tourist shops in Hawaii and throughout Asia. By 1990, total outlays on foreign travel exceeded $20 billion per year.

The generation reaching middle age in the 1980s had come of age in a time of intense political turbulence and astonishing economic transformation. Its members felt some discomfort at these trends. They, too, might travel abroad and fill their homes with bigger refrigerators and more powerful air conditioners. But they feared their children lacked their own core of serious commitment. They labeled the youth *shin-jinrui*, a term that can be translated as "new species" or even "aliens." An oft-cited example of "alien" behavior was the shocking decision of a young company man to reject an overtime assignment in favor of a date with his girlfriend. A related new label of the 1980s was *furiitaa*, roughly drawn from a German-English hybrid of "free arbeiter." It referred to phenomenon of young men, in particular, who rejected secure corporate jobs on the career track for the freedom of freelance, temporary assignments, which were abundantly available.

The behavior of the older generation, at its extreme, could not have been more different. One much-noted symbol of the pathology of workaholic, middle-age men, also a newly popularized word of the 1980s, was *karōshi*. It literally meant "death from overwork." The term was coined to describe cases where a man (invariably), with no particular history of disease, died suddenly of a heart attack or stroke, at a time when he was spending extraordinary, stressful hours—perhaps one hundred or more per week—at work. Social activists set up a "*karōshi* hotline" to offer legal advice to the families of victims, or those who feared themselves at risk. In 1987 the government liberalized its definition of occupational disease to open the way for survivors to put in claims for compensation. Based on calls to their hotline, activists

At the peak of the economic boom of the late 1980s (December 1989 in this photo), young "office ladies" and their male counterparts (who enjoyed no such catchy label) line up at the counter of a government office in Tokyo to pick up passports for overseas travel during the upcoming holiday season.
Courtesy of *Mainichi* newspaper.

estimated that the number of cases reached five hundred annually between 1988 and 1990. Only a handful were officially recognized by the Ministry of Labor for compensation: twenty-one cases in 1987, twenty-nine cases in 1988, and thirty in 1989.[16]

Beyond such extreme incidents and despite the flourishing of an "alien" youth culture, it was undeniable that Japanese people continued to work long and hard. Much overtime in Japan went unreported because of the pressure on employees to offer what people called "service overtime" to the firm. Official statistics, therefore, underestimated work hours. But even the government numbers showed that the average annual hours on the job increased from the late 1970s through the 1980s. By 1990 Japanese employees were working about twenty-two hundred hours per year. While the South Koreans outpaced them by a wide margin, this represented a roughly 10 percent margin over U.S. workers and an average of nearly 30 percent (roughly twelve weeks per year) more time on the job than Western Europeans.

Foreigners upset at record Japanese trade surpluses responded to such numbers with criticism and self-interested sympathy. "The Japanese work too hard," they said, and that must be the reason for their competitive advantage.[17] At home, some critics echoed these voices with calls for companies to lighten up on their demands. Others reacted with defensive pride. "What's wrong with hard work?" they asked. They turned the tables and accused Westerners of being lazy and complacent. For example, in 1992 the speaker of the lower house of the Japanese Diet, Sakurauchi Yoshio, claimed that "the source of the [trade] problem is the inferior quality of U.S. labor. . . . U.S. workers are too lazy. They want high pay without working."[18] Such rhetoric, roundly critized abroad, ironically brought to mind older Euro-American views of indolent colonial labor.

A similar division between criticism and celebration marked views of mass culture. Japanese intellectuals and social critics argued over the meaning of greater heterogeneity in a society increasingly divided into "micro-masses." These were identified in the 1980s as fragmented subsets of the larger society, now freed by affluence and a more flexible marketing and manufacturing system to pursue their own special interests and hobbies. The publishing industry launched hundreds of specialized weekly and monthly magazines catering to particular age groups and diversified tastes. Critics called this diversification superficial. The masses were simply "working like mad" to stay in place, pursuing the same mindless race for the latest and the newest, in the false belief that small differences mattered.[19] For some conservatives, despite evidence the employees worked extremely long hours by international standards, the consumerism that came with affluence signaled the hollowing out of the work ethic that had built postwar Japan into a world power. For some progressives, the materialistic population had turned lamentably apolitical and self-centered.

Not everyone agreed with this criticism. One leading intellectual, Tsurumi Shunsuke, argued that ordinary Japanese maintained a healthy balance between too much work and excessive play. They ridiculed "gung-ho company men" or "neurotic education mamas" who "put out stupendous effort to achieve high status." He praised them for a "strong belief that leading an average lifestyle and livelihood is sufficient."[20] Perhaps the most important contrarian thinker who embraced the social changes of the 1980s was Yoshimoto Takaaki. Echoing his position from the 1960 debate with Maruyama over the security treaty crisis, he and others took delight in a more playful, private, and often iconoclastic spirit of youth in particular, and mass culture more generally. They viewed this as the liberation of the subjective desires of ordinary people who might transcend simple materialism. They noted that advertisers, instead of preaching the practical virtues of particular products or even companies, created alluring images with no apparent link to the sponsor. Their writings were part of a debate in Japan over the character of a "postmodern" society and culture that paralleled similar debates in other advanced capitalist societies.[21]

Advertising images helped redefine the physical landscape of Japan in one important way. As agricultural employment fell below 10 percent of the work force by 1985, the steady transformation of rural Japan into a suburban space continued apace. But the advertising industry joined forces with the tourist and transportation industries to reverse this homogenizing trend of the high-growth era. They transformed rural Japan into a nostalgic homeland of the entire nation. In a famous advertising campaign of the 1970s, the populace was urged to "discover Japan" by riding the trains to the countryside. In the 1980s, the distance between modern cities and "traditional" villages was increased with a follow-up campaign extolling the charm of travel to "Exotic

Japan." With tax revenues swollen by the booming economy, dozens of prefectures, towns, and villages joined private developers in a rush to build not only golf courses but also museums and theme parks designed to bring tourists back "home."[22]

A second reversal of the homogenizing social trends of the high-growth decades took place in the realm of education. In the 1970s and 1980s, the impressive egalitarianism of the merit-based system of entrance exams for high school and college eroded dramatically. This was in part an ironic result of the refusal of public schools to simply and single-mindedly teach testing skills. Parents and children responded with an eager search for any advantage in the competition to win places in top schools. The private sector responded to meet their needs. Afterschool "cram schools" proliferated, in major cities especially. Ambitious high school students took four or five hours of afterschool classes to hone their test-taking skills, coming home exhausted at 9 or 10 P.M., only to face homework for their regular daytime classes. In addition, private high schools and even some private middle and elementary feeder schools developed justified reputations for placing graduates in leading national and private universities. Cram schools then emerged that specialized in paving the way to get into these private schools. Parental wealth conferred considerable advantage on the race to get ahead. The proportion of students from wealthy homes in top-ranked universities rose sharply.

Other troubling social trends included a rise in reports of brutal forms of bullying among schoolchildren. Pundits feared students were taking out their frustration at the stress of the exam race upon weaker classmates. And as real estate prices surged in the early 1980s, the difference in wealth between those with property and those without began to widen sharply.

But for most of the 1980s, problems such as the spreading gap between haves and have-nots appeared to most people in Japan as manageable, minor blemishes. As measured in opinion polls and falling voting rates, the populace of an ever more affluent nation was increasingly apolitical and complacent. As the economy continued to outperform its advanced capitalist competitors in North America and Western Europe between 1985 and 1990, the financial as well as productive power of Japanese corporations reached dizzying heights.

Complacency soon gave way to arrogance. Stock values soared, and private individuals joined the speculative action. They coined the term *zai-tekku* (financial technique), a play on the well-known *hai-tekku* (high-tech). By the end of 1989, the Nikkei stock index had tripled in just three years. Companies listed on the Tokyo stock exchange accounted for more than 40 percent of the total value of the entire world's stock markets. Land prices had doubled in the early 1980s. A few years later they doubled again, and tripled in some spots. Organized crime syndicates jumped into the land speculation business, sometimes strong-arming residents into selling them property that they could quickly resell for huge profits. By 1989 the aggregate value of real estate in Tokyo exceeded that of the entire United States by some accounts. Japanese investors bid up the market for European art to unprecedented levels. The French impressionists were a particular favorite. One businessman purchased two paintings, a Van Gogh and a Renoir, for the astonishing sum of $160 million.

Such excesses were not limited to youngsters, gangsters, or eccentric businessmen. Some of the sober great names in banking, such as Sumitomo and Fuji, jumped into flimsy ventures in truly reckless ways. In one notorious case, the Industrial Bank of Japan—the bluest of Japanese blue-chip banks, which had played a central role in financing the 1950s–1960s economic miracle—lent two billion dollars to a woman who ran a small chain of Osaka restaurants frequented by gangsters and their girl-friends. She used the money in stock speculation, guided by seances with a fortune teller. Her collateral turned out to be sloppily forged certificates of deposit from a local credit agency. In retrospect it is easy to see that these trends were combining to create a dangerous, unsustainable speculative bubble. But at the time, many people assumed that good times had come to stay.

Was this history from postwar recovery through undreamt wealth the story of a miracle and model? Was it the tale of the emergence of a threatening global monster? Or did it represent a sad loss of virtue and the erosion of traditional values? All these views were expressed, both in Japan and around the world. Underlying them all was the misleading notion that Japan was a place of remarkable, even unique, difference. We might better see experiences in Japan as fascinating but less exceptional. They were variants on an increasingly global theme of coming to grips with modernity and affluence.

17

Beyond the Postwar Era

The logic for dividing Japanese as well as global time around 1990 is compelling. The Berlin Wall came down in 1989 and the two Germanies were united in 1990. The Soviet empire disintegrated in 1989, and the Soviet Union itself collapsed in 1991. In Japan, the Shōwa emperor died on the eve of this season of European revolution, in January 1989. In July, the LDP suffered a crushing defeat in the upper house Diet election. The party lost its majority in that chamber for the first time since it was founded. In 1990, the speculative bubble of the 1980s burst in spectacular fashion, inaugurating over a decade of economic stagnation. Both the global context and the domestic spirit of the 1990s differed markedly from the 1980s.

THE END OF SHŌWA AND THE TRANSFORMATION OF THE SYMBOL MONARCHY

In September 1987, Emperor Hirohito underwent surgery to treat a swollen pancreas. In September 1988, he collapsed with internal bleeding. Widespread rumors that he was in fact suffering from cancer proved correct, although this was not confirmed by the government until after his death. The people of Japan were drawn into a lingering death watch through four excruciating months of hemorrhage and transfusions. The emperor died on January 7, 1989, and the Shōwa era was over. It had been the longest single reign in the history of the monarchy. The government immediately announced the new reign name of Heisei (literally, "attaining peace"). Hirohito's son, Crown Prince Akihito, officially took the throne on November 12, 1990.

The death of the emperor revealed some important continuities in the place of the imperial institution in Japan. During his months of decline, the major newspapers printed daily reports of the emperor's vital signs and bodily traumas: temperature and pulse and incidents of vomiting blood, rectal bleeding, and transfusion. Despite the coverup of the fact of cancer, this was a strangely invasive public spectacle of the death of a monarch whose private acts, thoughts, and physical condition were almost completely hidden from view for his entire life. Violating imperial privacy in this way was not a democratic innovation of postwar times; the practice of presenting the emperor's medical condition to the nation was a modern tradition invented at the time of the Emperor Meiji's death in 1912. Government officials who released this information sought to solidify an intimate link between their modern monarchs and the populace by bringing the emperors before the people in this extraordinary way at the close of their lives.

Calling for "self-restraint" because an emperor lay dying was another invented Meiji tradition revived in 1988. Officials urged people "voluntarily" to restrain everyday activities of celebration during the emperor's long final illness. The literary scholar Norma Field has written eloquently of this atmosphere of "coercive consensus." Neighborhood festivals and school field days were canceled. Happy slogans were deleted from television commercials. Field also describes the still-powerful taboo on criticizing the emperor for his wartime role. As the emperor lay dying in December, the mayor of Nagasaki explained that he believed "the emperor bears responsibility for the war." This was not a new or unusual opinion. But imperial defenders condemned Mayor Motoshima with unusual virulence. In a throwback to the oppressive politics of the 1930s, the mayor was shot in a failed assassination attempt in 1990.[1]

Alongside continuities, one finds important differences in the response to this monarch's death compared to the time of his father or grandfather. Citizens were free to ignore the spectacle. When television programming turned full time to coverage of the emperor's funeral, people emptied the shelves of video rental shops in search of something else to watch. Some also criticized the excesses of the government-enforced "self-restraint." Others protested state funding of the funeral because it included religious elements. The Nagasaki Citizens' Committee to Seek Free Speech strongly defended their mayor. The committee prepared a petition calling for an end to taboos in political discussion of the monarch. In a few months nearly four hundred thousand people signed it.[2] Such acts would have been unimaginable before the war.

The accession ceremony of the new Heisei emperor in November 1990 provoked a replay of the controversy over the proper boundary to government support of imperial ceremonies of religious character. State officials and conservative intellectuals took an expansive view of what the government might do to mark imperial rites of passage. Liberals and leftists, who feared any hint of a renewed link between the state and the Shinto religion, pushed for a narrow role. The new emperor himself pledged to respect the limited symbolic role defined for the monarch in the postwar constitution. Opinion polls showed that a vast majority of the population supported the emperor as a symbolic monarch, no more or less. Most seemed little concerned with the details of who paid for which ceremony.

Three years later another major imperial spectacle took place. In June 1993 Emperor Akihito's eldest son, Crown Prince Naruhito, followed in his father's footsteps and married outside the narrow circle of the court aristocracy. His bride was Owada Masako, the daughter of a top-ranked diplomat. The prince had courted her for nearly seven years. She was remarkable for her elite education on three continents: an undergraduate degree from Harvard and graduate studies at Oxford and at Tokyo University. She was equally unusual, as an imperial bride, for her career path. Until her engagement, she had worked for seven years as a young diplomat in the Foreign Ministry.

The massive media coverage of the wedding, and the delight of many that Prince Naruhito was finally to marry at age thirty-three, made it clear that the fate of the monarchy remained a matter of great public interest. But the public response intriguingly combined detachment and celebrity worship. Many young women lamented what they called the "waste" of a woman giving up an exceptional career, even for this marriage. Others worried over the impact of the confining palace life on the princess-to-be. For this somewhat dubious public, the media scripted the "royal wedding" as a Disneyesque Cinderella story. But the elaborate wedding festivities drew less intense interest than the 1959 wedding of the Emperor Akihito to Shōda Michiko.

The shift of the throne from object of awe to celebrity was also evident at the decade's end. In November 1999 the government sponsored an elaborate festival to celebrate the tenth anniversary of the enthronement of the Heisei emperor. Many of the young people in the crowd confessed they had come primarily to hear the performances of big-name rock stars.[3]

At the start of the second decade of Heisei, and the first of the new millennium, the imperial institution faced an intriguing dilemma. The Crown Prince and Princess remained childless for the first eight years of their marriage. But in December 2001, after a miscarriage two years earlier, the princess gave birth to a baby girl. The imperial household law limited succession to men, and since the prince's brother also had two daughters, there were no male heirs in the new generation. One logical solution would be to open the throne to women. Precedent could be found in the Tokugawa era and much earlier, when a total of ten women held the throne, eight in the 500s through 700s, two in the seventeenth and eighteenth centuries. Meiji government officials had seriously considered allowing female emperors when they wrote the constitution in the 1880s. Under the 1947 constitution, the Diet held the power to change the succession law. The birth of the imperial granddaughter in 2001 revealed that the throne remained a lightning rod for the hopes and fears of conservatives and reformers alike. Politicians and ordinary citizens weighed in with their views; some "traditionalists" objected, but the majority opinion, including that of key leaders in the LDP, favored revising the law to allow female emperors, and a change seemed likely. The throne no longer commanded fear and awe as before and during the war, but its future was a matter of great interest to most people.

THE END OF LDP HEGEMONY

The end of Shōwa marked the beginning of the end of the Liberal Democratic Party's long hegemony. Its powerful boss, Tanaka Kakuei, suffered a stroke in 1985 that effectively removed him from power. He died in 1993. Following the stroke, his top lieutenants continued to control the party, but their own rivalries caused turmoil. In addition, two major scandals weakened the party: the Recruit affair in 1989 and the Sagawa scandal in 1992. Perhaps most important, the end of the Cold War removed the external pressure that had forced the LDP to remain united despite long-standing factional rivalries.

The first major blows came in 1988–89. Prime Minister Takeshita and his allies drew sharp criticism for accepting favors from the Recruit corporation. In addition, Takeshita was hurt when he made an unpopular commitment to fiscal prudence. In December 1988 he and the Ministry of Finance had followed up on Prime Minister Nakasone's efforts to lower the growing burden of public debt by enacting a new consumption tax. He upset farmers by acceding to foreign pressure and allowing modestly expanded food imports. By May 1989 Takeshita's public approval rating was a microscopic 4 percent, the lowest in Japan's history. He resigned in disgrace.

His successor, Uno Sōsuke, faced a difficult battle in the House of Councillors (upper house) election scheduled for July. The 252 councillors serve six-year terms, and one half of them stand for reelection every three years. The LDP entered the contest with a bare majority. Uno's troubles were compounded with the revelation that he had for years kept a mistress. Even worse in the eyes of many, he had treated her shabbily when he ended the relationship.

The triple punch of sex scandal, money scandal, and an unpopular new tax gave an extraordinary boost to the opposition. In a fortunate coincidence, the Japan Socialist Party in 1986 had elected a woman, Doi Takako, as its chairperson for the first time. She led the party to victory in what the media dubbed the "madonna boom." Polls showed a gender gap at the ballot box: Female voters objected to Uno's behavior and the consumption tax. Female candidates won 22 of the 126 seats at stake (twelve women won seats from the JSP alone). The socialists won a total of 46 seats, compared to just 36 for the LDP, which lost a majority in one house of the Diet for the first time ever.

Fortunately for the ruling party, under the postwar constitution the House of Councillors is the weaker chamber of the Diet. Most importantly, it cannot veto a budget that is passed by the House of Representatives. As long as it maintained its majority in that chamber, the LDP could stay in power. Over the following months the JSP proved unable to turn its electoral success into an effective challenge to LDP policies. In the general election of February 1990 the Liberal Democrats actually expanded their majority in the House of Representatives (See Appendix B.)

The party took heart from this result and blithely ignored the warning signals of its 1989 debacle. Kanemaru Shin, career politician and long-time follower of Tanaka Kakuei, emerged as the new boss behind the scenes by taking charge of the Tanaka faction. His faction controlled the votes needed to elect the LDP president, who then became prime minister. Nicknamed "the Don," Kanemaru was the puppeteer who pulled the strings of the next two prime ministers, Kaifu Toshiki (1989–91) and Miyazawa Kiichi (1991–93).

Miyazawa was the polar opposite of Kanemaru. He had been a career finance ministry official before entering politics. He was fluent in English, with sophisticated knowledge of global finance and politics. He detested the deal-making, money-obsessed style of men like Kanemaru. But he followed the latter's orders in matters of policy and personnel in order to have his day in the sun as prime minister.

In 1992, the Sagawa Express scandal broke open, and Miyazawa's outlook grew cloudy. This was far bigger than the Recruit affair. The Sagawa company chieftain not only bought politicians with money to ensure favorable regulations for his industry but also used underworld connections to support his political allies and intimidate their opponents. Kanemaru was at the center of this dirty story. He met with crime family bosses to thank them for their help. He evaded taxes massively. Among other sins, he was discovered to have squirreled away one hundred kilograms of gold bars in his luxury apartment in central Tokyo.

Kanemaru's corruption was extreme, but shady practices had been part of the underside of LDP rule for decades. With the end of the Cold War, LDP supporters were less reluctant to criticize their party, and the media was emboldened to attack corrupt politicians. Kanemaru was forced to resign from the Diet late in 1992. Miyazawa faced widespread calls to reform the electoral system to reduce the role of money in politics. But he insisted that corrupt individuals caused problems, not a corrupt system. His complacent party pushed for no significant reform.

In the summer of 1993, the LDP castle finally crumbled. The opposition parties, as they often did, proposed a vote of no-confidence to protest the LDP failure to propose credible reforms. Because the opposition lacked the votes to prevail, this appeared to be a symbolic protest. But suddenly, a politician named Ozawa Ichirō jumped on the reform bandwagon. Ozawa emerged as a key, if inconsistent, player in the politics of the 1990s. Like Kanemaru, he was a Tanaka protégé. Younger than the Don, and impatient, he sought to seize his mentor's mantle with a bold stroke. He and his followers revolted by supporting the opposition's no-confidence measure. In a dramatic turnabout, it passed. The Miyazawa cabinet was forced to resign and call an election.

The LDP fared poorly. It fell well short of a majority of the seats. Ozawa and his group formed a new Japan Renewal Party, pledging reform of politics. They did well. Another reformist party did even better. This was the Japan New Party, led by Hosokawa Morihiro and founded the previous year. Hosokawa was an attractive political leader. His background was elite: His paternal line stretched back to one of Kyushu's most powerful daimyō clans, while his maternal grandfather was the wartime Prime Minister Konoe Fumimaro. But his style was open, and his rhetoric was populist. He won a substantial following with pledges to clean up the political process and implement policies to favor ordinary citizens. In a wild scramble after this election, Ozawa's Japan Renewal Party and Hosokawa's Japan New Party joined with the older opposition parties (the JSP and CGP) to cobble together the first non-LDP government since 1947. Ozawa built the coalition behind the scenes. Hosokawa served as prime minister. Committed to reform, he still faced difficult challenges in economics and foreign policy, as well as political resistance from a still-powerful LDP.

THE ECONOMIC BUBBLE BURSTS

One factor behind the LDP's fall from power was surely the end of Japan's economic glory days. The long stretch of world-beating economic growth ended as the 1990s began. The first sign of trouble was a stock market swoon. This resulted from a conscious policy decision by the powerful bureaucrats in the Ministry of Finance. In 1985, with the Plaza Accord of the G-7 ministers, they had embarked on a program to stimulate investment and domestic consumption. By the end of the decade, finance officials decided the resulting surge in land and stock prices had reached dangerous heights. They gradually tightened credit, hoping to curb speculative investment and gently deflate the bubble. From the fall of 1989 through the summer of 1990, they enacted a series of increases that more than doubled borrowing rates from 2.5 to 6 percent. Investors took notice. The Nikkei index of the Tokyo stock exchange (comparable to the Dow industrial average on Wall Street) fell by half, from a peak of nearly forty thousand yen in December 1989 to twenty thousand by October 1990.[4]

Falling stock prices left speculators stranded, unable to repay their loans. The

Osaka restauranteur-speculator noted in Chapter 16 was arrested for forging bank notes in 1991. A steel trading company that had branched out into stock trading went bankrupt. Higher interest rates likewise ruined dozens of real estate development schemes because the developers' estimated revenues could not cover the increase in new borrowing costs. These failures sparked a drop in land prices, which eroded the value of their land as loan collateral. Beginning in late 1990 with a huge golf course developer called Itōman, one property company after another went bust. A vicious cycle of failures, further price drops, and more failures replaced the spiraling cycle of rising land and stock values. The bubble had burst.

Despite the crash to earth of stock and land speculators, the underlying economy did not show immediate signs of trouble. The economic bureaucrats claimed to be squeezing out the excess without harming the core. Japan continued to run huge trade surpluses, on the order of forty billion to fifty billion dollars annually with the United States and twenty billion to thirty billion dollars with the European Union. In 1990 and 1991 Japan's GNP continued to grow at a brisk 4 percent per year. Corporate capital spending grew by 10 percent from 1990 to 1991. Industry seemed to be laying a strong foundation for a future once more focused on production, rather than speculation. Pundits around the world joked that "the cold war is over, and Japan has won."

Trade negotiators from the United States and other G-7 states were not laughing. They pushed Japanese officials to open their domestic markets further. The so-called Uraguay round of multilateral negotiations aimed to expand the General Agreement on Tariffs and Trade (GATT) to eliminate almost all remaining global trade restrictions, tariffs, and state subsidies. Japanese farmers were among the most protected and subsidized producers in the world. They and their political allies tried desperately to keep domestic markets closed. But the new GATT agreement finally reached in late 1993 committed Japan gradually to admit imports of rice and other farm goods.

Bilateral negotiations with the United States focused primarily on high-tech products. The Americans took a convenient view of the virtues of "free trade." They praised it with words, but they violated it with deeds by pushing Japan to set trade quotas. Some of these took the form of ceilings on the export of cars or steel. In addition, in 1991 one of the most controversial agreements set a floor for a minimum acceptable American share of Japan's semiconductor market: no less than 20 percent by the end of 1992. Japanese negotiators, no less conveniently than their opposite numbers, wrapped themselves in the rhetoric of free trade: They called the agreement merely a "target" at which private producers might aim. The Americans expected the Japanese government to enforce sufficient imports. The government denied that it intervened directly, but the target was somehow reached by the promised date.

The United States also pressured Japan to play a more active role as a military partner. The issue came to a head during the short Gulf War of 1991. The peace clause of Japan's constitution, as well as public opinion, ruled out sending troops to join the multinational expedition sent to resist the Iraqi occupation of Kuwait. As the Americans led the war with air raids and then an invasion to oust the Iraqis, they pushed Japan to support the effort in some way. Eventually the Japanese government contributed thirteen billion dollars toward the cost of the war. Although this was the largest donation of any nation outside the Persian Gulf area, the protracted process of reaching this decision left a bad taste on all sides. Many Japanese felt underappreciated. Many Americans felt the Japanese were selfish for depending on Middle Eastern oil while leaving others to fight to make sure the pipelines stayed open.

By the early 1990s, a pattern of American pressure met by Japanese resistance, then concession, had been deeply entrenched in both trade and military matters. Cynics noted the weakness of the JSP or CGP in domestic politics and called the United States "Japan's most powerful opposition party." But as matters turned out through the rest of the decade, the United States–Japan economic relationship never broke down into an open trade war. Despite numerous negotiations marred by angry threats and counterthreats, the two sides settled most of their disputes without imposing retaliatory tariffs or unilateral barriers. Ironically enough, the weakened Japanese economy and booming American one lowered the political volatility of chronic tensions.

After its initial collapse, Japan's stock market rallied in 1991. But the next year the collapse of the speculative stock market bubble spilled over into the rest of the economy. A recession began. Indices of industrial production, construction starts, and wholesale prices all started to fall. So did business and consumer confidence. The stock marked turned down once more; the Nikkei average fell to fourteen thousand by the summer of 1992. At this point Japanese authorities decided they had gone too far with their tight money program. They started to lower interest rates to revive the economy. Borrowing rates fell to levels rarely seen in Japan or elsewhere. By 1995 favored borrowers could have funds at a mere 2 percent; bank deposits earned less than 0.5 percent per year. But banks were frightened by their many bad loans of previous years. More ominously, their weak balance sheets limited their ability to make new loans even to solid customers. Investment stagnated. Industrial production actually fell by 11 percent from 1991 through 1994. The GNP rose 1 percent in 1993 and was virtually flat in 1994 (see Figure 17.1).

The Japanese economy faced a problem similar to the "savings and loan" crisis

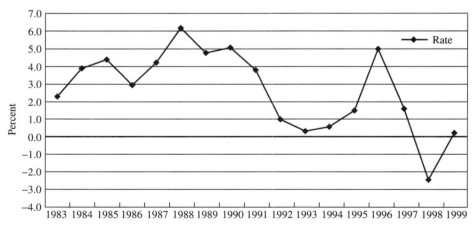

Figure 17.1   Real GNP Growth in Japan, 1983–99.
Source: Comparative Economic and Financial Statistics, Japan and Other Major Countries (Tokyo: International Department, Bank of Japan, December, 2000).

in the United States of the 1980s. Weak outside scrutiny had allowed banks to make careless, risky loans to land developers in particular. Many banks were technically insolvent. They were paralyzed by the inability to collect loans from failed ventures and by the collapse in value of land and stock held as collateral. As early as the summer of 1992, top Japanese officials saw the need for banks to clean the system by dumping bad debts. They began planning for a government bailout, along the lines of the plan implemented in the United States by the Resolution Trust Company. This body had used billions of taxpayer dollars to clean up the mess of bad debt of insolvent savings and loan institutions in the United States. But to do something similar would have required Japan's bureaucrats, banks, and major corporations to openly admit their mistakes. It would have meant the failure of some leading financial institutions. The government instead took only limited steps to address the banking crisis.

Weighted down by the debilitated financial system, the economy staggered through the first half of the 1990s. The government hoped to restore some confidence and energy to consumers and the private sector. It turned to public works projects to stimulate business, allocating billions of dollars to construct dams and highways. To help exports, it welcomed the cheapest yen in history, well under one hundred yen to a dollar in 1995. Signs of recovery did appear in 1995 and 1996. The strong American economy and cheap yen boosted exports, at the cost of increased political tensions over auto exports in particular. The GNP grew by 2 to 3 percent annually.

But recovery sat on a weak foundation. Although GNP increased, unemployment rose. Prices continued to fall. Wage earners feared that corporate cost-cutting might also cost them their jobs, eliminate bonuses, or take away pay hikes. Consumer spending remained rather weak, rising just 3 percent annually in 1995 and 1996. Banks, and nonbank lenders such as huge agricultural cooperatives, continued to carry massive amounts of nonperforming assets that distorted their balance sheets. These were mainly loans to real estate developers that were not being repaid and were unlikely to be recovered. It was impossible to trust the official statements of the extent of the bad loan problem because so many former regulators from the Ministry of Finance and other ministries sat in postretirement posts as directors of the suspect lenders. In 1995, some small banks failed, in an ominous sign that a larger problem remained. The bad debt of the agricultural cooperatives alone was estimated to stand at ten trillion yen (about one hundred billion dollars).

In this uncertain context, the government took a dangerous step in the name of fiscal prudence. Prime Minister Hashimoto Ryūtarō (1996–98) decided that increased budget deficits had to be controlled. Faced with an aging population and large future social security costs, in the summer of 1997 he increased the consumption tax from 3 to 5 percent. This dampened the already shaky confidence of consumers, slowed their spending, and choked off the incipient recovery.

Over these years of inconsistent performance and policy, the attitude toward the Japanese economy changed profoundly both at home and abroad. Observers began to identify deep structural problems and speak of systemic failure. Looking at the state, they criticized excess intervention in the private economy and called for "loosened regulation." Looking at private firms, they coined a new English-based word for their prescription, *risutora*. This meant "restructuring" by reducing the number of workers and closing unprofitable ventures. But the banking crisis suggests that the heart of the problem was a more complex mix of overprotection and insufficient regulation than simple slogans such as "loosened regulation" and "restructuring" implied.

The mid-1990s—and above all the year 1995—was also a time of declining confidence in the core institutions of the Japanese establishment. In January 1995 a major earthquake struck the port city of Kobe and its environs. Nearly sixty-four hundred people died and three hundred thousand lost their homes. Victims were heartened by the selfless work of thousands of volunteers—as many as twenty thousand per day in the month after the quake and five hundred to one thousand daily for many months to follow. But the evident lack of preparation on the part of national and local officials to respond to such a disaster—in a country where earthquakes are a familiar menace—shook popular confidence in the government.

Just two months later an act of terrorism on the Tokyo subway presented an even greater shock to a population proud of its low crime rate, the safety of major cities, and the efficiency of Japanese police in solving crimes. On a subway passing under the heart of the government business district at the height of the morning rush hour on March 20, 1995, members of a new religion called Aum Shinrikyō released small portions of deadly poisonous sarin gas. The group had been founded in 1987 by a legally blind former yoga teacher named Asahara Shōko, who combined anger at his own marginal background with a potent mix of self-styled "Eastern religious ideas"

Compounding the economic difficulties of the 1990s was the literal shock of the Kobe earthquake of January 1995. Thousands of people lost their lives. The city's major expressway toppled in this dramatic manner.
Courtesy of *Mainichi* newspaper.

and anti-Western rage. The group expanded rapidly through the early 1990s, claiming fifty thousand members by 1995 (although the numbers cannot be confirmed and might, in fact, have been declining at this point). The Aum terrorists, under the spell of their charismatic leader, were seeking to hasten the day of an expected apocalypse with this act. Twelve passengers were killed and nearly fifty-five hundred passengers were injured in the attack. Aum had already been implicated in earlier instances of suspicious deaths and disappearances. These facts, and the group's ability to obtain illegal arms and chemicals with ease, led to harsh criticism of the police authorities.

The attacks also provoked legal reforms designed to monitor religious organizations better. The Religious Corporations Law, which defined the legal relationship of religions to the state and society, was revised to give the Ministry of Education increased power to collect financial data on religions. Defenders of religious freedom worried that civil liberties would be sacrificed for the sake of public safety, but the step was relatively mild by international standards. The government in fact had gained relatively little new authority to move against groups other than Aum itself. Even so, legal changes in the wake of the gas attack did signal a shift in the basic assumption behind laws concerning religion in Japan. They now assume that the state has a duty to protect citizens from abuses by religious bodies, in contrast to the premise throughout the postwar era that the state was to be restrained from its potential to abuse religious freedom. It remains to be seen how this issue will be treated in practice.

Bureaucrats had generally kept a reputation for honesty through the scandals of the previous decade, which had tainted politicians and businessmen with charges of greed and corruption. This bureaucratic prestige declined sharply in the 1990s because of a new series of scandals. Most notorious was the revelation in 1996 that the Welfare Ministry had failed to ban the production of potentially lethal blood plasma products in the early 1980s. At the time, AIDS had just been discovered. Researchers were moving toward the conclusion that blood carried the disease and that to ensure purity blood products should be heated before use in transfusions. For several years American pharmaceutical corporations were the only producers of heated blood, and a Ministry of Welfare committee obstructed its import. Even after admitting imports of heated blood, the ministry continued to allow use of domestic nonheated blood plasma. For eighteen months, Japanese producers supplied hemophilia patients with unheated blood despite the availability of a safer foreign product. By the late 1980s, twenty thousand people, or 40 percent of the hemophilia patients in Japan, had tested HIV positive. Some of these victims were probably infected before heated blood was available. But the behavior of the Ministry of Welfare raised the suspicion that bureaucrats and doctors sacrificed public health simply to protect Japanese medical supply companies from foreign competition.[5]

In 1996, a reformist politician, Kan Naoto, took over as minister of welfare. Kan was an activist who had cut his teeth on anti–Vietnam War protests in the 1960s. In 1996 he was a leading member of a small reformist party (called New Party Sakigake) that was part of the governing coalition. He won public acclaim for bringing the problem out in the open and admitting the government's responsibility. The head of the Green Cross Company, which had continued selling nonheated blood despite knowing its risk, apologized to the public and the AIDS patients in dramatic fashion.

*In March 1996, seven years after the first lawsuits were filed against medical supply compa-
nies whose unheated blood products infected patients with the AIDS virus, HIV, the Green
Cross Company and three other defendants reached a settlement with the victims. Here, the
president of the Green Cross Company and its directors bow their heads to the floor in apology to the plaintiff victims. This and other scandals of the 1990s shook public confidence in
government bureaucrats, who regulated private industry and normally enjoyed high respect,
as well as business leaders and politicians, who had often been the target of popular
suspicion.*
Courtesy of *Mainichi* newspaper.

But the reputation of career bureaucrats had suffered a great blow. Over the following
years new revelations of illegal use of public funds by bureaucrats for lavish entertainment furthered eroded public respect for state officials.

THE JAPANESE DISEASE AT CENTURY'S END?

In the face of economic stagnation and scandal, calls for reform reached a crescendo
in the second half of the 1990s. At no time since the immediate postwar days was
the need for change so widely discussed. Predictions of collapse or transformation
and prescriptions for "the third opening" of Japan—after the Meiji and postwar revolutions—became well-worn clichés. But it is worth remembering that the first two
revolutions took place under the authoritarian governments of Meiji Japan and of
SCAP. In contrast, reforms of the democratic 1990s were anemic. Despite talk, no
political leaders came forward to create a consensus for reform or build the authority
to impose it.

Confusion in the political arena reflected and reinforced the lack of consensus.
One indication of the changed political climate was instability at the top. In the forty-

four years from the founding of the LDP in 1955 through the upheavals of 1989, twelve men served as prime minister for an average term of 3.7 years. Over the next twelve years, from 1989 through 2000, ten men held the office for an average tenure of just 1.2 years.

When the LDP gave way to a coalition cabinet in 1993, most observers predicted that something close to a two-party system was about to emerge. They expected a coherent rival to the LDP would come together. Its likely members were the breakaway reformers from the LDP such as Hosokawa and Ozawa, together with opposition moderates in the CGP, the Democratic Socialists, and some in the Japan Socialist Party. Although the old political map of left-right opposition indeed was redrawn completely over the next several years, this expectation was not met, at least in the short run. Instead, the LDP made a comeback.

The return of the LDP began most strangely. Hosokawa Morihiro resigned as prime minister after only eight months in office. The LDP had turned the tables by accusing this champion of clean government of dubious financial dealings. But the deeper reason for Hosokawa's quick fold was probably his fundamental distaste for the daily grind of political battle. Hata Tsutomu took over at the helm of the coalition government in April 1994. He was a reform-minded politician who had broken away from the LDP together with Ozawa Ichirō in 1993. But he lasted just two months in office. By this time LDP attacks and efforts to win back some of its runaway members had succeeded in undermining the tenuous unity of the new coalition.

In place of the anti-LDP coalition, in June 1994 the nation was treated to a stunning spectacle: the LDP formed a coalition government with the Japan Socialist Party, the largest opposition party and its long-standing ideological rival. What is more, the LDP agreed that the JSP president, Murayama Tomiichi, would serve as prime minister. This alliance was comparable, in American terms, to a situation in which a Republican president would name a Democrat as vice president.

Two factors led these strange bedfellows to their marriage of political convenience. The first was pure pragmatism. The socialists saw the LDP invitation to join hands as a last best chance to share power. The LDP, for its part, needed some opposition ally in order to put together a parliamentary majority. Party leaders were so alienated from the turncoat Ozawa that they preferred to join with their once-despised socialist rivals. The second enabling factor was the changed climate of global and domestic politics, the product of long secular shifts as well as dramatic recent events. Election rhetoric aside, for some time, the LDP and JSP Diet members had been working together in parliament to draft and pass legislation. The majority of laws that passed the Diet from the 1960s onward in fact had been supported by both parties, and this bipartisan parliamentary voting had become more frequent since the 1970s. The increasingly cooperative relations of labor unions and corporations had for some time dulled the edge of left-right antagonism. In addition, since the 1970s, the two parties had frequently supported the same candidate in local elections. Finally, the end of the Cold War and the triumph of global capitalism eliminated much of the basis for the mutual distrust of the two parties.

But even if the LDP-JSP alliance could be explained in this way, it remained surprising and troubling to Japanese voters. Above all, it damaged the socialists. People already viewed the LDP as a party of pragmatic deal-makers. LDP supporters expected political and economic favors more than ideological consistency. The JSP electoral support, in contrast, rested to a large extent upon principle: defense of the peace constitution, opposition to the United States–Japan military alliance, and distrust of cozy corporate ties to the state.

In exchange for joining the government, the JSP did win some reluctant LDP concessions in the ideological realm. Prime Minister Murayama offered the most forthright apologies on record for wartime atrocities such as the enslavement of "comfort women." The LDP on its own would have been less forthcoming. But the socialists were nonetheless widely seen to have abandoned principle for the sake of power. In short order, their political presence faded.

In January 1996, Prime Minister Murayama stepped down, ostensibly for personal reasons but facing strong pressure from his LDP allies. The prime minister's job went to Hashimoto Ryūtarō, an LDP stalwart and Tanaka loyalist. The LDP was clearly in charge of the government. The JSP remained in the ruling coalition as a weakened junior partner. Another coalition member was the small New Party Sakigake, led by reform-minded politicians including Kan Naoto, who won acclaim for his fight to expose the tainted-blood scandal.

In the fall of 1996, with an election looming in the House of Representatives, a shuffle of party alignment took place. The majority of the JSP, members of the New Party Sakigake such as Kan, and remnants of Hosokawa's New Party founded the Democratic Party of Japan (DPJ). These politicians hoped to displace Ozawa Ichirō's group as the major rival to the LDP. His breakaway faction of the LDP had been founded in 1993 as the Japan Renewal Party and renamed the New Frontier Party one year later. In the election that October, the DPJ did fairly well (52 seats), and Ozawa's group gained much support (156 seats). But the remnants of the JSP nearly evaporated. It fell from 70 to 15 seats. Its long life as the major opposition force was effectively over. The LDP made slight gains and came close to majority (239 of 500 seats).

After the election, Prime Minister Hashimoto managed to form the first exclusively LDP cabinet since 1993. The socialists left the coalition but agreed to support the government issue by issue. For the rest of the decade, the Liberal Democrats ran the government. Starting out just short of a majority, they formed a coalition with centrist and conservative allies rather than the socialists or other reformers. In 1998 Ozawa's political party broke in half. The splinter group joined the Democratic Party, and those remaining with Ozawa renamed their group yet again, this time as the Liberal Party. After five years of trying to build an opposition force, Ozawa now turned back to his roots, and his Liberal Party joined the LDP in a coalition government. In 1999 the CGP followed suit. Some Ozawa supporters rejoined the LDP outright, giving it a sole lower house majority for the first time in six years. On the surface, Japanese politics apparently had returned to business as usual: The LDP was in power, faced with a scattering of smaller parties in opposition.

But the LDP hegemony of the late 1990s was much weaker than that of the past. Despite its growing strength in the House of Representatives, the party did quite poorly in the 1998 House of Councillors house election. It ended up with an all-time low of 37 percent of the seats. Prime Minister Hashimoto's decision to raise taxes was blamed by voters for throwing the economy back into recession. The ballot was seen as a repudiation of his economic policy. He resigned, replaced by another LDP veteran,

Obuchi Keizō (1998–2000), who was initially ridiculed as a backroom political dealer "with all the pizzazz of cold pizza."[6] Obuchi presided with limited success over two years of aggressive deficit spending intended to revive the economy. In May 2000 he died of a stroke, probably brought on by exhaustion. His successor, Mori Yoshihiro, called a House of Representatives election in July 2000. The party suffered continued blame for the still weak economy. It fared poorly, falling short of a sole majority in the lower house once more. It continued in power only by virtue of its coalition with Ozawa's liberals and the CGP.

The Democratic Party did better than ever. It showed some potential to emerge finally as a strong opposition party. But continued rule by a weakened LDP, faced by a divided opposition, seemed more likely as the twenty-first century began. As in the United States, huge numbers of voters simply failed to vote, distrustful of all the parties. Facing intense pressure to reign in government spending, the LDP lacked the means to keep rewarding its traditional pork-barrel constituents. The Democrats, for their part, were sharply divided among themselves on key issues such as constitutional revision or the place of the military in the United States–Japan alliance. A major part of the problem for all parties, and for the bureaucracy and business elites as well, was a lack of consensus over how to revive the still stagnant economy. Reversing the rhetoric of the 1970s and 1980s, critics at home and abroad spoke of "a Japanese disease" marked by political paralysis in the face of major social and economic problems.

In the spring of 2001, Prime Minister Mori's approval rating fell to single-digit levels, and he resigned under pressure from his party, whose members feared an electoral disaster without some change in leadership. In a surprising outcome, a popular LDP politician from slightly outside the party mainstream, Koizumi Junichirō, was elected as party president and prime minister in Mori's place. He pledged dramatic changes in economic policy above all, and he surprised people further by appointing a record five women to his cabinet. But his promised harsh economic medicine threatened many key supporters of the LDP in rural Japan and top financial institutions. He faced major obstacles in the effort to impose his agenda of neoliberal reforms.

In addition to obvious economic problems of stagnant growth and a dysfunctional financial sector, as the decade and century ended Japanese politicians and the populace at large faced major social issues centered on demography and education. The baby bust of the 1980s continued unchecked through the '90s. It was unaffected by a modest new Welfare Ministry "baby bonus" offered to parents. The birthrate (the number of children an average woman would bear in her lifetime) fell to 1.34 in 1999. Demographers projected that with no change in these numbers and no increased immigration, the Japanese population would peak at 130 million in 2005 and fall to 55 million by the year 2100.

Some pointed to the benefits of population decline. Cities would be less crowded. Better housing would be available. Increasingly valuable female employees (and, presumably, their male counterparts) would be able to negotiate better conditions in the workplace. And, of course, a smaller population would be more ecologically correct.[7]

It was unlikely that demographic trends would proceed so neatly in one direction for a century, although it made sense to welcome a smaller population in the long run. But in the short run, these demographic projections were unlikely to be wrong, and many observers feared the impending burdens of adjusting to a smaller, older population. Fewer working people would lower social security revenues, while more elderly would increase the system's cost. Significant tax increases, or major benefit reductions, appeared unavoidable. And even if a more productive future economy brought relatively little net gain in employment, a falling population would bring on a labor shortage. A much publicized report of March 2000 predicted that Japan would have to bring in roughly six hundred thousand immigrant workers *per year*, for the foreseeable future, simply to maintain its current work force size. Fear of alienating voters by lowering benefits, and fear of choking recovery by raising taxes, made it politically difficult to address the social security issue. Fear of foreigners made it unlikely that Japan would soon become a major site of immigration.

Education and youth seemed to be in a chronic state of crisis as well in the 1990s. A series of reports by the Ministry of Education and authoritative bodies such as the Japan Productivity Center called for basic reform of higher education. Universities were widely condemned for lackluster teaching that failed to prepare young people to think critically or adapt to a changing global environment. Secondary education was criticized, as in the past, for excessive reliance upon rote learning. Experts and pundits also expressed heightened fear that schools were failing to inculcate proper social values. Abusive "bullying" and school phobia had been identified as social problems since the 1980s. In the 1990s a series of sensational crimes made the schools appear to be ever more volatile breeders of demented behavior. The fact that graduates of the engineering faculty of Tokyo University had been leaders in the Aum Shinrikyō organization and helped produce the poison gas shocked the public almost as much as the gas attack itself. In 1997 a fourteen-year-old middle school student murdered an eleven-year-old boy for no apparent reason. He deposited the victim's severed head in front of the murderer's school. In 1999 several cases of murder or torture by teenagers made front page news. People speculated that the hothouse environment of exam-centered education failed to impart any sense of morality to these youths.

Another notorious social issue of the 1990s was a new sort of youth prostitution, euphemistically termed "assisted dating" or "paid dating." Large numbers of teenage women made themselves sexually available to adult men for substantial fees. Those who studied the phenomenon were shocked to discover how "normal" most of these girls were. They were not poor. Their family lives were apparently calm. One critic wrote of two ninth graders who occasionally engaged in prostitution while attending an exclusive Christian girls' school famous for high academic standards:

> I would have been more comfortable if they had had bleached hair and rings in their noses and tongues. In fact, however, they were perfectly normal-looking young girls. They wore blue skirts and blazers with white blouses.

Analysts blamed materialism and shallow family relationships for a crisis of the soul that produced a widespread amorality. The result, they said, was "paid dating" for the sake of the cash to buy expensive clothes or simply to gain some attention and companionship.[8]

However troubling these social problems appeared over the decade, the combination of economic woes and a media eager for good stories probably conveyed to the Japanese people an exaggerated impression of social decay. Gruesome crimes were neither new nor unique to Japan. Critics made much of the "unprecedented" age of the Kobe schoolboy killer. But in fact, this was by no means the first juvenile killer in postwar history. In response to calls for stricter laws for juvenile crime, level-headed lawyers pointed out that the incidence of violent crimes by youth was not increasing dramatically. It had actually been greater in the 1950s and 1960s.[9]

Young people obsessed with cell phones sending email and music, flaunting out-landish fashions and hairstyles, were everywhere to be found in turn-of-the-century Japan. But youths—such as the "modern girls" and "modern boys" of the 1920s— who act differently from their parents (and upset them in the bargain) have been present throughout Japan's modern history. Taken as a whole, the youth of the 1990s may actually have been as socially responsible as their elders. In the wake of the Kobe earthquake, young people were prominent among the small army of volunteers who assisted the victims. Volunteerism in general appeared on the rise in the late 1990s. The government responded in 1998 with a new law to make it easier for citizens to organize nonprofit organizations. For the vast majority, Japan at the start of a new century remained a safe and livable society.

More than social ills, economic problems provided the major source of the widely held sense that Japan faced a systemic crisis. The recovery of 1995–96 came to a quick halt. A prolonged recession began the following year. Real GDP fell 2 percent from 1997 through 1998 and showed virtually zero growth in 1999 and 2000. Foreign observers wrote of Japan as "the system that soured" and described the 1990s as a "lost decade."[10] Many observers at home were no less gloomy (see Figure 17.2).

To address Japan's economic ills, the government took three important steps in the late 1990s. First, in November 1996 Prime Minister Hashimoto announced a com-prehensive program to deregulate financial markets, dubbed the "big bang." The as-sumption was that Japan's industry and technological progress were being obstructed by an inefficient financial system. Hashimoto's plan echoed similar programs imple-mented in the United States and Britain. It sought to ease complex regulations that hampered the banking, insurance, and securities industries.

Step two came in the fall of 1998, when the Diet passed the Financial Revitali-zation Law. This act created a Financial Reconstruction Commission (FRC) with a mandate to rebuild a banking system overwhelmed with bad debt. It was modeled on the American Resolution Trust Corporation of the 1980s. The FRC used public funds to take over insolvent banks and liquidate their bad debt. The Democratic Party, en-ergized by its summer election victory, played a significant role in negotiating with the LDP to draft the bill. This was a sign of the potential for a competitive party system to shape government policy. The law held promise of finally setting the banking system on a sound footing, although this would depend on the willingness of the commission directors to make aggressive use of their authority. For several years, authorities in fact remained reluctant to act. By 2001, the levels of bad debt held by major banks had scarcely diminished; by some accounts, debt had actually increased.

The third key state response to recession was a binge of deficit spending aimed at jump-starting the stagnant domestic economy. From 1997 to 2000, the government ran annual deficits of more than 8 percent of GDP. This spending prevented an even deeper recession, and by 2000, signs of an economic revival had appeared. Japan's "new economy" of high-tech and some manufacturing industries was growing briskly.

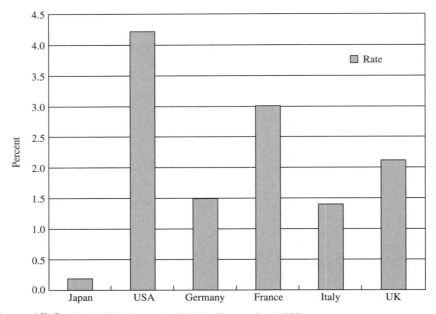

Figure 17.2   Real GDP Growth of Major Economies, 1999

Source: Comparative Economic and Financial Statistics, Japan and Other Major Countries (Tokyo: International Department, Bank of Japan, December 2000).

But the "old economy" sectors such as agriculture, transportation, retail sales, and heavy industries remained in decline, and domestic demand remained fairly weak. Electronic equipment companies, for example, saw labor productivity soar nearly 20 percent in 1999, while most other sectors experienced flat or declining efficiency. The gap between old and new economy sectors was deep.

Moreover, repeated fiscal deficits had piled up an extraordinary mountain of public debt. By the end of 2000 the sum of accumulated central and local government debt had surpassed 140 percent of GDP. No major economy had run such a proportion of debt for forty years. At the same time, the social security system was running a chronic deficit. It required major government transfers from general revenues to stay afloat. This cost would increase as the proportion of elderly continued to rise.

As the twenty-first century began, the government faced some very tough choices. It might take the politically tempting but economically risky step of encouraging moderate inflation. This would reduce the real burden of accumulated debt, as long as inflation did not spin out of control. It might also take the politically perilous steps of reducing expenditures, raising taxes, and restructuring the social security system. The prospect of continued stagnation and further banking crisis was real. And something like a public sector debt crisis loomed as an ominous possibility.[11]

While politicians pondered their options, the private sector faced great pressure to change as well. With the Japanese economy continuing to flounder, and the American economy continuing to grow smartly, at least through 2000, the rhetoric of the 1980s turned on its head. Observers no longer urged the United States, Europe, or the rest of the world to learn from Japan. Pundits in Japan and on Wall Street, in particular, rather urged Japan to adopt the so-called Anglo-American model. Managers were told that the shareholder should be king and that workers should be dismissed quickly when profits declined. Government was implored to limit regulations and enforce transparency and competition. The Japanese system had long taken a different approach. It stressed managerial autonomy rather than shareholder sovereignty. Personnel management was organization-oriented more than market-oriented. Rules were opaque and often informal. State regulation and guidance of the economy were extensive. Of course, Japan's economy had prospered grandly for forty years with these practices.[12]

As the twenty-first century began, despite a decade of weak performance and several years of pressure to reform, Japan's economic institutions had changed just modestly in the direction prescribed by free market reformers. Managers continued some moves toward greater flexibility, but these had been underway since the 1970s. Companies were relying more on temporary, part-time, and contract workers. As of 1999 more than one-quarter of all employees fell into these categories.[13] Corporations also continued to increase the proportion of employee pay that was linked to performance and to reduce the weight of seniority in setting pay and giving promotions.

But as hundreds of major firms announced plans to "restructure" themselves in the late 1990s, the lack of change was more impressive than any managerial or labor market revolution. Headlines blared news of plans to "reduce the work force at Company X by 20 percent" or "cut three thousand jobs at Company Y." But the fine print revealed that such cuts would be spread out over three to five years and would rely mainly on attrition and early retirement. In fact, of all those who left their jobs from 1993 through 1997, the vast majority retired or left of their own choice. Only 8 percent were "dismissed at the employer's convenience." This was lower than the level of involuntary dismissals during the oil-crisis recession of 1975.[14] Young workers moved around more than in the past, but Japan was unlikely to soon become a society of job-hoppers. A majority of companies in 2000 still set age limits on new hiring, a practice that was legal in Japan. Most would not look at a candidate older than forty.[15]

The move toward shareholder sovereignty was also limited. Observers in 2000 made much of the creation of new institutions to raise capital for young companies, such as NASDAQ Japan and the "Mothers" offshoot of the Tokyo stock exchange. But listings were limited. These exchanges did not grow quickly. Japanese businesses did not abandon wholesale the long-established practice of "cross-shareholding," by which allied companies held each other's shares through thick and thin to limit the control of outsiders. Despite extensive talk of the need for companies to emphasize return on equity, businesses were not giving dramatically more priority than in the past to shareholder dividends, as opposed to stabilizing employment or investing in research and development.[16]

Was the persistence of these practices of Japanese-style capitalism a sign of a structural paralysis in which entrenched interests prevented needed change? Such a harsh view seems partly justified. The government may well have manipulated statistical data on growth rates in the domestic economy in 1999–2000 to protect itself and build public confidence. Authorities surely downplayed the extent of the bad debt problem throughout the 1990s to help out leading banks and their customers. And it was a remarkable fact, given Japanese levels of education and popular interest in new technology, that in 2000 Japan ranked no better than thirteenth among industrialized nations in citizen access to the Internet. Only 21 percent of the population lived in "wired" households.[17] The major reason for this lag was probably the high cost of service, a result of the monopolistic structure of Japan's telecommunications system. The Japanese government appeared reluctant to change regulations that might allow domestic and foreign competitors to challenge the domination of the recently privatized giant NTT.

But the full picture was more complex. Practices and institutions under attack at the turn of the century had been lauded just a few years before as the secret to Japanese success. These included both long-term employment relations and the ability of managers to make costly investments on behalf of long-term growth, without constant pressure to satisfy the quarterly shareholder demand for profits. It is hard to imagine that practices that valued accumulated experience and long-term vision were in themselves impediments to success in the information-intensive economy of the twenty-first century. Japan's economic woes of the 1990s might have been above all the result of a series of disastrous macroeconomic policy decisions rather than the product of a fundamental systemic failure.

ISSUES FOR THE FUTURE

As the new century began, a variety of social, cultural, and international issues faced people in Japan, as around the world. For one, diversity in gender roles was greater than ever in the past, although the question of proper and acceptable roles for men and women remained contentious. Feminist writings reached wider audiences than in the past, in both the popular press as well as in academic circles. In the home, the divorce rate reached record levels, standing even with levels in France and Germany, although it was roughly half that of the United States. Some viewed more divorce as a sign of social breakdown. Others saw it a sign that women had been empowered. Divorces rose sharply among older couples. It is likely that legal changes making it easier for women to claim a share of property in divorce settlements encouraged this trend.[18]

In the schools, the year 1994 marked something of a turning point. The study of home economics was made compulsory for boys as well as girls. But in 1997 the Ministry of Education revealed its unease at the prospect of a more pluralistic view of family life when it censored the first textbooks prepared for co-ed home economics classes. The books had not, in the ministry's view, made it clear that heterosexual two-parent households were the preferable and proper structure for contemporary families.[19]

At work, opponents of sexual discrimination and harassment were less often ridiculed as cranky troublemakers, as they once had been. In a 1996 decision, the Tokyo District court awarded thirteen veteran female bank workers a total of nearly one million dollars to compensate for the "clear and extreme differences in promotions for men and women." The court concluded clearly, "The bank's personnel policies are definitely not permissible under current law."[20] A strong sign that the public now took sexual harassment seriously came in 1999. A young female campaign worker charged the well-known governor of Osaka, a former comedian named Yokoyama Knock, with making unwelcome advances as they were riding to attend a political engagement. The public was unwilling to laugh this off. Yokoyama admitted the charges and resigned his position. A criminal trial followed, and he was found guilty, sentenced to eighteen months in prison with a suspended sentence.

The Japanese government in the 1990s came to support a measure of increased gender equality. In 1995 the Diet passed a government bill to strengthen the Equal Employment Opportunity Law. It also created the Council for Gender Equality, one of whose members was a leading feminist scholar in the social policy field. In 1996 Prime Minister Hashimoto encouraged the council to draft the Basic Law for a Gender-Equal Society. This measure passed the Diet in 1999. The law offered a general commitment to enact measures that would enable men and women to participate as equals throughout society. Even some conservative leaders had come to think that gender equality, and fuller female participation in the work force, might be economically beneficial in a time of falling birthrates that were projected to lead to a labor shortage. But the belief remained powerful among many in the political and business elite that women should act mainly as good wives and mothers, while men should devote themselves to working to support their family. There was no guarantee that significant new policies would follow to give greater substance to the vision of a gender-equal society.[21]

A second issue for the future was the place of foreigners in Japanese society. During the labor-short boom years of the 1980s, the government opened the door slightly to immigration. A major revision of the immigrant law in 1990 allowed ethnic Japanese a preferential right to return from overseas. Thousands of Brazilian Japanese, in particular, took up the offer. Other foreigners came to Japan illegally in search of opportunities they could not find in their home countries of Iran, Bangladesh, China, and elsewhere in Asia. The migrant workers took jobs that native Japanese were now unwilling to perform, in particular manual labor dubbed "three-K" work: dangerous (*kiken*), dirty (*kitanai*), and difficult (*kitsui*). By the mid-1990s, authorities counted over 1.6 million foreign residents, legal and illegal, in Japan. The long-established communities of Korean and Chinese residents accounted for no more than six hundred thousand of this total. The majority, roughly one million, were relatively recent immigrants or visitors.

Even as the economy sagged throughout the 1990s and early 2000s, the number of immigrants continued to increase. Important questions remained. Would legal foreign residents, especially those with high skills and education, be given equality in job opportunities? One site of controversy was the school system, where foreign university professors complained of discriminatory treatment.[22] How generous would the government be in extending public services such as schooling and medical care to short-term migrants?

Media watchers criticized the tendency of the press to run negative stories that linked foreigners to crime. In April 2000 the nationalistic Tokyo governor Ishihara Shintarō offered a startling statement of fear of foreigners. In a speech to the Self Defense Forces, he told the troops to be ready to play a greater role in maintaining law and order within Japan because increased numbers of foreigners were committing crimes. He revived an early postwar term for Koreans in Japan and noted that in the event of a natural disaster such as an earthquake, "third-country people" might take advantage of the confusion to loot or harm Japanese people.[23] The echoes here of a rhetoric that tolerated the massacre of thousands of Koreans in just this circumstance in 1923 were unmistakable. In the controversy that followed, majority opinion roundly condemned Ishihara for his prejudice, but a significant minority shared his fears and saw nothing wrong with his statement. With the population declining and a labor shortage looming, the economy was likely to generate demand for far greater numbers of immigrant workers in the near future. The question of how people would responded to an increasingly multiethnic society remained to be answered.[24]

Equally uncertain was the future of Japan's global role. For over half a century, American troops had been stationed on Japanese soil in the face of significant misgivings and much strong opposition. The huge American presence in Okinawa was a particular sore point. In the 1990s three-quarters of the total American force in Japan was based there. The U.S. facilities covered one-fifth of the island. In 1995, three American servicemen kidnapped and raped a twelve-year-old Okinawan girl. This was among the most brutal of many crimes committed over the years by soldiers against civilians. It sparked some of the most vociferous anti-base protests in decades, both in Okinawa and on the main islands. The largest demonstrations drew eighty-five thousand people. American and Japanese officials scrambled with some success to mollify protestors over the following months and years. They developed plans to slightly reduce troop levels and shift some facilities to less populated areas of the island.

For Japanese citizens, the most persuasive reason for the United States–Japan alliance had long been to protect Japan from allegedly hostile communist regimes in the Soviet Union, China, and North Korea. The bases also served America's broader strategic goals, such as protection of oil supply lines from the Middle East to East Asia, which benefited Japan directly. Finally, more than fifty years after the end of World War II, Japan's Asian neighbors still expressed fear that Japan might rearm. The American military presence, in their view and that of American strategists, made this unnecessary and thus served, in a sense, to "contain" Japan even while protecting it.

The end of the Cold War undercut the argument that U.S. bases protected Japan from a communist threat. It helps explain the particular force of the anti-base protests of the mid-1990s. As moves toward reconciliation on the Korean peninsula gained force from the year 2000, the immediate military threat to Japan receded further. The American military presence on Japanese soil was certain to remain controversial.

Japan's own military role in the larger Asian region and beyond was a related matter of ongoing debate at home and abroad. After the Gulf War, the Japanese government authorized the participation of the Self-Defense Force (SDF) in peacekeeping operations of the United Nations. The first such SDF action came in Cambodia in 1992. Over the next four years, the SDF joined United Nations actions on four occasions, helping to supervise elections in Angola (1992), Mozambique (1993–95), and El Salvador (1994), as well as serving as observers of the truce on the Golan Heights between Israel and Syria (1996). These actions represented a significant expansion of Japan's international role.

Even so, the American government continued to pressure Japan to grant the SDF a more active role as military partner by expanding its mission beyond the narrow defense of the home islands. The Japanese government obliged in 1998 by writing more liberal "guidelines" for allowable SDF activity. According to the new guidelines, the SDF was to provide logistic support for American forces beyond Japan's borders in cases of "regional emergency." Newly authorized activities included inspection of third-party vessels as well as search-and-rescue missions of U.S. personnel or Japanese nationals abroad. In the wake of terrorist attacks on the United States on September 11, 2001, the Japanese government moved quickly—and in the face of considerable domestic opposition—to pass a new Anti-Terrorism Law enabling the SDF to join American operations in Afghanistan with various sorts of logistical support.

Despite their calls for a more forward Japanese military posture, Americans looked askance when Japanese officials sought a more forward economic role. Government leaders in 1997 proposed creating an Asian Monetary Fund to help Korea and other nations cope with their financial crisis, but the United States scornfully rejected the notion. This response revealed the ongoing tension between American desires to promote Japan as an ally while containing its military or economic power. Nonetheless, Japanese officials continued to pursue a more active foreign economic policy. They offered significant loan funding to help troubled business ventures survive throughout the region. National interest played a role because these funds often supported ventures linked to Japanese companies. But the loan terms were typically more generous than the aid provided by the American-dominated International Monetary Fund. Japan's more forward economic profile was generally welcomed by other Asian leaders.[25]

The subject of history itself remained one continuing impediment to this effort to build stable and constructive relationships throughout Asia. Ironically, as the war receded into the past, tensions came to the fore within Japan and abroad over historical understanding of Japanese imperialism and World War II. In 1991, renewed controversy erupted when three Korean former "comfort women," with support from feminists in Japan, brought legal suit against the Japanese government. The fact that brothels had been operated for the convenience of Japanese soldiers near the front lines in China and Southeast Asia was not in dispute. Nor was the fact that most of the "comfort women" were Korean. But the government continued to deny any official involvement of the military in setting up or supervising the brothels or in forcing women to work there. In early 1992, a Japanese historian uncovered government documents confirming that the military was closely involved in creating the wartime system of so-called comfort stations. The newly found evidence—together with evidence already available but not widely publicized—made it clear that the Japanese military played a direct role in setting up the comfort stations and that significant numbers of the women were slaves rather than prostitutes. Japanese Prime Minister Miyazawa Kiichi reversed the official position and admitted that the government had played a role in the system of sexual slavery. On a visit to Seoul in 1992 he offered an apology. Those surviving comfort women who came forward, as well as supporters in Japan and around the world, demanded compensation as well as an apology.

These and other charges of war crimes sparked a nationalist backlash over the course of the 1990s and into the new century. A new wave of "revisionist" historians condemned what they called a "masochist" historical consciousness that stressed the dark side of the Japanese past. Some went so far as to deny that the Nanjing Massacre of 1937–38 had taken place. They called for a history, in particular as taught in the schools, that would instill pride in the "Japanese people" by stressing achievements such as Japan's rapid emergence as an independent modern state. Echoing Hayashi Fusao's position in the 1960s, they characterized World War II as a noble endeavor to liberate Asia from the yoke of Western imperialism. They opposed teaching children about such subjects as the comfort women or massacres of civilians.

In 2001, the Association to Write New Textbooks wrote a textbook that took this narrowly nationalistic approach. The Japanese Ministry of Education forced the authors to tone down their rhetoric and correct factual errors in over one hundred places, but it ultimately approved the book for possible classroom use. Historians, teachers, and many citizens at home, as well as the public and the governments of China and South Korea in particular, sharply criticized this textbook and the government's decision to accept it. The first round of decisions by prefectural and municipal school boards came in the summer of 2001, and only a handful of schools (far less than 1 percent) actually adopted the text. But the issue of how to teach the past to young people in Japan was certain to remain controversial.

Such controversy over how to remember the bloody past of modern times was certainly a worldwide phenomenon. In an exhibit at the Smithsonian Museum featuring the airplane that dropped the bomb on Hiroshima, veterans' organizations in the United States in 1995 ultimately prevented a full discussion of the use of the atomic bombs. In Japan, against sharp criticism by many historians, organizations of war veterans and their kin in the 1990s pushed forward plans for the state-funded Memorial Hall for the War Dead with an exhibition that avoided discussion of Japan's wartime aggression. As the twenty-first century began, people in Japan were taking part in continued debate over how to characterize the modern history of nations and how to situate this as part of a global experience. How does one balance the desire to feel pride in one's heritage with the need to honestly examine inequality, injustice, and the operation of power in the past? And what, exactly, are the borders of any one person's heritage? Whether one considers the interaction and flow of ideas, of people, of goods, or of technologies, it is clear that themes of history and heritage cannot, in the end, be contained within national borders.

Appendix A
PRIME MINISTERS OF JAPAN, 1885–2001

Name of Prime Minister	Entered Office	Left Office
Itō Hirobumi	December 1885	April 1888
Kuroda Kiyotaka	April 1888	December 1889
Yamagata Aritomo	December 1889	May 1891
Matsukata Masayoshi	May 1891	August 1892
Itō Hirobumi	August 1892	September 1896
Matsukata Masayoshi	September 1896	January 1898
Itō Hirobumi	January 1898	June 1898
Ōkuma Shigenobu	June 1898	November 1898
Yamagata Aritomo	November 1898	October 1900
Itō Hirobumi	October 1900	June 1901
Katsura Tarō	June 1901	January 1906
Saionji Kimmochi	January 1906	July 1908
Katsura Tarō	July 1908	August 1911
Saionji Kimmochi	August 1911	December 1912
Katsura Tarō	December 1912	February 1913
Yamamoto Gonnohyōe	February 1913	April 1914
Ōkuma Shigenobu	April 1914	October 1916
Terauchi Masatake	October 1916	September 1918
Hara Kei (Takashi)	September 1918	November 1921
Takahashi Korekiyo	November 1921	June 1922
Katō Tomosaburō	June 1922	September 1923
Yamamoto Gonnohyōe	September 1923	January 1924
Kiyoura Keigo	January 1924	June 1924
Katō Kōmei (Takaaki)	June 1924	January 1926
Wakatsuki Reijirō	January 1926	April 1927
Tanaka Giichi	April 1927	July 1929
Hamaguchi Osachi	July 1929	April 1931
Wakatsuki Reijirō	April 1931	December 1931
Inukai Tsuyoshi	December 1931	May 1932
Saitō Makoto	May 1932	July 1934
Okada Keisuke	July 1934	March 1935
Hirota Kōki	March 1935	February 1937
Hayashi Senjūrō	February 1937	June 1937
Konoe Fumimaro	June 1937	January 1939

Name of Prime Minister	Entered Office	Left Office
Hiranuma Kiichirō	January 1939	August 1939
Abe Nobuyuki	August 1939	January 1940
Yonai Mitsumasa	January 1940	July 1940
Konoe Fumimaro	July 1940	October 1941
Tōjō Hideki	October 1941	July 1944
Koiso Kuniaki	July 1944	April 1945
Suzuki Kantarō	April 1945	August 1945

Postwar Prime Ministers, under Meiji Constitution	Entered Office	Left Office
Higashikuni Naruhiko	August 1945	October 1945
Shidehara Kijūrō	October 1945	May 1946
Yoshida Shigeru	May 1946	May 1947

Postwar Prime Ministers, under New Constitution	Entered Office	Left Office
Katayama Tetsu	May 1947	March 1948
Ashida Hitoshi	March 1948	October 1948
Yoshida Shigeru	October 1948	December 1954
Hatoyama Ichirō	December 1954	December 1956
Ishibashi Tanzan	December 1956	February 1957
Kishi Nobusuke	February 1957	July 1960
Ikeda Hayato	July 1960	November 1964
Satō Eisaku	November 1964	July 1972
Tanaka Kakuei	July 1972	December 1974
Miki Takeo	December 1974	December 1976
Fukuda Takeo	December 1976	December 1978
Ōhira Masayoshi	December 1978	July 1980
Suzuki Zenkō	July 1980	November 1982
Nakasone Yasuhiro	November 1982	November 1987
Takeshita Noboru	November 1987	June 1989
Uno Sōsuke	June 1989	August 1989
Kaifu Toshiki	August 1989	November 1991
Miyazawa Kiichi	November 1991	August 1993
Hosokawa Morihiro	August 1993	April 1994
Hata Tsutomu	April 1994	June 1994
Murayama Tomiichi	June 1994	January 1996
Hashimoto Ryūtarō	January 1996	July 1998
Obuchi Keizō	July 1998	April 2000
Mori Yoshihiro	April 2000	April 2001
Koizumi Junichirō	April 2001	

Appendix B
VOTE TOTALS AND SEATS BY PARTY, 1945–2000 LOWER HOUSE ELECTIONS

Election of April 10, 1946		
Party Name	**Votes (% of total)**	**Seats (% of total)**
Liberal Party (Jiyūtō)	13,506,000 (24.4)	140 (30.2)
Progressive Party (Shinpotō)	10,351,000 (18.7)	94 (20.3)
Japan Socialist Party (Nihon Shakaitō)	9,858,000 (17.8)	92 (19.8)
Co-operative Party (Kyōdōtō)	1,800,000 (3.2)	14 (3.0)
Japan Communist Party (Nihon Kyōsantō)	2,136,000 (3.8)	5 (1.1)
Independent	11,325,000 (20.4)	81 (17.4)
Others	6,473,000 (11.7)	38 (8.2)
Total	55,449,000	464

Election of April 25, 1947		
Party Name	**Votes (% of total)**	**Seats (% of total)**
Japan Socialist Party (Nihon Shakaitō)	7,176,000 (26.2)	143 (30.7)
Liberal Party (Jiyūtō)	7,356,000 (26.9)	131 (28.1)
Democratic Party (Minshutō)	6,840,000 (25.0)	121 (26.0)
People's Co-operative Party (Kokumin Kyōdōtō)	1,916,000 (7.0)	29 (6.2)
Japan Communist Party (Nihon Kyōsantō)	1,003,000 (3.7)	4 (0.8)
Independent	1,581,000 (5.8)	13 (2.8)
Others	1,490,000 (5.4)	25 (5.4)
Total	27,362,000	466

Election of January 23, 1949		
Party Name	**Votes (% of total)**	**Seats (% of total)**
Democratic Liberal Party (Minshujiyūtō)	13,420,000 (43.9)	264 (56.7)
Democratic Party (Minshutō)	4,798,000 (15.7)	69 (14.8)
Japan Socialist Party (Nihon Shakaitō)	4,130,000 (13.5)	48 (10.3)
Japan Communist Party (Nihon Kyōsantō)	2,985,000 (9.7)	35 (7.5)
People's Co-operative Party (Kokumin Kyōdōtō)	1,042,000 (3.4)	14 (3.0)
Labor Farmer Party (Rō-dōsha nōmintō)	607,000 (2.0)	7 (1.5)
Independent	2,008,000 (6.6)	12 (2.6)
Others	1,602,000 (5.2)	17 (3.6)
Total	30,593,000	466

Election of October 10, 1952		
Party Name	**Votes (% of total)**	**Seats (% of total)**
Liberal Party (Jiyūtō)	16,939,000 (47.9)	240 (51.5)
Reformist Party (Kaishintō)	6,429,000 (18.2)	85 (18.2)
Right Socialist Party (Nihon Shakaitō, Uha)	4,108,000 (11.6)	57 (12.2)
Left Socialist Party (Nihon Shakaitō, Saha))	3,399,000 (9.6)	54 (11.6)
Labor Farmer Party (Rō-dōsha nōmintō)	261,000 (0.7)	4 (0.9)
Japan Communist Party (Nihon Kyōsantō)	897,000 (2.6)	0 (0)
Independent	2,355,000 (6.7)	19 (4.1)
Others	949,000 (2.7)	7 (1.5)
Total	35,337,000	466

Election of April 19, 1953

Party Name	Votes (% of total)	Seats (% of total)
Yoshida Liberal Party (Jiyūtō [Yoshida-ha])	13,476,000 (39.0)	199 (42.7)
Reformist Party (Kaishintō)	6,186,000 (17.9)	76 (16.3)
Left Socialist Party (Nihon Shakaitō, Saha))	4,517,000 (13.1)	72 (15.4)
Right Socialist Party (Nihon Shakaitō, Uha))	4,678,000 (11.6)	66 (14.2)
Hatoyama Liberal Party (Jiyūtō [Hatoyama-ha])	3,055,000 (8.8)	35 (7.5)
Labor Farmer Party (Rōdōsha nōmintō)	359,000 (1.0)	5 (1.1)
Japan Communist Party (Nihon Kyōsantō)	656,000 (1.9)	1 (0.2)
Independent	1,524,000 (4.4)	11 (2.4)
Others	152,000 (0.4)	1 (0.2)
Total	34,602,000	466

Election of February 27, 1955

Party Name	Votes (% of total)	Seats (% of total)
Democratic Party (Minshutō)	13,536,000 (36.6)	185 (39.6)
Reformist Party (Kaishintō)	9,849,000 (26.6)	112 (24.0)
Left Socialist Party (Nihon Shakaitō, Saha)	5,683,000 (15.3)	89 (19.1)
Right Socialist Party (Nihon Shakaitō, Uha)	5,130,000 (13.9)	67 (14.3)
Labor Farmer Party (Rōdōsha nōmintō)	358,000 (1.0)	4 (0.9)
Japan Communist Party (Nihon Kyōsantō)	733,000 (2.0)	2 (0.4)
Independent	1,229,000 (3.3)	6 (1.3)
Others	497,000 (1.3)	2 (0.4)
Total	37,015,000	467

Election of May 22, 1958		
Party Name	Votes (% of total)	Seats (% of total)
Liberal Democratic Party (Jiyūminshutō)	22,977,000 (57.8)	287 (61.5)
Japan Socialist Party (Nihon Shakaitō)	13,094,000 (32.9)	166 (35.5)
Japan Communist Party (Nihon Kyōsantō)	1,012,000 (2.6)	1 (0.2)
Independent	2,381,000 (6.0)	12 (2.6)
Others	288,000 (0.7)	1 (0.2)
Total	39,752,000	467

Election of November 20, 1960		
Party Name	Votes (% of total)	Seats (% of total)
Liberal Democratic Party (Jiyūminshutō)	22,740,000 (57.6)	296 (63.4)
Japan Socialist Party (Nihon Shakaitō)	10,887,000 (27.6)	145 (31.0)
Democratic Socialist Party (Minshushakaitō)	3,464,000 (8.8)	17 (3.7)
Japan Communist Party (Nihon Kyōsantō)	1,157,000 (2.9)	3 (0.6)
Independent	1,119,000 (2.8)	5 (1.1)
Others	142,000 (0.3)	1 (0.2)
Total	39,509,000	467

Election of November 21, 1963		
Party Name	Votes (% of total)	Seats (% of total)
Liberal Democratic Party (Jiyūminshutō)	22,424,000 (54.7)	283 (60.7)
Japan Socialist Party (Nihon Shakaitō)	11,907,000 (29.0)	144 (30.8)
Democratic Socialist Party (Minshushakaitō)	3,023,000 (7.4)	23 (4.9)
Japan Communist Party (Nihon Kyōsantō)	1,646,000 (4.0)	5 (1.1)
Independent	1,956,000 (4.8)	12 (2.6)
Others	60,000 (0.1)	0 (0)
Total	41,017,000	467

Election of January 29, 1967		
Party Name	**Votes (% of total)**	**Seats (% of total)**
Liberal Democratic Party (Jiyūminshutō)	22,448,000 (48.8)	277 (57.0)
Japan Socialist Party (Nihon Shakaitō)	12,826,000 (27.9)	140 (28.8)
Democratic Socialist Party (Minshushakaitō)	3,404,000 (7.4)	30 (6.2)
Kōmei Party (Kōmeitō)	2,472,000 (5.4)	25 (5.1)
Japan Communist Party (Nihon Kyōsantō)	2,191,000 (4.8)	5 (1.0)
Independent	2,554,000 (5.5)	9 (1.9)
Others	101,000 (0.2)	0 (0)
Total	45,997,000	486

Election of December 27, 1969		
Party Name	**Votes (% of total)**	**Seats (% of total)**
Liberal Democratic Party (Jiyūminshutō)	22,382,000 (47.6)	288 (59.2)
Japan Socialist Party (Nihon Shakaitō)	10,074,000 (21.4)	90 (18.5)
Kōmei Party (Kōmeitō)	5,125,000 (10.9)	47 (9.7)
Democratic Socialist Party (Minshushakaitō)	3,637,000 (7.7)	31 (6.4)
Japan Communist Party (Nihon Kyōsantō)	3,199,000 (6.8)	14 (2.9)
Independent	2,493,000 (5.3)	16 (3.3)
Others	81,000 (0.2)	0 (0)
Total	46,990,000	486

Election of December 10, 1972		
Party Name	**Votes (% of total)**	**Seats (% of total)**
Liberal Democratic Party (Jiyūminshutō)	24,563,000 (46.8)	271 (55.2)
Japan Socialist Party (Nihon Shakaitō)	11,479,000 (21.9)	118 (24.0)
Japan Communist Party (Nihon Kyōsantō)	5,497,000 (10.5)	38 (7.7)
Kōmei Party (Kōmeitō)	4,437,000 (8.5)	29 (5.9)
Democratic Socialist Party (Minshushakaitō)	3,661,000 (7.0)	19 (3.9)
Independent	2,646,000 (5.0)	14 (2.9)
Others	143,000 (0.3)	2 (0.4)
Total	52,425,000	491

Election of December 5, 1976		
Party Name	**Votes (% of total)**	**Seats (% of total)**
Liberal Democratic Party (Jiyūminshutō)	23,654,000 (41.8)	249 (48.7)
Japan Socialist Party (Nihon Shakaitō)	11,713,000 (20.7)	123 (24.1)
Kōmei Party (Kōmeitō)	6,177,000 (10.9)	55 (10.8)
Democratic Socialist Party (Minshushakaitō)	3,554,000 (6.3)	29 (5.7)
Japan Communist Party (Nihon Kyōsantō)	5,878,000 (10.4)	17 (3.3)
New Liberal Club (Shin Jiyū Club)	2,364,000 (4.2)	17 (3.3)
Independent	3,227,000 (5.7)	21 (4.1)
Others	45,000 (0.1)	0 (0)
Total	56,613,000	511

Election of October 7, 1979		
Party Name	**Votes (% of total)**	**Seats (% of total)**
Liberal Democratic Party (Jiyūminshutō)	24,084,000 (44.6)	248 (48.6)
Japan Socialist Party (Nihon Shakaitō)	10,643,000 (19.7)	107 (20.9)
Kōmei Party (Kōmeitō)	5,283,000 (9.8)	57 (11.2)
Japan Communist Party (Nihon Kyōsantō)	5,626,000 (10.4)	39 (7.6)
Democratic Socialist Party (Minshushakaitō)	3,664,000 (6.8)	35 (6.3)
New Liberal Club (Shin Jiyū Club)	1,632,000 (3.0)	4 (0.7)
Social Democratic League (Shakaiminshurengō)	368,000 (0.7)	2 (0.4)
Independent	2,641,000 (4.9)	19 (3.7)
Others	69,000 (0.1)	0 (0)
Total	54,010,000	511

Election of June 22, 1980		
Party Name	**Votes (% of total)**	**Seats (% of total)**
Liberal Democratic Party (Jiyūminshutō)	28,262,000 (47.9)	284 (55.6)
Japan Socialist Party (Nihon Shakaitō)	11,401,000 (19.3)	107 (20.9)
Kōmei Party (Kōmeitō)	5,330,000 (9.0)	33 (6.5)
Democratic Socialist Party (Minshushakaitō)	3,897,000 (6.6)	32 (6.3)
Japan Communist Party (Nihon Kyōsantō)	5,804,000 (9.8)	29 (5.7)
New Liberal Club (Shin Jiyū Club)	1,766,000 (3.0)	12 (2.3)
Social Democratic League (Shakaiminshurengō)	402,000 (0.7)	3 (0.5)
Independent	2,057,000 (3.5)	11 (2.1)
Others	109,000 (0.2)	0 (0)
Total	59,029,000	511

Election of December 18, 1983		
Party Name	**Votes (% of total)**	**Seats (% of total)**
Liberal Democratic Party (Jiyūminshutō)	25,983,000 (45.8)	250 (48.9)
Japan Socialist Party (Nihon Shakaitō)	11,065,000 (19.5)	112 (21.9)
Kōmei Party (Kōmeitō)	5,746,000 (10.1)	58 (11.3)
Democratic Socialist Party (Minshushakaitō)	4,130,000 (7.3)	38 (7.4)
Japan Communist Party (Nihon Kyōsantō)	5,302,000 (9.3)	26 (5.1)
New Liberal Club (Shin Jiyū Club)	1,341,000 (2.4)	8 (1.6)
Social Democratic League (Shakaiminshurengō)	381,000 (0.7)	3 (0.6)
Independent	2,769,000 (4.9)	16 (3.1)
Others	62,000 (0.1)	2 (0.4)
Total	56,780,000	511

Election of July 6, 1986		
Party Name	**Votes (% of total)**	**Seats (% of total)**
Liberal Democratic Party (Jiyūminshutō)	29,875,000 (49.4)	300 (58.6)
Japan Socialist Party (Nihon Shakaitō)	10,412,000 (17.2)	85 (16.6)
Kōmei Party (Kōmeitō)	5,701,000 (9.4)	56 (10.9)
Japan Communist Party (Nihon Kyōsantō)	5,313,000 (8.8)	26 (5.1)
Democratic Socialist Party (Minshushakaitō)	3,896,000 (6.4)	26 (5.1)
New Liberal Club (Shin Jiyū Club)	1,115,000 (1.8)	6 (1.2)
Social Democratic League (Shakaiminshurengō)	500,000 (0.8)	4 (0.8)
Independent	3,515,000 (5.8)	9 (1.7)
Others	121,000 (0.2)	0 (0)
Total	60,449,000	512

Election of February 18, 1990		
Party Name	**Votes (% of total)**	**Seats (% of total)**
Liberal Democratic Party (Jiyūminshutō)	30,315,000 (46.1)	275 (53.7)
Japan Socialist Party (Nihon Shakaitō)	16,025,000 (24.4)	136 (26.6)
Kōmei Party (Kōmeitō)	5,243,000 (8.0)	45 (8.8)
Japan Communist Party (Nihon Kyōsantō)	5,227,000 (8.0)	16 (3.1)
Democratic Socialist Party (Minshushakaitō)	3,179,000 (4.8)	14 (2.7)
Social Democratic League (Shakaiminshurengō)	567,000 (0.9)	4 (0.8)
Independent	4,807,000 (7.3)	21 (4.1)
Others	58,000 (0.1)	0 (0)
Total	65,704,000	512

Election of July 18, 1993		
Party Name	**Votes (% of total)**	**Seats (% of total)**
Liberal Democratic Party (Jiyūminshutō)	23,000,000 (36.6)	223 (43.6)
Japan Socialist Party (Nihon Shakaitō)	9,687,000 (15.4)	70 (13.7)
Renewal Party (Shinseitō)	6,341,000 (10.1)	55 (10.8)
Kōmei Party (Kōmeitō)	5,114,000 (8.1)	51 (10.0)
Japan New Party (Nihon Shintō)	5,054,000 (8.0)	35 (6.8)
Japan Communist Party (Nihon Kyōsantō)	4,835,000 (7.7)	15 (2.9)
Democratic Socialist Party (Minshushakaitō)	2,206,000 (3.5)	15 (2.9)
New Harbinger Party (Shintō Sakigake)	1,658,000 (2.6)	13 (2.5)
Social Democratic League (Shakaiminshurengō)	461,000 (0.7)	4 (0.8)
Independent	4,385,000 (6.9)	30 (5.9)
Others	4,512,000 (7.1)	17 (3.3)
Total	62,804,000	511

Election of October 20, 1996		
Party Name	**Votes (% of total)**	**Seats (% of total)**
Liberal Democratic Party (Jiyūminshutō)	21,836,000 (38.6)	239 (47.8)
New Frontier Party (Shinshintō)	15,812,000 (28.0)	156 (31.2)
Democratic Party (Minshutō)	6,002,000 (10.6)	52 (10.4)
Japan Communist Party (Nihon Kyōsantō)	7,097,000 (12.6)	15 (3.0)
Social Democratic Party (Shakaiminshutō)	1,241,000 (2.2)	15 (3.0)
New Harbinger Party (Shintō Sakigake)	728,000 (13)	2 (0.4)
Democratic Reform League (Minkairen)	149,000 (0.3)	1 (0.2)
Independent	2,509,000 (4.4)	9 (1.8)
Others	1,110,000 (2.1)	0 (0)
Total	55,569,000	500

Election of June 25, 2000		
Party Name	Votes (% of total)	Seats (% of total)
Liberal Democratic Party (Jiyūminshutō)	25,733,000 (41.0)	233 (48.54)
Democratic Party (Minshutō)	17,323,000 (27.6)	127 (26.46)
New Komeitō (Shin Kōmeitō)	1,255,000 (2.0)	31 (6.46)
Liberal Party (Jiyūtō)	2,134,000 (3.4)	22 (4.58)
Japanese Communist Party (Nihon Kyōsantō)	7,594,000 (12.1)	20 (4.17)
Social Democratic Party (Shakaiminshutō)	2,385,000 (3.8)	19 (3.96)
Independent	3,075,000 (4.9)	15 (3.13)
Others	3,326,000 (5.3)	13 (2.7)
Total	62,764,000	480

Sources: Through 1996—*Asahi Nenkan*, various dates, as tabulated in J. A. A. Stockwin, *Governing Japan: Divided Politics in a Major Economy*, 3rd ed. (Oxford: Blackwell Publishers, 1999), pp. 158–61. Election of 2000—*Asahi Nenkan* (2000).

Notes

NOTES TO CHAPTER 1

1. Cited in Mikiso Hane, *Peasants, Rebels, and Outcastes: The Underside of Modern Japan* (New York: Pantheon Books, 1982), p. 8.
2. Engelbert Kaempfer, *Kaempfer's Japan*, ed. and trans. Beatrice M. Bodart Bailey (Honolulu: University of Hawaii Press, 1999), p. 271. Kaempfer was a German scholar who spent the years 1690 to 1692 with Dutch traders at their outpost in Nagasaki.
3. James Murdoch and George Sansom cited in George Elison, "The Cross and the Sword," in *Warlords, Artists, and Commoners: Japan in the Sixteenth Century*, ed. George Elison and Barwell L. Smith (Honolulu: University of Hawaii Press, 1981), pp. 67–68.
4. A. L. Sadler, *The Maker of Modern Japan: The Life of Tokugawa Ieyasu* (1937; reprint, Rutland, Vt.: Charles E. Tuttle Company, 1984), p. 25.
5. With the division of some domains and promotion of some direct vassals to daimyō status, the number of daimyō increased over time, stabilizing at about 260 in the eighteenth century.
6. A *koku* is a unit of measure equivalent to about 180 liters.
7. *The Journal of Townsend Harris* (Tokyo: Kinkōdō Shoseki, 1913), pp. 468–80.
8. James L. McClain, *Kanazawa: A Seventeenth-Century Japanese Castle Town* (New Haven, Conn.: Yale University Press, 1982), p. 151.
9. The regulations also had an unintended consequence important to historians. Like the data stored in parishes of early modern Europe, the population records collected in Japan's temple registers provided the raw materials in recent decades for sophisticated analysis of demographic and social history.
10. Bob Tadashi Wakabayashi, *Anti-Foreignism and Western Learning in Early-Modern Japan: The New Theses of 1825* (Cambridge: Harvard Council on East Asian Studies, 1986), p. 149.
11. John W. Hall, "Rule by Status in Tokugawa Japan," *Journal of Japanese Studies* 1, no. 1 (Fall 1974): 39–49.

NOTES TO CHAPTER 2

1. See John W. Hall, "The Castle Town and Japan's Modern Urbanization," in *Studies in the Institutional History of Early Modern Japan*, ed. John W. Hall and Marius Jansen (Princeton, N.J.: Princeton University Press, 1968).
2. Cited in Michael Cooper, *They Came to Japan: An Anthology of European Reports on Japan, 1543–1640* (Berkeley: University of California Press, 1965), p. 292.
3. All quotes are taken from Yasumi Roan, "Ryokō Yojinshū," as translated and introduced in Constantine N. Vaporis, "Caveat Viator: Advice to Travelers in the Edo Period," *Monumenta Nipponica* 44, no. 4 (Winter 1989): 461–83.

4.   Thomas C. Smith, *Native Sources of Japanese Industrialization, 1750–1920* (Berkeley: University of California Press, 1988), p. 51.

5.   For a discussion of literacy rates, see Ronald Dore, *Education in Tokugawa Japan* (Berkeley: University of California Press, 1965).

6.   Smith, *Native Sources*, pp. 20–21, 46–47.

7.   See Thomas C. Smith, *Nakahara: Family Farming and Population in a Japanese Village, 1717–1830* (Stanford, Calif.: Stanford University Press, 1977). A review of this book by Daniel Scott Smith in *Journal of Japanese Studies* 5, no. 1 (Winter 1979) offers some alternative interpretations of the data.

8.   Statement by Sugita Genpaku, cited in Harold Bolitho, "The Tempō Crisis," in *The Cambridge History of Japan*, vol. 5, *The Nineteenth Century*, ed. Marius Jansen (Cambridge: Cambridge University Press, 1989), p. 128.

9.   Cited in Smith, *Native Sources* pp. 25–26.

10.   Cited in Smith, *Native Sources* p. 29.

11.   Stephen Vlastos, *Peasant Protests and Uprisings in Tokugawa Japan* (Berkeley: University of California Press, 1986), p. 46. See also James W. White, *Ikki: Social Conflict and Political Protest in Early Modern Japan* (Ithaca, N.Y.: Cornell University Press, 1995), p. 157.

12.   Jennifer Robertson, "The Shingaku Woman," in *Recreating Japanese Women, 1600–1945*, ed. Gail Bernstein (Berkeley: University of California Press, 1991), p. 91.

13.   Kathleen S. Uno, "Women and Changes in the Household Division of Labor," in *Recreating Japanese Women*, p. 33.

14.   Uno, "Women and Changes in the Household Division of Labor," cites Isabella Bird, *Unbeaten Tracks in Japan* (New York: G.P. Putnam, 1880).

NOTES TO CHAPTER 3

1.   For more on this topic, see Herman Ooms, *Tokugawa Ideology Early Constructs, 1570–1680* (Princeton, N.J.: Princeton University Press, 1985).

2.   Samuel H. Yamashita, "The Writings of Ogyū Sorai," in *Confucianism and Tokugawa Culture*, ed. Peter Nosco. (Princeton, N.J.: Princeton University Press, 1984), pp. 161–165.

3.   Tetsuo Najita, *Visions of Virtue: The Kaitokudō Merchant Academy of Osaka* (Chicago: University of Chicago Press, 1987), pp. 1–17.

4.   Cited in Haruo Shirane, *Traces of Dreams: Landscape, Cultural Memory, and the Poetry of Basho* (Stanford, Calif.: Stanford University Press, 1998), p. 13.

5.   Cited in *Chushingura: The Treasury of Loyal Retainers*, trans. Donald Keene (New York: Columbia University Press, 1971), pp. 2–3.

6.   Thomas C. Smith, " 'Merit' as Ideology in the Tokugawa Period," ch. 7 in *Native Sources of Japanese Industrialization, 1750–1920* (Berkeley: University of California Press, 1988), pp. 156–172.

7.   Kate Wildman Nakai, "Tokugawa Confucian Historiography," in *Confucianism and Tokugawa Culture*, ed. Peter Nosco, (Princeton, N.J.: Princeton University Press, 1984), p. 86.

8.   Tsuji Tatsuya, "Politics in the Eighteenth Century," in *The Cambridge History of Japan*, vol. 4, ed. John W. Hall (Cambridge: Cambridge University Press, 1991), pp. 468–469.

9.   Kären Wigen, *The Making of a Japanese Periphery* (Berkeley: University of California Press, 1995), p. 169.

10.   Peter F. Kornicki, *The Book in Japan: A Cultural History from the Beginnings to the Nineteenth Century* (Leiden: Brill, 1998), pp. 300–306.

NOTES TO CHAPTER 4

1. Harold Bolitho, "The Tempō Crisis," in *Cambridge History of Japan*, vol. 5, *The Nineteenth Century*, ed. Marius Jansen (Cambridge: Cambridge University Press, 198–9), p. 157.

2. Edward Yorke McCauley, *With Perry in Japan: The Diary of Edward Yorke McCauley*, ed. Allan B. Cole (Princeton, N.J.: Princeton University Press, 1942), pp. 98–99.

3. McCauley, *With Perry in Japan.*

4. William G. Beasley, ed., *Select Documents on Japanese Foreign Policy, 1853–1868* (London: Oxford University Press, 1955), p. 102.

5. Patricia Sippel, "Popular Protest in Early Modern Japan: The Bushū Outburst," *Harvard Journal of Asiatic Studies* 37, no. 2 (1977): 273–322.

6. Cited in Anne Walthall, *The Weak Body of a Useless Woman: Matsuo Taseko and the Meiji Restoration* (Chicago: University of Chicago Press, 1998), p. 98.

7. Cited in George Wilson, *Patriots and Redeemers in Japan: Motives in the Meiji Restoration* (Chicago: University of Chicago Press, 1992), pp. 105–6.

NOTES TO CHAPTER 5

1. Basil Hall Chamberlain, *Things Japanese* (London: K. Paul, Trench, Trubner & Co., Ltd., 1891), p. 1.

2. Historian Thomas C. Smith has written a wonderful short essay on this topic: "Japan's Aristocratic Revolution"; see in Thomas C. Smith, *Native Sources of Japanese Industrialization 1750 to 1920* (Berkeley: University of California Press, 1988).

3. Yokoyama Toshio, *Japan in the Victorian Mind: A Study of Stereotyped Images of a Nation 1850–80* (Houndmills, Basingstoke, Hampshire: Macmillan, 1987), p. 109.

4. Tokutomi Kenjirō (penname, Roka), *Footprints in the Snow*, trans. Kenneth Strong (New York: Pegasus Books, 1970), p. 107. Originally published as *Omoide no ki*, 1901.

5. Tokutomi, *Footprints in the Snow*, p. 107.

6. Takeshi Fujitani, *Splendid Monarchy* (Berkeley: University of California Press, 1996), p. 36.

7. Kido Kōin, *The Diary of Kido Kōin*, vol. 2, Sidney D. Brown, trans. (Tokyo: Tokyo University Press, 1982)

8. Stephen J. Ericson, *The Sound of the Whistle: Railroads and the State in Meiji Japan* (Cambridge: Harvard Council on East Asian Studies Monographs, 1996), pp. 66–73.

9. The Ōkubo quote is cited in Sidney D. Brown, "Ōkubo Toshimichi: His Political and Economic Policies in Early Meiji Japan," *Journal of Asian Studies* Vol. 21, No. 2 (February 1963), p. 194. The statement on locks was made by Maeda Masano, cited in Thomas Smith, *Political Change and Industrial Development in Japan: Government Enterprise, 1868–1880* (Stanford: Stanford University Press, 1955), p. 39.

10. On the Taiwan expedition and the plan for colonization, see Robert Eskildsen, "Of Civilization and Savages: The Mimetic Imperialism of Japan's 1874 Expedition to Taiwan," *American Historical Review*, 107, no. 2 (April 2002): 388–418

11. For an interesting account of peoples on Japan's northern frontier, see Tessa Morris-Suzuki, "Becoming Japanese: Imperial Expansion and Identity Crises in the Early Twentieth Century," in *Japan's Competing Modernities: Issues in Culture and Democracy: 1900–1930*, ed. Sharon Minichiello pp. 157–80. (Honolulu: University of Hawaii Press, 1998)

12. One historian has suggestively called this a revolution of the "service intelligentsia." Thomas Huber, *The Revolutionary Origins of Modern Japan* (Stanford, Calif.: Stanford University Press, 1981).

NOTES TO CHAPTER 6

1. Furushima Toshio, *Nihon hōken nōgyōshi* (Tokyo: Kowa Shobo, 1947), p. 83.

2. Bob T. Wakabayashi, *Anti-Foreignism and Western Learning in Early Modern Japan: The New Theses of 1825* (Cambridge: Harvard Council on East Asian Studies Monographs, 1986), p. 211.

3. Soyejima Taneomi et al., "Memorial on the Establishment of a Representative Assembly," in *Japanese Government Documents*, ed. W. W. McLaren, published in *Transactions of the Asiatic Society of Japan* 42, Part 1 (1914) pp. 426–432.

4. Irokawa Daikichi, *The Culture of the Meiji Period* (Princeton, N.J.: Princeton University Press, 1985), p. 101.

5. Irokawa, *Culture of the Meiji Period*, p. 111.

6. Cited in Stephen Vlastos, "Opposition Movements in Early Meiji," in *The Cambridge History of Japan*, vol. 5, *The Nineteenth Century*, ed. Marius Jansen (Cambridge: Cambridge University Press, 1989), p. 411.

7. Cited in Richard Devine, "The Way of the King," *Monumenta Nipponica* (Spring 1979): 53. vol. 34, No. 1.

8. Cited in Masao Miyoshi, *As We Saw Them: The First Japanese Embassy to the United States (1860)* (Berkeley: University of California Press, 1979), p. 71.

9. These various essays are available in William Braisted, ed. and trans., *Meiroku Zasshi: Journal of the Japanese Enlightenment* (Cambridge: Harvard University Press, 1976).

10. Braisted, *Meiroku Zasshi*, p. 395, quotes Sakatani Shiroshi, "On Concubines," March 1, 1875.

11. Cited in Sharon Seivers, *Flowers in Salt* (Stanford, Calif.: Stanford University Press, 1983), p. 36.

12. Inoue Kiyoshi, *Jōyaku kaisei: Meiji no minzoku mondai* (Tokyo: Iwanami shoten, 1955), p. 117.

13. The original seven oligarchs (*genrō*) were Itō Hirobumi, Kuroda Kiyotaka, Matsukata Masayoshi, Ōyama Iwao, Saigō Tsugumichi, Yamagata Aritomo, and Inoue Kaoru. In the early 1900s, Katsura Tarō and Saionji Kimmochi were added to their ranks.

NOTES TO CHAPTER 7

1. See James Nakamura, *Agricultural Production and the Economic Development of Japan, 1873–1922* (Princeton, N.J.: Princeton University Press, 1966), and Henry Rosovsky, "Rumbles in the Rice Fields," *Journal of Asian Studies* (February 1968): 347–60. vol. 27, No. 2

2. Cited in Eleanor Hadley, *Antitrust in Japan* (Princeton, N.J.: Princeton University Press, 1970), p. 35.

3. Alexander Gerschenkron, *Economic Backwardness in Historical Perspective* (Cambridge: Harvard University Press, 1962), ch. 1, pp. 5–30.

4. For a more detailed account, see Steven J. Ericson, *The Sound of the Whistle: Railroads and the State in Meiji Japan* (Cambridge: Harvard Council on East Asian Studies, 1996).

5. Shibusawa Eiichi and Morimura Ichizaemon, both cited in Byron Marshall, *Capitalism and Nationalism in Japan* (Stanford, Calif.: Stanford University Press, 1967), pp. 35–36.

6. This report is cited in Hazama Hiroshi, *Nihon rōmu kanri shi kenkyū* (Tokyo: Ochanomizu shobo, 1978), p. 277.

7. E. Patricia Tsurumi, *Factory Girls: Women in the Thread Mills of Meiji Japan* (Princeton, N.J.: Princeton University Press, 1990), pp. 93, 97, 99.

8. Thomas C. Smith, *Native Sources of Japanese Industrialization 1750–1920* (Berkeley: University of California Press, 1988), p. 257.

9. Cited in Andrew Gordon, *The Evolution of Labor Relations in Japan* (Cambridge: Harvard Council on East Asian Studies, 1985), p. 83.

10. Donald Roden, *Schooldays in Imperial Japan: A Study in the Culture of a Student Elite* (Berkeley: University of California Press, 1980), pp. 165–73.

11. William P. Malm, "Modern Music of Meiji Japan," in *Tradition and Modernization in Japanese Culture*, ed. Donald Shively (Princeton, N.J.: Princeton University Press, 1971), p. 259–77.

12. John M. Rosenfield, "Western Style Painting in the Early Meiji Period and Its Critics," in *Tradition and Modernization in Japanese Culture*, pp. 181–219.

13. See Stephen Vlastos, *Mirror of Modernity: Invented Traditions of Modern Japan* (Berkeley: University of California Press, 1998).

14. See Irwin Scheiner, *Christian Converts and Social Protest in Meiji Japan* (Berkeley: University of California Press, 1970).

15. Statement by Tanabashi Ichirō, cited in Kenneth Pyle, *The New Generation in Meiji Japan: Problems of Cultural Identity, 1885–1895* (Stanford, Calif.: Stanford University Press, 1969), p. 66.

NOTES TO CHAPTER 8

1. For an interesting discussion of this topic, see David Howell, "Visions of the Future in Meiji Japan," in *Historical Perspectives on Contemporary East Asia*, ed. Merle Goldman and Andrew Gordon (Cambridge, Harvard University Press, 2000).

2. The *Times*, April 20, 1895, p. 7.

3. See Carol Gluck, *Japan's Modern Myths: Ideology in the Late Meiji Period* (Princeton, N.J.: Princeton University Press, 1985), pp. 135–36.

4. Cited in Gluck, *Japan's Modern Myths*, p. 137.

5. Cited in Howell, "Visions of the Future," p. 117.

6. See William Lockwood, *The Economic Development of Japan* (Princeton, N.J.: Princeton University Press, 1968), ch. 6.

7. Known remittances from Hawaii alone were 1.6 percent of Japanese exports. If we assume that some remittances were hidden from government statisticians and that a comparable amount came from emigrants to the continental United States, the total was over 3 percent. See Suzuki Jōji, *Nihonjin dekasegi imin* (Tokyo: Heibonsha, 1992), p. 67.

8. See Akira Iriye, *Pacific Estrangement: Japanese and American Expansionism, 1897–1911* (Cambridge: Harvard University Press, 1972), ch. 5.

9. Cited in J. M. Winter, "The Webbs and the non-White World: A Case of Socialist Racialism," *Journal of Contemporary History* (January 1974): Vol. 9. No. 1. 181–92.

10. Bob Tadashi Wakabayashi, *Anti-Foreignism and Western Learning in Early-Modern Japan: The New Theses of 1825* (Cambridge: Harvard Council on East Asian Studies, 1986) p. 149.

11. Hara's given name can be read as "Takashi" or as "Kei." He did not become president of the Seiyūkai until 1914, but from 1904 he was the de facto leader in the Diet, with Saionji presiding in the formal role of party president.

12. Tetsuo Najita, *Hara Kei and the Politics of Compromise* (Cambridge: Harvard University Press, 1967).

13. Natsume Soseki, *Kokoro* (New York: Regnery, 1957), p. 245.

14. Cited in Tetsuo Najita, *Hara Kei in the Politics of Compromise*, p. 147.

15. Tetsuo, *Hara Kei in the Politics of Compromise*, quoting Abe Shinnosuke.

16. Cited in Andrew Gordon, *Labor and Imperial Democracy in Prewar Japan* (Berkeley: University of California Press, 1991), pp. 106–7.

17. Miyachi Masato, *Nichiro sengo seijishi kenkyū* (Tokyo: Tokyo University Press, 1973), p. 226.

18. Vera Mackie, *Creating Socialist Women in Japan: Gender, Labour and Activistm, 1900–1937* (Cambridge: Cambridge University Press, 1997), pp. 60–62.

19. *Shakai shinbun*, March 8, 1908, p. 4, cited in Gordon, *Labor and Imperial Democracy*, pp. 74–75.

20. Cited in Matsumoto Gappei, *Nihon shakaishugi engeki shi* (Tokyo: Chikuma shobō, 1975), p. 406.

21. Sharon Nolte and Sally Hastings, "The Meiji State's Policy toward Women," in *Recreating Japanese Women*, ed. Gail Bernstein (Berkeley: University of California Press, 1991), pp. 163–64.

22. Cited in Richard Smethurst, *A Social Basis for Prewar Japanese Militarism: The Army and the Rural Community* (Berkeley: University of California Press, 1974), p. vii.

23. Miyachi Masato, *Nichiro sengo seijishi kenkyū* (Tokyo: Tokyo University Press, 1973), p. 24.

24. From "My Individualism," a speech given on November 25, 1914, cited in Natsume Soseki, *Kokoro: A Novel and Selected Essays* (Lanhan, Md.: Madison Books, 1992), p. 313.

NOTES TO CHAPTER 9

1. Industrial production figures are for plants with five or more operatives. See William Lockwood, *The Economic Development of Japan: Growth and Structural Change* (Princeton, N.J.: Princeton University Press, 1968), pp. 38–39.

2. Lockwood, *The Economic Development of Japan*, pp. 39, 56.

3. For an analysis of this problem, see Hugh T. Patrick, "The Economic Muddle of the 1920s," in *Dilemmas of Growth in Prewar Japan*, ed. James Morley (Princeton, N.J.: Princeton University Press, 1971), pp. 211–66.

4. Edward Seidensticker, *Low City, High City, Tokyo from Edo to the Earthquake* (New York: Knopf, 1983), pp. 3–7, for an English language account. He notes that cooking fires were not the sole cause of the conflagrations. Chemicals and electrical wiring were also culprits.

5. The words of the assassin of Mitsui Trading Company's CEO, Dan Takuma, in 1932. See John G. Roberts, *Mitsui: Three Centuries of Japanese Business* (New York: Weatherhill, 1973), p. 276.

6. See Ann Waswo, *Japanese Landlords: The Decline of a Rural Elite* (Berkeley: University of California Press, 1977) pp. 99, 108–9, and Nakamura Masanori, "Daikyōkō to nōson mondai," in *Iwanami kōza: Nihon rekishi, 19* (Tokyo: Iwanami shoten, 1976), p. 145.

7. See Ronald P. Dore, "The Meiji Landlord: Good or Bad," *Journal of Asian Studies* 18, no. 3 (May 1959): 343–355.

8. On the attitudes toward empire of landlords and the rural population, see Michael Lewis, *Becoming Apart: National Power and Local Politics in Toyama, 1868–1945* (Cambridge: Harvard University Asia Center, 2000).

9. Nagatsuka Takashi, *The Soil: A Portrait of Rural Life in Meiji Japan*, trans. Ann Waswo (Berkeley: University of California Press, 1993), p. 47.

10. Ann Waswo, *Modern Japanese Society, 1868–1994* (Oxford: Oxford University Press, 1996), p. 66.

11. Author's interview with Hideji Kamimura, October 14, 1992.

12. Kobayashi Takiji, *The Absentee Landlord* (Tokyo: University of Tokyo Press, 1973), p. 147.

13. Waswo, *Japanese Landlords*, pp. 99, 108–09. Tenants won all or part of their demands in 74 percent of the disputes.

14. About 280,000 of 700,000 employed persons. The total population of Tokyo at the time was slightly under two million.

15. They were considered family labor and were not counted in these surveys, which did, however, count female factory workers. This means that the total of 41 percent in the "trading and merchant" category undercounts the actual proportion.

16. Sheldon Garon, *Molding Japanese Minds* (Princeton, N.J.: Princeton University Press, 1997), pp. 52–57.

17. Andrew Gordon, *Evolution of Labor Relations in Japan* (Cambridge: Harvard Council on East Asian Studies, 1985), pp. 83, 85. Cites Kobayashi Sakutarō of Shibaura Engineering Works in *Taiheiyō shōkō sekai*, Nov. 15, 1908, p. 42, and *Jitsugyō shōnen*, Sept. 1, 1908, p. 9.

18. Matsunari Yoshie et al., *Nihon no sarariiman* (Tokyo: Aoki shoten, 1957), p. 31.

19. Matsunari et al., *Nihon no sarariiman*, p. 35.

20. Matsunari et al., *Nihon no sarariiman*, pp. 27–31. Margit Nagy, "Middle Class Working Women during the Interwar Years," in *Re-creating Japanese Women, 1600–1945*, ed. Gail Bernstein (Berkeley: University of California Press, 1991), pp. 199–216.

21. Takeuchi Yō, "Sarariiman to iu shakaiteki hyōshō," *Nihon bunka no shakaigaku: Gendai shakaigaku* 23 (1996): 132, cites Maeda Hajime, *Sarariiman monogatari* (Tokyo: Tōyō keizai shuppan, 1928), pp. 1–2, for the wages of male clerks. For wages of factory workers, see Naimushō tōkei kyoku, *Rōdō tōkei jitchi chōsa hōkoku*, vol. 4 1927, (reprint, Tokyo: Kōscikan, 1970) p. 6.

22. Matsunari et al., *Nihon no sarariiman*, pp. 46–57, on male and female organizing efforts.

23. From *Sata Ineko shū*, vol. 25 of *Gendai Nihon no bungaku* (Tokyo: Gakujutsu kenkyusho, 1971), pp. 255–56.

24. Cited in Watanabe Etsuji and Suzuki Yūko, eds., *Tatakai ni ikite: senzen jujin rōdō e no shōgen* (Tokyo: Domesu shuppan, 1980), p. 206.

25. Nihon rōdō undō shiryō hensan iinkai, ed., *Nihon rōdō undō shiryō*, vol. 10 (Tokyo: Tokyo University Press, 1975), p. 122.

26. Cited in Gordon, *Evolution of Labor Relations in Japan*, p. 36.

27. Cited in Gordon, *Evolution of Labor Relations in Japan*, pp. 85–86.

28. Cited in Andrew Gordon, *Labor and Imperial Democracy in Prewar Japan* (Berkeley: University of California Press, 1991), p. 40.

29. Stephen Large, *The Rise of Labor in Japan: The Yūaikai* (Tokyo: Sophia University Press, 1972), p. 142.

30. Nihon rōdō undō shiryō hensan iinkai, ed, *Nihon rōdō undō shiryō*, vol. 10, p. 440.

31. Nihon rōdō undō shiryō hensan iinkai, ed, *Nihon rōdō undō shiryō*, vol. 10, p. 424. This was the peak in percentage of the work force (7.9 percent). In absolute numbers, the peak was 1936, when 420,600 were enrolled in unions (6.9 percent).

32. In the United States, about 13 percent of the nonagricultural work force had joined unions by early 1935 prior to the grant of legal protection under the Wagner Act.

33. Thomas C. Smith, *The Native Origins of Japanese Industrialization* (Berkeley: University of California Press, 1988); pp. 236–270.

34. Cited in Gordon, *Evolution of Labor Relations in Japan*, p. 146.

35. A low estimate of the death toll is 2,700, the result of Yoshino Sakuzō's investigation. Official Korean sources calculate a higher figure of 6,400. The Japanese Ministry of Justice reported only 243 deaths, unquestionably far too low. See Kang Tok-san, *Kantō daishinsai*

(Tokyo: Chūō Kōronsha, 1975), on numbers killed. For newspaper reports, see *Kantō daishinsai to chosenjin*, vol. 6 of *Gendai shi shiryo*, Part I (Tokyo: Misuzu Shobo, 1963). Changsoo Lee and George Devos, *Koreans in Japan* (Berkeley: University of California Press, 1981), p. 23, on the police atrocities.

36. On the department store, see Louise Young, "Marketing the Modern: Departments Stores, Consumer Culture, and the New Middle Class in Interwar Japan," *International Labor and Working Class History* 55 (Spring 1999): 52–70.

37. Young, "Marketing the Modern," p. 56.

38. Takeuchi, "Sarariiman," p. 127.

39. Ariyoshi Hiroyuki and Hamaguchi Haruhiko, eds., *Nihon no shin chūkansō* (Tokyo: Waseda University Press, 1982), p. 1.

40. Laurel Rasplica Todd, "Yosano Akiko and the Taisho Debate over the 'New Woman,' " in *Re-creating Japanese Women*, pp. 175–98.

41. Miriam Silverberg, "The Modern Girl as Militant," in *Re-creating Japanese Women*, pp. 239–66; p. 242 for citation to "legs."

42. Henry DeWitt Smith II, *Japan's First Student Radicals* (Cambridge: Harvard University Press, 1972), p. 137.

43. Matsunari et al, *Nihon no sarariiman*, pp. 44–45, cites *Tokyo Asahi Shinbun*, Feb. 17, 1918. *Mochi* are sticky rice cakes traditionally prepared for the New Year holiday.

44. Takeuchi, "Sarariiman," p. 131. Tanuma Hajime, *Gendai no chūkan kaikyū* (Tokyo: Ōtsuki shoten, 1958), p. 6.

45. *Hara Kei nikki*, June 13, 1910, cited in Ariyoshi and Hamaguchi, eds., *Nihon no shin chūkansō*, p. 4.

46. Yoshino Shinji, *Rōdō hōsei kōwa* (Tokyo: Kokumin daigaku kai, 1925), p. 14.

47. Miriam Silverberg, "The Modern Girl as Militant," pp. 248, 258–59, 264.

48. Garon, *Molding Japanese Minds*, pp. 60, 71.

49. Garon, *Molding Japanese Minds*, pp. 73–74.

50. Inagaki Tatsurō and Shitamura Toshio, eds. *Nihon bungaku no rekishi*, vol. 11 (Tokyo: Kadokawa Shoten, 1968), p. 364.

51. Gregory J. Kasza, *The State and the Mass Media in Japan* (Berkeley: University of California Press, 1988), p. 88.

52. On this topic, see Harry D. Harootunian, *Overcome by Modernity: History, Culture and Community in Interwar Japan* (Princeton, N.J.: Princeton University Press, 2000).

NOTES TO CHAPTER 10

1. See Hara Takeshi, *Taishō Tennō* (Tokyo: Asahi shinbunsha, 2000), for an important revision of the standard view that the Taishō monarch was sickly and mentally disturbed for his entire life. For the Maruyama recollection, see p. 11.

2. Cited in Andrew Gordon, *Labor and Imperial Democracy in Prewar Japan* (Berkeley: University of California Press, 1993) p. 56.

4. John W. Dower, *Embracing Defeat: Japan in the Wake of World War II* (New York: W.W. Norton, 1999), pp. 314–15.

5. See Herbert Bix, *Hirohito and the Making of Modern Japan* (New York: HarperCollins, 2000), Part I, on the education and worldview of the young emperor.

6. Edward Behr, *Hirohito* (New York: Vintage, 1990), p. 65; Bix, *Hirohito and the Making of Modern Japan*, pp. 214–20.

7. Hugh Byas, *Government by Assassination* (New York: A.A. Knopf, 1942).

8. Gordon, *Labor and Imperial Democracy* p. 136.

9. See Vera Mackie, *Creating Socialist Women in Japan: Gender, Labour, and Activism, 1900–1937* (New York: Cambridge University Press, 1997). Also, Laura Rasplica Rodd, "The Taishō Debate over the 'New Woman,' " in *Recreating Japanese Women, 1600–1945*, ed. Gail Bernstein (Berkeley: University of California Press, 1991), p. 194, and E. Patricia Tsurumi, "Visions of Women and the New Society in Conflict: Yamakawa Kikue versus Takamure Itsue," in *Japan's Competing Modernities: Issues in Culture and Democracy, 1900–1930*, ed. Sharon Minichiello (University of Hawaii Press, 1998), pp. 335–57.

10. See Tetsuo Najita, "Some Reflections on Idealism in the Political Thought of Yoshino Sakuzō," in *Japan in Crisis: Essays on Taishō Democracy*, ed. Bernard S. Silberman and H.D. Harootunian. (Princeton, N.J.: Princeton University Press, 1974), p. 56.

11. Eguchi Keiichi, ed., *Shimupojiumu Nihon rekishi: Taishō demokurashii* (Tokyo: Gakuseisha, 1976), p. 129, quotes Yokota.

12. Yoshimi Kaneko, *Kindai Nihon josei shi* (Tokyo: Kagoshima shupparkai, 1971), p. 146, cites Hara.

13. Sheldon Garon, *The State and Labor in Japan* (Berkeley: University of California Press, 1987), pp. 62–68; Andrew Gordon, *Evolution of Labor Relations in Japan*, (Cambridge, Ma: Harvard Council on East Asian Studies, 1985) pp. 210–11.

14. Sheldon Garon, *Molding Japanese Minds: The State in Everyday Life* (Princeton, N.J.: Princeton University Press, 1997), pp. 52–53.

15. Ōhara Shakai Mondai Kenkyūjo, ed., *Nihon rōdō nenkan* (Tokyo: pub, 1925), pp. 509–13; Richard Smethurst, *Agricultural Development and Tenancy Disputes in Japan, 1870–1940* (Princeton, N.J.: Princeton University Press, 1986), p. 355.

16. On Japan and World War I, see Fred Dickinson, *War and National Reinvention: Japan in the Great War, 1914–1919* (Cambridge: Harvard University Asia Center, 1999), pp. 93–116.

17. Prime Minister Tanaka presided over a meeting in Tokyo in 1927 that produced a memorandum on Japan's East Asian policy that was later dubbed the "Tanaka Memorial." During and after World War II, the allied powers claimed that this memorial was a blueprint for Japanese conquest of Asia and the world, but this view has since been largely discredited.

18. As quoted in Roger Daniels, *The Politics of Prejudice: The Anti-Japanese Movement in California and the Struggle for Japanese Exclusion* (Berkeley: University of California Press, 1962), p. 101.

19. Estimates of the death toll vary. Japanese authorities admitted about 500 killed, 1,400 injured, and 12,000 arrested. Korean estimates run as high as 7,600 killed and 50,000 arrested.

20. George Wilson, *Radical Nationalist in Japan: Kita Ikki, 1883–1937* (Cambridge: Harvard University Press, 1969), p. 82.

21. See Bix, *Hirohito and the Making of Modern Japan*.

NOTES TO CHAPTER 11

1. For a detailed discussion of economic policy of these years, see Hugh T. Patrick, "The Economic Muddle of the 1920s," in *Dilemmas of Growth in Prewar Japan*, ed. James Morley (Princeton, N.J.: Princeton University Press, 1971), pp. 252–55.

2. These quotations found in Eguchi Keiichi, *Toshi shōborujoa undō shi no kenkyū* (Tokyo: Miraisha, 1976), pp. 418–9, 430–31, 438–9.

3. Sumiya Mikio, *Shōwa kyōkō* (Tokyo: Yūhikaku, 1974).

4. Suzuki Yūko, *Jokō to rōdō sōgi* (Tokyo: Renga shobō shinsha, 1989), pp. 16–17.

5. For these quotations, and more on this topic, see Sheldon Garon, *Molding Japanese Minds: The State in Everyday Life* (Princeton, N.J.: Princeton University Press, 1997), pp. 106–111.

6. Henry D. Smith, *Japan's First Student Radicals* (Cambridge: Harvard University Press, 1972), pp. 199–230.

7. Ōya Sōichi, "1930 nen no kao," *Chūō kōron* (December 1930): 303–4.

8. On this incident, see Stephen Pelz, *Race to Pearl Harbor: The Failure of the Second London Naval Conference and the Onset of World War II* (Cambridge: Harvard University Press, 1974).

9. See Ugaki Kazushige, *Ugaki Kazushige Nikki*, vol. 1 (Tokyo: Misuzu Shobō, 1968) pp. 747, 758–60, 766–7, 782–3, and Andrew Gordon, *Labor and Imperial Democracy*, (Berkeley, Ca.: University of California Press, 1991) pp. 266–7.

10. Louise Young, *Japan's Total Empire* (Berkeley: University of California Press, 1998), pp. 55–114, chapter on "War Fever."

11. "Suzuki Teiichi nikki: Shōwa 8 nen," *Shigaku zasshi* (January 1978): 87, No. 1 93.

12. Keynes had, however, set out some of his key ideas in earlier publications, and it is possible that Takahashi was familiar with these.

13. William Lockwood, *The Economic Development of Japan* (Princeton, N.J.: Princeton University Press, 1968), pp. 64–77 offers a detailed overview of the economic trends of this period.

14. Chalmers Johnson, *MITI and the Economic Miracle* (Stanford, Calif.: Stanford University Press, 1982).

15. On agrarian policy and its impact, see Kerry Smith, *A Time of Crisis: Japan, the Great Depression, and Rural Revitalization* (Cambridge.: Harvard Asia Center, 2001).

16. Susan Beth Weiner, "Bureaucracy and Politics in the 1930s: The Career of Gotō Fumio," (Ph.D. diss., Harvard University, 1984), p. 144.

17. Gordon, *Labor and Imperial Democracy*, pp. 310–5.

18. Two of Kobayashi's works are available in English, in Takiji Kobayashi, *The Factory Ship and the Absentee Landlord* (Seattle: University of Washington Press, 1973).

19. Frank O. Miller, *Minobe Tatsukichi: Interpreter of Constitutionalism in Japan* (Berkeley: University of California Press, 1965), pp. 217–8.

20. Garon, *Molding Japanese Minds*, pp. 61, 70–76.

21. Gregory J. Kasza, *The State and the Mass Media in Japan: 1918–1945* (Berkeley: University of California Press, 1988), pp. 88, 252–3.

NOTES TO CHAPTER 12

1. Alvin Coox, *Nomonhan: Japan against Russia 1939* (Stanford, Calif.: Stanford University Press, 1985), is the definitive study of this war. On casualty totals, see pp. 914–5.

2. Andrew Gordon, *The Evolution of Labor Relations in Japan* (Cambridge: Harvard Council on East Asian Studies, 1985), pp. 300–310.

3. Cited in Thomas R. H. Havens, *Valley of Darkness: Japanese Society in World War II* (New York: W.W. Norton, 1978), p. 108.

4. Havens, *Valley of Darkness*, p. 109, for this and the previous quote of a government bureaucrat. In fact, Tōjō was wrong about the United States, which never took the legal step of drafting women into factories, although many American women were encouraged to take on industrial jobs and did so.

5. Details of the election are found in Ben-Ami Shillony, *Politics and Culture in Wartime Japan* (Oxford: Clarendon Press, 1981), p. 26.

6. Haruko Cook and Theodore Cook, *Japan at War: An Oral History* (New York: New Press, 1992), p. 180.

7. Kuruma Samezō worked at the Ōhara Institute of Social Research. His wartime labors produced a set of index cards that were destroyed in the Tokyo air raids, but after the war he finally completed the work; it was published in Japanese and German in the 1970s.

8. The author was Yamanoguchi Baku. Translated by Steve Rabson in *Stone Lion Review* 1 (Spring 1978): 28.

9. On the modernity debate of wartime, see Tetsuo Najita and H. D. Harootunian, "Japanese Revolt against the West," in *The Cambridge History of Japan*, vol. 6, ed. Peter Duus (Cambridge: Cambridge University Press, 1988), pp. 758–67. Quotes in this paragraph from p. 759. A more difficult but important study is Harry Harootunian, *Overcome by Modernity: History, Culture, and Community in Interwar Japan* (Princeton, N.J.: Princeton University Press, 2000).

10. Najita and Harootunian, "Japanese Revolt against the West," p. 763.

11. Shillony, *Politics and Culture in Wartime Japan*, p. 142.

12. Shillony, *Politics and Culture in Wartime Japan*, p. 143.

13. Shillony, *Politics and Culture in Wartime Japan*, p. 144.

14. Shillony, *Politics and Culture in Wartime Japan*, pp. 144–5.

15. Cited in John W. Dower, *Empire and Aftermath: Yoshida Shigeru and the Japanese Experience* (Cambridge,: Council on East Asian Studies Monographs, 1979), p. 290.

16. Cited in Dower, *Empire and Aftermath*, p. 265.

17. John W. Dower, *War without Mercy* (New York: Pantheon Books, 1986), p. 48.

18. No firm count of the comfort women is possible. George Hicks, "The 'Comfort Women,' " in *The Japanese Wartime Empire, 1931–1945*, ed. Peter Duus, Ramon H. Myers, and Mark R. Peattie (Princeton, N.J.: Princeton University Press, 1996), pp. 305–23, offers the estimate of 100,000; Watanabe Kazuko, "Militarization, Colonialism, and the Trafficking of Women: 'Comfort Women' Forced into Sexual Labor for Japanese Soliders," *Bulletin of Concerned Asian Scholars* 26, no.4 (Oct.–Dec. 1994):3–17, estimates 200,000.

19. Noguchi Yukio, *1940-nen taisei: saraba "senji keizai"* (Tokyo: Tōyō Keizai Shinpōsha, 1995), was a best-selling popular account. Numerous scholars in Japan and elsewhere had developed the idea of a transwar political economy in the previous fifteen or so years.

NOTES TO CHAPTER 13

1. For a fuller discussion of the surrender, see John W. Dower, *Embracing Defeat: Japan in the Wake of World War II* (New York: W.W. Norton, 1999), pp. 34–39. For the text of the surrender, see Robert J. C. Butow, *Japan's Decision to Surrender* (Stanford, Calif.: Stanford University Press, 1967), pp. 1–4.

2. This is the very apt phrase of Theodore Cohen, a midlevel SCAP official. He was referring to the stance of the Japanese cabinet in 1946, but the statement applies equally to the emperor and his attitude. See Theodore Cohen, *Remaking Japan: The American Occupation as New Deal* (New York: The Free Press, 1987), p. 262.

3. Dower, *Embracing Defeat*, pp. 187–8.

4. Dower, *Embracing Defeat*, pp. 139–48.

5. For example, see "Drastic Steps Set to Fight Food Lack," *Japan Times*, June 6, 1946.

6. Kawasaki rōdō shi hensan iinkai, ed., *Kawasaki rōdō shi* (Kawasaki: pub, 1987), pp. 7–8, 410.

7. Cohen, *Remaking Japan*, pp. 171, 179.

8. Dower, *Embracing Defeat*, pp. 145, 156 for the quotes in this paragraph.

9. Allied Council members were the United States, Great Britain, the Soviet Union, and

China. Far Eastern Commission members were Burma, Canada, China, France, India, the Netherlands, New Zealand, Pakistan, the Phillipines, the Soviet Union, the United Kingdom, and the United States.

10.   The supreme commander's bureaucracy was also abbreviated GHQ (General Headquarters). Thus the occupation leadership was variously labeled SCAP, SCAP-GHQ, or simply GHQ.

11.   Three died during the trial, and the two men found guilty only of conspiracy to wage war received finite prison terms of seven and twenty years.

12.   On MacArthur's evangelism in Japan, see Ray A. Moore, "Reflections on the Occupation of Japan," *Journal of Asian Studies* 38, no.4 (August 1979): 724, 729, and Richard Finn, *Winners in Peace: MacArthur, Yoshida, and Postwar Japan* (Berkeley: University of California Press, 1992), pp. 62–63.

13.   Dower, *Embracing Defeat*.

14.   Cited in Bruce Cumings, "Japan in the World System," in *Postwar Japan as History,* ed. Andrew Gordon (Berkeley: University of California Press, 1993), p. 40.

15.   Thomas R. H. Havens, *Fire across the Sea: The Vietnam War and Japan, 1965–1975* (Princeton, N.J.: Princeton University Press, 1987), p. 93. Nippon Kōkan, *Nippon Kōkan 40 nen shi* (Kowasahi: 1952) (place: pub, year), p. 382.

16.   John W. Dower, *Empire and Aftermath: Yoshida Shigeru and the Japanese Experience* (Cambridge: Harvard Council on East Asian Studies, 1980, p. 316. Nippon Kōkan, *Nippon Kōkan 40 nen shi*, p. 382.

17.   Dower, *Empire and Aftermath*, p. 306.

NOTES TO CHAPTER 14

1.   Cited in Chalmers Johnson, *MITI and the Japanese Miracle: The Growth of Industrial Policy* (Stanford, Calif.: Stanford University Press, 1982), p. 3. As noted in Chapter 11, a similar expression was actually used by the economist Arisawa Hiromi to describe the Japanese economy in the 1930s, but the *Economist* story appears to be the first postwar application of the term.

2.   Johnson, *MITI and the Japanese Miracle*, p. 16.

3.   On TV prices and market penetration, see Simon Partner, *Assembled in Japan: Electrical Goods and the Making of the Japanese Consumer* (Berkeley: University of California Press, 1999), pp. 140, 166, 247. If American televisions in the year 2000 were priced as a comparable multiple of income, they would cost between $8,000 and $10,000 each! On overall trends in consumer spending, see Charles Yuji Horioka, "Consuming and Saving," in *Postwar Japan as History*, ed. Andrew Gordon (Berkeley: University of California Press, 1993).

4.   Leonard Lynn, "Institutions, Organizations and Technological Innovation: Oxygen Steelmaking in the U.S. and Japan" (Ph.D diss. 1980), pp. 124–33, 252.

5.   Irokawa Daikichi, *Shōwa shi: sesō hen* (Tokyo: Shogakkan, 1990), pp. 25–32, on births, weddings, deaths, funerals, and other rituals.

6.   Irokawa, *Shōwa shi: sesō hen*, p. 27.

7.   Walter Edwards, *Modern Japan through its Weddings: Gender, Person, and Society in Ritual Portray* (Stanford, Calif.: Stanford University Press, 1989).

8.   Thomas P. Rohlen, "Is Japanese Education Becoming Less Egalitarian? Notes on High School Stratification and Reform," *Journal of Japanese Studies* 3, no. 1 (Winter 1977): 41.

9.   See Sakiko Shioda, "Innovation and Change in the Rapid Economic Growth Period," in *Technology Change and Female Labor in Japan*, ed. Masanori Nakamura (Tokyo: United Nations University, 1994), pp. 163–4.

10. Erdman Palmore, *The Honorable Elders: A Cross-Cultural Analysis of Aging in Japan* (Durham, N.C.: Duke University Press, 1975), p. 48.

11. Ezra Vogel, *Japan's New Middle Class: The Salary Man and His Family in a Tokyo Suburb* (Berkeley: University of California Press, 1963), brought this term to prominence in the English-speaking world.

12. Vogel, *Japan's New Middle Class*, pp. 175–8.

13. See Anne Allison, *Nightwork: Sexuality, Pleasure, and Corporate Masculinity in a Tokyo Hostess Club* (Chicago: University of Chicago Press, 1994).

14. Classic and recent studies of middle classes in urban Japan include Ronald Dore, *City Life in Japan: A Study of a Tokyo Ward* (Berkeley: University of California Press, 1958); Theodore C. Bestor, *Neighborhood Tokyo* (Stanford, Calif.: Stanford University Press, 1989); and Jennifer Roberston, *Native and Newcomer* (Berkeley: University of California Press, 1991).

15. See Takafusa Nakamura, *The Postwar Japanese Economy: Its Development and Structure* (Tokyo: University of Tokyo Press, 1981), p. 183.

16. Koji Taira, *Economic Development and the Labor Market in Japan* (New York: Columbia University Press, 1970), p. 175, shows that workers at companies of 4 to 9 employees received 50 percent of wages given to those at firms with over 1,000 workers. Those at companies of 50 to 99 workers received 63 percent of large firm wages.

17. On these legal battles and their results, see Frank Upham, "Unplaced Persons and Struggles for Place," in *Postwar Japan as History*, ed. Andrew Gordon (Berkeley: University of California Press, 1993), pp. 335–7.

18. See Upham, "Unplaced Persons," pp. 327–32.

19. Sheldon Garon, "Luxury Is the Enemy: Mobilizing Savings and Popularizing Thrift in Wartime Japan," *The Journal of Japanese Studies* 26, no.1 (Winter 2000): 41–78, has some discussion of postwar savings also.

20. On this movement, see Andrew Gordon, "Managing the Japanese Household: The New Life Movement in Postwar Japan," *Social Politics* 4, no. 2 (Summer 1997): 245–83.

21. The direct cause-and-effect relationship might be spurious, as the wedding came just as the television manufacturing industry was taking off in any case.

22. This is the so-called Engel coefficient. Charles Horioka, "Consuming and Saving," in *Postwar Japan as History*, pp. 264–273.

23. The two major surveys on class structure and identity are Naikaku sōridaijin kanbō chōkan kōhō shitsu, *Kokumin seikatsu ni kan suru yoron chōsa* (Tokyo: Naikaku sōridaijin kanbō chōkan kōhō shitsu, 1958–present), and 1975-nen SSM Zenkoku Chōsa Iinkai, ed., *Shakai kaisō to shakai idō: 1975-nen SSM zenkoku chōsa hōkoku* (Tokyo: 1978). For English language discussion of this survey and its implications, see Koji Taira, "The Middle-Class in Japan and the United States," *Japan Echo* 6, no.2 (1979): 18–28, and Shigeru Aoki, "Debunking the 90%-Middle-Class Myth," *Japan Echo* 6, no. 2 (1979): 29–33.

24. These statements are taken from Yoshimoto Takaaki, "The End of a Fictitious System," in *The Myth of Democracy* (October 1960) and Maruyama Masao, "8/15 and 5/15," *Chūō Kōron* (August 1960), both translated in Theodore DeBary, *Sources of the Japanese Tradition*, rev. ed. (New York: Columbia University Press, forthcoming).

25. Yoshimo, "The End of a Fictitious System," and Maruyama, "8/15 and 5/15," in DeBary, *Sources of the Japanese Tradition*, rev. ed.

26. Matsushita Keiichi, "The Emperor System of the Masses," *Chūō kōron* 74, no. 5 (April 1959); portions are translated in DeBary, *Sources of the Japanese Tradition*, rev. ed.

NOTES TO CHAPTER 15

1.   Together they won a total of 33.4 percent of the 467 seats. Right socialists won 67 seats; left socialists won 89 seats.

2.   Laura Hein, "Growth versus Success," in *Postwar Japan as History* ed. Andrew Gordon (Berkeley: University of California Press, 1993), pp. 111–112.

3.   For a good account of such groups, and the tension between "maternalism" and "equality" as grounds for action, see Kathleen S. Uno, "The Death of 'Good Wife, Wise Mother'?" in *Postwar Japan as History*, pp. 308–12.

4.   Uno, "The Death of 'Good Wife, Wise Mother'?," p. 309.

5.   Economic Planning Agency, *New Long-Range Economic Plan of Japan (1961–1970): Doubling National Income Plan* (Tokyo: 1961).

6.   Chalmers Johnson, *MITI and the Japanese Miracle* (Stanford, Calif.: Stanford University Press, 1981), is the most important work on the developmental state.

7.   Sheldon Garon and Mike Mochizuki, "Negotiating Social Contracts," in *Postwar Japan as History*, pp. 148–55.

8.   Andrew Gordon, *Wages of Affluence* (Cambridge,: Harvard University Press, 1998), p. 47.

9.   Andrew Gordon, "Contests for the Workplace in Postwar Japan," in *Postwar Japan as History*, p. 377.

10.   Kumazawa Makoto, "Suto-ken suto: 1975 nen Nihon," in *Sengo rōdō kumiai undō shiron*, ed. Shimizu Shinzō (Tokyo: Nihon hyōronsha, 1982) pp. 486–8. On public sector unions from 1949 through 1975, see Hyōdō Tsutomu, "Shokuba no rōshi kankei to rōdō kumiai," in *Sengo rōdō kumiai undō shiron*, pp. 245–58.

11.   On the global context, see Charles Maier, "The Politics of Productivity: Foundations of American International Economic Policy after World War II," in *Between Power and Plenty: Foreign Economic Policies of the Advanced Industrial States*, ed. Peter Katzenstein, (Place: Madison University of Wisconsin Press, 1978).

12.   Dōmei Kaigi is an abbreviation of Zen Nihon Rōdō Sōdōmei Kumiai Kaigi; the All Japan Conference of Federated Labor Unions.

13.   Ishida Hirohide, "Hoshutō no bijiyon," *Chūō kōron* 78, no. 1 (January 1963): 88–97.

14.   In Japanese, "Betonamu ni heiwa o! Shimin rengō."

15.   On the anti-war protests in general, see Thomas R. H. Havens, *Fire across the Sea: The Vietnam War and Japan, 1965–1975* (Princeton, N.J.: Princeton University Press, 1987). For these numbers, see pp. 133 and 207.

16.   On the Narita protests, see David Apter and Sawa Nagayo, *Against the State* (Cambridge: Harvard University Press, 1984).

17.   These all had precedents in the prewar era.

18.   Minobe's father was Minobe Tatsukichi, the scholar of constitutional law at Tokyo University of the prewar era introduced in Chapter 11, who was ousted from his academic position by right-wing critics for his slightly liberal views of the emperor's position.

19.   Unions in eight public enterprises participated: Japan National Railway, Tobacco Monopoly, Postal Service, Nippon Telephone and Telegraph, Government Printing Office, National Mint, Alcohol Sales Office, Forestry Division.

20.   Kumazawa Makoto, "Suto-ken suto," in *Sengo rōdō kumiai undō*, pp. 491–503, on the course of the strike and reasons for its failure.

21.   On this episode, see "CIA Spent Millions to Support Japanese Right in '50s and '60s," *New York Times* (October 9, 1994), and "CIA Keeping Historians in the Dark about Its Cold War Role in Japan," *Los Angeles Times* (March 20, 1995).

22.   E. O. Reischauer, "The Broken Dialogue with Japan," *Foreign Affairs* (October 1960): 11–26.

23. Chalmers Johnson, *Blowback: The Costs and Consequences of American Empire* (New York: Metropolitan Books, 2000), p. 36.

NOTES TO CHAPTER 16

1. For a dramatic telling of the automobile story, see David Halberstam, *The Reckoning* (New York: William Morrow, 1986).

2. This incident is examined in a prize-winning documentary film by Christine Choy and Renee Tajima, *Who Killed Vincent Chin?* (1988).

3. Theodore H. White, "The Danger from Japan," *New York Times Magazine* (July 28, 1985), pp. 18–23, 27, 37–43, 57–58.

4. The participants were Canada, France, Germany, Great Britain, Italy, Japan, and the United States. Canada participated from the second meeting.

5. For a powerful statement of this position, see Ienaga Saburō, *The Pacific War* (New York: Pantheon, 1978), translated from a 1968 Japanese book titled *Taiheiyō sensō*.

6. Ronald Dore, *Stock Market Capitalism, Welfare Capitalism: Japan and Germany versus the Anglo Saxons* (Oxford: Oxford University Press, 2000), p. 225.

7. The Japanese term is *genryō keiei*.

8. Paul Lillrank and Noriaki Kano, *Continuous Improvement* (Ann Arbor: Center for Japanese Studies, the University of Michigan, 1989), p. 1.

9. Karatsu Hajime, "Japanese Know-How for American Industry," *Japan Echo* XIII, no. 4 (1986): 64. Translated from "Beikoku keizai no hatan" ("The Collapse of the American Economy"), *Voice* (October 1986):115–25. Note the much gentler title for the English version.

10. For an analysis and overview of such work, see Peter N. Dale, *The Myth of Japanese Uniqueness* (London: Croon Helm & Nissan Institute for Japanese Studies, University of Oxford, 1986). For reference to these specific examples, see pp. 16, 23, 65–67, 72–73, 189–90.

11. Takeo Doi, *The Anatomy of Dependence* (Tokyo: Kodansha International, 1973), originally published as *Amae no kōzō* (Tokyo: Kobundō, 1971).

12. Ezra F. Vogel, *Japan as Number One* (Cambridge: Harvard University Press, 1979). The Japanese translation was published that same year. It reportedly sold over one million copies, and was the best-selling work of translated nonfiction ever in Japan.

13. Jacob Schlesinger, *Shadow Shoguns: The Rise and Fall of Japan's Postwar Political Machine* (New York: Simon and Schuster, 1997), p. 120.

14. See Sheldon Garon, *Molding Japanese Minds* (Princeton, N.J.: Princeton University Press, 1997).

15. See Prime Minister's Office, *Kankō hakusho* (Tokyo: pub, 1991), pp. 37–40.

16. See National Defense Council for Victims of Karoshi, ed., *Karōshi: When the "Corporate Warrior" Dies* (Tokyo: Mado-sha, 1990), pp. 7, 12.

17. See "Friendly New U.S. Line in Trade Talks Strikes Some Japanese as Self-Serving," *Wall Street Journal*, September 14, 1989, p. A17.

18. *New York Times*, January 21, 1992, Section D, p. 1.

19. Kumazawa Makoto, *Portraits of the Japanese Workplace* (Boulder, Colo.: Westview Press, 1996), p. 249.

20. Tsurumi Shunsuke, *Sengo Nihon no taishū bunka-shi* (A History of Mass Culture in Postwar Japan) (Tokyo: Iwanami shoten, 1984), pp. 189–90, cited in Kumazawa, *Portraits of the Japanese Workplace*, p. 249. Translated into English as *A Cultural History of Postwar Japan, 1945–1980* (London: KPI, 1987).

21. See Marilyn Ivy, "Formations of Mass Culture," in *Postwar Japan as History*, ed, Andrew Gordon (Berkeley: University of California Press, 1993), pp. 253–55, on these debates.

22. Ivy, "Formations of Mass Culture," pp. 251, 256, on the ad campaigns. On rural

tourist development projects, see Jennifer Robertson, "It Takes a Village: Internationalization and Nostalgia in Postwar Japan," in *Mirror of Modernity*, ed. Steven Vlastos (Berkeley: University of California Press, 1999), pp. 110–29.

NOTES TO CHAPTER 17

1. Norma Field, *In the Realm of a Dying Emperor: Japan at Century's End* (New York: Vintage Books, 1991), pp. 19–25, on the emperor's illness and resulting "self-restraint." Chapter III has the story of the statement by Mayor Motoshima of Nagasaki and the ensuing controversy.

2. Field, *In the Realm of a Dying Emperor*, pp. 233–4.

3. See "Ibento kankaku ki ni itta," *Sankei Shinbun*, November 11, 1999, p. 28.

4. For an account of these decisions and their consequences, see Richart Taggart Murphy, *The Weight of the Yen: How Denial Imperils America's Future and Ruins an Alliance* (New York: Norton, 1996), Part III.

5. On the response to AIDS in Japan and this incident, see Eric A. Feldman, *The Ritual of Rights in Japan: Law, Society and Health Policy in Japan* (Cambridge: Cambridge University Press, 2000).

6. This phrase, coined by John F. Neuffer, an American political and economic analyst living in Japan, was first quoted in a *New York Times* story of July 23, 1998, and very quickly caught widespread attention.

7. See B. Meredith Burke, "Japan's Baby Bust: A Brighter Prospect Than Ours?," *The Japan Digest*, July 11, 2000, p. 5.

8. The quote is from Kuronuma Katsushi, *Enjo kōsai* (Tokyo: Bungei Shunjū, 1996), quoted in Kawai Hayao, "The Message from Japan's Schoolgirl Prostitutes," *Japan Echo* 24, no. 2 (June 1997). Kawai is a well-known psychiatrist and public commentator who is among those blaming the phenomenon on shallow relationships and a crisis of the soul.

9. "Shōnen kuaku jiken, piiku wa 40 nen mae," *Asahi Shinbun*, October 11, 2000, p. 38.

10. Richard Katz, *Japan: The System That Soured: The Rise and Fall of the Japanese Economic Miracle* (Armonk, N.Y.: M.E. Sharpe, 1998), and "The Lost Decade," *Newsweek*, July 27, 1998.

11. See David Asher and Robert H. Dugger, "Could Japan's Financial Mount Fuji Blow Its Top?" *Working Paper Series*, MIT Japan Program, May 15, 2000.

12. For a good summary of these prescriptions and an analysis of recent trends, see Ronald Dore, *Stock Market Capitalism, Welfare Capitalism: Japan and Germany versus the Anglo Saxons* (New York: Oxford University Press, 2000).

13. *The Japan Digest*, June 27, 2000, p. 3.

14. Dore, *Stock Market Capitalism, Welfare Capitalism*, p. 105.

15. *The Japan Digest*, June 27, 2000, p. 4.

16. Dore, *Stock Market Capitalism, Welfare Capitalism*, pp. 111–23.

17. *The Japan Digest*, July 27, 2000, p. 5.

18. *The Japan Digest*, June 30, 2000, pp. 3–4.

19. "Kōkō no katei kyōkasho 4 satsu ga fugōkaku," *Asahi Shinbun*, July 5, 1997, p. 25.

20. "Shōkaku danjo sabetsu 'yurusarenu,' " *Asahi Shinbun*, International Satellite edition, November 28, 1996, p. 22.

21. Mari Osawa, "Government Approaches to Gender Equality in the mid-1990s," *Social Science Japan Journal* 3, no. 1 (2000):3–19.

22. Ivan Hall, *Cartels of the Mind: Japan's Intellectual Closed Shop* (New York: W.W. Norton, 1998).

23. "Third country persons" (*san koku jin*) referred to people in the occupation era who

were neither Japanese nor SCAP personnel, and came to refer particularly to residents of the former colonies of Korea and Taiwan.

24. For a full treatment of ethnicity and foreigners in Japan, see John Lie, *Multiethnic Japan* (Cambridge: Harvard University Press, 2001).

25. See Edith Terry, *How Asia Got Rich: Japan and the Asian Miracle* (Armonk, N.Y.: M.E. Sharpe, 1998).

Select Bibliography

I. GENERAL

Dower, John. *Embracing Defeat: Japan in the Wake of World War II.* New York: W.W. Norton and Co., 1999.

————. *Japan in War and Peace: Selected Essays.* New York: The New Press, 1993.

Duus, Peter, ed. *The Twentieth Century.* Vol. 6 of *The Cambridge History of Japan.* Cambridge: Cambridge University Press, 1989.

Goldman, Merle, and Andrew Gordon, eds. *Historical Perspectives on Contemporary East Asia.* Cambridge: Harvard University Press, 2000.

Gluck, Carol, and Stephen R. Graubard, eds. *Shōwa: The Japan of Hirohito.* New York: W. W. Norton and Co., 1992.

Hardacre, Helen. *Shintō and the State, 1868–1988.* Princeton, NJ.: Princeton University Press, 1989.

Iriye, Akira. *China and Japan in the Global Setting.* Cambridge: Harvard University Press, 1993.

Jansen, Marius B., ed. *The Nineteenth Century.* Vol. 5 of *The Cambridge History of Japan.* Cambridge: Cambridge University Press, 1989.

Johnson, Chalmers. *MITI and the Japanese Miracle: The Growth of Industrial Policy, 1925–1975.* Stanford, Calif: Stanford University Press, 1982.

Najita, Tetsuo. *Japan.* Englewood, N.J.: Prentice Hall, 1974.

Najita, Tetsuo, and Victor Koschmann. *Conflict in Modern Japanese History: The Neglected Tradition.* Princeton, N.J.: Princeton University Press, 1982.

Totman, Conrad. *Early Modern Japan.* Berkeley: University of California Press, 1993.

II. TOKUGAWA JAPAN

A. Society, Population and the Economy

Bix, Herbert P. *Peasant Protest in Japan, 1590–1884.* New Haven, Conn.: Yale University Press, 1986.

Crawcour, S. "The Tokugawa Period and Japan's Preparation for Modern Economic Growth." *Journal of Japanese Studies* 1, no.1 (Autumn 1974):113–35.

Howell, David L. *Capitalism from Within: Economy, Society, and the State in a Japanese Fishery.* Berkeley: University of California Press, 1995.

Jannetta, Ann Bowman. *Epidemics and Mortality in Early Modern Japan.* Princeton, N.J.: Princeton University Press, 1987.

McClain, James L. *Kanazawa: A Seventeenth-Century Japanese Castle Town.* New Haven, Conn.: Yale University Press, 1982.

Smith, T. C. *The Agrarian Origins of Modern Japan.* Stanford, Calif.: Stanford University Press, 1959.

————. *Native Sources of Japanese Industrialization, 1750–1920*. Berkeley and Los Angeles: University of California Press, 1988.

Totman, Conrad. *The Green Archipelago: Forestry in Preindustrial Japan*. Berkeley: University of California Press, 1989.

Vlastos, Stephan. *Peasant Protests and Uprisings in Tokugawa Japan*. Berkeley: University of California Press, 1986.

Wigen, Kären. *The Making of a Japanese Periphery, 1750–1920*. Berkeley: University of California Press, 1995.

B. Politics

Bolitho, Harold. *Treasures among Men: The Fudai Daimyō in Tokugawa Japan*. New Haven, Conn: Yale University Press, 1974.

Hall, John W., and Marius B. Jansen, eds. *Studies in the Institutional History of Early Modern Japan*. Princeton, N.J.: Princeton University Press, 1968.

Nakai, Kate Wildman. *Shogunal Politics: Arai Hakuseki and the Premises of Tokugawa Rule*. Harvard East Asian Monographs 134. Cambridge: Harvard University, Council on East Asian Studies, 1988.

Toby, Ronald. *State and Diplomacy in Early Modern Japan: Asia in the Development of the Tokugawa Bakufu*. Princeton, N.J.: Princeton University Press, 1984.

Totman, Conrad. *Politics in the Tokugawa Bakufu*. Cambridge: Harvard University Press, 1967.

Webb, Herschel. *The Japanese Imperial Institution in the Tokugawa Period*. New York: Columbia University Press, 1968.

C. Thought and Culture

Dore, Ronald. *Education in Tokugawa Japan*. Berkeley: University of California Press, 1965.

Elison, George. *Deus Destroyed*. Cambridge: Harvard University Press, 1974.

Harootunian, H. D. *Things Seen and Unseen: Discourse and Ideology in Tokugawa Nativism*. Chicago: University of Chicago Press, 1988.

Kelly, William W. *Deference and Defiance in Nineteenth-Century Japan*. Princeton, N.J.: Princeton University Press, 1985.

Maruyama, M. *Studies in the Intellectual History of Tokugawa Japan*. Translated by Mikiso Hane. Princeton, N.J.: Princeton University Press, 1974.

Najita, Tetsuo. *Visions of Virtue in Tokugawa Japan*. Chicago: University of Chicago Press, 1987.

Ooms, Herman. *Tokugawa Ideology: Early Constructs, 1570–1680*. Princeton, N.J.: Princeton University Press, 1985.

Wakabayashi, Bob Tadashi. *Anti-Foreignism and Western Learning in Early-Modern Japan: The New Theses of 1825*. Cambridge: Harvard University, Council on East Asian Studies, 1986.

III. THE BAKUMATSU AND MEIJI RESTORATION

Craig, Albert M. *Chōshū in the Meiji Restoration*. Cambridge: Harvard University Press, 1961.

Harootunian, H. D. *Toward Restoration: The Growth of Political Consciousness in Tokugawa Japan*. Berkeley: University of California Press, 1970.

Huber, Thomas. *The Revolutionary Origins of Modern Japan*. Stanford, Calif.: Stanford University Press, 1981.

Jansen, Marius B. *Sakamoto Ryōma and the Meiji Restoration*. Stanford, Calif.: Stanford University Press, 1961.

Walthall, Anne. *The Weak Body of a Useless Woman: Matsuo Taseko and the Meiji Restoration*. Chicago: University of Chicago Press, 1998.

Wilson, George M. *Patriots and Redeemers in Japan, Motives in the Meiji Restoration*. Chicago: University of Chicago Press, 1992.

IV. MEIJI ERA

A. Society, Population, and the Economy

Hirschmeier, Johannes. *The Origins of Entrepreneurship in Meiji Japan*. Cambridge: Harvard University Press, 1964.

Moulder, Frances. *Japan, China and the Modern World Economy*. New York: Cambridge University Press, 1977.

Reischauer, Haru Matsukata. *Samurai and Silk: A Japanese and American Heritage*. Cambridge: Harvard University Press, 1986.

Rosenstone, Robert A. *Mirror in the Shrine: American Encounters with Meiji Japan*. Cambridge: Harvard University Press, 1988.

Smith, Thomas C. *Political Change and Industrial Development in Japan: Government Enterprise, 1868–1880*. Stanford, Calif.: Stanford University Press, 1955.

Tsurumi, E. Patricia. *Factory Girls: Women in the Thread Mills of Meiji Japan*. Princeton, N.J.: Princeton University Press, 1990.

Wray, William D. *Mitsubishi and the N.Y.K., 1870–1914: Business Strategy in the Japanese Shipping Industry*. Cambridge: Harvard University, Council on East Asian Studies, 1984.

B. Politics and Foreign Policy

Akita, George. *Foundations of Constitutional Government in Modern Japan, 1868–1900*. Cambridge: Harvard University Press, 1967.

Conroy, Hilary. *The Japanese Seizure of Korea, 1868–1910*. Philadelphia: University of Pennsylvania Press, 1960.

Hackett, R. F. *Yamagata Aritomo in the Rise of Modern Japan, 1838–1922*. Cambridge: Harvard University Press, 1973.

Hall, Ivan. *Mori Arinori*. Cambridge: Harvard University Press, 1973.

Jones, Hazel L. *Live Machines: Hired Foreigners and Meiji Japan*. Vancouver: University of British Columbia, 1980.

Pittau, J. *Political Thought in Early Meiji Japan, 1868–1889*. Cambridge: Harvard University Press, 1967.

C. Thought and Culture

Bartholomew, James R. *The Formation of Science in Japan*. New Haven, Conn.: Yale University Press, 1989.

Gluck, Carol. *Japan's Modern Myths: Ideology in the Late Meiji Period*. Princeton, N.J.: Princeton University Press, 1985.

Irokawa, Daikichi. *The Culture of the Meiji Period*. Translated and edited by Marius B. Jansen. Princeton, N.J.: Princeton University Press, 1985.

Ketelaar, James Edward. *Of Heretics and Martyrs in Meiji Japan: Buddhism and Its Persecution*. Princeton, N.J.: Princeton University Press, 1990.

Kinmonth, Earl H. *The Self-Made Man in Meiji Japanese Thought: From Samurai to Salary Man*. Berkeley: University of California Press, 1981.

V. IMPERIAL ERA

A. Politics, Foreign Policy, Colonialism, and Imperialism

Berger, Gordon. *Parties Out of Power in Japan, 1931–1941*. Princeton, N.J.: Princeton University Press, 1977.

Bix, Herbert. *Hirohito and the Making of Modern Japan*. New York: HarperCollins Publishers, 2000.

Borg, Dorothy, ed. *Pearl Harbor as History: Japanese American Relations, 1931–1941*. New York: Columbia University Press, 1973.

Choi, Chungmoo. *The Comfort Women: Colonialism, War, and Sex.* Durham, N.C.: Duke University Press, 1997. [*Positions* special issue 5, no. 1 (Spring 1997)].

Coox, Alvin D. *Nomonhan: Japan against Russia, 1939.* Stanford, Calif.: Stanford University Press, 1985.

Crowley, James. *Japan's Quest for Autonomy.* Princeton, N.J.: Princeton University Press, 1966.

Dickinson, Frederick R. *War and National Reinvention: Japan in the Great War, 1914–1919.* Cambridge: Harvard University Asia Center, 1999.

Dower, John. *Empire and Aftermath: Yoshida Shigeru and the Japanese Experience.* Cambridge: Harvard University Council on East Asia Studies, 1979.

Duus, Peter. *The Abacus and the Sword: The Japanese Penetration of Korea, 1895–1910.* Berkeley: University of California Press, 1995.

———. *Party Rivalry and Politics: Change in Taishō Japan.* Cambridge: Harvard University Press, 1968.

Fogel, Joshua, ed. *The Nanjing Massacre in History and Historiography.* Berkeley: University of California Press, 2000.

Fujitani, Takeshi. *Splendid Monarchy: Power and Pageantry in Modern Japan.* Berkeley, Los Angeles, and London: University of California Press, 1996.

Iriye, Akira. *After Imperialism: The Search for a New Order in the Far East, 1921–1931.* Harvard University Press, 1965.

Lewis, Michael. *Becoming Apart: National Power and Local Politics in Toyama, 1868–1945.* Cambridge: Harvard University Press, 2000.

Morley, James W., ed. *Dilemmas of Growth in Prewar Japan.* Princeton, N.J.: Princeton University Press, 1971.

Najita, Tetsuo. *Hara Kei and the Politics of Compromise, 1905–1915.* Cambridge: Harvard University Press, 1967.

Ogata, Sadako. *Defiance in Manchuria: The Making of Japanese Foreign Policy.* Berkeley: University of California Press, 1964.

Peattie, Mark. *Ishiwara Kanji and Japan's Confrontation with the West.* Princeton, N.J.: Princeton University Press, 1975.

Pelz, Stephen. *The Race to Pearl Harbor.* Cambridge: Harvard University Press, 1971.

Silberman, Bernard, and H. D. Harootunian, eds. *Japan in Crisis: Essays on Taishō Democracy.* Ann Arbor: Center for Japanese Studies, the University of Michigan, 1999.

Smith, Henry D. *Japan's First Student Radicals.* Cambridge: Harvard University Press, 1972.

Titus, David. *Palace and Politics in Prewar Japan.* New York: Columbia University Press, 1974.

Wilson, George. *Radical Nationalist in Japan: Kita Ikki, 1863–1937.* Cambridge: Harvard University Press, 1969.

Yamanouchi, Yasushi, Victor J. Koschmann, and Ryūichi Narita, eds. *Total War and "Modernization."* Ithaca, N.Y.: East Asia Program, Cornell University, 1998.

Young, Louise. *Japan's Total Empire: Manchuria and the Culture of Wartime Imperialism.* Berkeley: University of California Press, 1998.

B. Economy

Barnhart, Michael A. *Japan Prepares for Total War: The Search for Economic Security 1919–1941.* Ithaca, N.Y.: Cornell University Press, 1987.

Ericson, Steven J. *The Sound of the Whistle: Railroads and the State in Meiji Japan.* Cambridge: Council on East Asian Studies, Harvard University Press, 1996.

Lockwood, William M., ed. *The State and Economic Enterprise in Japan.* Princeton, N.J.: Princeton University Press, 1965.

Marshall, Byron. *Capitalism and Nationalism in Prewar Japan: The Ideology of the Business Elite.* Stanford, Calif.: Stanford University Press, 1967.

Molony, Barbara. *Technology and Investment: The Prewar Japanese Chemical Industry*. Cambridge: Council on East Asian Studies: Harvard University Press, 1990.

Patrick, Hugh, ed. *Japanese Industrialization and Its Social Consequences*. Berkeley: University of California Press, 1976.

Smith, Kerry. *A Time of Crisis: Japan, the Great Depression, and Rural Revitalization*. Cambridge: Harvard University Press, 2001.

Wray, William D., ed. *Managing Industrial Enterprise: Cases from Japan's Prewar Experience*. Cambridge: Harvard University, Council on East Asian Studies, 1990.

C. Society and Culture

Barshay, Andrew E. *State and Intellectual in Imperial Japan: The Public Man in Crisis*. Berkeley and Los Angeles: University of California Press, 1989.

Bernstein, Gail. *Japanese Marxist: A Portrait of Kawakami Hajime, 1879–1946*. Cambridge: Harvard University Press, 1976.

Dore, Ronald. *British Factory–Japanese Factory: The Origins of National Diversity in Employment Relations*. Berkeley: University of California Press, 1973.

Dower, John W. *War without Mercy: Race and Power in the Pacific War*. New York: Pantheon Books, 1986.

Fogel, Joshua. *Politics and Sinology: The Case of Naitō Konan (1866–1934)*. Cambridge: Harvard University Press, 1984.

Garon, Sheldon. *Molding Japanese Minds: The State in Everyday Life*. Princeton, N.J.: Princeton University Press, 1997.

———. *The State and Labor in Modern Japan*. Berkeley: University of California Press, 1987.

Gordon, Andrew. *The Evolution of Labor Relations in Japan: Heavy Industry, 1853–1955*. Cambridge: Harvard University, Council on East Asian Studies, 1985.

Havens, Thomas. *Farm and Nation in Japan*. New Haven, Conn.: Yale University Press, 1975.

Hoston, Germaine A. *Marxism and the Crisis of Development in Prewar Japan*. Princeton, N.J.: Princeton University Press, 1986.

Lewis, Michael. *Rioters and Citizens: Mass Protest in Imperial Japan*. Berkeley: University of California Press, 1990.

Mackie, Vera. *Creating Socialist Women in Japan: Gender, Labour, and Activism, 1900–1937*. New York: Cambridge University Press, 1997.

Maruyama, Masao. *Thought and Behavior in Modern Japanese Politics*. London and New York: Oxford University Press, 1963.

Minichiello, Sharon, ed. *Japan's Competing Modernities: Issues in Culture and Democracy, 1900–1930*. Honolulu: University of Hawaii Press, 1998.

Mitchell, Richard H. *Thought Control in Prewar Japan*. Ithaca, N.Y.: Cornell University Press, 1976.

Nolte, Sharon H. *Liberalism in Modern Japan: Ishibashi Tanzan and His Teachers, 1905–1960*. Berkeley: University of California Press, 1986.

Pyle, Kenneth. *The New Generation in Meiji Japan: Problems of Cultural Identity 1885–1895*. Stanford, Calif.: Stanford University Press, 1969.

Roden, Donald. *Schooldays in Imperial Japan: A Study in the Culture of a Student Elite*. Berkeley: University of California Press, 1980.

Sievers, Sharon L. *Flowers in Salt: The Beginnings of Feminist Consciousness in Modern Japan*. Stanford, Calif.: Stanford University Press, 1983.

Smith, Robert J., and Ella Lury Wiswell. *The Women of Suye Mura*. Chicago: University of Chicago Press, 1983.

Tanaka, Stefan. *Japan's Orient: Rendering Pasts in History*. Berkeley: University of California Press, 1993.

Tsutsui, William M. *Manufacturing Ideology: Scientific Management in Twentieth-Century Japan*. Princeton, N.J.: Princeton University Press, 1998.

Uno, Kathleen S. *Passages to Modernity: Motherhood, Childhood, and Social Reform in Early Twentieth Century Japan*. Honolulu: University of Hawaii Press, 1999.

Vlastos, Stephen, ed. *Mirror of Modernity: Invented Traditions of Modern Japan*. Berkeley: University of California Press, 1998.

Waswo, Ann. *Japanese Landlords: The Decline of a Rural Elite*. Berkeley: University of California Press, 1977.

VI. POSTWAR AND CONTEMPORARY JAPAN

A. Government and Politics

Allinson, Gary D. *Japanese Urbanism: Industry and Politics in Kariya, 1872–1972*. Berkeley: University of California Press, 1975.

———. *Suburban Tokyo: A Comparative Study in Politics and Social Change*. Berkeley: University of California Press, 1979.

Dower, John. *Embracing Defeat: Japan in the Wake of World War II*. New York: W.W. Norton and Co., 1999.

George, Timothy. *Minamata: Pollution and the Struggle for Democracy in Postwar Japan*. Cambridge: Harvard Asia Center, 2000.

Gordon, Andrew, ed. *Postwar Japan as History*. Berkeley: University of California Press, 1993.

Gordon, Beate Sirota. *The Only Woman in the Room*. Tokyo, New York, and London: Kodansha International, 1997.

Hein, Laura E. *Fueling Growth: The Energy Revolution and Economic Policy in Postwar Japan*. Cambridge: Council on East Asian Studies, Harvard University Press, 1990.

Masumi, Junnosuke. *Contemporary Politics in Japan*. Translated by Lonny E. Carlisle. Berkeley: University of California Press, 1995.

———. *Postwar Politics in Japan, 1945–1955*. Translated by Lonny E. Carlisle. Berkeley: University of California, Institute of East Asian Studies, Center for Japanese Studies, 1985.

Moore, Joe. *Japanese Workers and the Struggle for Power, 1945–1947*. Madison: University of Wisconsin Press, 1983.

Nakamura, Masanori. *The Japanese Monarchy, 1931–1991: Ambassador Grew and the Making of the "Symbol Emperor System."* Armonk, N.Y.: M.E. Sharpe, 1992.

Packard, George R. *Protest in Tokyo: The Security Treaty Crisis of 1960*. Princeton, N.J.: Princeton University Press, 1966.

Pempel, T. J. *Policy and Politics in Japan: Creative Conservatism*. Philadelphia: Temple University Press, 1982.

Pharr, Susan J. *Losing Face: Status Politics in Japan*. Berkeley: University of California Press, 1990.

Samuels, Richard J. *"Rich Nation, Strong Army": National Security and the Technological Transformation of Japan*. Ithaca, N.Y.: Cornell University Press, 1994.

Ward, Robert E., and Yoshikazu Sakamoto, eds. *Policy Planning during the Allied Occupation of Japan*. Princeton, N.J.: Princeton University Press, 1981.

B. Economy and Society

Allinson, Anne. *Nightwork: Sexuality, Pleasure, and Corporate Masculinity in a Tokyo Hostess Club*. Chicago: University of Chicago Press, 1994.

Bestor, Theodore C. *Neighborhood Tokyo*. Stanford, Calif.: Stanford University Press, 1989.

Brinton, Mary C. *Women and the Economic Miracle: Gender and Work in Postwar Japan*. Berkeley: University of California Press, 1993.

Dore, Ronald P. *British Factory—Japanese Factory: The Origins of National Diversity in Industrial Relations*. Berkeley: University of California Press, 1973.

Edwards, Walter. *Modern Japan through Its Weddings: Gender, Person, and Society in Ritual Portrayal*. Stanford, Calif.: Stanford University Press, 1989.

Fowler, Edward. *San'ya Blues: Laboring Life in Contemporary Japan*. Ithaca, N.Y., and London: Cornell University Press, 1996.

Gordon, Andrew. *The Wages of Affluence: Labor and Management in Postwar Japan*. Cambridge: Harvard University Press, 1998.

Hardacre, Helen. *Marketing the Menacing Fetus in Japan*. Berkeley: University of California Press, 1997.

Hunter, Janet, ed. *Japanese Women Working*. London and New York: Routledge, 1993.

Ishida, Hiroshi. *Social Mobility in Contemporary Japan*. Stanford, Calif.: Stanford University Press, 1993.

Johnson, Chalmers. *MITI and the Japanese Miracle: The Growth of Industrial Policy, 1925–1975*. Stanford, Calif.: Stanford University Press, 1982.

Kondo, Dorinne K. *Crafting Selves: Power, Gender, and Discourses of Identity in a Japanese Workplace*. Chicago: University of Chicago Press, 1990.

Kumazawa, Makoto. *Portraits of the Japanese Workplace: Labor Movements, Workers and Managers*. Edited by Andrew Gordon and translated by Andrew Gordon and Mikiso Hane. Boulder, Colo.: Westview Press, 1996.

LeBlanc, Robin. *Bicycle Citizens: The Political World of the Japanese Housewife*. Berkeley: University of California Press, 1999.

McCormack, Gavan, and Yoshio Sugimoto, eds. *Democracy in Contemporary Japan*. Armonk N.Y.: M.E. Sharpe, 1986.

Nakamura, Takafusa. *The Postwar Japanese Economy: Its Development and Structure*. Tokyo: University of Tokyo Press, 1981.

Nakane, Chie. *Japanese Society*. Stanford, Calif.: Stanford University Press, 1972.

Norbeck, Edward, and Margaret Lock, eds. *Health, Illness, and Medical Care in Japan: Cultural and Social Dimensions*. Honolulu: University of Hawaii Press, 1987.

Ogasawara, Yūko. *Office Ladies and Salaried Men: Power, Gender, and Work in Japanese Companies*. Berkeley: University of California Press, 1998.

Partner, Simon. *Assembled in Japan: Electrical Goods and the Making of the Japanese Consumer*. Berkeley: University of California Press, 2000.

Patrick, Hugh, and Henry Rosovsky, eds. *Asia's New Giant: How the Japanese Economy Works*. Washington, D.C.: Brookings Institution, 1976.

Pharr, Susan J. *Political Women in Japan: The Search for a Place in Political Life*. Berkeley: University of California Press, 1981.

Price, John. *Japan Works: Power and Paradox in Postwar Industrial Relations*. Ithaca, N.Y.: Cornell University Press, 1997.

Robertson, Jennifer. *Native and Newcomer: Making and Remaking a Japanese City*. Berkeley: University of California Press, 1991.

Rohlen, Thomas P. *Japan's High Schools*. Berkeley: University of California Press, 1983.

———. *For Harmony and Strength: Japanese White-Collar Organization in Anthropological Perspective*. Berkeley: University of California Press, 1974.

Smith, Robert J. *Kurusu: The Price of Progress in a Japanese Village, 1951–1975*. Stanford, Calif.: Stanford University Press, 1978.

Upham, Frank K. *Law and Social Change in Postwar Japan*. Cambridge: Harvard University Press, 1987.

Vogel, Ezra F. *Japan's New Middle Class: The Salary Man and His Family in a Tokyo Suburb*. Berkeley: University of California Press, 1971.

C.　Thought and Culture

Burkman, Thomas W. *The Occupation of Japan: Arts and Culture*. Norfolk, Va.: Liskey Lithograph, 1988.

Cary, Otis, ed. *War-Wasted Asia: Letters, 1945–46*. Tokyo and New York: Kodansha International, 1975.

Field, Norma. *In the Realm of a Dying Emperor: A Portrait of Japan at Century's End*. New York: Pantheon Books, 1991.

Kersten, Rikki. *Democracy in Postwar Japan: Maruyama Masao and the Search of Autonomy*. London and New York: Routledge, 1996.

Koschmann, Victor. *Revolution and Subjectivity in Postwar Japan*. Chicago: University of Chicago Press, 1996.

Krauss, Ellis S. *Japanese Radicals Revisited: Student Protest in Postwar Japan*. Berkeley: University of California Press, 1974.

Lifton, Robert J. *Death in Life: The Survivors of Hiroshima*. New York: Random House, 1968.

Olson, Lawrence. *Ambivalent Moderns: Portraits of Japanese Cultural Identity*. Lanham, Md.: Rowman and Littlefield Publishers, Inc., 1992.

Treat, John Whittier. *Writing Ground Zero: Japanese Literature and the Atomic Bomb*. Chicago: University of Chicago Press, 1995.

Tsurumi, Shunsuke. *A Cultural History of Postwar Japan, 1945–1980*. London: KPI Limited, 1987.

D.　Japan and the World

Buckley, Roger. *U.S.–Japan Alliance Diplomacy, 1945–1990*. Cambridge: Cambridge University Press, 1992.

Encarnation, Dennis J. *Rivals beyond Trade: America versus Japan in Global Competition*. Ithaca, N.Y.: Cornell University Press, 1992.

Havens, Thomas H. *Fire across the Sea: The Vietnam War and Japan, 1965–1975*. Princeton, N.J.: Princeton University Press, 1987.

Hein, Laura, and Mark Selden, eds. *Living with the Bomb: American and Japanese Cultural Conflicts in the Nuclear Age*. Armonk, N.Y.: M.E. Sharpe, 1997.

Miyoshi, Masao. *Off Center: Power and Culture Relations between Japan and the United States*. Cambridge: Harvard University Press, 1991.

Nagai, Yōnosuke, and Akira Iriye, eds. *The Origins of the Cold War in Asia*. New York: Columbia University Press, 1977.

Pyle, Kenneth B. *The Japanese Question: Power and Purpose in a New Era*. Washington, D.C.: The AEI Press, 1992.

Schonberger, Howard B. *Aftermath of War: Americans and the Remaking of Japan, 1945–1952*. Kent, Ohio: The Kent State University Press, 1989.

Index